9/02

INDICTMENT
AT THE HAGUE

INDICTMENT AT THE HAGUE

THE MILOSOVIĆ REGIME AND CRIMES OF THE BALKAN WAR

NORMAN CIGAR AND PAUL WILLIAMS

NEW YORK UNIVERSITY PRESS
New York and London

Published in association with
THE PAMPHLETEER'S PRESS

NEW YORK UNIVERSITY PRESS
New York and London

Published in association with
THE PAMPHLETEER'S PRESS
Stony Creek, CT

Norman Cigar wishes to state that the views expressed in this study are entirely his own and do not necessarily reflect the views or policies of the U.S. Government, the Department of Defense, or the U.S. Marine Corps University.

Library of Congress Cataloging-in-Publication Data
Cigar, Norman L.
Indictment at The Hague : the Milošević regime and crimes of the Balkan Wars / Norman Cigar and Paul Williams.
p.   cm.
Includes bibliographical references.
ISBN 0-8147-1626-1 (cloth : alk. paper)
1. Serbia—Politics and government—1992– 2. Milošević, Slobodan, 1941– 3. Yugoslav War, 1991–1995—Atrocities. 4. Kosovo (Serbia) —History—Civil War, 1998– —Atrocities. I. Williams, Paul.
II. Title.DR2051 .C54 2002
949.703—dc21   2001056819

Design by Toki Design, San Francisco

Manufactured in the United States of America
10 9 8 7 6 5 4 3 2 1

DEDICATED TO

THE BOSNIAN INSTITUTE
— London, England —

(www.bosnia.org.uk)

IN THE MIDST OF THE BOSNIAN GENOCIDE A NUMBER OF SMALL groups in several countries gathered together to oppose the maelstrom that was then sweeping the Balkans. Among the views they articulated was the principle that the perpetrators of the genocide and other crimes against humanity should be held accountable. They also held to a simple, yet basic proposition, that peace for Bosnia could only come about if it was a "just peace". This included a juridical process that would bring the perpetrators of war crimes in the Balkans to trial.

At a time when world leaders were busy imagining a hundred ways in which Bosnia might be partitioned such a view seemed utterly utopian. Yet, these foolish men and women never strayed from this path. A decade after the Bosnian genocide began the Hague Tribunal is bringing the perpetrators of Srebrenica and so many other terrible acts of murder to trial. Not all those indicted have been arrested. Many are still sought.

Yet, it must be said that in this instance not all the "big fish" have gotten away—as they so often do. Senior figures of the Milošević regime in Serbia and its offshoots in Bosnia are standing trial for war crimes—including Milošević himself. Among other charges, he stands indicted for genocide

When it counted most to be a clear voice amidst a wilderness of moral compromise, the Bosnian Institute could be heard. Although the Institute and its leadership were not the only ones to show courage and protest the inaction of the so-called "international community", their analysis was among the most penetrating. A special appreciation in this regard is offered to Quintin Hoare, Branka Margas and Noel Malcolm.

TABLE OF CONTENTS

ACKNOWLEDGMENTS

THE AUTHORS WISH TO EXPRESS THEIR GRATITUDE TO QUINTIN Hoare and Noel Malcolm of the Bosnian Institute, London, for their valued encouragement, permission to use the study done originally for the Bosnian Institute in 1996, and initiative in securing a grant from the Open Society Institute to support the publication of this book. At the same time, the authors also wish to thank Aryeh Neier, President of the Open Society Institute, and Elise van Oss, Special Assistant to the President of OSI, for their commitment to human rights and their generosity in providing support to the Bosnian Institute to make this project possible. We must also express our appreciation to Bianca Jagger who graciously recommended this project to the OSI.

We are also grateful to Michael Sells of Haverford College for his valuable assistance in tracking down obscure documents relating to Bosnia and for providing the appropriate references. His website on War Crimes in Bosnia-Herzegovina is a veritable archive of reports and documents on the conflict in the Balkans and proved an invaluable resource. Likewise, we wish to thank Smail Cekić, Director of the Institute for Research on Crimes against Humanity and International Law, Sarajevo, for providing several documents which we used in the study.

The authors would also like to thank Jennifer Harris, Karina Michael, Samantha Williams, Bethany McAndrew, and Knox Thames of the American University for their research assistance, Abigail Taylor for her administrative and research support, Danielle McClellan for copyediting and proofreading the manuscript, and Jasmina Basirević for her painstaking work in inserting the hundreds of diacritics for the Bosnian, Croatian and Serbian names and places mentioned in this book.

Finally, we would like to express our gratitude to Rabia Ali for her professional and dedicated editorial work as she revised and successfully updated this study despite the constantly changing developments which occurred throughout the editing phase, so that if the resulting case study can be of use for some years to come it is largely through her unstinting efforts and editorial talent. Our special thanks are also due to Lawrence Lifschultz without whose commitment and initiative this book would not have happened.

INTRODUCTION

IVO BANAC
YALE UNIVERSITY

THE MILOŠEVIĆ STORY HAS ALL THE ELEMENTS OF INDUSTRIOUS mediocrity, which seems to be the necessary ingredient for evildoing. It is also linked with the decadence of a regime that created the conditions for its violent downfall. The ideology of Yugoslav communism was predicated on an opportunistic idea that only the Communists stood in the way of the "dark past," that is, of internecine carnage among the peoples of Yugoslavia on a scale that could match the traumatic period of the Second World War. In order to fulfill this prophylactic responsibility, the Communists needed to attain the fullness of power, which they proceeded to apply generously to suppress nationalism — "the most dangerous class enemy."

In fact, the Communist war against "nationalism" very frequently was no more than combat against free speech and free display of national identity. It tended to legitimize the symbols of resistance that, in themselves, were as imbued with intolerance as the regime itself. It also engendered a competition for national "self-defense" among the republic leaderships of Yugoslavia-although not among all of them and not to the same degree, but sufficiently so to make the advocacy of nationalism a necessary substitute to the declining fortunes of Communist ideology. As usual, the Communists monopolized every bit of political casting: They were simultaneously both the inquisitors of "nationalism" as well as the guardians of a Yugoslav "nation."

Milošević was presented with a window of opportunity in the 1980s when the Communist organization of Serbia started making demands after a long period of colonization by Tito. In 1972, Tito purged the liberal leadership of the League of Communists of Serbia (SKS), getting rid of the only elite group in twentieth-century Serbian history that wanted to order Yugoslavia in a genuinely federalist fashion. The dregs of the Serbian leadership went along with Tito's constitution of 1974, which nominally empowered the six republics and Serbia's two autonomous provinces (Kosovo and Vojvodina), but in fact were nursing a grudge against the "parcelization" of Serbia, that is, the increase in what they regarded as interference by Vojvodina and, especially, Kosovo. Then, in 1980, Tito was dead and the great game of dismantling his constitution commenced.

Miloševic's role in Serbia's de-Titoization initially was modest. An apparatchik from the provinces, Milošević was regarded as a reliable and alert party worker. His career started in the SKS student organization at the Law Faculty of the University of Belgrade, where in the 1960s he stunned learned regime jurists with an objection to the proposed new constitutional name of the state-Federative Socialist Republic of Yugoslavia. No, said Milošević, stress should be put on the socialist content. In the corrected proposal, which ultimately was adopted, the country was renamed Socialist Federative Republic of Yugoslavia (SFRJ).

Milošević climbed fast at the side of Ivan Stambolić, Serbia's prospective party leader of the younger generation, whose ties to the republic's party leadership were significantly personal. His uncle, Petar Stambolić, was the topmost SKS leader in Serbia during the length of the postwar period. With Stambolic's backing, Milošević rose fast in Belgrade's party organization, soon becoming the director of the powerful Beogradska banka, the most important bank in the country, and, in 1984, the president of the SKS Belgrade organization. In 1986, again with Stambolic's backing, Milošević became the president of the SKS Central Committee, that is, the head of the party in Serbia. He was the only candidate for the position over the objections of Draža Marković, Serbia's veteran Communist warhorse, and the uncle of his wife Mira Marković.

By that time the leadership of Serbia, with Stambolić in the position of the republic's new president, was deeply embroiled in attempts at a revision of Yugoslavia's constitution. Specifically, after the Kosovar student demonstrations in 1981, Belgrade was presented with an argument against the autonomy of Kosovo and Vojvodina. Greater autonomy, the argument went, inevitably means greater instability. The campaign against the "constitution-defenders" had already ended in the purge of Mahmut Bakalli, the senior Albanian leader in Kosovo, and put the party leaders of Slovenia and Croatia on the defensive. Stambolić, however, did not anticipate that the campaign would be turned against his leadership.

In April 1987, Milošević went to Kosovo, where he was to address the Serbs of the predominantly Serb Kosovo Polje community near Priština. There was a mêlée at the site, the predominantly Albanian police being none too gentle with the audience. Milošević improvised a crowd-pleasing sentence: "Nobody has the right to beat you." The pronoun was interpreted ethnically and became the political program in the crafting of anti-Albanian measures. Milošević returned from Kosovo as the new national leader, asking the slackers in the Serbian party to account for themselves. The party media of Belgrade was enlisted in his service. By September 1987, the less reckless SKS leaders, including Ivan Stambolić, were forced to resign. Milošević had discovered the formula for success. The politics of resentment (initially against Albanians, later against the Slovenes, Croats, and Bosnians) could be generated by media manipulation, enlistment of the national intelligentsia, and mass demonstrations. The chief beneficiary would be the new national elite that emerged out of the outworn SKS cocoon.

By the end of the 1980s, Milošević had transformed the ruling structure of Serbia. Whereas in the Communist Eastern Europe the crisis of communism meant the collapse of the *ancien regime* and a transition to democracy and the free market, in Serbia Milošević preserved the old system in the new guise. The Communist concentration of party, state, police, military, judicial, and media power was retained with a new ideological mission at hand. Nationalism, redefined as resistance to Titoist bureaucrats, afforded new opportunities for regime continuity. But it was a typically apparatchik nationalism, with a significant admixture of state socialism. The essence of Milošević's politics, however, was not nationalism, but the retention of power by any and all means.

Milošević's attempts to change the Titoist rules engendered opposition in the other Yugoslav republics and hastened their search for an alternative. The calls for an exit from a federation that was threatened by Milošević were soon to follow. This, in turn, afforded Milošević with an opportunity to enlist the support of the Yugoslav People's Army (JNA) against "separatism" and pluralism. The JNA became the agency for Milošević's subversion of the other republics, the arms from the JNA depots being delivered by Milošević's security operatives to the reliable Serb minority leaders in Croatia and Bosnia. The "defense" of Yugoslavia and state socialism was nationalized by becoming a Serb nationalist cause.

Milošević would not have succeeded in his game had he not enlisted like-minded leaders of the other republics in a campaign that inevitably led to armed conflict. From his initial goal of reimposing centralism on the whole of Yugoslavia he shifted to a goal of creating a Serb national state out of several Yugoslav republics and several other republic fragments (Great Serbia). The goal of Croatia's post-Communist president, Franjo Tudjman, too, was a nationally homogeneous state. Since the two goals could be accomplished only by a partition of Bosnia, the two opponents started cooperating in what would become a sort of a war by agreement. Closer investigations will tell to what extent Milošević's war plans had Tudjman's prior agreement; it is certain, however, that the style of Milošević's war making was mimicked by Tudjman's forces.

Foreign observers frequently succumb to elaborate theories about how Yugoslavia's past acted itself out in the conflicts of the 1990s. This is a false lead that cannot account for what was essentially recent, planned, and simply criminal activity. With the Serbian party-state at his disposal, Milošević created instruments for every occasion. The JNA was used for initial "legal" gambits. The secret police created a web of dependents organized into various parties, a typical example being the Serb Democratic Party (SDS) of Radovan Karadžić in Bosnia-Hercegovina. The dirty work was assigned to the various paramilitary organizations—the Tigers of Željko Ražnatović-Arkan, the White Eagles of the Serbian Renaissance Movement, the Chetniks of Vojislav Šešelj—which Milošević supplied with weapons and, occasionally, with personnel from his security apparatus. In the meanwhile, the propaganda machine of the state used TV broadcasts and the press to create the most negative images of Milošević's operational targets.

The Vukovar operation was typical. In the fall of 1991, during the war against Croatia, the JNA laid siege to this easternmost Croatian city on the Danube. Vukovar was no strategic target. Its systematic destruction served the cause of national homogenization—the crafting of "uni-national" states. First, the JNA's artillery barraged the city prompting a mass exodus of Croats and the growth of hatred between the communities. Meanwhile the Milošević media vilified the defenders of Vukovar as bloodthirsty fascists of the Second World War vintage. Then, after the city was thoroughly destroyed and left defenseless, the JNA marched into Vukovar in November 1991 and facilitated the execution of the wounded and other captured Croatian prisoners (Ovcara massacre). The paramilitary units undertook the liquidations. The political "solution" in the guise of the Republic of Serbian Krajina (RSK) came afterwards and was offered to the international community as a fair outcome of conflict.

The Bosnian pattern was less "labor intensive." The paramilitaries embarked on a random campaign of executions of Muslim civilians in Eastern and Northwestern Bosnia, with rapes and concentration camps (Omarska, Manjaca) being organized to heighten the sense of hopelessness. The terror was accompanied by the destruction of Muslim mosques, a symbolic overthrow of legitimacy. This engendered mass flights of civilian population—the so-called "quail effect"—and accomplished the goal of what was felicitously referred to as "ethnic cleansing." Then came the creation of the parastates (Republika Srpska, followed by the Croat Herzeg-Bosna) and the maintenance of military pressure on Sarajevo. The international community's decision not to intervene was reinforced with plans for the partition of Bosnia that were not dissimilar from the parastate pattern designed by Milošević's intervention (Owen-Stoltenberg plan, Contact Group plan). Meanwhile Milošević maintained his taciturn composure, letting the state media offer leads on his thinking. His legitimacy was increased when the international mediators came courting his favors on behalf of what they took to be peace.

Serbia's domestic opposition could not be a counterpart to Milošević as most of these oppositional politicians shared his nationalist conceptions, in many cases more sincerely. Matters were not improved when Milošević's hand became weakened. Sanctions and isolation chipped at his flank. His growing corruption weakened the image of the selfless patriot. By 1995, the Clinton administration targeted Croatia for a proxy role in Bosnia. With U.S. tactical support, the Croatian forces succeeded in retaking the Krajina parastate and much of the neighboring parastate of Republika Srpska. Milošević was forced into a retreat. At the Dayton agreements (1995) he facilitated the make-do plan that stopped the war at the cost of Bosnia's delayed political reintegration. The Serbian opposition hastened to attack Milošević for accepting the half loaf.

In a sense they hastened his next crisis. The Albanian movement that generated Milošević's rise in the 1980s was dutifully quiescent in the 1990s. Milošević stripped Kosovo of autonomy in 1989, expelled Albanians from all positions of power, and cleansed all official institutions of Albanian influence. The result was an apartheid society in which Albanians developed counter-institutions entirely according to their own design, but divested of all official sanction and legitimacy. For example, students attended alternative Albanian schools and received diplomas that had no legal standing. Milošević made no attempt at undue harassment of Kosovar Albanian counter-society as it deepened the isolation of Albanians, who refused to participate in the Serbian political society.

This policy could satisfy the Albanians for as long as they could envisage some denouement at the horizon. After the Dayton conference, which did not address the issue of Kosovo, the younger generation of Albanians concluded that their grievances could be addressed only by direct action. This led to the creation of the Kosovo Liberation Army (UÇK) and the beginning of skirmishes between the Kosovar Albanian guerrillas and the Milošević authorities. Milošević's way of dealing with the new Albanian challenge was not dissimilar from his style of warfare as practiced in Croatia and Bosnia. This time, however, the "enemy" was compact and the confrontation was direct, largely without the benefit of various paramilitary guises. Moreover, the response of the international community was swift, both diplomatically (Rambouillet meeting) and militarily (NATO intervention, 1999).

It was argued, and compellingly so, that the NATO intervention failed to perform the most beneficial service to Serbia by effecting the change of the regime. This objective could have been accomplished only by the use of infantry at a cost of perhaps significant losses. Moreover, it would have necessitated NATO's involvement in a the step-by-step construction of Serbia's civil society. Needless to say, it would have included the total dismantling of the Milošević's regime. Such a road was not followed, but the change of the regime occurred all the same—under conditions that agreed with the needs of the domestic opposition. The Belgrade turnabout of October 2000 thus remains a negotiated revolution that engaged the services of the former Milošević loyalists who had lost the belief in his ability to lead Serbia out of total isolation.

The Hague indictment against Milošević and his principal accomplices for war crimes in Kosovo played an important role in the sobering of the Belgrade political elite. Their decision to have him arrested in March 2001 was a measure, in part, aimed at preempting Milošević's testimony before an impartial international tribunal, where his accounting of fourteen years of state crime, it was feared, inevitably would compromise untold associates and fellow travelers. Without such an accounting, however—and the realization that Milošević could not have destroyed so many lives without a broad social acceptance of his policies—Serbia cannot expect an inner healing that is a precondition for her future course. In June 2001, under increasing international pressure, the regime in Belgrade agreed to deliver Milošević to the Hague Tribunal which, finally, also issued indictments against him for the commission of war crimes in Croatia and in Bosnia-Herzegovina.

Slobodan Milošević left a wasteland in his wake. His misdeeds are apparent to the naked eye, from the rubble of Vukovar to the empty spaces where once stood some of Bosnia's most magnificent mosques (Aladža in Foča, Ferhadija in Banja Luka), from the empty Serb homesteads in the environs of Knin to the destroyed villages of Drenica in Kosovo. But no human eye can detect the pain of hundreds of thousands, not least of the all the pain visited upon the Serbs themselves by one of their own. After the Gazimestan rally of June 1989, where Milošević declared his intention of waging war against the other republics of Yugoslavia, Kosovar Albanian leader Ibrahim Rugova observed that whenever a small nation attempted to impose its hegemony over the region it precipitated its own tragedy. No matter how he personally meets his end, Milošević shall remain one of the most villainous figures in the history of the South Slavs. It is the task of an impartial international court to demolish his justifications.

I

IN DECEMBER 1992, AS THE TIDE OF ETHNIC CLEANSING engulfed Bosnia-Herzegovina, the Department of State of the United States identified Slobodan Milošević, President of Serbia—along with several paramilitary leaders such as Željko Ražnatović ("Arkan") and Vojislav Šešelj—as a suspected war criminal.[1] And yet, in the years that followed, the international community's reluctance to intervene and—more significantly—its refusal to lift the arms embargo that was crippling Bosnia-Herzegovina's ability to defend itself allowed the Serb forces, armed and supported by the Milošević regime, to continue their campaign unchecked. Instead, through this entire period, and with full knowledge of the extent of war crimes being committed in Bosnia and

Croatia, the international community (principally through its American and British representatives) continued to negotiate with Slobodan Milošević, producing successive peace plans that might meet with his approval. This process culminated in the Dayton Accords signed in the United States in 1995, which, in effect, conferred legitimacy on the Milošević regime's war aims by conceding the virtual partitioning of Bosnia-Herzegovina and, therefore, its destruction as a multiethnic state. Milošević's subsequent campaign to secure Serb dominace in Kosovo was an entirely predictable consequence of the 'peace' imposed on Bosnia.

At the turn of the century, however, a decade of war waged by the Milošević regime in the Balkans reached its dénouement when the International Criminal Tribunal for the former Yugoslavia, established by the United Nations in 1993, issued the first of its indictments against Slobodan Milošević for war crimes. In 1999, beginning with Kosovo, it indicted Milošević for "planning, ordering, or carrying out deportations and murders during the Serb forces' campaign to drive Kosovar Albanians from their homes, which killed thousands along the way." In June 2001, the new regime in Belgrade, under increasing international pressure, deported Milošević to The Hague. In the next six months the Tribunal issued two further indictments against Milošević for the commission of war crimes in his earlier campaigns against Croatia and Bosnia-Herzegovina. The indictment on Bosnia was the most comprehensive of all: it charged Milošević not only with "crimes against humanity, grave breaches of the Geneva Conventions and violations of the laws or customs of war", but also with the commission of "genocide".[2]

The indictment of Slobodan Milošević for the war crimes committed in Bosnia and Croatia had been long overdue. This study, making a case and elaborating the grounds for his indictment, was first initiated in 1996 when there appeared to be little, if any, prospect that the international community would promote an investigation, must less a formal indictment of Milošević on charges of war crimes. Nevertheless, an examination of available evidence had convinced us that there was a case to answer. The present book is an extension of that first study, containing additional evidence that has appeared in the public domain since then. More and more documentary and personal proof is likely to emerge over time, providing further corroborating evidence for what we feel has always been a logical case to investigate and prosecute. With the formal indictments now in existence, this work in its revised form should be read as a 'case study' which delineates the legal principles and the clear and extensive evidence defining the nature and legal responsibility of Slobodan Milošević for war crimes committed in Croatia and Bosnia-Herzegovina. In brief, the object here is to analyze the legal and evidentiary facets which eventually formed the basis of the indictment of Milošević by the International Criminal Tribunal for the former Yugoslavia at The Hague.

As the chapters that follow demonstrate, Slobodan Milošević can be held personally responsible under international law for war crimes committed by Yugoslav federal forces, the forces of the Republic of Serbia, and Serbian paramilitary units in Croatia and Bosnia, whether working separately or in joint operations among themselves, or with the Bosnian Serb Army (BSA), or with the Army of the Republic of the Serbian Krajina. The atrocities committed by Serbian forces were part of a planned, systematic, and organized campaign to secure territory for an ethnically "pure" Serb state by clearing it of all non-Serb populations. In the past decade a growing body of evidence in the public domain has clearly indicated that government agencies subordinate to Slobodan Milošević, at the federal as well as the republic level, were extensively involved, providing both support and direction to this campaign. There is also sufficient evidence that not only was Milošević fully aware of the overall activity of these organizations, but that he also knew and approved of the support the agencies under his control were providing to these organizations. Therefore, as we have long argued, under the rules of procedure and evidence of the International Criminal Tribunal for the Former Yugoslavia, there is sufficient evidence in the public domain to support the indictment of Slobodan Milošević on charges of genocide, crimes against humanity, violation of the laws and customs of war, and grave breaches of the Geneva Conventions of 1949. The indictments issued by the Tribunal corroborate the validity of such an argument.

The delineation of Slobodan Milošević's responsibility for war crimes in the former Yugoslavia—specifically the crimes that took place during the Bosnian and Croatian phases of the war—is important for several reasons. First, attaching liability for war crimes will serve as a reminder to other prospective war criminals that their actions will not be granted *de facto* immunity by the world community. Secondly, despite the fall of the Milošević regime indictments for war crimes may well act as an immediate deterrent for a number of Serbian paramilitary units that remain active. If use of these units is not ultimately delegitimized, they may continue to terrorize non-Serb civilians within Bosnia, Montenegro, and in the Republic of Serbia itself. There is substantial historical evidence to support such a view.

For example, while officials claimed that Arkan's Serbian Volunteer Guard, *Srpska dobrovoljacka garda* (SDG), would be demobilized, since it had accomplished its mission, there were hints that its maintenance in some form for future requirements might be necessary to serve as a cover for Serbia's own direct involvement. According to Borislav Pelević, Vice President of Arkan's Serbian Unity Party and Deputy Commander of their paramilitary force, "The SDG will pull out of the Republic of the Serbian Krajina along with the army, but it will not be demobilized; rather, it will help the Serbian people wherever it is threatened." Pelević promised, "If, God forbid, fighting breaks out in Kosovo, we will set up the guard again and place it in the service of the Serbian people." Pelević noted as early as 1995 that in the future more attention would be paid to Hungarians in Vojvodina, the Muslims in the Sandžak, and to Kosovo, where "the documents of all 500,000 [Albanian] immigrants [*sic*] [should] be checked." Indeed, the events in Kosovo were foretold. The official government news agency *Tanjug* noted in early 1996, three years before the mass expulsions, that Arkan was turning his attention to Kosovo. In a move clearly designed to intimidate the Kosovar Albanian population, Arkan issued a new threat to "solve" the problem of "Albanian separatism" by "emigration."[3] Arkan announced on 25 March 1999 that he had reactivated the Serbian Volunteer Guard and that the following day there would be a meeting to select individuals who would "immediately put themselves at the disposal of the army and the police."[4] Arkan's Tigers were reported to be operating in Kosovo thereafter and to have been responsible for additional atrocities.[5]

In Kosovo, unlike the case of Croatia and Bosnia, there was no benefit for the Serbian government to rely on paramilitary forces for plausible denial of its own involvement, since Kosovo was within Serbia's legal control. Therefore, it was not surprising that Arkan's group and other paramilitary units in Kosovo were often openly attached to the police and army and were employed in some of the more repulsive aspects of ethnic cleansing of civilians. In fact, Arkan stressed that he did not have "paramilitary units" but that his "units of volunteers" in Kosovo were "all the time under the command of [the] Yugoslav Army."[6] In a move perhaps intended to deter Arkan in Kosovo, as events spiraled out of control, on 31 March 1999 the Tribunal made public an indictment that it had drawn up against him on 30 September 1997.

Finally, the indictment and trial of Milošević and senior members of his regime, and thus the documenting of the commission of and responsibility for war crimes, can serve to educate the citizens of the international community so that they understand how and why these crimes occurred as well as ensure that such events are not forgotten or denied by the protagonists as time passes. Furthermore, the establishment of individual responsibility serves to reinforce the principle that nations or entire populations of a particular society are not collectively responsible for the war crimes resulting from the genocidal policies of a specific individual or group of individuals.[7] The Serbian leadership consistently engaged in blanket denials of any responsibility. Milošević, for example, told the BBC in 1995, "There is no one who can believe what is mentioned as an organized genocide, even organized from Belgrade, even organized by me! It is really out of consideration!"[8]

On a number of occasions the Prosecutor for the International Criminal Tribunal for the Former Yugoslavia had declared that it was a prosecution strategy to investigate "lower-level persons directly involved in carrying out the crimes in order to build effective cases against the military and civilian leaders who were party to the overall planning and organization of those crimes."[9] Consistent with this objective, this study identifies the areas where the Tribunal, through its several indictments, established a solid legal and factual foundation for building an even more extensive case against Slobodan Milošević than was advanced in the context of actions perpetrated by Serbian forces in Kosovo.

In order to assess Milošević's responsibility, we begin, first, with a review of the prevailing international law governing liability for the commission of war crimes. We then proceed to elaborate the evidence available in the public domain, which, under the rules of procedure and evidence of the Tribunal, forms the basis for the case against Slobodan Milošević. The objective is to show how Milošević could be held individually responsible—both on the basis of *direct responsibility* and *command responsibility*—for the commission of war crimes in the territory of the former Yugoslavia, and, furthermore, how specific actions that took place in Croatia and Bosnia established the grounds for his indictment and trial. However, before we explore the legal and factual basis for such an indictment of Milošević and others within the Serbian leadership, it is essential to set forth a set of basic facts and definitions, and to identify the sources of information upon which this inquiry is based.

The International Criminal Tribunal for the Former Yugoslavia (the Tribunal) was created by the United Nations Security Council on 25 May 1993 for the purpose of prosecuting those individuals responsible for grave breaches of international humanitarian law in the former Yugoslavia. The Tribunal was to consist of a Prosecutor and his staff, Chambers, including two Trial

Chambers and an Appeals Chamber (Court), and a Registry.[10] The Tribunal was to have competence and jurisdiction to prosecute any person responsible for war crimes committed in the territory of the former Yugoslavia since 1 January 1991. At the time of this writing it had issued 40 indictments and charged 73 individuals with the commission of war crimes in the former Yugoslavia.[11]

In establishing a case for a broader indictment and trial of Slobodan Milošević by the Tribunal, this inquiry relies upon the standards set forth in the statute of the Tribunal and utilizes the previous indictments of the Tribunal—in particular, those against Radovan Karadžić and Ratko Mladic—as guiding precedents.[12] We do not address some of the fundamental questions relating to the applicability of the laws and customs governing the conduct of war since the Tribunal has concluded that sufficient evidence existed to establish that, from 1991, a state of armed conflict and partial occupation did exist in the Republic of Bosnia-Herzegovina and Croatia, and widespread and systematic or large-scale attacks did occur against civilian populations. The Tribunal further declared that these civilian victims were protected by the laws of war, and that the civilian and military authorities responsible for the commission of atrocities were required to abide by the laws and customs of war.[13]

Slobodan Milošević exercised significant political power in the territory of the former Yugoslavia since the late 1980s. In September 1987, at the Eighth Central Committee Plenum in Serbia, he became the president of the Central Committee of Serbia's ruling party, then known as the League of Communists of Serbia and subsequently renamed the Socialist Party of Serbia (*Socijalisticka Partija Srbije* or SPS). In May 1989 he also became the president of the Collective Presidency of Serbia. After the elections in December 1990, he became the country's sole president. Milošević was re-elected in December 1992.[14] Prior to the dissolution of the former Yugoslavia, Slobodan Milošević was able to establish control over four of the federal units (Serbia, Montenegro, Vojvodina, and Kosovo).[15] After the dissolution of the former Yugoslavia and the creation of the Federal Republic of Yugoslavia (*Savezna Republika Jugoslavija*), consisting of the republics of Serbia (including Vojvodina and Kosovo) and Montenegro, he retained his position as the president of Serbia and exercised legal control over all republic-level agencies. In addition, he exercised actual and, in some instances, official control over the newly reorganized Yugoslav federal agencies. The result was an extensive and interlocking system of state agencies responsive to Milošević's authority.

After the dissolution of the former Yugoslavia, Serbia and Montenegro transformed the Yugoslav People's Army (*Jugoslovenska Narodna Armija* or JNA) into the Army of Yugoslavia or Yugoslav Army (*Vojska Jugoslavije* or VJ). The JNA had operated widely in Croatia and Bosnia and continued these operations after its transformation into the Yugoslav Army and into two other successors, the Bosnian Serb Army and the Army of the Republic of the Serbian Krajina. A United Nations report published in 1992 described the transparent transition of the JNA into the Bosnian Serb Army:

> From late May 1992, when the JNA ostensibly had left BiH [Bosnia and Herzegovina] territory as far as its members originating from out-side BiH were concerned [officially on May 4, 1992], the remaining Serbian military in the region of Banja Luka (as well as in other regions) officially converted the remaining JNA into the Army of the SRBiH [Bosnian Serb Republic-Herzegovina].... The transformation essentially was characterized by a change of name and insignia. The Army SRBiH was to be commanded by General Ratko Mladić.
> When he was appointed to his new duty in the first half of May 1992, General Ratko Mladić was still commander of the [JNA's] Knin Corps (based in the Croatian Krajina).... The overall command structure, the lion's share of the military personnel, the weaponry and the ammunition of the JNA, remained in place with the Army of SRBiH. In Banja Luka, the 5th Corps of the JNA thence became the 1st [Bosnian] Krajina Corps. The commander was Major General Momir Talić (who had previously been the deputy commander of the 5th Corps).... When the SRBiH changed its name on August 12, 1992 to the Republic of Srpska, the Army [of] SRBiH changed its name and acronym to VRS (*Vojska Republike Srpske*, the Army of the Republic of Srpska).[16]

Although the former Yugoslavia had a number of related federal forces, such as the federal police and customs service, these forces were depleted by the defection of a number of their members to the republic-level forces of the successor republics while the remnants of these forces were largely subsumed into the forces of the Republic of Serbia and were controlled by Slobodan Milošević.

Other agencies involved in activities related to the conflict in the territory of the former Yugoslavia include Serbia's Ministry of Internal Affairs (*Ministarstvo Unutrašnjih Poslova* or MUP), Serbia's Ministry of Defense and

Territorial Defense (the former republic-level reserve defense authority), and to a lesser extent, the state transportation system and the Ministry of Information. The Republic of Serbia maintained its own police force consisting of some 120,000 active duty and reserve police officers, a secret service, and, until the defense reorganization of 1993, a Territorial Defense System. The command and control of the police force was exercised by the Republic of Serbia Ministry of Internal Affairs which was directly responsible to the president of Serbia, Slobodan Milošević. Throughout much of the 1990's the Republic of Serbia's Ministry of Internal Affairs was headed by Zoran Sokolović. The Ministry includes the Department (*Resor*)—formerly Service (*Služba*)—of Public Security, which was headed by Radovan Stojcić Badža, who during this period also served as Deputy Minister of Internal Affairs, and the State Security Service, the SDB (Služba državne bezbednosti), essentially the secret police, which was headed by Jovica Stanišić during most of the period under consideration here. Badža was gunned down in Belgrade's Mamma Mia pizzeria in April 1999 by unknown assailants. Stanišić was removed from his post in 1998. The assets needed to support military operations or paramilitary groups were almost exclusively in the hands of the Republic of Serbia. For example, most large firms (including armaments factories), banks, the media, and the transportation infrastructure are owned by the Republic of Serbia and often have been managed by individuals who, at the same time, held office in the Serbian government. In many instances, government ministers participated on the board of directors of these companies.[17]

Serbian paramilitary forces active during the war in the former Yugoslavia represented an eclectic set of organizations with several dozen operating in Bosnia at one time, and differed in size, capabilities and discipline. They ranged from forces numbering only a few dozen men to some with several thousand. Determining a precise number of those who participated in paramilitary units is difficult in the absence of access to official documents, and various paramilitary leaders have given self-serving claims of the numbers who served under their command. Milika Ceko Dacević, founder of the Serbian Guard paramilitary formation affiliated with Vuk Draškovic's SPO, claimed, "I was the commander of all volunteer units in Bosnia, that is some 11,000 personnel were under my command."[18] Vojislav Šešelj, for his part, claimed, "We sent tens of thousands of volunteers to many fronts."[19] The Yugoslav Army, on the other hand, estimated that, in 1993, Šešelj had 8,000 armed personnel.[20] Some were little better than armed gangs while others have had greater discipline and training and even a limited conventional military capability.

Among the larger Serbian paramilitary formations which operated were the Serbian Volunteer Guard or SDG (*Srpska dobrovoljacka garda*), also known as the Tigers, commanded by Arkan; the Chetniks commanded by Vojislav Šešelj; the White Eagles (*Beli orlovi*) commanded by Mirko Jović; and the Serbian Guard (*Srpska garda*) led by Vuk Drašković. Mirko Jović's party was the Serbian National Reform or SNO (*Srpska narodna obnova*) and the White Eagles was its paramilitary formation. The Eagles' first combat commander was Dragoslav Bokan. Vuk Drašković and his wife Danica set up the Serbian Reform Movement, SPO (*Srpski pokret obnove*), as their political party. Šešelj, Drašković, and Jović had all been members of a single organization—the SNO—but quickly split to form separate parties and paramilitary units.[21]

Arkan's SDG was especially important for its size and its considerable equipment in comparison to most of the other paramilitary formations. Borislav Pelević, Arkan's deputy and director for training, claimed that by early 1994 ten thousand men had undergone training at the organization's encampment.[22] The discipline and relative capability of the SDG suggested that at least some, if not most, of the cadre and rank-and-file of the SDG may actually have been police or army personnel seconded to paramilitary units. Although reliable numbers are often difficult to come by, there were reports of 3,000 men under arms at any one time. Judging from photographs published in the press of the ceremonies in 1995 marking the fifth anniversary of its establishment, the SDG had some light armor, as well as an extensive motorized capability. One source also attributed tanks and heavy artillery to Arkan's order of battle.[23]

While several political leaders—including Vuk Drašković, Mirko Jović, and Milan Paroški—along with Vojislav Šešelj claimed to be "Chetnik" and the political heirs of the Second World War Chetnik Serbian nationalist movement, Šešelj appropriated the name for his paramilitary forces formally and preempted the others. Originally, Šešelj's party was called the Serbian Chetnik Movement (*Srpski cetnicki pokret*), but then was renamed the Serbian Radical Party or SRS (*Srpska radikalna stranka*).

In the ethnic cleansing of Bosnia and Croatia, the paramilitary groups played a key role, far out of proportion to their numbers. Yet, Milošević consistently downplayed the role and impact of these formations. Milošević appears to have adopted this pose in an effort to diminish his personal responsibility for the activities of these groups, and denied any involvement with them. Asked in mid-1995 about the role of paramilitary organizations operating in Bosnia, Milošević was quick to insist, "You know, all those kinds of paramilitary formations were totally marginal in the war....There were never more than a couple of thousand all together." [24] Even Serbia's Parliament had gone on record by claiming that any reports of armed groups from Serbia operating in Bosnia had "no basis in fact." [25]

The larger paramilitary formations were usually affiliated with a political party and their ideological outlook ranged virtually across the entire political spectrum, although some of the smaller paramilitary groups seemed to have had no driving ideology or goals beyond plunder. Virtually all of the larger paramilitary groups were affiliated to a political party, and some of their leaders—such as Šešelj, Arkan, Drašković, and Paroški—sat as deputies in Serbia's Parliament or at least ran for office, as was the case with Captain Dragan. The political parties often used affiliated paramilitary groups as "enforcers" during political campaigns. For example, according to Dejan Lucić, a senior SPO official, Captain Dragan (real name Daniel Sneden), "supervised the voting" for Vuk Drašković's SPO during the 1990 elections. [26] Nevertheless, a common denominator for all the main paramilitary organizations, and ultimately the one that was perhaps key to their success, was their link to Slobodan Milošević and the Serbian agencies under his control.

This inquiry has drawn on evidence consisting in large part of reports made public by the United Nations, Western governments, and non-governmental organizations as well as statements made by Serbian government officials, military personnel, and paramilitary commanders as published in the Yugoslav press. In addition, press releases and official indictments of the Hague Tribunal were utilized to establish certain fundamental facts.

There is, doubtless, substantial additional information in existence, which, if made available, would support an even stronger case. Communications intercepts, human intelligence, and overhead imagery collected by foreign government agencies could also provide compelling corroborative evidence. At the time of this writing, despite the efforts of the Tribunal, much of this evidence still lay outside the public domain.

Access to official Serbian documents (written instructions, minutes of meetings, and receipts), other unofficial records such as photos and videos, and the testimony of government and paramilitary agent officials would be instructive. Documents captured by Bosnian military forces became available at public archives in Sarajevo, and formed the basis of a pending civil suit filed at the Hague by the Bosnian government. In this inquiry, we have made use of a few selected documents from the Sarajevo archives.

Furthermore, by early 1996, the paramilitary leader, Vojislav Šešelj, was offering to testify against Slobodan Milošević at the Tribunal. Serbian authorities seemed concerned about the prospect and reportedly refused to extend Šešelj's passport.[27] One of Šešelj's lieutenants, Branislav Vakić claimed that he had documents showing cooperation between Serbia's police and their paramilitary units. Some of the documents, he said, "I gave to Šešelj, if needed at the Hague."[28] Ultimately, Šešelj was accommodated by Milošević, and in 1998 he was officially incorporated into the ranks of the Serbian government as Deputy Prime Minister as his Serbian Radical Party entered a coalition with Milošević's ruling party.[29]

Other paramilitary officials and military officers publicly noted that they had in their possession documentary evidence that could be used to bolster testimony about Milošević's linkages to paramilitary organizations and their war crimes. During a sham legal proceeding in Belgrade intended to show Serbia's concern about "human rights" violations, lawyers for Vojin Vucković Žuca, the indicted commander of the "Igor Markovic" units, better known as the "Yellow Wasps" paramilitary force, claimed he had acted as an operative of the Serbian police and threatened to call specific police officials as witnesses. Žuca clearly fell out of favor or was being offered as a scapegoat. However, his legal team warned that the court "does not have enough valid proof, and, if it does offer sufficient valid proof, it will find itself in a situation in which they will reveal more than is desired." Similarly, Colonel Veselin Šljivancanin and other Yugoslav Army officers, after being indicted by the International Criminal Tribunal, threatened to reveal documents that were in their possession and that would implicate Slobodan Milošević if they were extradited to the Hague.[30] With the extradition and indictment of Milošević himself, it would not be long before he would have to answer for the war crimes committed in Bosnia-Herzegovina and Croatia.

NOTES

1. Acting Secretary of State Lawrence Eagleburger, "The Need to Respond to War Crimes in the Former Yugoslavia," *U.S. Department of State Dispatch*, 28 December 1992, pp. 923-24.

2. See the Document Section for the texts of the Indictments on Croatia and Bosnia-Herzegovina.

3. A.R.P., "Garda odlazi s vojskom" [The Guard Will Pull Out Along with the Army], *Evropske Novosti* (Frankfurt), 16 November 1995, p. 5. *Evropske Novosti* is the foreign edition of the pro-Milošević Belgrade daily *Vecernje Novosti*. Regarding Pelević's comments on Vojvodina, Sandžak, and Kosovo see the interview with Borislav Pelević by Vojislav Tufegdžić, '*Ne priznajem kapitulaciju*' [I Do Not Recognize Capitulation], *Intervju* (Belgrade), 13 October 1995, p. 60. For Pelević 's remarks on Kosovo see D. P., "Demobilization of Tigers at the Beginning of April," Naša Borba (Belgrade), 25 January 1996, cited on p. 2, *Foreign Broadcast Information Service (FBIS) Eastern Europe (EEU)-96-018*, 26 January 1996, p. 70. For Arkan's remark on his solution for the Kosovar Albanian problem see Belgrade *Tanjug* Domestic Service, 13 February 1996, *FBIS-EEU-96-032*, 15 February 1996, p. 71. See also "The Serbian Voluntary Guard Is Being Disbanded" *Naša Borba* , 27 March 1996, *FBIS-EEU-96-061*, 28 March 1996, p. 56.

4. Quoted in "Arkan: Garda je spremna" [Arkan: The Guard Is Ready], *Vijesti* (Podgorica, Montenegro), 26 March 1999, at www.vijesti.cg.yu.

5. See U.S. Department of State, *The Ethnic Cleansing of Kosovo* fact sheet, 4 June 1999, at www.state.gov/www/regions/eur/rpt_990604_kosovo_ethnic.html; Jack Kelley, "Remorseless Troops Tell about Pillaging Kosovo," *USA Today*, 22 July 1999, p. 10-A; and "11 Child Victims-But Warlord Arkan Denies Blame," *Daily Record and Sunday Mail* (Glasgow), 16 June 1999, at www.ic24.net/mgn/DAILY_RECORD/NEWS/P7S1.html

6. Interview with Arkan by Diane Sawyer, ABC-TV, *Good Morning America*, 3 April 1999. For accounts of the ethnic cleansing in Kosovo, see U.S. Department of State, *Erasing History: Ethnic Cleansing in Kosovo, May 1999*, at www.state.gov/www/regions/eur/rpt_9905_ethnic_ksvo_toc.html; and U.S. Department of State, *Ethnic Cleansing in Kosovo: An Accounting*, December 1999, at www.state.gov/www/global/human rights/kosovoii/homepage.html.

7. The need to establish individual responsibility in order to avoid conclusions of collective guilt has been highlighted by both the United Nations Secretary-General and the Chief Prosecutor for the International Criminal Tribunal for the Former Yugoslavia. See Press Statement by the Prosecutor, Justice Richard Goldstone, 25 July 1995.

8. Milošević speaking in 1995 on the "Gates of Hell" episode from the BBC's *Death of Yugoslavia* series 1995.

9. Press statement by the Prosecutor, Justice Richard Goldstone, 25 July 1995.

10. Article 11 of the Statute of the International Criminal Tribunal for the Former Yugoslavia, 25 May 1993, p. 13 [hereinafter Statute of the Tribunal].

11. Articles 1 and 8 of the *Statute of the Tribunal*, pp. 5 and 11.

12. Indictment of Dragan Nikolić for Grave Breaches of the Geneva Conventions, Violations of the Laws or Customs of War, and Crimes Against Humanity (Tribunal Document IT-94-2-I, 7 November 1994 ; hereinafter Indictment of Dragan Nikolic); Indictment of Željko Meakić for Genocide, Grave Breaches of the Geneva Conventions, Violations of the Laws and Customs of War, and Crimes Against Humanity (No Tribunal Document number available, 13 February 1995 ; hereinafter Indictment of Željko Meakić); Indictment of Miroslav Kvocka, Dragoljub Prcac, Mladen Radić, Momcilo Gruban for Grave Breaches of the Geneva Conventions,

Violations of the Laws and Customs of War, and Crimes Against Humanity (No Tribunal Document number available, 13 February 1995; hereinafter Indictment of Miroslav Kvocka, Dragoljub Prcac, Mladen Radić, Momcilo Gruban); Indictment of Slobodan Miljković, Blagoje Simić, Milan Simić, Miroslav Tadić, Stevan Todorović, and Šimo Žarić for Grave Breaches of the Geneva Conventions, Violations of the Laws or Customs of War, and Crimes Against Humanity, (Tribunal Document IT-95-9-I, 29 June 1995, hereinafter Indictment of Slobodan Miljković, Blagoje Simić, Milan Simić, Miroslav Tadić, Stevan Todorović, and Šimo Žaric); Indictment of Goran Jelišić and Ranko Cesić for Genocide, Grave Breaches of the Geneva Conventions, Violations of the Laws and Customs of War, and Crimes Against Humanity, Tribunal Document IT-95-10 I, 30 June 1995 [hereinafter Indictment of Goran Jelišić and Ranko Cesic]; Indictment of Duško Šikirica, Damir Došen, Dragan Fuštar, and Dragan Kulundžija for Grave Breaches of the Geneva Conventions, Violations of the Laws or Customs of War, and Crimes Against Humanity (Tribunal Document IT-95-8-I, 19 July 1995 ; hereinafter Indictment of Duško Šikirica, Damir Došen, Dragan Fuštar, and Dragan Kulundžija); Indictment of Milan Martić for Violations of the Laws or Customs of War, (Tribunal Document IT-95-11-I, 24 July 1995; hereinafter Indictment of Milan Martic); Indictment of Radovan Karadžić and Ratko Mladić for Genocide, Crimes Against Humanity and Violations of the Law or Customs of War (Tribunal Document IT-95-5-I, 25 July 1995; hereinafter Indictment of Radovan Karadžić and Ratko Mladić #1). Indictment of Ivica Rajić for Grave Breaches of the Geneva Conventions, and Violations of the Law or Customs of War (Tribunal Document IT-95-12-I, 23 August 1995; hereinafter Indictment of Ivica Rajic); Indictment of Dario Kordić, Tihomir Blaškić, Mario Cerkez, Ivan Šantić, Pero Skopljak, and Zlatko Aleksovski (Tribunal Document IT-95-14-I, 2 November 1995; hereinafter Indictment of Dario Kordić, Tihomir Blaškić, Mario Cerkez, Ivan Šantić, Pero Skopljak, and Zlatko Aleksovski); Indictment of Mile Mrkšić, Miroslav Radić, and Veselin Šljivancanin for Grave Breaches of the Geneva Conventions, Violations of the Laws or Customs of War, and Crimes Against Humanity (Tribunal Document IT-95-13-I, 7 November 1995; hereinafter Indictment of Mile Mrkšić, Miroslav Radić, and Veselin Šljivancanin); Indictment of Radovan Karadžić and Ratko Mladić for Genocide, Crimes Against Humanity and Violations of the Law or Customs of War (Tribunal Document IT-95-18-I, 14 November 1995; hereinafter Indictment of Radovan Karadžić and Ratko Mladić #2). Indictment of Djordje Djukić for Crimes Against Humanity and a Violation of the Laws and Customs of War (Tribunal Document IT-96-20-I, 29 February 1996; hereinafter Indictment of Djordje Djukic); and Indictment of Zejnil Delalić, Zdravko Mucić and Hazim Delić for Grave Breaches of the Geneva Conventions, and Violations of the Laws and Customs of War (Tribunal Document IT-95-21-I, 20 March 1996; hereinafter Indictment of Zejnil Delalić, Zdravko Mucić and Hazim Delic).

13. *Ibid*

14. On Slobodan Milošević's rise to and consolidation of power, see Slavoljub Djukić, *Izmedju slave i anateme* [Between Glory and Anathema], Belgrade: Filip Višnjić 1994; Ivan Stambolić, *Put u bespuce* [Path into the Uncharted], Belgrade: Radio B92 1995; Nebojša Popov, "*Srpski populizam; Od marginalne do dominante pojave*" [Serbian Populism; From a Marginal to a Dominant Phenomenon], special insert in *Vreme* (Belgrade), 24 May 1993; and Branka Magaš, *The Destruction of Yugoslavia*, London: Verso 1993.

15. Noel Malcolm, *Bosnia: A Short History*, London: Macmillan 1994, pp. 223-24.

16. *Final Report of the United Nations Commission of Experts Established Pursuant to Security Council Resolution 780* (1992); Annex V; *The Prijedor Report*, para 187.

17. See S. Jovicić, "Personalna unija politike i ekonomske moci" [Personal Union of Politics and Economic Power], *Naša Borba*, 9 April 1996, www.yurope.com/zines/nasa-borba.

Companies owned by the Republic of Serbia, such as Jugopetrol and JAT, were used frequently to channel funds in order to foster a non-official image for such purposes as media campaigns abroad. This overlapping system of Republic of Serbia state ownership and control is illustrated by the status of the airports (including even the ones in Montenegro), which are owned by the state airline JAT, which is in turn owned by the Republic of Serbia. JAT was made a public company owned by the Republic of Serbia by a law enacted by the Parliament of the Republic of Serbia in February 1992 and signed by Slobodan Milošević. A subsequent decree in December 1995 reaffirmed that all assets for common use-such as roads-as well as all assets that carry out public services are the property of the Serbian state. As part of the consolidation of state control, JAT personnel were purged and replaced by politically reliable individuals. See Branka Plamenac, "Ciji ce biti aerodromi Podgorica i Tivat" [Whose Are the Airports in Podgorica and Tivat Going to Be?], *Monitor* (Podgorica, Montenegro), 23 February 1996, pp. 8-9.

Indicative of the level of Slobodan Milošević's control and involvement over the state economic sector in Serbia was the statement of Nikola Sajnović, then Minister for Energy: "As if a soldier, I reported not only to the government, but also to President Milošević, once a week." Interview with Nikola Šajnović by Vladan Dinić and Sredoje Šimić, "Price o kradji zlata iz Bora su izmišljotina [Stories About Theft of Gold from Bor Are an Invention], *Svedok* (Belgrade), 20 March 2001, p. 5.

18. See interview with Milika Ceko Dacević by B.A. and B.B., "Život za gusle" [A Life for Fiddles], *NIN* (Belgrade), 21 April 1995, p. 12. According to the Serbian Guard's field commander, in 1991 about 7,000 personnel were in training, although not all may have deployed. Aleksandar Knežević and Vojislav Tufegdžić, *Kriminal koji je izmenio Srbiju* [Crime Which Changed Serbia], Belgrade: *Radio* B92, 2nd edition 1995, p. 28. Earlier, the commander of the Serbian Guard, Djordje Božović, had boasted that 40,000 volunteers had already shown up. Interview with Djordje Božović by Slavica Lazić, "Bicemo vojska moderne i humane Srbije" [We Will Be the Army of a Modern and Humane Serbia], *Srpska rec* (Belgrade), 5 August 1991, p. 15. Yet, another paramilitary leader Captain Dragan claimed 1,200 in his force in 1991. Interview with Captain Dragan by Aleksandar I. Popović, "Nisam Buntovnik" [I Am Not a Rebel], Pogledi (Kragujevac, Serbia), 29 November 1991, p. 29.

19. Interview with Vojislav Šešelj by Željka Godec, "Svim Srbima iz Hrvatske porucio bih da se isele" [I Would Suggest to All Serbs from Croatia to Leave], *Globus* (Zagreb), 12 May 1995, p. 51.

20. Miloš Vasić and Filip Švarm, "Cetnicki Votergejt" [Chetnik Watergate], *Vreme*, 15 November 1993, p. 25.

21. Regarding the size and formation of Arkan's Tigers see B. Trivić, "Diskont života" [Discount on Lives], *Stav* (Novi Sad, Yugoslavia), 7 February 1992, p. 29. In 1995 one of Arkan's top officials gave a figure of 2,000 as the size of the organization's force. Interview with Mihajlo Ulemek, a colonel in the SDG, and Arkan's deputy in Western Bosnia, by Gordana Jovanović, "Srbin sam, tim se dicim" [I Am a Serb and Proud of It], *Intervju*, 3 November 1995, p. 20.

22. Quoted in Radovan Pavlović, "Zašto su Arkanovi 'tigrovi' uvukli kandže" [Why Arkan's Tigers Pulled in Their Claws], *Politika*, 30 March 1994, p. 12. Borislav Pelević elsewhere gave a figure of over 10,000 for late 1995, although that number also included former Krajina Army personnel and forcibly mobilized refugees. Interview "I Do Not Recognize Capitulation," 13 October 1995, p. 58.

23. Radovan Pavlović, "Mnogo vojske pod jednom komandom" [Many Armies under One Command], *Politika* (Belgrade), 11 November 1993, p. 9. All in all, it was a large-scale

operation requiring significant logistic support (fuel, food, ammunition, and spare parts), as well as funding. *Politika* is a state-owned daily.

24. Interview with Slobodan Milošević by James R. Gaines, Karsten Prager, Massimo Calabresi, and Marguerite Michaels, "I Am Just an Ordinary Man," *Time*, 17 July 1995, p. 29.

25. Reported by Belgrade TV News, 4 November 1992.

26. Dejan Lucić is quoted in Vojislav Tufegdžić, "Elita u podzemlju" [Elite in the Underworld], *Intervju*, 25 November 1994, p. 61. On the criminal background of the leadership of the SPO's Serbian Guard, see Aleksandar Knežević and Vojislav Tufegdžić, *Kriminal koji je izmenio Srbiju* [Criminality Which Has Transformed Serbia], 2nd ed., Belgrade: Radio B-92 1995 pp. 5-52.

27. M. M. "Šešelj Denied Passport," *Naša Borba* , 17 January 1996, p. 9; *FBIS-EEU-96-012*, 18 January 1996, p. 103.

28. Interview with Branislav Vakić by Predrag Popović, 'Branislav Vakić: Kako smo Frenki i ja osvajali Srebrenicu' [Branislav Vakić: How Frenki and I Conquered Srebrenica], Svet, 13 November 1995, p. 8. Vakić was commander of paramilitary unit commander under Šešelj. He held the rank of 'warlord' (*vojvoda*) and later served as a deputy in the Serbian Parliament.

29. Šešelj remains in parliament today as leader of an opposition party.

30. Interview with Colonel Veselin Šljivancanin by Krešimir Meler, "Naredjenje je stiglo sa Dedinja" [The Order Came from Dedinje], *Svijet* (Ljubljana), 25 April 1996, p. 20.

II

A PERSON IS INDIVIDUALLY RESPONSIBLE FOR THE COMMISSION of a crime of war if he commits a clearly definable war crime or aids and abets in the commission of such a war crime. An individual is also to be held legally responsible if he is complicit in the commission of genocide, has command responsibility for individuals or organizations that commit war crimes, or if he fails to prevent or punish the commission of war crimes by those individuals or organizations over which he has authority. The military tribunals in the Nuremberg and Tokyo war crimes trials established substantial precedent relating to the prosecution of suspected war criminals.[1] Building on these precedents, the United Nations Security Council and the Yugoslav

Tribunal chose to create a self-contained set of rules of procedure and evidence for the indictment and prosecution of suspected war criminals.[2] The following review of individual responsibility for the commission of war crimes is therefore limited to the statute, rules of procedure and evidence adopted by the Tribunal, with reference to supporting customary international law or international conventions.

According to the statute of the Tribunal the following acts were to be considered crimes of war for which a person may be held individually responsible and over which the Tribunal had jurisdiction:

GRAVE BREACHES OF THE GENEVA CONVENTIONS OF 12 AUGUST 1949: These include the willful killing, torture, or inhumane treatment causing great suffering or serious injury to people protected by the conventions, as well as the extensive destruction and appropriation of property. Such breaches, not justified by military necessity and carried out unlawfully and wantonly, further include compelling prisoners of war or civilians to serve in the forces of a hostile power; willfully depriving a prisoner of war or a civilian of the rights to a fair and regular trial; unlawfully deporting, transferring, or confining civilians; and taking civilian hostages.[3]

VIOLATIONS OF THE LAWS OR CUSTOMS OF WAR: These include the employment of weapons calculated to cause unnecessary suffering; the wanton destruction of population centers not justified by military necessity; the attack on undefended population centers; the seizure of, destruction, or willful damage done to institutions of religion, charity, education, and the arts and science; the willful destruction or damage of historic monuments and works of art and science; and the plunder of public or private property.[4]

GENOCIDE: This is defined as the intentional attempt to destroy, in whole or in part, a national ethnic, racial, or religious group by killing members of the group, causing serious bodily or mental harm to members of the group, deliberately inflicting on its members conditions of life calculated to bring about the group's physical destruction in whole or in part, imposing measures to prevent births within the group, or forcibly transferring children of the group to another group. Punishable crimes of genocide also include conspiracy to commit genocide, direct and public incitement to commit genocide, attempts to commit genocide, and complicity in genocide.[5]

CRIMES AGAINST HUMANITY: These include the following acts committed against any civilian population in times of international or internal armed conflict: murder, extermination, enslavement, deportation, imprisonment, torture, rape, persecution on political, racial and religious grounds, and other inhumane acts.[6]

A person may be held individually responsible for grave breaches of the Geneva Conventions, violations of the laws or customs of war, crimes of genocide, and crimes against humanity on the basis of, one, *direct responsibility*, two, *command responsibility*, and, three, *complicity-based responsibility*. A person is individually responsible for the commission of a war crime if he commits, plans, instigates, orders, or otherwise aids and abets in the planning, preparation or execution of any of the acts listed above.[7] This form of individual responsibility is usually referred to as *direct responsibility*. The Tribunal has indicted concentration camp guards and commanders, local political and military leaders, paramilitary leaders, and national political and military leaders (Radovan Karadžić and Ratko Mladic) for war crimes on the basis of direct responsibility.[8]

A person also is individually responsible for the commission of a war crime if he knew or had reason to know that his subordinates or agents were about to commit one of the acts listed above, or had done so, and if he failed to take necessary and reasonable measures to prevent such acts or to punish the perpetrators of those acts.[9] This form of individual responsibility is usually referred to as *command responsibility*. The Tribunal has indicted concentration camp commanders, local political and military leaders, and national political and military leaders (Radovan Karadžić and Ratko Mladic) for war crimes on the basis of command responsibility.[10]

If a person commits, directs, or aids and abets in the commission of genocide, or fails to prevent or punish his subordinates who commit, direct, or aid and abet genocide, he is individually responsible for the war crime of genocide. A person is additionally responsible for the war crime of genocide if he is complicit in the commission of genocide.[11] In most instances, this latter responsibility is referred to as *complicity-based responsibility*. The tribunal has indicted concentration camp commanders on the basis of direct responsibility and complicity-based responsibility for genocide. It has indicted national political and military leaders (Radovan Karadžić and Ratko Mladic) on the basis of both direct responsibility and command responsibility.[12]

The Tribunal also indicted Radovan Karadžić and Ratko Mladić as individually responsible for the commission of war crimes on the basis that they or their subordinates permitted others to commit the war crime of extensive, wanton and unlawful destruction of Bosnian Muslim and Bosnian Croat property—a grave breach of the Geneva Conventions.[13] Although not specifically provided for in the statute of the Tribunal, this indictment serves as a precedent for extending complicity-based responsibility beyond the crime of genocide to include other war crimes.

The Tribunal may indict an individual on the basis of direct responsibility, command responsibility, or complicity-based responsibility for the commission of a war crime upon the presentation of a *prima facie* case by the Prosecutor.[14] According to the rules of procedure and evidence of the Tribunal, a *prima facie* case may be established where "there is sufficient evidence to provide reasonable grounds for believing that a suspect has committed a crime within the jurisdiction of the Tribunal."[15] Evidence that may be presented to establish a *prima facie* case includes "any relevant evidence which [the Court] deems to have probative value" and that is not excludable by the Court on the basis that "its probative value is substantially outweighed by the need to ensure a fair trial."[16] The Tribunal is not bound by national rules of evidence and, accordingly, there is no automatic rule against the admission of hearsay or circumstantial evidence.[17]

To present a *prima facie* case that a person is *individually, or directly, responsible* for the commission of a war crime on the basis that he committed, planned, instigated, ordered, or otherwise aided and abetted in the planning, preparation, or execution of a war crime, it must be established that a criminal act has been committed and that the accused person either committed or affirmatively assisted in the commission of that act, or alternatively that forces under the effective control of the accused either committed or affirmatively assisted in the commission of that act.[18]

To present a *prima facie* case that a person is individually responsible for war crimes by virtue of his *command responsibility*, it must be established that a criminal act has been committed, the accused was in a position of superior authority to those who committed the war crime, the accused knew or had reason to know that persons subject to his superior authority were about to commit the war crime, and the accused failed to prevent or punish the perpetration of the crime.

To establish that the accused was in a position of superior authority, it must be demonstrated that the persons committing the offense were under the command or control of the accused, such that the accused had the ability to prevent them from committing illegal acts and to see that the offenders were punished. Specifically, the individual had the authority to issue orders to his subordinates not to commit illegal acts and the authority to see that offenders were punished.

To establish that the accused knew or should have known of the commission of the war crime, it must be demonstrated that the accused had *actual, constructive*, or *imputed* notice of the crime. *Actual notice* occurs when the accused individual sees the commission of the war crimes or is informed of their commission on a timely basis thereafter. Actual knowledge may be demonstrated either by direct or circumstantial evidence. *Constructive notice* occurs where the number of crimes is of such a great number that a reasonable person could come to no other conclusion than that the accused individual must have known of the offenses or of the existence of an understood and acknowledged routine for their commission. *Imputed notice* occurs when the accused individual should have known of the commission of the crime but displayed such serious personal dereliction as to constitute willful and wanton disregard of the possible consequences of his reckless behavior. To establish the act of omission, it must be demonstrated that the accused failed to take such appropriate measures as were within his power to prevent and punish the commission of the war crime.

Therefore, to present a *prima facie* case that a person is individually responsible for the crime of genocide either on the basis of direct responsibility or command responsibility, the circumstances set forth in either of the immediately preceding two paragraphs must be met. To establish a *prima facie* case that a person is individually responsible for complicity in genocide, it must be established that he failed to act to prevent the commission of genocide where he had a legal duty and effective opportunity to do so.

In order to establish that Slobodan Milošević may be held individually responsible for the commission of war crimes in the former Yugoslavia, this study investigates his potential liability on the basis of both *direct* and *command* responsibility.

To establish direct responsibility, two questions need to be addressed. First, it is necessary to determine whether Milošević may be considered to have directed, planned, or instigated the commission of war crimes by virtue of his effective control over Serbian forces and their paramilitary forces. Second, we must establish whether Milošević may be considered to have aided and abetted, or directed the aiding and abetting of, the commission of war crimes in Bosnia and Croatia by virtue of the fact that Serbian forces under his effective control aided and abetted the commission of war crimes by Serbian paramilitary units, the Bosnian Serb Army, and the Army of the Republic of the Serbian Krajina. With respect to command responsibility, this study investigates whether Slobodan Milošević may be considered to have failed to prevent or punish the commission of war crimes by forces under his authority and control, when he knew or had reason to know that those forces were about to commit or had committed war crimes.

In order to reduce the risk of repetition, the issue of Slobodan Milošević's responsibility for the crime of genocide is not separately explored in this text. Instead, we highlight the relevant sections where there is sufficient evidence to establish a *prima facie* case that Slobodan Milošević is individually responsible for crimes of genocide on the basis of direct responsibility, command responsibility, and/or complicity-based responsibility.

In short, in this study we address the following questions. First, we ask whether Serbian forces and their affiliated paramilitary formations committed war crimes in Bosnia and Croatia. Second, we address the question whether Milošević and senior figures in the Belgrade regime were individually responsible for ordering, planning, or instigating the commission of war crimes in Bosnia and Croatia by virtue of their effective control over Serbian military and paramilitary forces. Third, we ask whether Slobodan Milošević was individually responsible for aiding and abetting the commission of war crimes in Bosnia and Croatia by virtue of the fact that Serbian forces under his effective control aided and abetted the commission of war crimes by Serbian paramilitary forces, the Bosnian Serb Army, and the Army of the Republic of Serbian Krajina. Finally, we inquire whether Milošević, as a superior authority, was individually responsible for the war crimes committed by Serbian forces and associated paramilitary units by virtue of his command responsibility for the acts of those forces. In the chapters that follow each of these questions is separately addressed.

NOTES

1. For a comprehensive review of the precedents set by the Nuremberg and Tokyo war crimes trials, as well as other instances of prosecution of suspected war criminals, see Colby, "War Crimes," 23 Michigan Law Review 482 (1924); Horwitz, "The Tokyo Trial," 465 International Conciliation (1950); Telford Taylor, Nuremberg and Vietnam: An American Tragedy (1970); Richard Falk, Gabriel Kolko & Robert Lifton, Editors, Crimes of War (1971);] Howard, "Command Responsibility for War Crimes," 21 Journal of Public Law 7 (1972); Friedman, Editor, The Law of War: A Documentary History (1972); Parks, "Command Responsibility for War Crimes," 62 Military Law Review 1 (1973); Note, "Command Responsibility for War Crimes," 82 Yale Law Journal 1274 (1973); Campbell, Jr., Military Command Liability for Grave Breaches of National and International Law: Absolute or Limited? (1974); Piccigallo, The Japanese on Trial - Allied War Crimes Operations in the East 1945-49 (1979); and Weston D. Burnett, "Command Responsibility and a Case Study of the Criminal Responsibility of Israeli Military Commanders for the Pogrom at Shatila and Sabra,"107 Military Law Review 71 (1985).

2. See "Statute of the Tribunal, and Rules of Procedure and Evidence of International Criminal Tribunal for the Former Yugoslavia" (February 1994; most recent updated version, 18 January 1996) [hereafter referred to as "Tribunal Rules of Procedure and Evidence"].

3. Article 2 of the Statute of the Tribunal, p. 5. The new military code, the Yugoslav Federal Defense Law, adopted in 1993, reaffirmed a commitment for the Yugoslav Army to be bound by international legal norms, "All citizens who in whatever capacity participate in armed combat would be bound to respect the rules of international military law" (Chapter I, Article 3).

4. Article 3 of the Statute of the Tribunal, p. 7.

5. Article 4 of the Statute of the Tribunal, p. 7. See also Convention on the Prevention and Punishment of the Crime of Genocide (entered into force on 12 January 1951).

6. Article 5 of the Statute of the Tribunal, p. 9.

7. Article 7, para 1 of the Statute of the Tribunal, p. 9.

8. It appears that all persons, except for Zejnil Delalić and Zdravko Mucić, indicted by the Tribunal have been indicted in part on the basis of direct responsibility. See Indictment of Zejnil Delalić, Zdravko Mucić, and Hazim Delić.

9. Article 7, para 3 of the Statute of the Tribunal, p. 9; and Report of the Secretary General issued pursuant to para 2 of Security Council Resolution 808, paras 53-57, pp. 213-14 (1993).

10. See Indictment of Radovan Karadžić and Ratko Mladić #1; Indictment of Radovan Karadžić and Ratko Mladić #2; Indictment of Milan Martić; Indictment of Ivica Rajić; Indictment of Mile Mrkšić, Miroslav Radić, and Veselin Šljivancanin; Indictment of Duško Šikirica, Damir Došen, Dragan Fuštar, and Dragan Kulundžija; Indictment of Željko Meakić; Indictment of Miroslav Kvocka, Dragoljub Prcac, Mladen Radić, and Momcilo Gruban; Indictment of Dragan Nikolić; Indictment of Blagoje Simić; Indictment of Dario Kordić, Tihomir Blaškić, Mario Cerkez, Ivan Šantić, Pero Skopljak, and Zlatko Aleksovski; and Indictment of Zejnil Delalić, Zdravko Mucić and Hazim Delić.

11. Article 4, para 3 of the Statute of the Tribunal, p. 7.

12. See Indictment of Goran Jelišić and Ranko Cesić, para 17, p. 3; Indictment of Željko Meakić, para 18, p. 5; Indictment of Duško Šikirica, Damir Došen, Dragan Fuštar, and Dragan Kulundžija, para 12, p. 4; Indictment of Radovan Karadžić and Ratko Mladić #1, para 33, p.12; and Indictment of Radovan Karadžić and Ratko Mladić #2, para 51, p. 11.

13. Indictment of Radovan Karadžić and Ratko Mladić #1, para 41, p.16.37.22.

14. Article 18, para 4 of the Statute of the Tribunal, pp. 17-19.

15. Rule 47 (A) of the Tribunal Rules of Procedure and Evidence, p. 26. See also "Review of the Indictment of Zejnil Delalić, Zdravko Mucić and Hazim Delić," by Judge Claude Jorda, March 1996 p. 2 [hereinafter "Review of the Indictment of Zejnil Delalić, Zdravko Mucić and Hazim Delic"]. After submission by the Prosecutor, a Judge of the Trial Chamber reviews the indictment, and if he determines that a *prima facie* case has been established by the Prosecutor, he confirms the indictment. Article 19 of the Statute of the Tribunal, p.19.

16. Rule 89 (C) & (D) of the Tribunal Rules of Procedure and Evidence, p. 51.

17. Rule 89 (A) of the Tribunal Rules of Procedure and Evidence, p. 51.

18. See infra, section IV.

III

THE COMMISSION OF WAR CRIMES BY SERBIAN FORCES AND AFFILIATED PARAMILITARY FORMATIONS IN BOSNIA AND CROATIA

THE FIRST REQUIREMENT OF A *PRIMA FACIE* CASE FOR AN indictment of an individual on charges of war crimes is to establish that a war crime, in fact, has been committed. The United Nations, foreign governments, the international and local media, and international humanitarian organizations compiled numerous reports containing extensive, detailed and credible evidence related to war crimes committed by regular Serbian forces and paramilitary formations under the control of the Belgrade authorities. At the time of this writing, the Tribunal had also issued fifty-eight indictments containing numerous, detailed accounts of war crimes committed in the territory of the former Yugoslavia. Although many of these crimes were committed by Bosnian Serb forces, the Tribunal noted in a number of circumstances that Serbian forces and paramilitary units they controlled were also involved in the commission of war crimes.[1]

Therefore, rather than providing an exhaustive catalog of war crimes committed by Serbian forces in the former Yugoslavia, it is sufficient for the purposes of this study to provide a few illustrative examples of war crimes committed by Serbian forces, agencies, and paramilitary forces, and to refer the reader to the great body of public information documenting the commission of war crimes by these forces. It should be noted here that these crimes entailed crimes against both prisoners of war and civilians, and included criminal acts of killing, expulsion, rape, detention in concentration camps, forced labor, torture, mutilation, and the looting and destruction of property. All were perpetrated on a large and systematic scale, often with an exceptional degree of brutality.[2]

The Yugoslav federal forces, in particular the JNA and its successor, the Yugoslav Army, were active in the commission of war crimes in both Croatia and Bosnia. Prior to the transformation of sections of the JNA into the Army of the Republic of the Serbian Krajina and the Bosnian Serb Army, the JNA directly participated in the initial seizures of territory and subsequent ethnic cleansing in Croatia and Bosnia. In many instances, the JNA would operate in a symbiotic relationship with local forces and paramilitary organizations: it would provide a secure environment within its area of control enabling lightly armed local forces and Serbian paramilitary groups, frequently under the command of the JNA, to commit systematic and widespread war crimes with impunity.[3] For instance, in early 1992, Goran Hadžić, president of the self-proclaimed Autonomous Region of Krajina, reported to General Tomislav Simović, the Serbian Minister of Defense: "Theft is flourishing. A tank rolls down the street and liberates it, and the infantry follows, since the infantry [is there to] plunder, and then the volunteers follow with a truck and 'cleanse the area.'"[4]

In addition to providing a secure environment for the commission of war crimes by local and paramilitary units, JNA personnel actively participated in the commission of war crimes themselves. For example, looting became so widespread that, in a meeting in the office of the Serbian Minister of Defense, one official mused rhetorically, "Tell me of even one reservist, especially if he is an officer, who has spent more than a month at the front and has not brought back a fine car filled with everything that would fit inside the car."[5] After the formal transformation of sections of the JNA into the Army of the Republic of the Serbian Krajina and the Bosnian Serb Army—which, in many ways, continued to operate as a Yugoslav Army task force for Bosnia[6]—the JNA ordered a number of high-ranking JNA officers to remain behind to assist the Bosnian Serb and Krajina Serb forces in their operations.[7] These operations frequently entailed the commission of war crimes. In other instances, Yugoslav Army forces returned to Bosnia or Croatia to assist the Bosnian Serb and Bosnian Croat forces in their commission of atrocities. Two prominent examples of the involvement or support of JNA and Yugoslav Army forces in the commission of war crimes are the siege and ethnic cleansing of Vukovar and the siege and ethnic cleansing of the "safe area" of Srebrenica.

VUKOVAR

According to the official records of the Tribunal, in late August 1991 the JNA laid siege to the city of Vukovar, Croatia, and launched a sustained artillery assault on the city. The assault resulted in the unlawful killing of hundreds of civilians and the unnecessary destruction of most of the city's buildings. On 18 November, the JNA forces, in concert with Serbian paramilitary units, captured and occupied the city. On 20 November 1991, again acting in concert with Serbian paramilitary forces, the JNA removed 400 men from the Vukovar hospital and subsequently killed 260 of them.[8] These men had been subjected to extensive beatings, execution, and burial in a mass grave.[9] As a result of these atrocities, the Tribunal indicted three JNA officers for grave breaches of the Geneva Conventions, violations of the laws or customs of war, and crimes against humanity.[10] To date, the Yugoslav Army has refused requests to place these officers in the custody of the Tribunal, and those in official control of the Yugoslav Army have failed to punish the officers for their crimes. This failure itself constitutes the commission of a war crime under the doctrine of command responsibility. In fact, the Yugoslav Army officially promoted two of the officers charged with war crimes committed in Vukovar.[11]

SREBRENICA

On 16 April 1993, the UN Security Council declared the town of Srebrenica a United Nations "safe area." From April 1993 until July 1995, Bosnian Serb forces besieged and repeatedly shelled this "safe area." From 6 July 1995 until 11 July 1995, in coordination with Yugoslav Army units and Serbian paramilitary groups deployed from Serbia, it mounted a full-scale attack on Srebrenica.[12] Following their capture of the "safe area" some Yugoslav

Army forces participated in the Bosnian Serb Army's systematic slaughter of its inhabitants with the objective of ethnically cleansing the region of its Bosnian Muslim population.[13] In the words of Judge Fouad Riad of the Tribunal:

> After Srebrenica fell to besieging Serbian forces in July 1995, a truly terrible massacre of the Muslim population appears to have taken place. The evidence tendered by the Prosecutor describes scenes of unimaginable savagery: thousands of men executed and buried in mass graves, hundreds of men buried alive, men and women mutilated and slaughtered, children killed before their mothers eyes, a grandfather forced to eat the liver of his own grandson. These are truly scenes from hell, written on the darkest pages of human history.[14]

As Srebrenica was overrun by the Bosnian Serb, a column of refugees fled along the main road to Tuzla. Before they could reach the relative safety of Tuzla, however, they were attacked by armor, artillery, anti-aircraft guns, and automatic weapons. Those who were not killed in the initial assault "were slowly slaughtered by a group of Serbian soldiers using knives."[15] The victims included women and children. Thousands of other inhabitants of Srebrenica surrendered to "Serbian military forces" and were taken to assembly points where they were summarily executed.[16] Others fled to the United Nations base at Potocari. Unable to secure the assistance of the Dutch peacekeepers, they were ordered onto buses by the Serbian military forces, taken to nearby fields and rivers and summarily executed. Women were raped and killed and, in many instances, "children had their throats slit before their mother's eyes."[17] As a result of the Serbian campaign against Srebrenica, "the Muslim population of the enclave was virtually eliminated."[18]

Although the Tribunal has not yet indicted members of the Yugoslav Army, or those who exercise power, influence, and control over the Yugoslav Army, it did indict Bosnian Serb political and military authorities for grave breaches of the Geneva Conventions, violations of the laws or customs of war, crimes against humanity, and genocide for the Srebrenica massacre. It is therefore reasonable to assume that the activities of the Yugoslav Army in supporting the Srebrenica massacre—and in this sense the BSA could be viewed as an extension of the Yugoslav Army—as well as those who were in control of these forces similarly amount to grave breaches of the Geneva Conventions, violations of the laws or customs of war, crimes against humanity, and genocide. Apart from the general support which the BSA received from the Yugoslav Army, there were reports that the Yugoslav Army's Chief of the General Staff, General Momcilo Perišić, "was on a mountaintop across the border in Yugoslavia, sending instructions and counsel to General Ratko Mladić, the commander of Bosnian Serb Military forces" as well as of "the presence of Yugoslav Army personnel."[19]

There is also substantial evidence that forces from the Republic of Serbia operating in Croatia and Bosnia committed war crimes against civilian populations. According to a United Nations report, for example, in 1992 special police units from Niš (Serbia) that were stationed in Banja Luka participated in the takeover of the town of Prijedor and the subsequent war crimes committed upon its population.[20] Similarly, in June 1995 the 101st Police Battalion was deployed from Serbia to operate against the Bihac pocket in an operation that included the siege and shelling of the civilian population.[21] The forces and agencies of the Republic of Serbia also maintained concentration camps within the territory of the Republic of Serbia. According to reports by the German Federal Intelligence Service, from 1992 non-Serbs from Bosnia were held in concentration camps such as Aleksinac in Serbia where conditions included forced labor in a coalmine.[22] As noted above, such actions are a grave breach of the Geneva Conventions and crimes against humanity.

In 1995, when Srebrenica and Žepa were ethnically cleansed, several hundred Muslim survivors were forced to flee across the border to Serbia. They were met at Bajina Bašta by officials of the Republic of Serbia Ministry of Health and of the Republic's Commissariat for Refugees. Bratislava Morina, Serbia's Commissar (komesar) for Refugees, had characterized the treatment meted out to these survivors as Serbia's having "again extended a helping hand."[23] Subsequent reports indicated that these refugees were abused in the detention camps in which they were held in Serbia until international pressure led to their release.[24] The state-run media also aided Belgrade's propaganda campaign that accompanied the ethnic cleansing which included staged filming by Novi Sad Television of arrests and forced "confessions" in Bosnia as well as a general legitimization of the government's policy of ethnic cleansing.[25]

On a number of occasions, security forces belonging to the Republic of Serbia exercised direct control over operations conducted in Croatia and Bosnia. In many cases, they also engaged in joint operations with Serbian paramilitary organizations also operating in Croatia and Bosnia. For instance, when asked if he had cooperated with the Serbian Security Service, the paramilitary commander Vojislav Šešelj replied:

Yes, but only on matters related to the war in the Serbian Republic of Krajina and the Serbian Republic [of Bosnia]...Our volunteers took part in combat as part of special units of the police from here [Serbia], under the command of Mihalj Kertes, in Eastern Slavonija and on the territory of the Serbian Republic [of Bosnia]. Also, we fought on many battlefields alongside Frenki Stamatović, who is the head of the intelligence service of Serbia's SDB [State Security Service]. Our people liberated the area around Srebrenica, and tightened the noose around that city.[26]

In a subsequent press conference, Vojislav Šešelj confirmed that his paramilitary forces had fought under the command of Serbia's Ministry of Internal Affairs' Special Forces, and named individual police officials who commanded his units.[27] Vojislav Šešelj also stated that his Chetniks and Arkan's SDG had operated jointly with the Red Berets from Serbia's Security Service when Zvornik was seized and its population cleansed in 1992.[28] As Branislav Vakić, one of Vojislav Šešelj's lieutenants noted, Serbia's police and Vojislav Šešelj's Chetniks also operated together in the Skelane area of eastern Bosnia. Branislav Vakić added that he was "under the direct command of Obrad Stefanović, the commander of the Special Forces of the Republic of Serbia's Ministry of Internal Affairs, and under that of his deputy, Frenki Simatović. All of that is documented, and there are many witnesses who will confirm that." In fact, Vakić, was fulsome in his praise of the operational-level cooperation. He stated, "I can say that those MUP [Ministry of Internal Affairs] fellows performed like heroes in combat, like true Chetniks. Our wish is that in case of war we again have such cooperation with the army and police."[29]

Frequently the Serbian forces responsible for the commission of war crimes were commanded by high-ranking officers. These included Franko Simatović, Deputy of Serbia's State Security. For example, Ljubiša Petković, Šešelj's principal commander on the ground early in the war, noted, "Frenki, as is probably true of the majority of MUP personnel, took part in combat operations along with our fighters and with the JNA."[30] Radovan Stojčić Badža, the Deputy Minister of Internal Affairs and Head of the Department of Public Security, was also reported to have commanded Special Forces in the Vukovar area, and the "Slavonija, Baranja, and Western Srijem Staff" which shared responsibility with the JNA for operations in eastern Croatia. There was additional confirmation of the presence in Bosnia of forces from the Republic of Serbia, who directed operations of Arkan's forces. According to one of Arkan's staff officers, also present in the Banja Luka area at the time was "Colonel Filip," allegedly a member of the Republic of Serbia's Special Forces. Furthermore, there were also reports of special police units from the Republic of Serbia's Ministry of Internal Affairs, which were deployed from Pec and Priština to Banja Luka, and included Franko Simatović, Deputy of Serbia's State Security.[31]

In some instances forces and agencies from the Republic of Serbia created a formal structure for directing the operation of Croatian or Bosnian Serb and Serbian paramilitary units in Croatia and Bosnia. For example, Serbia set up a Territorial Defense organization under Radovan Stojcić Badža in occupied areas of eastern Croatia to command and provide training and support for the reserve forces and paramilitary units operating there. Slobodan Miljković, who was indicted for war crimes by the Tribunal, noted that he had been an SRS volunteer who belonged to a special unit operating in Eastern Croatia. The "Slavonija, Baranja, and Western Srijem Staff (Štab)," with Badža in charge, ordered them to transfer from the JNA to the local police after the January 1992 United Nations-brokered ceasefire. One of the provisions of the ceasefire was that only Serbian police, not the army, would be allowed in the United Nations-protected zones.[32] Elsewhere evidence shows how two colonels, on active duty in the JNA, were transferred from the Center for Military Schools in Belgrade to the Territorial Defense General Staff in Baranja.[33] The funds for the Krajina Territorial Defense, paid in cash, came through the office of Serbia's Defense Minister, General Tomislav Simović.[34] The links are clear.

Serbian paramilitary forces played a special role in the commission of war crimes. They have taken a significant part in the perpetration of ethnic cleansing, genocide, and plunder—actions which were at the heart of their mission and, in many respects, their *raison d'être*. Even General Ratko Mladić, the chief of the Bosnian Serb Army's General Staff was quite candid about the operations carried out by paramilitary groups. According to Mladić, "There is no need to set up paramilitary units such as we had in 1992 and in part of 1993. Most consisted of 'great patriots' who never absented themselves from TV screens, as well as 'liberators' who were able to 'do it all.' However, their groups and paramilitary units in general hovered around gold shops, banks, and well-stocked self-service stores, and there is not a single hill which they held or liberated. All they did was plunder well."[35] *Vojska*, the Yugoslav Army's official organ, reported that, "in Foca, there are units which could be called paramilitary agents. Despite all their services, it is sad that some units do their duty only when they feel like it, and they most feel like it when they are near 'war booty.'"[36] Although the regular JNA, Yugoslav Army, and Bosnian Serb Army systematically targeted civilian populations, it was often the paramilitary units who conducted the campaign of "ethnic cleansing." Serbian paramilitary units were often attached directly to regular army units for this specific purpose. For example, one Chetnik unit had been under the operational control of a battalion of the Bosnian Serb Army since 1992. The paramilitary unit's commander understood his mission thus: "We take care of relations with the Muslims. We only have one Muslim family left which does not want to leave....Of course, we permitted those Muslims who lived in my area of responsibility and who expressed a desire to cross over to Alija [Izetbegovic] to do so." He was able to report, "this area is [now] ethnically clean.'"[37]

In a number of its indictments the Tribunal took note of the involvement of Serbian paramilitary forces in the commission of war crimes. In one particular instance, the Tribunal alleged that from 17 April 1992 Serbian military and political authorities from Bosnia and elsewhere in the former Yugoslavia permitted Serbian paramilitary units from Serbia to enter detention camps and beat and kill prisoners.[38] The Tribunal also issued an indictment against Slobodan Miljković, the Deputy Commander of the Gray Wolves paramilitary based out of Serbia, for war crimes related to the seizure of Bosanski Šamac and the subsequent ethnic cleansing of its population.[39]

In an attempt to minimize their responsibility for the commission of war crimes, commanders of paramilitary groups sought to claim credit for military successes while blaming rival paramilitary commanders for the atrocities accompanying those military actions. For instance, while Vojislav Šešelj blamed Arkan for the looting of Bijeljina, he sought credit for himself rather than Arkan for the takeover of the town. Šešelj likewise claimed that it was Mirko Jović's White Eagles who were responsible for attacks on refugees for which Šešelj's Chetniks had been blamed. He also accused Arkan of looting in Slavonija in 1991. In 1993, Arkan sued Šešelj for defamation of character in relation to such accusations. Perhaps feeling his case to be weak, Arkan subsequently directed his lawyer to withdraw his libel suit against Šešelj, although he gave as his motive the need for unity and a sense of patriotism.[40] While such attempts to shift the blame did little to absolve the paramilitary commanders of their responsibility for the commission of war crimes, they have brought into the public domain substantial information relating to the activities and atrocities of Serbian paramilitary forces.

As noted by the United Nations Commission of Experts, Arkan's SDG was one of the most active paramilitary groups and was responsible for some of the worst acts of violence against civilians.[41] Arkan (real name Željko Ražnatovic) was a Serb from Montenegro. Born in Slovenia in 1952, Arkan was the son of a Yugoslav Air Force officer. After a record of juvenile delinquency at home, he emigrated abroad, where he made a career of crime. Before his return to Yugoslavia there were outstanding warrants for his arrest for armed bank robbery, murder, car theft, and house robbery in several West European countries. He was gunned down in Belgrade's Intercontinental Hotel on 15 January 2000. Although there has been much speculation, the motive for this murder remains to be established, although fear of a disclosure by Arkan of potentially embarrassing linkages with the Belgrade government may have played a role. A number of other former paramilitary commanders—including Slobodan Miljković and Branislav Lainović mentioned in this study—have been assassinated in Serbia over the past few years, eliminating potentially awkward witnesses.

In response to allegations that he also had targeted dissidents abroad, Arkan claimed that he had been acting at the behest of Yugoslavia's security services. Once back in Yugoslavia, he continued his violent behavior, but also established a significant business empire. He also organized the "Tough Guys," a hooligan fan club in support of the Belgrade "Red Flag" soccer team. The club served later as the nucleus for the SDG.[42] In Bosnia, Arkan's SDG played a significant role in the takeover and cleansing of such towns as Zvornik, Bijeljina, Bratunac, Prijedor, and Foca, and in the Potocari massacre following the fall of Srebrenica.[43] In the case of the Bijeljina and Janja area of eastern Bosnia at the beginning of the war, for example, Arkan himself was reportedly present during the intimidation and expulsion of Muslims and Gypsies. Indicative of the type of operations that the SDG often undertook was the fact that, according to Arkan, in five months in 1991 the SDG had engaged in eighty-seven combat actions in Croatia, but had suffered only five killed. This suggested that most of these were actions against civilians, although they may have been masked as "combat" for public consumption.[44]

Typically, one of Arkan's lieutenants described the takeover of the town of Bijeljina, in which Arkan's paramilitary agent took part, thus: "Bijeljina is a short, sweet story. The job there was done in eight hours, with only two of ours wounded."[45] On the other hand, when there was significant fighting, the paramilitary forces from Serbia proper often fared poorly, as was the case with the SPO's Serbian Guard on the Gospić front in Croatia. When they suffered a few killed, they beat a hasty retreat, much to the dismay of local Serb paramilitary units.[46] The United Nations Commission of Experts characterized Arkan's (and Šešelj's) mode of operation thus:

> Upon entering a village, sometimes under the cover of shelling, particularly in those counties where they were operating simultaneously with the JNA, Šešelj's and Arkan's troops would begin their reign of terror. In an overwhelming majority of the counties in which Šešelj's and Arkan's troops were operating, there are allegations of killing of civilians, rape, looting, destruction of private or cultural property, and prison camps. In some instances specific individuals were targeted, such as prominent non-Serb leaders or intellectuals.[47]

Arkan's men often acted with exceptional and calculated brutality. In the town of Bratunac, for example, again as noted by the United Nations Commission of Experts, Muslim men were subjected to brutal abuse.

> [B]eatings with iron rods and wooden poles. Some prisoners were taken to an "investigation room" where they were forced to trample over their fellow inmates' dead bodies. Mutilation also occurred; ears, noses and genitals were cut off, and the sign of the cross was cut into prisoners' flesh. While being tortured, the prisoners were made to sing Chetnik songs.[48]

That such behavior was considered acceptable and sanctioned was corroborated by the fact that preparation for harsh policies was part of the training that Arkan's paramilitary units received. One of the Russian mercenaries in Arkan's SDG recalled his training prior to deployment, "The philosophy of brutality drummed into the heads of the fighters of each Serbian patriot is that of being totally merciless toward the enemy; he does not have the right to spare their children, women, or the elderly. This startled our [Russian] gunmen."[49] Moreover, within the SDG, discipline was reportedly good—a matter of special pride for Arkan—thereby indicating that criminal acts were very much part of a deliberate policy rather than isolated actions by irresponsible individuals. Arkan publicly claimed, "My discipline is fifty times better than in the JNA...That is one of the reasons for our success. This war is to be won through discipline."[50]

In some instances, ethnic cleansing by members of Arkan's paramilitary group took on a long-term, institutionalized form, as in the Bijeljina area. There, one of Arkan's subordinates, Major Vojkan Djurković, ran what was euphemistically known as the "State Commission for the Free Transfer of the Civilian Population" whose basic function was the systematic expulsion of non-Serbs. According to Djurković, "After a time, the [Bosnian Serb] People's Deputies, Milan Teslić and Vojo Kupresanin, expanded the Commission in the name of the [Serb Democratic Party] Deputies Club, and later the Commission was approved also by the Parliament of the Serbian Republic [of Bosnia]."[51] In an interview published under the headline "I Am A Humanitarian," Djurković denied that his activities constituted ethnic cleansing. "In effect," claimed Arkan's deputy, "What is going on is a classic population migration or, in effect, respect for the population's freedom of movement. If an individual has exchanged his property, if he takes with him the members of his family, and if he goes to where he wants, then this in no way is ethnic cleansing."[52]

Djurković argued that he should instead be praised for allowing some people to depart for free if they could not pay the mandatory fee. He claimed: "Travel costs an average of 100 dinars per person. Let me add, however, that our Commission had social-humanitarian feelings and transferred for free many who did not have the money. For example, the Gypsy community from Janja, which we moved for free."[53] Reconfirming Arkan's command relationship over Major Vojkan Djurković, Arkan promoted him to Lieutenant Colonel of the SDG in October 1995.[54]

During a fact-finding trip to the region, U.S. Assistant Secretary of State for Human Rights, John Shattuck, confirmed that Arkan's forces were deeply involved in the large-scale campaign of ethnic cleansing that took place in northern Bosnia in September and October 1995 as the Serbs consolidated their control in preparation for a territorial settlement. The State Department characterized the events as "a systematic pattern of ethnic cleansing, of beatings, of rape, of murder, and of severe mistreatment of Muslims and Croatians, including of the elderly and the infirm." Muslims were forced to wear white armbands and to have distinguishing signs affixed to their houses for identification, and there were reports of forced labor camps and of several hundred civilians being killed in the process.[55]

According to a UN Security Council report, Arkan's men allegedly were active in Banja Luka, Bosanski Novi, Prijedor, Sanski Most, and other towns during a campaign lasting several months; much of this was confirmed in

INDICTMENT AT THE HAGUE

the *Report to the Secretary-General Pursuant to Security Council Resolution 1019*. According to this document, "The presence of paramilitary forces, in particular units of Arkan and, to a lesser degree, of Šešelj, was observed in the whole area during the period described." It accused Arkan's forces of "harassment, killing, and rape, and provoking mass expulsions."[56]

In addition to the substantial amount of documentation relating to the war crimes committed by Arkan's Tigers, there was a significant chronicling of the atrocities committed by Vojislav Šešelj's Chetniks, Mirko Jović's White Eagles, Vuk Drašković's Serbian Guard, and Milan Martic's Knindžas. According to the *Final Report of the United Nations Commission of Experts*, Vojislav Šešelj's Chetnik forces were actively involved in the commission of war crimes in Bosnia. One specific example of atrocities recorded by the Commission of Experts is cited below:

On 17 May 1992, Šešeljovci entered Divić in Zvornik County [Bosnia] and began to loot and pillage Muslim property for nine days. On 26 May 1992, the residents of Divić were loaded onto buses supposedly headed to Olovo. Instead the buses went to Tuzla and on to Zvornik.... On 29 May 1992, the 174 male residents from Divić were moved to a movie theater in a cultural center in Celopek, seven kilometers north of Zvornik. The prisoners were threatened with death unless they could come up with 2,000 DM per person, which they did. Nevertheless, the prisoners were still beaten, tortured, sexually abused, and killed.[57]

The UN Report also catalogued the widespread atrocities committed by Mirko Jović's White Eagles forces.

On 13 April 1992, the city of Višegrad was occupied by the Užice Corps. This group consisted of JNA soldiers, reservists, Užice territorial defense forces, and White Eagles...The corps then broadcast a message instructing the residents to return to Višegrad and assuring their safety...The JNA then blocked all roads leading out of Višegrad with help from the White Eagles and Užice Corps. Soldiers at the roadblocks would take away Muslims, whose names appeared on a master list. Between 18 and 25 May, the Užice Corps left Visegrad, leaving it to fall under the control of the White Eagles, Chetnik gangs and Šešelj's forces....After the retreat of the Užice Corps, the killing and torturing of Muslims began. Residents could not leave the city without permission. Many Serbs were seen throwing bound Muslims into the river to drown them. In early June, many girls were taken to the hotel Vilina Vlaš, interrogated, and raped. Some of the females were not returned.[58]

After the massacre of Muslims in the town of Gacko, members of the Serbian Guard paramilitary bragged about the rape and torture. The Serbian Guard was the paramilitary wing of Vuk Drašković's Serbian Reform Movement (Srpski pokret obnove-SPO). Danica Drašković, the leader's wife recounted the following: "I listened to members of the Serbian Guard...as they told how they had raped a thirteen-year old Muslim girl, all twenty of them, and how they had then placed her on a tank and drove her around, and laughed about how all that was left of her was a skeleton...There are no Ustaše knives there [in Gacko]. There was no battle there, no Serbs had been massacred.... You have not presented a single comparable example of a similar massacre of the Serbs as has occurred [to the Muslims] in Nevesinje, Trebinje, or Foca."[59]

Milan Martić, police chief and later president of the Republic of Serbian Krajina, organized a militia that subsequently became the Krajina's police force.[60] His force—sometimes known as the Knindžas (Ninjas from Knin)—took part in actions in the occupied territories in Croatia and in Bosnia. For example, according to the UN Report, during their assault against the Bosnian village of Carakovo in late July 1992, "Some of the Serbs gave commands such as 'Burn down!' and 'Kill!' It was like a hunt, as one survivor recounts, in which the nearby forest was also searched for non-Serbs. Hundreds of people were killed-shot, burnt alive, beaten, or tortured to death in other ways."[61] According to the UN Report, Martic's personnel also took part in the takeover of Prijedor, Bosnia, and in the atrocities committed there.[62]

Although the Bosnian Serb Army and the Army of the Republic of the Serbian Krajina were not under the official control of Slobodan Milošević, it is important to take note here of the war crimes these forces committed. This is important because, as will be discussed below, Slobodan Milošević may be held individually responsible for the war crime of directing or permitting forces under his control to aid and abet the commission of war crimes by the Bosnian Serb Army and the Army of the Republic of the Serbian Krajina.

As was widely reported, the Bosnian Serb Army engaged in "ethnic cleansing" throughout Bosnia. A U.S. Department of State report summarized actions by Bosnian Serb forces at the first stages of the Bosnian war.

In early 1993, the Bosnian Serb Army, supported by paramilitary forces from Serbia and Montenegro, moved to complete ethnic cleansing campaigns in eastern Bosnia. The Bosnian Serb Army virtually destroyed the hamlet of Cerska, chasing its residents into forests and minefields, and subjected Srebrenica, Goražde, and Žepa to strangulation and intense shelling. International protective forces which reached the enclaves in March described conditions as the worst they had ever seen and noted that there were virtually no residents left to help.[63]

Activities of the Bosnian Serb Army also included the siege of numerous towns and the targeting of civilians. In the case of Sarajevo, for example, the United Nations Commission of Experts reported that, by 1993, nearly 10,000 persons, including over 1,500 children, had been killed or were missing, and that 56,000 persons, of whom nearly 15,000 were children, had been wounded.[64] John Gannon, the Central Intelligence Agency's Deputy Director for Intelligence, testified at a hearing held by the U.S. Congress and made the following statement.

The Bosnian Serb Army...has been a central participant in ethnic cleansing campaigns against Muslims and Croats. Bosnian Serb Army units have conducted systematic ethnic cleansing operations, controlled detention camps, and methodically destroyed Muslim villages...Bosnian Serb Army forces have often operated in conjunction with Serb paramilitary units identified as perpetrators of some of the worst atrocities of the Balkan conflict. The Bosnian Serb Army has operated many of the detention camps that have held primarily Muslim and Croat civilians...Bosnian Serb Army-run camps, notorious for their alleged brutality and death tolls, included facilities at Manjaca and Batković ....Bosnian Serb Army forces in both the January-April 1993 Srebrenica offensive and the April 1994 Gorazde attack, for example, razed Muslim villages well after Bosnian Serb troops had control of the areas surrounding them.[65]

With regard to war crimes committed by the Army of the Republic of the Serbian Krajina, a U.S. Department of State report presented the following description.

In the occupied UNPA's [United Nations Protected Areas], "authorities" of the self-proclaimed and internationally unrecognized "Republic of Serbian Krajina (RSK)" controlled all military and police functions...These forces were heavily augmented from time to time by "volunteers" provided by the Government of Serbia/Montenegro and by Serbian criminal warlords from other parts of the former Yugoslavia...All these forces were directly involved in a continuing pattern of serious human rights abuses against non-Serbian populations as well as other Serbs...Some of the Krajina Serb "authorities" continued to be among the most egregious perpetrators of human rights abuses against the residual non-Serb population, as well as Serbs not in agreement with nationalistic policy. Human rights violations included killings, disappearances, beatings, harassment, forced resettlement, or exile-all part of the systematic campaign of 'ethnic cleansing' designed to ensure Serbian dominance of the areas.[66]

In sum, a review of availabe information concerning the commission of war crimes in the territory of the former Yugoslavia provides sufficient grounds for concluding that extensive and systematic war crimes were committed by Yugoslav federal forces, forces and agencies of the Republic of Serbia, and various paramilitary formations subordinate to Serbia. The question of the extent to which Slobodan Milošević and his closest associates were both individually and collectively responsible for the commission of these crimes is addressed in the following pages.

NOTES

1. See e.g., Review of the Indictment of Radovan Karadžić and Ratko Mladić for Genocide, Crimes Against Humanity and Violations of the Law or Customs of War, Tribunal Document IT-95-18-I, by Judge Fouad Riad, p. 3 (16 November 1995) [hereinafter Review of the Indictment of Radovan Karadžić and Ratko Mladić #2], citing the involvement of JNA forces and Serbian paramilitary agents in the massacre at Srebrenica. See also Indictment of Slobodan Miljković, Blagoje Simić, Milan Simić, Miroslav Tadić, Stevan Todorović, and Šimo Žarić paras 6, 21-26, pp. 2, 4-6, charging Slobodan Miljković, the commander of the Gray Wolves paramilitary unit from Serbia, with numerous counts of grave breaches of the Geneva Conventions, violations of the laws or customs of war, and crimes against humanity.

2. Among the main reports chronicling war crimes are: United Nations Security Council, *Final Report of the United Nations Commission of Experts Established Pursuant to Security Council Resolution 780 (1992)*, Document S/1994/674, especially Annex III. A, *Special Forces*, and Annex IV, *The Policy of Ethnic Cleansing*, 28 December 1994, internet edition at gopher://gopher.rgc.apc.org7030/11/annexes; and the summary version, *Final Report of the United Nations Commission of Experts Established Pursuant to Security Council Resolution 780 (1992)*; Security Council document S/1994/674, 27 May 1994; Reports by Tadeusz Mazowiecki, Special Rapporteur for the United Nations, internet edition at www.emse.fr/~maillot/HTML/PERSO/E/YUGO/MAZOWIECKI.CN4_1992-S-1-9 html; United States Senate, Committee on Foreign Relations, *The Ethnic Cleansing of Bosnia-Hercegovina*; A Staff Report, Washington, DC: GPO, (August 1992); U.S. Department of State, *Report on War Crimes in Former Yugoslavia*. Supplemental United States Submission of Information to UN Security Council in Accordance with Paragraph 5 of Resolution 771 (1992) and Paragraph 1 of Resolution 780 (1992) (eight reports); Human Rights Watch, *Yugoslavia: Human Rights Abuses in the Croatian Conflict*, New York: Vol. 3, No. 14, September 1991; War Crimes in Bosnia-Hercegovina: Bosanski Samac, New York: Vol. 6, No. 5, April 1994; Bosnia-Hercegovina; Sarajevo, New York: Vol. 6, No. 15, October 1994; Bosnia-Hercegovina; "Ethnic Cleansing" Continues in Northern Bosnia, New York: Vol. 6, No. 16, November 1994; Former Yugoslavia: War Crimes Trials in the Former Yugoslavia, New York, vol. 7, No. 10, June 1995; Helsinki Watch, War Crimes in Bosnia-Hercegovina, vol. I, New York: August 1992, vol. II, New York: April 1993; Amnesty International, *Bosnia-Herzegovina: "You Have No Place Here"-Abuses in Bosnian Serb-Controlled Areas*, (London: 1994); *Bosnia-Herzegovina/Living for the Day: Forcible Expulsions from Bijeljina and Janja*, (London: 1994); U.S. Department of State, Human Rights Practices annual reports for Bosnia-Herzegovina, Serbia-Montenegro, and Croatia; and Tilman Zlch, ed., "'Ethnische Sšuberung'-Vôlkermord for Grobserbien"; Ein Dokumentation ["Ethnic Cleansing" and Genocide for "Greater Serbia"; Documentation], (Zurich: Luchterhand Literaturverlag 1993).

3. This symbiotic relationship calls to mind the operational procedure the Nazis used in occupied areas of Eastern Europe. In a studied division of labor, the Einsatzgruppen, the Order Police (Ordnungspolizei), and locally raised and often unruly light auxiliary forces such as the Volksdeutsche Selbstschutz in Poland, normally went into action once the more heavily-armed Wehrmacht combat forces had secured an area, thereby enabling the lighter forces to operate. Yitzhak Arad, Shmuel Krakowski, and Shmuel Spector, eds., *The Einsatzgruppen Reports*, New York: Holocaust Library 1989; Christopher R. Browning, *Ordinary Men; Reserve Battalion 101 and the Final Solution in Poland*, New York: Harper Perennial 1993; and Christian Jansen and Arno Weckbecker, Der '*Volksdeutsche Selbstschutz' in Polen* 1939/40, Munich: R. Oldenbourg 1992.

4. Dobrila Gajic-Glišić, *Srpska vojska; Iz kabineta ministra vojnoga* [The Serbian Army; From the Minister of Defense's Office], Cacak: Marica i Tomo Spasojević 1992, p. 144. Mrs. Gajic-Glišić was the administrative assistant to General Tomislav Simović, the Serbian Minister of Defense, and published minutes of meetings held during her tenure. Serbia's Ministry of Defense was a headquarters organization, with no standing troops as such, but cooperated with Serbia's Territorial Defense in fielding and equipping reserve forces. This agency was abolished when Slobodan Milošević established effective control over the regular army.

5. Ibid., p. 155.

6. On the JNA's initial actions in Bosnia and the continuing links between Belgrade and the Bosnian Serb Army, see Ed Vulliamy, "Serbian Lies World Chose to Believe," The Guardian (London), 29 February 1996, p. 12. See also *Final Report of the United Nations Commission of Experts Established Pursuant to Security Council Resolution 780 (1992); Annex V; The Prijedor Report*, para 187.

7. For example, Colonel General Momcilo Perišić, who later became the Chief of the General Staff of the Yugoslav Army, has stated that, "after the withdrawal of the JNA, I stayed behind for a month and a half longer until the [Serb] Herzegovinians could be trained on the equipment which remained behind." Interview with Colonel General Perišić by Dada Vujasinović, "Komandant života i smrti" [Commander of Life and Death], *Duga* (Belgrade), reprinted in *Vesti* (Frankfurt), 11 August 1993, p. 18.

8. Indictment of Mile Mrkšić, Miroslav Radić, and Veselin Šljivancanin, para 26, p. 9.

9. Indictment of Mile Mrkšić, Miroslav Radić, and Veselin Šljivancanin, paras 1-14, pp. 1-8. See also Blaine Harden, "Serbs Accused of 1991 Croatia Massacre: U.S. Doctors Believe 200 Wounded Men Were Taken from Hospital and Shot," *The Washington Post*, 26 January 1993, p. A-13. JNA sources gave the number of those who surrendered at Vukovar as 300 Croatian military personnel, 2,000 "unarmed Croatian military," and 5,000 civilians. Colonel Nebojša Pavković, *Narodna armija*, 30 December 1991, p. 19. Other JNA sources have also mentioned 300 individuals from Croatia's Albanian community (whom the JNA labeled "Albanian mercenaries") taken in Vukovar's hospital who were not seen again. Nikola Ostojić, "Vukovar - slobodan grad" [Vukovar: A Free City], *Narodna armija*, 23 November 1991, p. 15.

10. Indictment of Mile Mrkšić, Miroslav Radić, and Veselin Šljivancanin, para 26, pp. 9-10.

11. Indictment of Mile Mrkšić, Miroslav Radić, and Veselin Šljivancanin, paras 15 and 17, p. 8.

12. Confirmation of the Indictment of Radovan Karadžić and Ratko Mladić #2, pp. 3-4; and Michael Dobbs and R. Jeffrey Smith, "U.S. Gives Investigators New Evidence of Bosnian Serb War Crimes," *Washington Post*, 29 October 1995, p. A36.

13. Confirmation of the Indictment of Radovan Karadžić and Ratko Mladić #2, pp. 3-4. See also David Rohde, "Bosnia Muslims Were Killed by the Truckload," *Christian Science Monitor*, 2 October 1995, pp. 1, 6-7; and Angelo Ascoli, "Il mondo grida: Fermate il genocidio della Bosnia" [The World Cries: Stop the Genocide in Bosnia], Oggi (Milan), 26 July 1995, pp. 12-15. For the testimony of one of the perpetrators on the Serb side, see Renaud Girard, "Bosnie: la confession de Dražen, criminel de guerre" [Bosnia: Confession by Dražen, War Criminal], Le Figaro (Paris), 8 March 1996, pp. 1, 4, 26; and the Tribunal's 1996 indictment of Dražen Erdemović, to which the latter pleaded guilty, at www.un.org/icty/indictment/english/erd-ii960529e.htm. Also see the United Nations report, *Report of the Secretary-General Pursuant to General Assembly Resolution 53/35 (1998); Srebrenica Report*, released 15 November 1999; Jan Willem Honig and Norbert Both, *Srebrenica: Record of a War Crime* (New York: Penguin,

1996); David Rohde, *Endgame: The Betrayal and Fall of Srebrenica* (New York: Farrar, Straus & Giroux, 1997).

14. Press Release of the International Criminal Tribunal for the Former Yugoslavia, Tribunal Document CC/PIO/026-E (16 November 1995).

15. Confirmation of the Indictment of Radovan Karadžić and Ratko Mladić #2, p. 2.

16. *Ibid.*

17. *Ibid.*

18. Confirmation of the Indictment of Radovan Karadžić and Ratko Mladić #2, p. 3.

19. Cabell Bruce, "Belgrade Blamed, Accused of Directing Attacks on Safe Haven," *Newsday*, 12 August 1995, p. A7, which is based on unidentified "intelligence officials" from western countries. The *Review of Indictment Pursuant to Rule 61 v Karadzić and Mladić*, 16 November 1995, mentions the presence of Yugoslav Army elements at Srebrenica.

20. *Final Report of the United Nations Commission of Experts Established Pursuant to Security Council Resolution 780 (1992); Annex V; The Prijedor Report*, para 276.

21. Disgruntled veterans of this operation spoke about it after their return to Serbia. Milovan Brkić, "'Oluja' oduvala Pauka'" [The Storm Slammed into the Spider], *Srpska rec*, 11 September 1995, pp. 46-47. According to a Corps Commander of the Army of the Republic of the Serbian Krajina,the "Pauk" [Spider] Operation was planned and commanded by the Yugoslav Army's Main Staff in Belgrade, and included forces from the Yugoslav Army and Serbia's Security Service. Milisav Sekulić, *Knin je pao u Beogradu* [Knin Fell in Belgrade]. (Bad Vibel: Nidda Verlag, 2000), pp. 91-92

22. "Eindeutiger Beweis," [Unambiguous Proof], *Der Spiegel* (Hamburg), 23 October 1995, pp. 170-71. Croatian soldiers and civilians taken prisoner in Vukovar in 1991 by the JNA were also sent to prison camps in Serbia (Sremska Mitrovica). See Branka Mitrović, "Neizvesnost I posle petka" [Uncertainty Even After Friday], *Borba*, 12 August 1992, p. 9; and Branka Mitrović, "Obicni ostaju za kraj" [The Ordinary Ones Remain until the End], *Borba*, 13 August 1992, p. 10.

23. Quoted in M. M., "Bekstvo u mir," [Flight to Peace], Evropske Novosti, 3 August 1995, p. 5.

24. Ed Vulliamy, "Serbs Run Secret Camps," The Guardian (London), 17 January 1996, p. 2. Refugees from Žepa who subsequently came to the United States complained that they had been beaten by prison guards while they were held in camps in Serbia. Joe Wyatt, "New Home, Hope," *Amarillo Sunday News-Globe* (Amarillo, Texas), 4 February 1996, pp. 11A and 17A.

25. See Human Rights Watch, *War Crimes in Bosnia-Hercegovina: Bosanski Šamac*, pp. 9-10.

26. Interview with Vojislav Šešelj by C[vijetin] M[ilivojevic], "Spreman cekam hapšenje" [I Am Ready, Awaiting Arrest], *Spona*, 18 December 1993, p. 15.

27. " Šešelj: Ne plašim se Haga" [I Am Not Afraid of the Hague], *Politika*, 12 September 1993, p. 8.

28. Šešelj speaking in 1995 on the "Gates of Hell" episode from the BBC's *Death of Yugoslavia* series, 1995.

29. Interview with Vakić, "Branislav Vakić: How Frenki and I Conquered Srebrenica," p. 8. See also interview with Branislav Vakić by Srboljub Bogdanović, "Odloženi nokaut" [Postponed Knock-out], *NIN*, 10 March 1995, p. 15.

30. Quoted in Vasić and Švarm, "Chetnik Watergate," 15 November 1993, p. 24. Note that, "Simatovic" is sometimes found as "Stamatovic" in the Serbian press.

31. See the interview with Ulemek, "I Am a Serb and Proud of It," p. 20, and Gordana

Igrić, "Arkan u Sajgonu" [Arkan in Saigon], *NIN*, 29 September 1995, p. 13. Regarding Simatović see D. Petrović and N. Todorović, "Serb Republic Cannot Exist if People Leave," *Naša Borba*, 20 October 1995, p. 3, in *FBIS-EEU-95-204*, 23 October 1995, pp. 33-34.

32. D. Petrović, "Badža u prvom izvlacenju' dobio najviši moguci cin" [Badža on His First Try Achieved the Highest Possible Rank], Naša Borba , 1 April 1996. See also interview with Slobodan Miljković by Dragan Alempijević, "Živ ne idem u Hag!" [I Will Not Go to the Hague Alive!], *Telegraf*, 27 September 1995, p. 10.

33. Gajic-Glišić, *Srpska vojska*, p. 298.

34. 79. *Srpska vojska*, p. 126. The staff of Serbia's Ministry of Defense had drafted the public appeal by which the Krajina's President, Goran Hadžić, requested help from the Serbian people in Serbia. *Srpska vojska*, p. 61.

35. Interview with General Mladić by [Colonel] Milovan Milutinović, "Narodu ne treba pricati ono što želi cuti, vec mu treba reci istinu" [The People Must Not Be Told What They Want to Hear, But Rather the Truth], *Srpska Vojska* (Sarajevo, Serbian area), 25 June 1995, p. 11. *Srpska Vojska* is the Bosnian Serb Army's official organ.

36. M. Petrović, "Opasna primirja" [Dangerous Truces], *Vojska* (Belgrade), 7 October 1993, p. 12.

37. Chetnik Major Slavko Aleksić quoted in *Javnost* (Pale), reprinted in "Ljudi i vreme" [People and Time], *Vreme*, 31 May1993, p. 54.

38. Indictment of Slobodan Miljković, Blagoje Simić, Milan Simić, Miroslav Tadić, Stevan Todorović, and Šimo Žarić , para 5, p. 1. See also Indictment of Radovan Karadžić and Ratko Mladić #2.

39. Indictment of Slobodan Miljković, Blagoje Simić, Milan Simić, Miroslav Tadić, Stevan Todorović, and Šimo Žarić , para 6, p. 2.

40. Interview with Vojislav Šešelj by Robert Coban, "Više me ne optužuju za ratne zlocine" [They No Longer Accuse Me of War Crimes], Svet, 28 April 1995, p. 6. Cited in Miloš Vasić, "Noc kratkih noževa" [Night of the Short Knives], *Vreme*, 8 November 1993, p. 9. Interview with Vojislav Šešelj by Radmila Dubljević, "Izvinjenja nece biti" [There Will Be No Apology], *Evropske Novosti*, 29 December 1993, p. 7. S. S., "Arkan tužio Šešelja" [Arkan Sues Šešelj], *Evropske Novosti*, 5 January 1994, p. 9; and Interview with Arkan's lawyer, Toma Fila, by Predrag Popović, "Bez pardona" [Without Pardon], Svet, 18 March 1996, p. 13.

41. *Final Report of the United Nations Commission of Experts, Add. 2 (Vol. I), Annex IV; The Policy of Ethnic Cleansing*, paras 1-6.

42. U[roš] K[omlenovic], "Arkanzas" [Arkansas], *NIN*, 1 May 1992, p. 29.

43. *Report of the Secretary-General Pursuant to Security Council Resolution 1019 (1995) on Violations of International Humanitarian Law in the Areas of Srebrenica, Žepa, Banja Luka and Sanski Most, UN Security Council document S/1995/988*, 27 November 1995, para 35.

44. See Amnesty International, *Bosnia-Herzegovina: Living for the Day: Forcible Expulsions from Bijeljina and Janja*, London: 1994. See Milošević, "The Cobra's Bite," p. 3. Šimo Dubajić, "Manjak od trideset dugih cevi" [A Shortage of Thirty Rifle Barrels], Duga, 1-14 February 1992, p. 54. Šimo Dubajić was a hardline leader of the initial Serb movement in Croatia and later became Chief of the General Staff of the Serbian Guard.

45. Interview with Ulemek, "I Am a Serb and Proud of It," p. 19. This was not unusual. Captain Dragan, for example, had claimed that out of his paramilitary force of 1200, there had been only four killed in action. Interview "I Am Not a Rebel," p. 29.

46. Šimo Dubajić, "Manjak od trideset dugih cevi" [A Shortage of Thirty Rifle Barrels], Duga, 1-14 February 1992, p. 54.

47. *Final Report of the United Nations Commission of Experts, Vol. I, Annex III. A, Special Forces*; para 105.

48. *Final Report of the United Nations Commission of Experts, Vol. I, Annex III. A, Special Forces*; para 74.

49. Evgeniy Vostrukhov, "Umeret' v Yugoslaviy" [To Die in Yugoslavia], Izvestiya (Moscow), 25 November 1992, p. 3.

50. Interview with Arkan "Vec imam kucu na Dedinju" [I Already Have a House on Dedinje Hill], *NIN*, 13 December 1991, p. 12.

51. Interview with Vojkan Djurković by Pero Simić, "Ja sam humanista" [I Am a Humanitarian], Intervju, 25 November 1994, p. 25. See also Amnesty International, *Bosnia-Herzegovina: Living for the Day: Forcible Expulsions from Bijeljina and Janja; and Bosnia-Hercegovina; "'Ethnic Cleansing' Continues in Northern Bosnia"* (New York: Vol. 6, No. 16, November 1994, pp. 33-34).

52. *Intervju*, 25 November 1994, p. 28.

53. *Intervju*, 25 November 1994, p. 29.

54. Gordana Lazarević, "Karadžici, pravoslavni šeici od Bosne" [The Karadžices: Orthodox Sheikhs from Bosnia], *Intervju*, 3 November 1995, p. 6.

55. Reported by Nicholas Burns, U.S. Department of State Daily Press Briefing, 20 October 1995. According to a UN Security Council report, Arkan's men allegedly were active in Banja Luka, Bosanski Novi, Prijedor, Sanski Most, and other towns during a campaign lasting several months; much of this was confirmed in *Report to the Secretary-General Pursuant to Security Council Resolution 1019 (1995)*, paras 44, 49-53, 69-73.

56. *Report to the Secretary-General Pursuant to Security Council Resolution 1019* (New York: 1995), para 73.

57. *Final Report of the United Nations Commission of Experts, Vol. I, Annex III. A, Special Forces*, paras 53 and 54. See also paras 34-36, 42, 53-54, 57-58, 108, 130, and 133. One of Šešelj's men recounts how they implemented ethnic cleansing in the Sarajevo area. Nebojša Jevrić, "Krivci iz plavo-crveno-sivog rukava" [The Culprits with the Blue-Red-Gray Sleeves], *Duga*, 25 June-8 July 1994, pp. 25-26. See also Human Rights Watch (Helsinki), *War Crimes in Bosnia-Hercegovina: Bosanski Šamac*, pp. 7-8.

58. *Final Report of the United Nations Commission of Experts, Vol. I, Annex III. A, Special Forces*, paras 10 and 11. See also paras 34, 35, and 133. The White Eagles were also known for executing prisoners. As their combat commander, Dragoslav Bokan, noted, "I feel sorry for the young Ustaše [Croatians] when we take them away to be executed." p. 46. Interview with Dragoslav Bokan by Dada Vujasinović, "Firer mekog srca" [Fuhrer with a Soft Heart], *Duga*, 29 March-11 April 1992, p. 46.

59. From the minutes of a session of the SPO, "'Osma sednica' Srpskog pokreta obnove; Pokušaj samoubistva" [The "Eighth Session" of the Serbian Renewal Movement: An Attempt at Suicide], Srpska rec, 10 May 1993, p. 21.

60. On July 25 1995, Milan Martić was indicted by the Tribunal for ordering the launch of Orkan rockets into three Croatian cities, including Zagreb. See Indictment of Milan Martić.

61. *Final Report of the United Nations Commission of Experts Established Pursuant to Security Council Resolution 780 (1992); Annex V; The Prijedor Report*; para 305.

62. *Final Report of the United Nations Commission of Experts Established Pursuant to Security Council Resolution 780 (1992); Annex V; The Prijedor Report*; paras 159, 197, 276, and 305. See also Helsinki Watch, *War Crimes in Bosnia-Hercegovina*, vol. II, pp. 80-81. They

were also active in the Derventa area of Bosnia, R. Vujatović, "Probijaju obruc" [They Are Breaking Through the Encirclement], *Politika Ekspres* (Belgrade), 19 June 1992, p. 7.

63. U.S. Department of State, *Human Rights Practices 1993*, internet edition at gopher:// dosfan.lib.uić.edu:70/OF-1%3A6197%3ABosnia %20%26%20Herzegovina.

64. *Final Report of the United Nations Commission of Experts Established Pursuant to Security Council Resolution 780 (1992); Annex VI; Study of the Battle and Siege of Sarajevo,* especially para 13.

65. Testimony in a briefing "Ethnic Cleansing and Atrocities in Bosnia" to the Senate Select Committee on Intelligence and the Senate foreign relations Committee, 9 August 1995; at www.odci.gov/cia/public_affairs/speeches/bosnia_handout.html. The public report on the internet included samples of satellite imagery highlighting the potential of this type of compelling evidence as part of an all-source information package for such cases.

66. U.S. Department of State, *Croatia Human Rights Practices 1993*, Washington, DC, 31 January 1994, internet edition at gopher://dosfan.lib.uic.edu:70/OF-1%3A6197%3ACroatia.

IV

UNDER INTERNATIONAL LAW A PERSON IS INDIVIDUALLY RESPONSIBLE for the commission of a war crime on the basis of direct responsibility if he commits a war crime or if forces under his effective control commit a war crime.[1] The Tribunal created a solid legal and factual foundation for indicting individuals responsible for planning and orchestrating the commission of war crimes. This was done through a series of indictments that establish individual responsibility both on the basis of direct evidence of the ordering of the commission of war crimes by the accused, and on the deductive basis that by virtue of his effective control over the forces committing the atrocities the accused ordered the commission of the war crimes.

With respect to direct evidence of the ordering of war crimes, the Tribunal indicted Milan Martić on the basis of evidence that he directly ordered the firing of Orkan rockets equipped with cluster bombs into Croatian population centers.[2] In the indictment of Dario Kordić and Tihomir Blaškić, both individuals were charged with direct responsibility (and command responsibility) for war crimes committed by military forces or paramilitary units under their direction and control. In some instances, the responsibility of Kordić and Blaškić was derived from direct evidence that by their acts they committed crimes against humanity.[3] In other instances, their responsibility was deduced from the fact that military forces subject to their "power, influence, and control" committed grave breaches of the Geneva Conventions and violated the laws and customs of war.[4]

In the indictment of Mile Mrkšić, Miroslav Radić and Veselin Šljivancanin, the Tribunal possessed no specific evidence that Mile Mrkšić and Miroslav Radić directly ordered JNA and Serbian paramilitary units under their command to commit the war crimes charged. Nevertheless, the Court deduced that these two commanders ordered, permitted, or participated in the commission of the war crimes by virtue of their "position of authority."[5] In the indictment of Djordje Djukić, the Tribunal deduced that Djukić directly participated in the planning, preparation, and execution of war crimes on the basis of his position on the Military Staff of the Bosnian Serb Army, which had responsibility for planning, preparing, and executing Bosnian Serb Army operations in Bosnia.[6]

In its review of the indictment of Radovan Karadžić for war crimes committed by forces under his control during the Srebrenica massacre, the Court found that Karadžić exercised "effective military control over the Bosnian Serb forces, as the commander and political leader of the Bosnian Serb administration" and that "he had, apparently, total authority and responsibility for the strategy and actions employed by the Bosnian Serbs in Bosnia-Herzegovina."[7] The Court then determined that "in these circumstances, it was possible to conclude that, 'the direct responsibility' of [Radovan Karadžic] could arise from planning, instigating, ordering, committing, or aiding and abetting the alleged crimes.'"[8]

On the basis of the precedent set by the Tribunal through these indictments it is possible to determine that available evidence establishes reasonable grounds for holding Slobodan Milošević individually responsible for ordering, planning, or instigating the war crimes committed by Serbian federal and republic forces and paramilitary units over which he exercised official and effective control. Even in the absence, so far, of a concrete, direct order from Milošević commanding forces under his control to commit war crimes, there is substantial evidence that he was involved in directing the day-to-day operations of forces that were responsible for the commission of war crimes and that—by a system of "commander's intent"—he authorized and instigated the commission of war crimes.

Throughout 1991 Milošević was in close contact with the JNA leadership, coordinating the operations of the JNA in Slovenia and Croatia. This collaboration is evident from the diary of Borisav Jović who was Serbia's representative on the Federal Presidency at the time. Jović's diary offers a chronicle of Milošević's numerous meetings with the military.[9] Significantly, on 5 July 1991, Slobodan Milošević and Borisav Jović had a meeting with General Veljko Kadijević (the Federal defense minister) and demanded that the JNA proceed with specific steps and deployments. They warned him, "If he did not immediately move into action in Slovenia, we would be lost in Serbia, after which the army, too, would collapse." As Borisav Jović added, "We were blunt. [General] Veljko [Kadijevic] accepted the requests without discussion."[10] When Veselin Šljivancanin, the JNA colonel responsible for security on the Vukovar front, asked the commander in charge of the operation, Lieutenant-Colonel General Života Panić, about the heavy shelling of that besieged city by the army, he claims he was told that "that is the order from Dedinje," a reference to the exclusive Belgrade suburb where Slobodan Milošević lived.[11] Again, according to Šljivancanin, it was "a very popular politician" who ordered Vojislav Šešelj to execute wounded prisoners who surrendered at Vukovar after the city fell. Šljivancanin estimates that about 1,600 prisoners were executed over a three-day period at Vukovar.[12]

As for the operations of Serbian paramilitary forces, according to Vojislav Šešelj on numerous occasions Milošević directly requested (molba) the deployment of Šešelj's paramilitary units in certain areas that were occupied by Bosnian Serb or Serbian forces.[13] Invariably, after their deployment, these forces engaged in acts of ethnic cleansing and plunder. Colonel Veselin Šljivancanin, indicted for the Vukovar massacre, claimed that Borisav Jović, then Slobodan Milošević's right-hand man, had ordered him to provide logistic support to the Serb paramilitary groups.[14] As the indictment of Djordje Djukić showed, the ordering or provision of logistic support to forces responsible for war crimes is sufficient to establish a basis for individual responsibility for those war crimes.[15]

There were also indications of a significant degree of coordination, beginning in the early days of the Bosnian crisis, between Milošević and other key players, such as Radovan Karadžić, the JNA, and the Montenegrin leadership. This was illustrated by a Belgrade press report of a recording of a telephone conversation between Slobodan Milošević and Radovan Karadžić in September 1991:

> [Milošević to Karadžic], "Contact [JNA General Nikola] Uzelac; he will tell you everything . . .If you have any problems, get in touch with me."
> [Karadžić to Milošević], "I have problems with [the city of] Kupres ...some of the Serbs there are not very obedient."
> [Milošević to Karadžic], "Don't worry, we will easily take care of that...just contact Uzelac. . .You will get everything; don't worry...we are the strongest....Don't worry....As long as there is the Army, no one can do anything to us....Don't worry about Herzegovina....Momir [Bulatović, president of Montenegro] told [his] people 'he who is not ready to die for Bosnia, let him take five steps forward'. No one stepped forward."[16]

This early cooperation with Karadžić also extended to Serbia's Ministry of Internal Affairs, an agency under Slobodan Milošević's direct authority. According to Radmilo Bogdanović, the Minister of Internal Affairs, "He [Karadžić] was working patriotically, and sought our help in organizing the Serbs, and we looked favorably on that. He was often in my office."[17] Karadžić and Milošević, in fact, were in constant contact in the early days of the planning stage. According to Karadžić, "As for my personal or official links with Mr Milošević, they are systematic, sometimes on a daily basis, by telephone."[18]

Apart from the day-to-day involvement with forces responsible for the commission of war crimes, Slobodan Milošević operated by a system of "commander's intent" whereby general goals were set within which subordinates could, provided that they contributed to the overall achievement of those goals, act on their own initiative. As Serbia's Minister of Defense, General Tomislav Simović, explained when asked about Slobodan Milošević's support for Arkan, all that was important was that he was contributing to official goals:

> As far as I know, the aforementioned 'Arkan' is acting with the direct blessing of the [Republic of] Serbia government in the areas of

Slavonija, Western Srijem, and Baranja. It is also known that they are not the only volunteers [there]. I would not differentiate between criminals and patriots, but rather between those who contribute to the interests of their nation and those who do not, and one knows where criminals fit in.[19]

Significantly, General Tomislav Simović and Slobodan Milošević were reported to be in daily contact via a "special phone"—even when the latter was abroad, in one case at a conference in the Hague—and they also would meet privately.[20] After one such meeting, Simović's office initiated the recruitment of retired army colonels for the specific mission of setting up a Serb Territorial Defense Unit in Croatia.[21] In a similar instance, the Ministry of Defense, after consultation with Milošević, authorized the training of paramilitary units and funding of their equipment and salaries by the forces of the Republic of Serbia.[22]

Although, at the time of this writing, any direct order by Slobodan Milošević for the commission of war crimes had surfaced in the public domain, according to an unnamed U.S. Department of Defense official, "We have unequivocal intelligence that Milošević has his hand in the cookie jar....It's as good as what we had on the Soviets during the Cuban missile crisis." Even the evidence reviewed here indicates that there is nevertheless sufficient evidence to establish that Slobodan Milošević *directly ordered* the commission of war crimes by forces under his control.[23] Furthermore, there also is sufficient evidence to prove Milošević's individual responsibility for the commission of war crimes on the basis that forces *under his power, influence, and control* committed widespread and systematic war crimes.

Indictments issued by the Tribunal, as noted above, indicated that a person may be held individually responsible for the crimes committed by forces over which he exercises power, influence, and control. In order to establish a legal and factual basis for indicting those responsible for planning and orchestrating the commission of war crimes, the Tribunal used these indictments to elaborate on the various indicia of a person's ability to exercise power, influence and control.

Thus in the indictment of Ivan Šantić, the accused was considered to exercise "power, influence, authority, and control over the political and strategic military aims of the HVO [Croatian Defense Council, the nationalist Bosnian Croat political-military organization]" by virtue of his position as the mayor of a local municipality in the region where the war crimes occurred.[24] Similarly, in the indictment of Dario Kordić, the accused was considered to exercise power, influence, and control over the HVO military forces on the basis that he "held various political positions from time to time, culminating in his position as Vice President of the Croatian Community of Herceg-Bosna [self-styled para-state established by the nationalist Bosnian Croat leadership] and HVO," and "by virtue of his political power base in Central Bosnia."[25]

In the case of Mario Cerkez, the Tribunal found sufficient evidence to conclude that Cerkez exercised control over armed forces responsible for war crimes on the basis that according to the Decree of the Armed Forces of the Croatian Community of Herceg-Bosna, he was responsible for the "combat readiness of the troops under his command, the mobilization of the armed forces and police units, and the authority to appoint commanders."[26] In the indictment of Radovan Karadžić, the accused was considered to exercise control over forces responsible for the Srebrenica massacre on the basis that he was the founding member and president of the Serbian Democratic Party and that he was authorized under the Bosnian Serb Constitution and Bosnian Serb Act on People's Defense to command the army and have the authority to appoint, promote and discharge officers.[27]

The Tribunal further elaborated on specific acts from which it might be inferred that a person exercised control over forces responsible for the commission of war crimes. In the indictment of Dario Kordić and Ivan Šantić the Tribunal found that they demonstrated their "power, influence, authority, and control" over civil and military matters by, *inter alia*, controlling municipal and governmental functions, issuing orders that were directly or indirectly of a military nature, negotiating and countermanding cease-fire agreements, negotiating with the United Nations, issuing orders for the arrest or release of influential Muslim prisoners, and negotiating the passage of relief convoys or United Nations vehicles through check-points in central Bosnia.[28] In the indictment of Radovan Karadžić, power, influence, and control over civil and military matters was demonstrated by, inter alia, his acting internationally as the president of the Republika Srpska, including participating in international negotiations, and making and implementing agreements relating to cease-fires and humanitarian relief.[29]

On the basis of the criteria established by the tribunal in these indictments, it is clear that Slobodan Milošević did exercise power, influence, and control over the Yugoslav federal forces, the forces and agencies of the Republic of

Serbia, and Serbian paramilitary units responsible for the commission of war crimes in the former Yugoslavia. He exercised this power by virtue of the public and party offices and positions that he occupied, including president of Serbia, president of the SPS ruling party, and membership on the Yugoslav Supreme Defense Council, his political power base in the region, and his responsibility for representing Yugoslavia in international negotiations.

Milošević's control over Yugoslavia and its federal institutions was established when the institutions of the Republic of Serbia, under his official and actual control, absorbed or pre-empted federal institutions and their functions. Therefore, actual power and political control in the Federal Republic of Yugoslavia came to reside in the Republic of Serbia where Milošević emerged as the dominant figure controlling federal and republic agencies and supported by trusted subordinates in all key positions. Although the new Yugoslavia, established when the former Yugoslavia disintegrated in 1992, became a federal state incorporating Serbia and Montenegro, Montenegro's role was that of a junior, and often silent, partner in the asymmetrical relationship.[30] As Borisav Jović explained it, the decision to establish the new state of Serbia and Montenegro as the Federal Republic of Yugoslavia rather than as an independent and enlarged Serbia was motivated predominantly by a desire to benefit from legal continuity in order to inherit state-owned property and representational seats in international bodies. At the same time, the Serbian leadership wanted to avoid having to undergo an accreditation process before the international community as a new state, especially in the area of minority and human rights.[31]

As such, federal officials under the new system were largely executive agents for governance by Slobodan Milošević. Indeed, as the SPS's official organ, *Epoha*, clarified, the intent of the federal set-up for the new Yugoslavia (Serbia and Montenegro) was that "the principle of consensus is avoided, and the president of the Republic [of Yugoslavia] is more of a representative of the [latter] state, rather than having executive-political powers [*funkcije*]."[32] As Montenegro's Premier Milo Djukanović, frustrated by the neglect of Montenegro's interests, declared, "There is, therefore, a host of questions on which the federal state is not fulfilling its role, thereby giving ample arguments to those who claim that the federal state is only a farce, and that the federal state is only an agency of the Serbian government."[33] Not surprisingly, in order to resolve contentious issues with the federal government, Premier Djukanović found that he had to deal directly with Milošević rather than the federal president, Zoran Lilić.[34]

The process of the absorption of federal agencies by the Republic of Serbia began, in some cases, even before Yugoslavia's breakup in 1991. As one well-informed source described it, "Everything remains—Yugoslavia, the federal agencies, [the federal] Parliament, [the federal] government, the President of the Republic [of Yugoslavia]—but only on one condition, that it be known that it is Slobodan Milošević who is the boss in the house."[35] For example, by 1990, as Yugoslavia progressively disintegrated, parts of the state security apparatus, such as the Federal Security Service and the Federal Research and Documentation Center, were absorbed by their counterparts in the Republic of Serbia.[36] Similarly, in 1993, Serbia's Ministry of Internal Affairs absorbed its federal counterpart. Serbia's police, with 40,000 personnel at the time, was far larger than the federal police, with 2,000 personnel in Serbia. Mihalj Kertes, the Deputy Minister of Internal Affairs, transformed the federal police (SSUP) into Serbia's MUP and, similarly, "republicanized" the federal secret service as well. Vukašin Jokanović, the Federal Minister of Internal Affairs, described the process of "republicanization" of the Federal security apparatus thus: "The situation necessitated that the ministries of internal affairs in the member republics of the Socialist Federal Republic of Yugoslavia, after the secession and war on part of the former Yugoslav territory, in accordance with the republic laws adopted, take over the largest share of security matters on their territories."[37]

Remaining federal structures became at the time a layer of government that largely existed on paper and were simply ignored by Serbia's leadership in making decisions and implementing policy. Thus, for instance, the Premier of Montenegro, Milo Djukanović, complained, "It is completely true that there are many examples of the elementary ignoring of federal state institutions on the part of influential politicians from Serbia, and even on the part of the Republic [of Serbia] agencies."[38] In similar vein, federal Premier Radoje Kontić stated that "the federal government is absolutely powerless to manage the economy, since the most important levers are in the hands of the [two] republics."[39]

An additional illustration of this locus of power was provided by Vukašin Jokanović, Yugoslavia's federal Minister of Internal Affairs, who was technically in charge of the federal police and was also the state-appointed examiner charged with investigating the activities of failed independent banks. In the representative case of the Dafiment Bank, which had provided multi-million dollar loans to companies owned by the Republic of Serbia, Jokanović discovered that his attempts to investigate the activities of the bank were blocked by republic-level agencies. "These activities are within the jurisdiction of the republic-level ministries," he explained. "The federal ministry has its coordination role, that is, it can suggest, initiate, and coordinate the activities of the republic-level ministries. It can raise questions, but actual concrete action rests with the republics."[40] No doubt, a lack of desire to bring everything to light in the murky financing of paramilitary units was also a factor limiting the probe.

While some institutions, such as the Yugoslav Army, technically continued to exist as federal structures, Milošević engineered their subservience to the agencies of the Republic of Serbia under his direct control. In the case of the army, he established his control in the wake of the JNA's dismal showing in Slovenia and Croatia. In May 1992, through behind-the-scene maneuverings, he eliminated the army's autonomy and purged thirty-eight of its generals without coordinating his action with the JNA leadership. Branko Kostić, the federation's vice president, felt compelled to counter the widespread (and reasonable) perception within the JNA's ranks that Milošević was behind the mass retirements, but he only ended up reconfirming that Milošević did have a hand, after all, as a member of the Supreme Military Council. Thus according to the army press, Kostić wanted to "deny stories according to which the president of Serbia, Slobodan Milošević, and General Vuk Obradović, supposedly, were behind these personnel changes. In Kostic's words, such 'interpretations' are completely arbitrary....The decision on the retirements was taken by the Presidency of the SFRY, in agreement with the Supreme Military Council, of which both Slobodan Milošević and Momir Bulatović, as presidents of Serbia and Montenegro, are members."[41] In fact, it was reported that by January 1991 Milošević had already discussed with General Tomislav Simović the need to retire certain JNA generals.[42] Additional officers were retired subsequently in accordance with the objective of ensuring a more loyal Yugoslav army.

In practice, Milošević had progressively established effective de facto control over the JNA even before the fighting began in 1991 through his control over the rump Yugoslav Presidency (Serbia, Montenegro, Kosovo and Vojvodina). Very quickly, Serbia also found itself providing virtually all of the manpower and resources which the JNA needed to pursue its combat operations, guaranteeing a decisive say in military affairs. As Major-General Aleksandar Vasilijević, Chief of the JNA's Counterintelligence Branch (KOS), noted: "I already told you several times and hope that you keep in mind that the Army did not do anything, anything at all, behind the backs of the government leadership. That is a fact." Milošević would also convene senior officers directly without going through the official JNA chain of command. Asked whether Milošević was, in fact, the "commander-in-chief" [vrhovni komandant] of the JNA throughout the 1991 war, General Vasilijević replied: "As far as I know, you are correct."[43]

Thus Slobodan Milošević demonstrated his power and control over the army by continuing to intervene with the leadership of the army to influence decisions he considered vital to his interests, and this included decisions on personnel matters. For example, the Yugoslav Army's spokesman, Colonel Ljubodrag Stojadinović, who had criticized the condition of the army in public, was ousted at Milošević's request. According to Colonel Stojadinović he was in the office of the Chief of the General Staff of the Yugoslav Army, Colonel General Momcilo Perišić, when Milošević called and elicited a "yes, yes, yes" response from General Perišić.[44] Stojadinović confirmed later that it was "The decision of Slobodan Milošević and of his wife" that he be sacked from the Army. Milošević had instructed Zoran Lilić: "Get rid of that officer from the Army within 24 hours." When Perišić had balked, and had pointed out it would take three months to complete the process, Milošević had replied "No, throw him out immediately; it is up to you how you do it." Likewise, later, according to General Perišić, "When I began to disturb Milošević, I was replaced."[45]

From late 1991 until the adoption of the December 1992 Yugoslav Federal Constitution, the Presidency of the rump Yugoslavia (Serbia and its then dependent partners Kosovo, Vojvodina, and Montenegro) had legal authority over the JNA, through the Supreme Military Council [*Vrhovni vojni savet*]. According to Article 135 of the Federal Republic of Yugoslavia's Constitution, adopted in December 1992, "The president [of the Federal Republic of Yugoslavia] commands the Army of Yugoslavia in peacetime and in wartime in accordance with the decisions of the Supreme Defense Council [*Vrhovni savet odbrane*]." The same article further provides that the Supreme Defense Council shall consist of the Federal President and the Presidents of Montenegro and of Serbia—that is Slobodan Milošević, who sat ex officio and participated formally in the command relationship over the Yugoslav Army.

The Supreme Defense Council dealt with some of the most significant issues affecting the Yugoslav Army and defense policy, such as the assessment of "the current political-military situation in the territory of the former Yugoslavia," budget issues, and the promotion, posting, and retirement of key personnel. Its charter extended to such matters as discipline and the military personnel's ethics. Moreover, its decisions seemed to be final for, as Zoran Lilić, federal president at the time, pointed out, "absolutely every decision by the Supreme Defense Council was accepted and carried out in the time and manner which had been projected by the Supreme [Defense] Council."[46] According to a report of the official records of the Council, Slobodan Milošević personally took part in the deliberations of the Supreme Defense Council.[47] As a member of the Council, he was legally entitled to directly gather information about the Yugoslav Army and, on a number of occasions, he demonstrated this authority. For example, in his capacity as "a member of the Supreme Defense Council," he inspected the Zvecan military barracks of the Third Army and the Priština Corps (in Kosovska Mitrovica), where "the officers...briefed President Milošević."[48] With the defeat by Milo Djukanović of Milošević's ally Momir Bulatović as Montenegro's president in the December 1997 elections, Milošević consolidated his control of the Supreme Defense Council even more openly to a point where Montenegro's new president was eventually excluded from even participating in decision-making and did not attend meetings of the Supreme Defense Council after November 1998. During the Kosovo War, Milošević began to use the title of Supreme Commander (*Vrhovni komandant*) of the Army, although the title is not found in the Yugoslav Constitution and was never granted formally.[49]

As Slavoljub Djukić, one of his biographers saw it, Slobodan Milošević had established his predominant position within the Serbian political structure by the late 1980s, and from that time enjoyed a virtual monopoly over political decision-making.[50] Whatever the overlapping jurisdiction between the federal and republic constitutions, the lack of clarity was insignificant as long as power was personalized and concentrated in one individual—Slobodan Milošević, who, for all intents and purposes, could be seen as the capstone to both the Republic of Serbia and the federal power structures. As reported by Djukić, when Milan Panić marveled at the fact that Milošević was willing to let someone else be the president of Yugoslavia, Milošević replied, "Milan, it is not important what position I hold. I am for the Serbs a sort of Khomeini."[51] Given his hold on power, the focus of decision-making within the system stayed with Slobodan Milošević personally. Thus, when Slobodan Milošević decided to become President of the Federal Republic of Yugoslavia in 1997—restricted as he was by the Constitution to only two terms as president of Serbia (Article 86)—power in the state simply moved to the federal level to accommodate his new position.

Until his ouster in 2000, the most serious challenge to Slobodan Milošević's power base was attempted during the brief interlude in 1992–93 when

California-based businessman Milan Panić and writer Dobrica Cosić became, respectively, premier and president of the new Federal Republic of Yugoslavia shortly after its establishment. It was a transparent attempt by Milošević to assuage world opinion in the wake of the imposition of economic sanctions by installing what he thought would be respectable figureheads. Commenting on her husband's selection of Milan Panić as Premier and impending removal, Mira Marković stated that his "nomination and selection to be Premier of the Yugoslav government was motivated by the hope that by his personality or his activity he could help lift the sanctions....If his personality and activity do not get the sanctions lifted for us, then I do not see any motive for his presence on the Yugoslav political scene."[52] As one of Dobrica Cosic's advisers, Svetozar Stojanović, noted, it was Slobodan Milošević and his top officials who insisted that Dobrica Cosić become federal president. As it was, Slobodan Milošević was able to impose his candidate, Vladislav Jovanović, as federal foreign minister (as well as being the Republic of Serbia's foreign minister) over Milan Panic's objections.[53]

Efforts by Panić and Cosić to assert their power at the federal level at the expense of Slobodan Milošević, however, failed utterly and led to their ouster and, in the process, highlighted Milošević's overwhelming power.[54] Illustrative of the power that Milošević wielded was the fact that he controlled even Dobrica Cosić's official car, driver, and security officers.[55] The federal president and premier were also confirmed by the Miloševic-dominated Parliament. Subsequently, Milošević selected as federal president a more pliant official, Zoran Lilić, who did not contest his patron's power despite the constitutional authority theoretically vested in his office. As noted by Slavoljub Djukić, "Zoran Lilić had all the honors of the President of the joint state [of Yugoslavia], but it was the Serbian president who governed Yugoslavia."[56] Other senior government officials, perhaps anxious to exculpate their own role in events, have confirmed Milošević's consolidation of power and dominance. For example, as Zoran Lilić was to note when asked if he had been a puppet in his post as President, "The then post of President of the Federal Republic of Yugoslavia was a ceremonial one, not a puppet one. It was logical for it to seem that the President of the Federal Republic of Yugoslavia had the role of implementing the orders and taskings of Slobodan Milošević, since he could not do anything else."[57] In describing Milošević's governing style, General Momcilo Perišić stated the following: "One must know that he possesses the capability to impose his will. He acts ruthlessly with arguments, which he uses like weapons. He simply did not let anyone open his mouth. I was for a long time an observer of how he pushed opponents to the wall... They could not even come up for air... He established and watchfully controlled all levers of government, the police, and finances. A second lever was propaganda... A third lever were the carefully selected aides. What was expected of them was only loyalty and obedience. They did not have to bother their heads, since he was there. In that manner, he assured for himself consensus, which in public was presented as a sign of collective wisdom."[58]

With all effective power vested in his person, from 1991 onwards, Slobodan Milošević also exercised control over the conduct of Yugoslav foreign policy. For example, in 1992, he moved to quash the agreement reached between Dobrica Cosić and the Croatian president Franjo Tudjman under the auspices of the United Nations and European Community negotiators in Geneva.[59] Subsequently, he prevented Cosić from negotiating with Croatia by ordering the police from the Republic of Serbia to detain, question, and expel Croatia's representatives at the border.[60] After the removal of Cosić, "without opposition, [Milošević] usurped the conduct of domestic and foreign policy for the Federal Republic of Yugoslavia."[61] Montenegro's premier, Milo Djukanović, confirmed Milošević's controlling role in foreign affairs by noting that, "Slobodan Milošević, as the undisputed leader of the Serbs, played a significant role in the foreign policy of Yugoslavia....This did not correspond to the Constitution, but it was probably due to the needs of the time and its specific problems."[62]

Indicative of Milošević's primacy in decision-making is the fact that he was the principal interlocutor in all substantive meetings with officials from the United Nations, the European Union and the United States in dealing with the crisis in the former Yugoslavia and was recognized as the key to the resolution of the conflict.[63] The former federal president, Zoran Lilić, himself emphasized Milošević's dominant role in the political process that surrounded the end of the war in Bosnia in 1995. Speaking in late October 1995, Lilić noted that, "On that path that we took, without doubt, Slobodan Milošević played the greatest role. I believe that recognition must be emphasized loudly and clearly to Serbia...[for] our peaceful foreign policy."[64] Montenegro's former Minister of Foreign Affairs, Nikola Samardžić, recalls that when the-President of Montenegro, Momir Bulatović had accepted the Carrington Plan at the Hague Conference, recognizing the independence of successor states, without Milošević's approval, Milošević rose from his seat, came up behind the Montenegrin delegation, and said with menacing sarcasm: "I'll give you an independent Montenegro," inducing Bulatović to reverse his vote.[65] According to Zvonimir

Trajković, Milošević's adviser from 1990 to 1992, Milošević's governing style involved "no serious discussions. There are no discussions, understand? They [i.e., advisers] only go to see him to get decisions already made, and then must implement what they are told to do."[66]

On occasion, even when he was still only president of Serbia, Milošević spoke officially and directly not only in the name of Serbia but also for Yugoslavia—as was the case in talks with a visiting state security delegation from China. The statement that Milošević's office released on this occasion noted, "*Yugoslavia* views China's efforts for peace in Bosnia as support to its own efforts for a lasting peace....*Yugoslavia* highly appreciated China's objective and principled position (emphasis added)."[67]

It is important to note that Milošević also demonstrated his power, influence, and control over the political and military authorities of the Republika Srpska by negotiating on behalf of the Bosnian Serbs the Dayton Accords in Dayton, Ohio, and at the follow-up talks in Paris. Zoran Lilić, who was the president of Yugoslavia during that period, was notably absent from any of these negotiations. The joint document agreed to between the Bosnian Serbs and Milošević in August 1995 recognized Milošević as the head of a delegation that would negotiate a peace for the Bosnian Serbs. Significantly, according to Point 5 of the agreement, Milošević was empowered to determine the structure of the negotiating team representing Yugoslavia.[68] "He has the last word. He asks the questions, which he then proceeds to answer himself," said a Bosnian Serb, testifying to Milošević's dominance, which was evident at a preliminary meeting on 19 October 1995 with the Bosnian Serb delegation in Belgrade in preparation for negotiations with the Contact Group.[69] In a revealing gesture at the Dayton talks, Milošević told a U.S. negotiator that it would be a "waste of your time" to seek the views of the senior Bosnian Serb official at the talks. Members of the Bosnian Serb delegation complained that they were kept uninformed by Milošević.[70] Milošević acted on behalf of the Bosnian Serbs not only at Dayton. For example, he also represented them in dealings with Fikret Abdić. According to Zoran Lilić who, as the federal president of Yugoslavia at the time, was on a state visit to Libya: "Mr. Slobodan Milošević, the President of the Republic of Serbia, brokered the establishment of permanent peace between Bosnia's Serbs and the Muslims of Western Bosnia [*i.e.*, Fikret Abdic]."[71]

The consolidation of his power over federal institutions and agencies, including the Yugoslav Army, was made possible by the power, both legal and actual, that, as president of Serbia, Slobodan Milošević, exercised over the forces and agencies of the Republic of Serbia. According to Article 8 of the constitution of the Republic of Serbia adopted in July 1990, as the president of the Republic of Serbia, Slobodan Milošević was the chief of state. As chief of state, he had extensive legal powers in Serbia, including the command of the army during war and peacetime; the power to issue decrees with the force of law in times of war or threat of war or threat to national unity; and the authority to order mobilization of the armed and security forces (Article 83). He was further authorized to conduct the foreign affairs of Serbia (Articles 82 and 83); appoint and remove the heads of executive agencies (Article 83), which themselves are empowered to "carry out the overall decisions of the Republic Presidency" (Article 95); and bestow decorations and awards, as well as grant amnesty (Article 83).

While other organs of government, such as the republic's parliament, were also accorded powers under the Constitution, they in fact played a limited role in governing the Republic of Serbia. As both the president of Serbia as well as the president of the ruling Socialist Party of Serbia (SPS), Milošević exercised control over all levers of government and power. The SPS controlled both the republic and federal legislatures as well as the federal presidency, and—from the 1987 Eighth Session of the League of Communists of Serbia, as it was known until 1990 when it changed its name to the SPS, until the elections of 2000—Milošević controlled the entire party structure. Even senior figures in the SPS were dismissed summarily when they disagreed with him or when they became political liabilities, as happened in the December 1995 purge that included SPS vice-presidents Borisav Jović and Mihajlo Marković.

Following the purge, in an open letter addressed to the Party's Central Council, Marković pointed out that Milošević had bypassed the Council itself in dismissing the individuals and had not bothered to respect even the formalities of a debate within the party body as Tito had allowed under such circumstances.[72] Slobodan Jovanović, one of Milošević's advisers and a former Vice-President of the SPS, confirmed that when Milošević evicted Mihajlo Marković and others from the SPS "[He] read out [the decision]; there was no discussion. That was done very quickly." The SPS's function was to be a pliable instrument of Milošević's will. Loyal members, such as the SPS's leader in Serbia's parliament, attested to the centrality of Milošević's role, "Up to now, we have won the elections because of the consistent fulfillment of our platform and because of our president's policy."[73]

The SPS provided Slobodan Milošević with an alternate, parallel channel of information and control reaching into every facet of Serbia's political, security and economic system at both the republic and federal levels. His power as the president of the party also extended to SPS members in the army or in federal civilian posts, who were his trusted subordinates within the party hierarchy, regardless of the formal government organizational relationship.[74] According to a former senior official of the orthodox Communist SK-PJ party (*Savez Komunista-Pokret za Jugoslaviju*-League of Communists Movement for Yugoslavia), the SPS's information and control functions were facilitated by some 50,000 SPS *apparatchiki* in key positions in the government bureaucracy, police, state-run firms and party administration.[75]

There is significant evidence that Slobodan Milošević used his position as head of the SPS and its extensive network of *apparatchiki* to maintain control over key decisions affecting Serbian paramilitary units and government agencies. For example, as noted by Dobrila Gajic-Glišić, the administrative assistant to the Serbian Minister of Defense, the ruling SPS's Central Council "had the final say in the matter of personnel for the defense agencies; apparently all parties in power act that way. Not one of whom they did not approve could now be accepted. Radmila Andjelković [a member of the SPS's Central Council] almost daily would forward some letters recommending her personnel....At every session of the government, either the Minister [General Simovic], or his assistants had to be present, and on everything that was discussed there it was necessary to get the SPS's opinion beforehand."[76]

In addition to these formal party linkages, Slobodan Milošević was also able to rely on the SK-PJ to exercise power, influence and control over the army, police and government structures. The SK-PJ was founded in 1990 by the JNA leadership as an orthodox Communist Party when they felt that the ruling League of Communists of Yugoslavia had become too liberal. In tandem with his process of bringing the transformed army under his direct control, Milošević's wife, Mira Marković, consolidated her own dominant position within the SK-PJ. Typical of the close ties between the SPS and the SK-PJ was the fact that the SK-PJ and the SPS both shared the building-owned by the SK-PJ-of the former Central Committee of the League of Communists of Serbia. A member of the JUL Politburo was at the same time a member of the SPS.[77] A former senior official of the SK-PJ confirmed that Milošević's wife, Mira Marković, was the key link in the close SK-PJ relationship with the SPS.[78] Later, Mira Marković was the driving force behind the creation of JUL

(*Jugoslovenska Udružena Levica*—United Yugoslav Left), a front of twenty-three, so-called, leftist micro-parties, of which only the SK-PJ was a credible political organization,[79] and she was Secretary-General of JUL's Politburo (*Direkcija*), which became essentially an extension of Slobodan Milošević's power structure.[80] As such, the SK-PJ and JUL provided Milošević additional informal—but effective—parallel conduits of information and yet another mechanism for control.[81] This was especially important in relation to the army and the police force of the Republic of Serbia who—apart from the SPS—could only be members of the SK-PJ and JUL.[82] This also extended to the Bosnian Serb Army, many of whose senior officers were reputed to be members of the SK-PJ.

Other than the Yugoslav Army and the forces of the Republic of Serbia, Milošević also exercised control over the paramilitary groups responsible for the commission of war crimes in Bosnia and Croatia. His power over the paramilitary forces stemmed from the fact that these were formal units of the command structure of the Yugoslav federal forces and almost exclusively relied upon Serbian forces and agencies for essential support.

As a result of their close connection to and dependence on the government of the Republic of Serbia, the paramilitary groups became an important tool for Milošević and served as an extension of his official policy apparatus. For instance, Slobodan Milošević used paramilitary forces to coerce the resignation of more moderate Serb leaders who, as was the case in Croatia, were interested in working out a deal peacefully. Vojislav Vukcelić, one of founders of the Serb nationalist movement in Croatia, claims that, while Radio Belgrade attacked them, Vojislav Šešelj and Milan Paroški arrived in Baranja in mid-April 1991 along with Stanko Cvijan, Serbia's Minister for Serbs Outside of Serbia, to threaten the moderates.[83] Of course, according to a Russian mercenary who worked for Arkan and escorted convoys delivering fuel to the Bosnian Serb Army, the paramilitary groups could also be used for more mundane activities with which the Republic of Serbia did not want to be seen as involved officially.[84]

Dealing through the paramilitary organizations provided Milošević with an effective, if blunt and imperfect, instrument to carry out some of the more odious acts in support of his broader strategic goals, which required the evacuation, disappearance, or neutralization of entire non-Serb communities as territorial control was established and expanded. At the same time, the outwardly intangible links with Slobodan Milošević and the image of the paramilitary groups as seemingly unofficial and uncontrolled elements offered the advantage of providing plausible denial, thereby allowing Milošević to plead that he was unaware of and not responsible for the actions of paramilitary forces. Of course, the need to obscure any linkages in itself suggested an implicit acknowledgment by Milošević that the paramilitary units' activities were beyond the pale of international legal norms and something better hidden from view.

Although the paramilitary organizations sometimes proved to be inconvenient to Milošević, especially whenever their existence became part of a broader challenge to his position by domestic political opponents, this did not diminish his critical role in and ultimate accountability for their existence and activity. Arkan and his SDG paramilitary forces offer a case study that is especially illustrative of Milošević's involvement and responsibility in this arena. In many ways, the SDG could be described as Milošević's "household paramilitary unit," a semi-official force with direct ties to, and good relations with, the Serbian government. Arkan had been anxious from the early days to emphasize that he was not a rogue element, but that his paramilitary group had been subordinated to the Serbian authorities, and to Slobodan Milošević in particular. As Arkan stressed, "Let us understand each other. We are not talking about just any paramilitary units. Every member of those units must, first of all, be responsible to the Serbian people and must respect the Parliament and the president of the Republic."[85] Arkan, perhaps as a defensive mechanism to avoid being made a scapegoat, insisted frequently in public, as he did in a 1999 interview, "I and my men have always operated within the framework of decisions taken by the Yugoslav Army, of which we were a component, a special force."[86] And, Arkan continued to emphasize his linkages with the authorities, noting that "The 'Tigers' are now undergoing training in Army centers."[87] He also insisted that when he had operated in Croatia he had been "under the command of the Territorial Defense, "We were always under command. Stories about some paramilitary acting on its own are simply insinuations."[88] Mihajlo Ulemek, one of Arkan's deputies, also confirmed that senior officers from Serbia's State Security Service were frequently present in Arkan's headquarters in Erdut and lower-ranking personnel had as their duty to "follow and control" Arkan.[89]

In July 1991, the Serbia-controlled Yugoslav presidency enacted what was at the time a little-publicized measure authorizing the inclusion of paramilitary units within the JNA structure.[90] Then, on 10 December 1991, the presidency enacted additional legislation granting regular status within the JNA, with all related benefits, to all paramilitary forces.[91] In accordance with this legislation, paramilitary groups—such as Arkan's SDG and Vojislav Šešelj's Chetniks—while operating in Croatia, continued to communicate and deal directly with Serbian government agencies in Belgrade. Officials of the Serbian Radical Party (*Srpska radikalna stranka* or SRS) have stressed that Vojislav Šešelj's forces were under the operational control of the army. According to Jovan Glamocanin, vice-president of the SRS, for example, "It is well known that we did not have any military organization of our own. Our volunteers were always within the structure of the Serbian army and under its command."[92]

The Tribunal, in its indictment of Mile Mrkšić, Miroslav Radić and Veselin Šljivancanin, had also confirmed that the Serbian paramilitary units operated under the control and supervision of JNA forces. In this particular indictment, the Tribunal declared that the paramilitary units that took part in the siege of Vukovar and the subsequent beating and execution of 260 captives from the Vukovar hospital were under the command or supervision of Colonel Mile Mrkšić, who commanded the JNA Guards Brigade based out of Belgrade; Captain Miroslav Radić, who commanded a special infantry unit of the Guards Brigade; and Major Veselin Šljivancanin, who commanded a military police battalion.[93]

While formally participating in the command structure of the JNA, paramilitary groups also functioned informally within the command structure of the forces and agencies of the Republic of Serbia and responded to requests by the Serbian Government to become involved in the Croatian and Bosnian conflicts. Speaking of Serbia's relations to the war in Croatia and Bosnia, Mihajlo Marković, then a vice president in Slobodan Milošević's SPS, noted that, in the Serbian government, "We talked not only about humanitarian aid, money, food, and medicines, and not only arms and ammunition (all of which we sent in abundant quantities), but in those days we also talked of help from Serbian [paramilitary forces]." As he explained it, "Of course, we will not declare war, this state cannot enter the war, and there is no need for it to do so. After all, we also sent them [paramilitary forces] earlier."[94]

Vojislav Šešelj, commander of the Chetniks paramilitary unit, detailed the control of his units by Serbian forces and named particular Serbian authorities under which his units operated:

> Our volunteers fought as part of special units of the police from [Serbia], under the command of Mihalj Kertes in Eastern Slavonija, while on the territory of the Serbian Republic [of Bosnia] this was under the

command of Radovan Stojčić Badža [deputy minister of the Republic of Serbia's Ministry of Internal Affairs]. Also, [we fought with] Frank Stamatović (Frenki), who is the head of the intelligence branch of Serbia's SDB [Služba državne bezbednosti-State Security Service]; we fought together on many battlefields....Our cooperation goes back to just before the battle for Borovo Selo, when 'Thompsons' [submachine guns] arrived from the MUP for Borovo Selo.[95]

Dragoslav Bokan, the former operational commander of the White Eagles, confirmed this command relationship between the Republic of Serbia and its paramilitary forces by noting that when his White Eagles went to Borovo Selo, Croatia, in 1991, "they were met by the authorities of [the Serbian-controlled] Territorial Defense, who provided arms....There was an agreement...that all units would be under the direct control of the Territorial Defense....In any event, we no longer had direct control over our boys from the moment the Territorial Defense took them over."[96]

In order to conceal its control over paramilitary units, the Republic of Serbia claimed that various paramilitary formations were receiving support and orders from other sources, such as the local Territorial Defense in those areas of Croatia controlled by Serbs. In fact, the Territorial Defense units allegedly providing support and direction were fictional organizations set up by Serbia's Ministry of Defense for the specific purpose of masking its support of paramilitary organizations. It was General Tomislav Simović's office that put out the call for volunteers to report to the municipal authorities for inclusion in Serbia's Territorial Defense. Some paramilitary leaders, however, such as Captain Dragan, refused to accept what they thought were low ranks being offered in the Territorial Defense.[97] When Serbia's former Minister of the Interior, Radmilo Bogdanović, was asked about the existence of paramilitary units, he said, "Paramilitary formations existed at one time but, later, that was regularized by the Defense Law, so that the personnel were classified as volunteers and were within the Territorial Defense system on the territory of the former Croatia, and also within the organization of the Serbian Republic [of Bosnia] Army. I don't want to talk any further about that!"[98] And yet, despite efforts to disguise Serbia's links with paramilitary forces, in some circumstances, Serbian forces permitted themselves to be photographed with commanders of Serbian paramilitary units wearing the exact same uniforms. For example, Radovan Stojčić Badža, then already a senior official in the police force of the Republic of Serbia, was photographed with Arkan in front of the putative Territorial Defense facility with a sign that identifies it as the "Center for Special Training of Volunteers from the Serbian Region of Slavonija, Baranja, and [Western] Srem," a Serb-controlled area of Croatia.[99]

In sum, according to the statute and the subsequent indictments of the Tribunal, a person may be held individually responsible for the commission of war crimes by those subject to his power, influence, and control. A review of the available evidence indicates that Slobodan Milošević exercised both official and actual power, influence, and control over Yugoslav federal forces, most notably the Yugoslav Army (JNA), as well as the forces and agencies of the Republic of Serbia, and even the Serbian paramilitary forces themselves. Milošević derived this power from his political power base in the government and the public and party offices and positions that he held: he was the president of Serbia, the president of the SPS ruling party, a member of the Yugoslav Supreme Defense Council, and represented Yugoslavia in international negotiations. The available evidence, therefore, shows that—by a system of "commander's intent"—he authorized and instigated the commission of war crimes.

In addition, as the following pages show, Slobodan Milošević could also be held individually responsible for aiding and abetting the commission of war crimes on the basis that Serbian forces under his power, influence, and control aided and abetted the commission of war crimes by Serbian paramilitary units, the Bosnian Serb Army, and the Army of the Republic of the Serbian Krajina.

NOTES

1. Given the complexity of the relationship between direct responsibility and command responsibility, there is some confusion in international law whether the "effective control" over forces responsible for the commission of war crimes imputes liability under the approach of direct responsibility or command responsibility. The limited confusion between direct responsibility and command responsibility of an accused for war crimes committed by those under his effective control is not significant to the outcomes of this study, since the question is more of a technical legal concern of whether this responsibility is derived from article 7(1) or 7(3) of the statute. Consistent with what it believes is the current practice of the Tribunal, this study has chosen to place the issue of such responsibility under article 7(1). See Indictment of Dario Kordić, Tihomir Blaškić, Mario Cerkez, Ivan Šantić, Pero Skopljak, and Zlatko Aleksovski.

2. Milan Martić was indicted both under article 7(1) for directly ordering an unlawful attack against the civilian population of Zagreb, (for which the Tribunal has specific evidence), and separately under article 7(3) on the basis of command responsibility for knowing or having reason to know that a subordinate was about to commit and did commit a war crime. Although the primary weight of the case against Milan Martić rests on the evidence of his ordering the unlawful attack, it is notable that the Tribunal additionally charged him with command responsibility. Indictment of Milan Martić, paras 15-18, pp. 2-3. See also Indictment of Ivica Rajić.

3. Indictment of Dario Kordić, Tihomir Blaškić, Mario Cerkez, Ivan Šantić, Pero Skopljak and Zlatko Aleksovski, charges at paras 23, p. 6, and counts at para 35, p. 10.

4. Indictment of Dario Kordić, Tihomir Blaškić, Mario Cerkez, Ivan Šantić, Pero Skopljak, and Zlatko Aleksovski, charges at paras 24-25, p. 6, and counts at para 36, p. 11.

5. Specifically, Judge Fouad Riad of the Court stated: "Considering it appears from the relevant parts of the record that the soldiers who carried out this operation were under the authority of Captain Miroslav Radić, Major Veselin Šljivancanin and Colonel Mile Mrkšić, all of whom were members of the Yugoslav People's Army (JNA). By virtue of their position of authority, these three individuals allegedly ordered, permitted, or participated in the above described acts." Confirmation of the Indictment of Mile Mrkšić, Miroslav Radić and Veselin Šljivancanin by Judge Fouad Riad, p. 1 (7 November 1995) [hereinafter Confirmation of the Indictment of Mile Mrkšić, Miroslav Radić and Veselin Šljivancanin]. See also Indictment of Mile Mrkšić, Miroslav Radić and Veselin Šljivancanin, paras 23 and 24, p. 9, wherein the indictment alleges that Mile Mrkšić, Miroslav Radić, and Veselin Šljivancanin are criminally responsible both on the basis of individual responsibility as provided in Article 7(1) of the Tribunal Statute, and on the basis of command responsibility provided in Article 7(3) of the Tribunal Statute. In the preliminary facts section of the indictment, it appears that specific evidence of direct orders to commit war crimes is available only for Veselin Šljivancanin, and that the indictment infers the ordering, planning, instigation, or aiding and abetting of war crimes by Mile Mrkšić and Miroslav Radić on the basis of their positions of authority. Indictment of Mile Mrkšić, Miroslav Radić and Veselin Šljivancanin, para 9, p. 2, and paras 15 and 17, p. 8.

6. Indictment of Djordje Djukić, paras 2-3, pp. 2-3.

7. Review of the *Indictment of Radovan Karadžić and Ratko Mladić* #2, p. 3.

8. Review of the Indictment of Radovan Karadžić and Ratko Mladić #2, p. 3. See also the indictment of Radovan Karadžić and Ratko Mladić on the basis of both direct responsibility and command responsibility for crimes against humanity. Indictment of Radovan Karadžić and Ratko Mladić #1, para 33, p. 12.

9. Borisav Jović, *Poslednji dani SFRJ* [The Last Days of the Socialist Federal Republic of Yugoslavia], (Belgrade: Politika, 1995) pp. 349, 370-71, 387, 389, 394, 420.

10. Jović, *Poslednji dani SFRJ* [The Last Days of the Socialist Federal Republic of Yugoslavia], p. 349.

11. Interview with Colonel Veselin Šljivancanin by Krešimir Meler, "Naredjenje je stiglo sa Dedinja" [The Order Came from Dedinje], *Svijet* (Ljubljana), 25 April 1996, p. 20.

12. Ibid., p. 21. Earlier Šljivancanin had claimed that he had registered and ensured that all prisoners had returned safely home and claimed that perhaps it was the Croatian government which killed them when they arrived home. Interview with then-Lieutenant Colonel Veselin Šljivancanin by S. Djokić, "Pothranjivanje mržnje" [Stirring Up Hate], *Vojska*, 14 October 1993, p. 9.

13. Šešelj speaking in 1995 on the "Gates of Hell" episode from the BBC's *Death of Yugoslavia* series, 1995.

14. Interview with Colonel Šljivancanin, "The Order Came from Dedinje," p. 20.

15. Djordje Djukić was indicted for the direct commission of war crimes in Bosnia on the basis of his membership on the Main Staff of the Bosnian Serb Army, which was responsible for the planning, preparation, and execution of the Bosnian Serb Army operations in Bosnia. Djordje Djukic's responsibilities specifically related to the Bosnian Serb Army's logistical operations, including regulating the requirements for logistic supplies, proposing appointments of personnel, issuing orders regarding the supply of material and regulating its transfer, and making decisions on the removal of material and technical equipment from the stocks of the Bosnian Serb Army. Indictment of Djordje Djukić, paras 2-3, pp. 2-3.

16. Milenko Vucetić, "Prolog i epilog" [Prologue and Epilogue], *Srpska rec*, 24 May 1993, p. 8. In fact, as Andjelko Grahovac, of the founders of the SDS in Bosnia-Herzegovina stated: "In the beginning we, in fact, did go together [i.e., with Karadžić] for meetings with Milošević. That was in 1991 and 1992, when we set up the autonomous regions, and I was Premier of the Autonomous region of the Krajina until the end of 1991. Milošević decided about everything." Interview with Andjelko Grahovac, "Milošević nas je zloupotrebljavao" [Milošević Misused Us], *Reporter* (Banja Luka),, 27 December 2000, online edition at ww.reportermagazin.com/rep/ rep140/0006.htm. In November 1991, Radovan Karadžić also sent a delegation which included Major Gvozden (who was responsible for coordinating and arming the Bosnian Serb forces) to General Simović, Serbia's Minister of Defense. Gajic-Glišić, Srpska vojska, pp. 260-64

17. Interview with Radmilo Bogdanović by Nenad Stefanović, "Logistika službe za volju naroda" [The Logistics of Service for the People's Will], *Duga*, 7-20 January 1995, p. 23.

18. Interview with Radovan Karadžić by Dada Vujasinović, "Država koja se razmnožava" [A State Which Is Multiplying Itself], *Duga*, 26 October-10 November 1991, p. 19.

19. Interview with General Tomislav Simović by Bogoljub Pejcić, "Bogohulno je cekati na prisilnu mobilizaciju" [It Is Blasphemy to Wait for Compulsory Mobilization], Srpska rec, 25 November 1991, p. 18.

20. Gajic-Glišić, *Srpska vojska*, p. 60, p. 110.

21. Gajic-Glišić, *Srpska vojska,* p. 61.

22. Gajic-Glišić, *Srpska vojska*, pp. 98-99.

23. Karsten Prager, "Message from Serbia," *Time*, 17 July 1995, p. 26.

24. Indictment of Dario Kordić, Tihomir Blaškić, Mario Cerkez, Ivan Šantić, Pero Skopljak, and Zlatko Aleksovski, paras 16 and 30, pp. 4 and 7-8.

25. These positions included the municipal President of the Croatian Democratic Union of Bosnia and Herzegovina in the municipality of Busovaca, and an ex officio position on the Presidency of the Croatian Community of Herceg-Bosna. Indictment of Dario Kordić, Tihomir

Blaškić, Mario Cerkez, Ivan Šantić, Pero Skopljak and Zlatko Aleksovski, paras 8-9, p. 3. See also indictment of Dario Kordić, Tihomir Blaškić, Mario Cerkez, Ivan Šantić, Pero Skopljak, and Zlatko Aleksovski paras 10 and 16, p. 3-4.

26. Indictment of Dario Kordić, Tihomir Blaškić, Mario Cerkez, Ivan Šantić, Pero Skopljak, and Zlatko Aleksovski para 14 p. 4.

27. Indictment of Radovan Karadžić and Ratko Mladić #2, paras 35-36, p. 8.

28. Indictment of Dario Kordić, Tihomir Blaškić, Mario Cerkez, Ivan Šantić, Pero Skopljak, and Zlatko Aleksovski paras 11 and 17, p. 3-4.

29. Indictment of Radovan Karadžić Ratko Mladić #2, para 38, p. 8. See also Indictment of Radovan Karadžić and Ratko Mladić #1, para 7, p.2.

30. The population ratio is itself indicative of the relationship: in 1991, Serbia (including Kosovo and Vojvodina) had 9.8 million people, while Montenegro had only 615,000. Indicative of the control that Serbia could exercise over its partner in the Federation, in 1995, the head of Montenegro's secret service, Boško Bojović, and two of his top aides simply transferred to the Republic of Serbia secret service, despite causing a public stir and embarrassing the Montenegrin leadership. Marko Lopušina, "Dva oka u neocešljanoj glavi" [Two Eyes in an Uncombed Head], *Intervju*, 4 August 1995, p. 25.

31. According to Borisav Jović, "Maintaining the continuity of Yugoslavia gives Serbia and Montenegro great advantages in their future functioning as states within the international community." If Serbia were independent and wanted recognition, he added, "this would lead it to a very unenviable international situation," in which Serbia would be "blackmailed and humiliated in a manner which would act destructively against the unity and survival of its present territory." In particular, according to Borisav Jović, if Serbia sought accreditation as a new state the international community would have sought the same rights for the Albanians and Hungarians in Serbia as for the Serbs in Croatia. Interview with Borisav Jović by Teodor Andjelić and Ivica Dacić, "Samo smelošcu i uspešnošcu protiv corsokaka opozicije" [Only with Daring and Success Against the Dead-End of the Opposition], Epoha (Belgrade), 25 February 1992, p. 12.Ivica Dacić, who later became the official spokesman and also a vice President of the SPS, reinforced these points, "The reasons for the creation of a third Yugoslavia also lie in the possibility that if Serbia established itself as a state it would be subjected to strong international pressure to split up in practice its territory into even more parts than the three former ones [Serbia, Kosovo, and Vojvodina] through the granting of special status to the ethnic minorities." Ivica Dacić, "Prvi Ustav trece Jugoslavije" [The First Constitution of the Third Yugoslavia], *Epoha*, 7 April 1992, p. 13.

32. Dacić, "The First Constitution of the Third Yugoslavia," p. 11.

33. Interview with Milo Djukanović by L[uka] M[icetic], "Farsa od savezne vlade" [A Farce of a Federal Government], *NIN*, 18 August 1995, p. 21.

34. Ibid., p. 22.

35. Djukić, *Between Glory and Anathema*, p. 254.

36. According to a former employee of the Security Service and an expert on Yugoslav security matters, Andreja Savić. Interview by Marko Lopušina and Momir Ilić, "Savezna policija je uhodila Srbiju" [The Federal Police Spied on Serbia], *Intervju*, 28 November 1994, p. 29.

37. Blaine Harden, "Serbian Police Seize Ministry in Belgrade Power Struggle," *Washington Post*, 20 October 1993, pp. A27 and A31. Marko Lopušina, "*Junaci epohe: Dosije Mihalj Kertes*" [The Heroes of Our Time: The Mihalj Kertes Dossier], *Intervju*, 19 August 1994, pp. 18 and 21. Interview with Vukašin Jokanović by Jelica Rocenović, "Kosovo samo u Srbiji" [Kosovo-Only in Serbia], *Intervju*, 1 March 1996, p. 7.

38. Interview with Milo Djukanović by Luka Miceta, 'Crnogorski model' [Montenegrin Model], *NIN*, 15 September 1995, p. 23.

39. Quoted in "Kljuc drže republike" [The Republics Hold the Key], *Vesti,* 2 July 1993, p. 7.

40. Interview with Vukašin Jokanović by Ljiljana Habjanovic-Djurović, "Imena su kod nadležnih organa" [The Authorities with Jurisdiction Have the Names], *Duga*, 4-17 February 1995, p. 13.

41. Jović, *Poslednji dani SFRJ*, p. 453. "Penzionisanje generala ne treba dramatizovati" [One Should Not Overdramatize the Retirement of the Generals], *Narodna armija*, 14 May 1992, p. 4.

42. Gajic-Glišić, Srpska vojska, p. 302.

43. Interview with Major-General Aleksandar Vasilijević by Svetislav Spasojević, "Ko je vrhovni komandant: Cosić ili Miloševic" [Who is the Supreme Commander: Cosić or Miloševic?], *NIN*, 3 July 1992, pp. 55-56.

44. Ljubodrag Stojadinović, *Film koji je zapalio Jugoslaviju [The Movie That Set Yugoslavia on Fire]*, Belgrade: Studio Design, 1995, p. 184. Interview with Ljubodrag Stojadinović by Vanja Bulić, "Patriota ne umire vec živi za otadžbinu" [A Patriot Does Not Die, But Rather Lives for His Fatherland], *Duga*, 28 April-11 May 2001, pp. 8-9.

45. Interview with Momcilo Perišić, "Nisam haški pacijent" [I Am Not the Hague's Patient], *Glas javnosti*, 25 May 2001, online edition at www.glas javnosti.co.yu/arhiva/2001/05/25/srpski/I01052401.shtml

46. Speech by Zoran Lilić, "Vojska za mir i bezbednost zemlje" [An Army for Peace and for the Country's Security], *Vojska*, 30 June 1994, p. 7. As of mid-1994, twelve sessions of the Supreme Defense Council had been held. Ibid., p. 6. The Council, exercising its oversight function, recorded explicitly its satisfaction that "the Army of Yugoslavia is successfully implementing the decisions of the Supreme Defense Council." "Za mirno rešenje sukoba u BiH" [For a Peaceful Solution to the Conflict in Bosnia-Herzegovina], *Vojska*, 18 August 1994, p. 3.

47. A partial list of confirmed sessions of the Supreme Defense Council which Slobodan Milošević attended in person includes: 12 and 14 June 1993, "Podmladjivanje generalskog kadra" [Making the General Officer Corps Younger], *Vojska*, 22 July 1993, p. 4; 23 and 25 August 1993, "Penzionisana 42 generala" [42 Generals Retired], *Vojska*, 2 September 1993, p. 4; 11 June 1993, "Vojska štednjom doprinosi stabilizaciji" [The Army through Savings Contributes to Stabilization], *Vojska,* 14 July 1994, p. 3; 9 August 1994, "Za mirno rešenje sukoba u BiH" [For a Peaceful Solution to the Conflict in Bosnia-Herzegovina], *Vojska*, 18 August 1994, p. 3; 2 November 1994, "Borbena gotovost primerena potrebama zemlje" [Combat Readiness Suitable to the Country's Needs], *Vojska*, 10 November 1994, p. 4; undated, "Vojni budžet" [Military Budget], *Vojska*, 15 December 1994, p. 4; undated January 1995, "Priprema se zakon o amnestiji" [The Amnesty Law Is Being Prepared], *Vojska*, 25 January 1995, p. 4; 15 February 1995, "Razmatrana vojnopoliticka situacija" [The Political-Military Situation Is Examined], *Vojska*, 23 February 1995, p. 4; 13 June 1995, "Postavljenja i unapredjenja" [Postings and Promotions], *Vojska*, 15 June 1995, p. 4; undated March 1996, "SRJ dosledna u realizovanju obaveza" [The Federal Republic of Yugoslavia is Consistent in Fulfilling its Obligations], *Vojska*, 28 March 1996, p. 4; and 23 April 1996, Belgrade *Tanjug* Domestic Service, 23 April 1996, *FBIS-EEU-96-080*, 26 April 1996, p. 53.

48. Lj. Bašcarević, "Predsenik Republike Srbije posetio Kasarnu Zvecan" [The President of the Republic of Serbia Visited the Zvecan Barracks], *Vojska*, 27 July 1995, p. 4.

49. See Ljubodrag Stojadinović, "Krnji Vrhovni savet odbrane; nepostojeci vrhovni komandant" [The Rump Supreme Defense Council; The Non-Existent Supreme Commander], *Glas javnosti*, 13 December 1999, at www.glas-javnosti.co.yu/danas/srpski/p99121201.shtm.

50. Slobodan Milošević "had the power" (p. 244); "he had full power" and "great power" (p. 123); Serbia is "a country where Slobodan Milošević is the sole institution" (p. 280). Milošević also ensured that potential competitors for power within the system were removed (p. 304). Djukić, *Between Glory and Anathema*.

51. Cited in an interview with Slavoljub Djukić, by Sava Dautović, "Slobodan Milošević: I pogaca i nož" [Slobodan Milošević: Both Loaf of Bread and Knife], *NIN*, 14 October 1994, p. 30.

52. Interview with Mira Marković by Aleksandar Janković, "Ja cu uvek biti na levoj strani" [I Will Always Be on the Left], *Student* (Belgrade), October 1992, reprinted in Mira Marković, *Odgovor* [Reply], Belgrade: BMG, 1993, p. 203.

53. *Autoritet bez vlasti* [Authority without Power], Belgrade: Filip Višnjić, 1993, p. 6, p. 9.

54. One of the best accounts of the power struggle is found in Djukić, *Between Glory and Anathema*, pp. 235-284.

55. Ibid., p. 291.

56. Ibid., p. 304

57. Interview with Zoran Lilić by Goran Djogić, "SPS je skidao moje glasove" [The SDS Removed My Votes], *Reporter* (Banja Luka), 22 November 2000, online edition at www.reportermagazin.com/rep135/0017.htm

58. Quoted in Djuro Zagorac, "Pregolema je srpska tuga u ocima" [The Serbian Sadness in the Eyes Is Too Great], *Profil*, number 32 [no date], 2001, online edition at www.profil.co.yu/prikazitekst.asp?Tekst=255

59. Interview with Dobrica Cosić by Milan Nikolić, "Pogled na buducnost" [A Look into the Future], Milan Nikolić, ed., *Šta je stvarno rekao Dobrica Cosić* [What Dobrica Cosić Really Said], Belgrade: Draganić, 1995, p. 263.

60. Ibid., p. 266.

61. Ibid., p. 266.

62. Interview with Milo Djukanović, "Milošević Rules Only Serbia," *Vesti* (Bad Vilbel, Germany), 9 April 1996, p. 19; *FBIS-EEU-96-074*, 16 April 1996, p. 71.

63. The flavor of Milošević's long-established central role in decision-making in Belgrade is well illustrated by someone who dealt with him extensively. Former U. S. Ambassador to Yugoslavia Warren Zimmermann, "The Last Ambassador: A Memoir of the Collapse of Yugoslavia," *Foreign Affairs*, March/April 1995, pp. 2-20. According to Borisav Jović, "There were also situations when he [i.e., Milosevic] made decisions on his own, especially when he assessed that that decision was necessary but that it would elicit opposition. Then he would avoid consultations." Interview with Borisav Jović by Dragan Bujošević, "Milošević je patron JUL-a "[Milošević Is JUL's Patron], *NIN*, 20 December 1996, p. 19.

64. "Afirmacija politike mira" [The Establishment of the Policy of Peace], *Vojska*, 2 November 1995, p. 5.

65. Interview with Nikola Samardžić by Milisav Nenadović, "Nikola Samardzić: bivši šef diplomatije Crne Gore" [Nikola Samardzić: Former Head of Montenegro's Diplomacy], *Vijesti* (Podgorica), 13 October 2000, online edition at www.vijesti.cg.yu/naslovna.ohtml?akcija=vijest&id=15886

66. Interview with Zvonimir Trajković by Dragan Belić and Momcilo Djorgović, "Srecna je okolnost da je Jovica Stanišić dovoljno ozbiljan I odgovoran covek"[It Is a God Thing that

Jovica Stanišić Is a Sufficiently Serious and Responsible Individual], *Nedeljni telegraf* (Belgrade), 12 February 1997, p. 16.

67. Belgrade *Tanjug* in English, 19 June 1995, *FBIS-EEU-95-118*, 20 June 1995, p. 48.

68. "Pet tacaka" [Five Points], *Vreme*, 4 September 1995, p. 8.

69. As reported by a Bosnian Serb participant, in Jovan Janjić, "Aparat u kvaru" [The Machine. Is Broken], *NIN*, 27 October 1995, p. 17.

70. Michael Dobbs, "After Marathon Negotiations, an Extra Mile to Reach Peace," *Washington Post*, 23 November 1995, p. A32.

71. Interview with Zoran Lilić "Nakunnu ihtiraman khassan li-sadiqina al-wafiy al-Qhadhdhafi" [We Feel Special Respect Toward Our Faithful Friend Al-Qadhdhafi], *Al-Jamahiriya* (Tripoli, Libya), 10 August 1994, p. 5.

72. "Akademik Mihajlo Marković: Otvoreno pismo Glavnom odboru Socijalisticke partije Srbije" [Academician Mihajlo Marković: Open Letter to the Central Council of the Socialist Party of Serbia], *Telegraf*, 19 December 1995, p. 4. Borisav Jović, when asked if there was a number two man in the SPS, stressed the gap below Milošević, replying that "Probably there should be a first, then, dot, dot, dot, then a sixth or seventh man; perhaps that is needed for the benefit of authority, for image. In my time, those dots did not exist. If there is a number two man now, I do not know. Some believe that there is a number two woman [i.e., Milošević's wife]." Interview with Borisav Jović by Bojana Lekić, *Radio B92* (Belgrade), 11 September 1999, online at www.b92.net/intervju/11_09__jović.shtml. Interview with Slobodan Jovanović, "Izbegavao sam prejake izraze" [I Avoided Over-Strong Declarations], *Reporter*, 3 May 2000, online edition at www.reporter.co.yu/rep106/0028.htm.

73. Interview with Gorica Gajević, "Rano je za izbore" [It Is Too Early for Elections], *NIN*, 27 October 1995, p. 11.

74. Djukić describes the high degree of control that Slobodan Milošević enjoyed over the SPS, with his elimination of potential rivals. *Between Glory and Anathema,* pp. 304-05. This is also confirmed by Stojanović, *Autoritet bez vlasti*, p. 18.

75. Interview with Zoran Cicak, "Obnovicemo bratsvo i jedinstvo" [We Will Renew Brotherhood and Unity], *Intervju,* 2 September 1994, p. 18.

76. Gajic-Glišić, *Srpska vojska*, p. 127.

77. Interview with General Stevan Mirković (Retired) by Sandra Petrušić, "Mira uzela sve" [Mira Took Everything], *Srpska rec*, 16-30 August 1993, p. 47.

78. Interview with Slobodan Cerović by Vanja Bulić, "Svi ljudi na istoj ulici" [All the People on the Same Street], *Duga*, 27 May-9 June 1995, p. 11. Borisav Jović noted that it was Milošević who had established JUL: "First, let me say that it is correct that JUL was established and developed under his [*i.e.,* Milošević's] aegis." Interview with Borisav Jović by Dragan Bujošević, "Milošević je patron JUL-a" [Milošević Is JUL's Patron], *NIN,* 20 December 1996, p. 20. And, according to Jović, Milošević had added: "Listen, let me tell you... I personally established the JUL and personally run its activities." Borisav Jović, "Naš poslednji razgovor" [Our Last Conversation], *NIN*, 26 October 2000, p. 20.

79. Asked whether he could see any difference between the SK-PJ and JUL, Dragomir Drašković, the former president of the SK-PJ answered, "Up to now, I too have not detected any difference," Interview with Dragomir Drašković by Zoran Stanić, "Hteo sam da JUL bude crveno vino, ali su ga oni razblažili vodom!" [I Wanted JUL to Be Red Wine, But They Have Weakened It with Water!], *Svet*, 25 December 1995, p. 6.

80. As noted in an interview with the President of JUL, Ljubiša Ristić, who was essentially a figurehead,"There is no mystery whatsoever about her [Mira Marković's] role in JUL. She is

JUL's moving spirit. It is she who invented it and who mobilized people to act as a movement." Interview with Ljubiša Ristić by Vladan Dinić, "Ni Milošević ni Tudjman ne znaju tacno šta se desilo u Krajini i oko nje" [Neither Milošević nor Tudjman Knows Exactly What Happened in the Krajina and Surrounding It], *Telegraf,* 23 August 1995, p. 13. Typically, JUL was given extensive access to Serbia's television.

81. Significantly, the SPS tolerated dual membership in JUL for its followers, thereby indicating a close relationship also with the broader front organization. When asked whether some members of the SPS were also members of JUL, the SPS's spokesman noted that since JUL was a coalition of leftist parties, "then, of course, among them are individuals who belong to the SPS, since the SPS is also a party of the Left." Interview with Ivica Dacić by Slobodan Savić, "Pukotine u jedinstvenom nastupu Srba" [Cracks in the Serbs' United Front], *Intervju,* 21 April 1995, p. 8. When JUL, in 1995, celebrated the anniversary of its founding, Slobodan Milošević and other officials of the Republic of Serbia government were prominently in attendance at the festivities. As Milorad Vucelić, a Vice-President of the SPS, noted, Milošević used multiple channels of command and control to maximize his power. "Even when I was head of that agency [i.e., Serbian Radio and Television], various people acted without my knowledge, with 'double links.' That was, in any event, Milošević's concept of governing. He would always run an institution with two or three parallel lines, since he did not trust anyone." Interview with Milorad Vucelić, "Prijatelje ne menjam zbog politike" [I Do Not Change Friends Because of Politics], *Glas javnosti,* 21 October 2000, online edition at www.glas-javnosti.co.yu.

82. Zoran Cicak, then spokesman for JUL, noted that his membership in JUL gave him ready access to information from the police and army, since many Communists were still serving in the ranks of both forces, "As a politician, I am engaged in collecting, collating, and using information.... As far as the police is concerned, they have a lot of information because of the nature of their work. I can always get the information I need. It is simple; in that service, as well, there are Communists and leftists and it is completely natural for them to help me. Incidentally, that also holds true for the army." Interview with Zoran Cicak by Nenad Stefanović, "Tajna crvene ruke" [Secret of the Red Hand], *Duga,* 4-17 February 1995, p. 17.

83. Interview with Vojislav Vukcelić by Ružica Ranitovic-Jović, "Vlak ce proci kroz Knin" [The Train Will Pass through Knin], *Srpska rec,* 15 August 1994, pp. 26-27.

84. Vostrukhov, "'Umeret' v Yugoslaviy" [To Die in Yugoslavia], p. 3.

85. Quoted in Slobodan Milošević (a namesake of President Milosevic), "Ubod kobre ruši stara gledanja" [The Cobra's Bite Destroys Old Ways of Looking at Things], *Ilustrovana Politika* (Belgrade), 4 November 1991, p. 3. *Ilustrovana Politika* is a state-run magazine.

86. Interview with Arkan, "Quella vittima di nome Arkan" [That Victim Named Arkan], Panorama (Milan), 2 July 1999, at www.mondadori.com/panorama/area_2/2699_1.html. As Arkan also told an American television audience, "I don't have the paramilitary-I don't have. Excuse me, I don't have paramilitary units. I am I was, all the time, under the command of Yugoslav Army... those are units of volunteers in a case of war." Interview with Arkan by Diane Sawyer, "King of Tigers," ABC News, 3 April 1999, online at www.abcnews.go.com/sections/world/dailynews/kosovo990402_arkan.html

87. Interview with Arkan by Tamara Zamyatina, "Komandir serbskikh 'tigrov' Arkan" [The Commander of the Serbian "Tigers" Arkan], *Komsomol 'skaya Pravda* (Moscow), 29 May 1999, at www.kp.ru

88. Interview with Arkan by Cvijeta Arsenić, "Nismo izgubili ni jednu bitku" [We Did Not Lose a Single Battle], *Srpsko jedinstvo* (Belgrade), June-July 1996, p. 6. *Srpsko jedinstvo* was Arkan's own magazine.

89. Interview with Mihajlo Ulemek by Marko Lopušina, "Arkan ubijen jer je postao pretnja porodici Milošević i policiji" [Arkan Was Killed Because He Became a Threat to the MiloševicFamily and to the Police], *Nedeljni telegraf*, 17 January 2001, online edition at www.nedeljnitelegraf.co.yu/novi/ulemek.html204 Aleksandar Cirić, "Svi smo mi dobrovoljci" [We Are All Volunteers], *Vreme*, 31 May 1993, p. 21.

90. Aleksander Cirić, "Svi smo mi dobrovoljci" [We Are All Volunteers], *Vreme*, 31 May 1993, p. 21.

91. Interview with Major General Tomislav Radovanović, chief of the JNA's legal branch, as quoted in Stanoje Jovanović, "I dobrovoljci vojna lica" [Volunteers Are Part of the Army Too], *Narodna armija*, 22 December 1991, p. 14. Colonel-General Života Panić, at the time Commander of the JNA's 1st Military District, also admitted that "The JNA successfully substituted for the lack of recruits in the units with territorial personnel, reservists, and volunteers - all in a single combat organization and under a single command of commanders and command structures of JNA units." Interview with Života Panić by Ivica Dacić, "Nepoznati rat" [The Unknown War], *Epoha* (Belgrade), 17 December 1991, p. 9.

92. Interview with Jovan Glamocanin by Vesna Bjekić, "Kako dokazati nevinost" [How to Prove One's Innocence], *Spona* (Frankfurt), 14 October 1993, p. 14. As Captain Dragan also stressed, "Every military force is under someone's command. I always had a commander, whether it was Dule Orlović, General Novaković, or General Mrkšić. We did not, then, have zones where uncontrolled units would roam." Interview with Dragan Vasiljković (Captain Dragan) by Boris Gajić, "Ako u Srbijj krene gradjanski rat, bice krvaviji od svih dosadasnjih" [If Civil War Breaks Out in Serbia , It Will Be the Bloodiest of All the Wars Up to Now, *Nezavisne novine* (Banja Luka), 9 March 2000, online edition at www.nnbl.co.yu/akou.htm.

93. Indictment of Mile Mrkšić, Miroslav Radić and Veselin Šljivancanin, para 26, p. 9.

94. Speech by Mihajlo Marković at the SPS Central Council, 24 August 1995, "Telegraf provalio izvode sa sednice Glavnog Odbora SPS" [Telegraf Got Its Hands on Extracts from a Session of the SPS Central Council], *Telegraf*, 12 December 1995, p. 5. He compared the Serbian "volunteers" to those that China used during the Korean War.

95. Interview with Šešelj, "I Am Ready, Awaiting Arrest," p. 15.

96. Interview with Dragoslav Bokan by Dejan Anastasijević, "Cerupanje orlova" [Plucking the Eagles' Feathers], *Vreme*, 22 November 1993, p. 20.

97. Captain Dragan's letter to General Simović to that effect was published. Gajic-Glišić, *Srpska vojska*, p. 104.

98. Interview with Radmilo Bogdanović by Biljana Sacić, "Milicije nikad nije dovoljno" [There Are Never Enough Policemen], *Intervju*, 23 December 1994, p. 16.

99. The photo, taken by Matija Koković, was published in Aleksandar Knežević, "Najbolji policajci, najgora policija" [The Best Policemen, the Worst Police], *Intervju*, 2 September 1994, p. 12. The photo, however, includes the ultra-nationalist Russian writer Edvard Limonov and probably dates from December 1991, when he visited the area.

V

A KEY INSTRUMENT OF THE CAMPAIGN FOR ETHNIC CLEANSING IN Bosnia and some of the worst perpetrators of atrocities in the region were Serbian paramilitary groups. If they were aided and abetted in the commission of war crimes by Serbian forces and agencies under the official control of Slobodan Milošević, then, under international law, Milošević may be held individually responsible for the crimes committed by these paramilitary forces.[1] To establish that Serbian forces and agencies "aided and abetted" the commission of war crimes, it must be demonstrated that they, in some manner, facilitated the commission of war crimes by the paramilitary groups. In order to attach responsibility for aiding and abetting paramilitary units through the provision of weapons and supplies, prior to their commission of war crimes, it is necessary to further demonstrate that Milošević had notice that these paramilitary units would be likely to commit war crimes.

Prior to the indictments against Milošević, the Tribunal has issued at least one indictment solely on the basis of aiding and abetting and had noted in two other indictments that individuals who "permit others" to engage in war crimes are themselves individually responsible for those crimes. In the case of General Djordje Djukić, the Tribunal's indictment was based "on the accused's role in aiding, as the head of logistics, the Bosnian Serb Army in its operations which included the shelling of civilian targets during the Bosnian Serb siege of Sarajevo between May 1992 and December 1995."[2] In the case of Radovan Karadžić and Ratko Mladić, the Tribunal based its indictment in part on the observation that subordinates "were about to destroy or permit others to destroy the property of Bosnian Muslim or Bosnian Croat civilians."[3] In the case of Slobodan Miljković, Blagoje Simić and Milan Simić, these political authorities were indicted for "permitting units of paramilitary soldiers from Serbia to enter the detention camps to kill and beat the prisoners."[4]

While in most national jurisdictions the act of permitting others to commit war crimes in areas under a person's control might not fall within the compass of 'aiding and abetting' those crimes, it is useful to note that in the Djukić case, the sole act of aiding and abetting the commission of war crimes through the organization of the provision of logistical support was deemed sufficient by the Tribunal to issue an indictment. In the other two cases, the definition of aiding and abetting encompasses the complicity-based act of permitting others to carry out those crimes when it appears that the accused had the opportunity to prevent such a crime.[5]

Based on these precedents, a review of even the partial evidence publicly available clearly would have indicated that the forces and agencies of the Republic of Serbia as well as the Yugoslav federal forces subject to the power, influence and control of Slobodan Milošević, on a substantial number of occasions, did direct, aid, and abet and were complicit in the commission of war crimes in Bosnia or Croatia by Serbian paramilitary groups. The activities of Serbia's forces and agencies were central in areas such as financing, provision of arms, recruitment, training, logistical support (including transportation to areas of operations), medical care, social benefits, and joint planning and operations. Without such help, the ability of the paramilitary forces to operate would have been severely limited or, in many cases, made impossible.

Yugoslav federal forces and the forces and agencies of the Republic of Serbia had sufficient notice that Serbian paramilitary units were likely to commit war crimes if they were armed and supported and provided access to the conflicts in Bosnia and Croatia. Even before the war started in Croatia, based on the fact that these paramilitary units had previously committed atrocities in Vojvodina and other areas of the Republic of Serbia, often at the behest of these agencies, Serbia's forces and Slobodan Milošević were fully cognizant of the mode of operation by paramilitary formations under their control. Additional notice-in some instances, during parliamentary debate-was provided by the fact that the commanders of these paramilitary groups had openly expressed their desire to engage in acts of ethnic cleansing.

In 1991, prior to the outbreak of hostilities in Croatia, Arkan's Tigers had been active against the non-Serb communities in Vojvodina in an effort to force them out. One of Arkan's lieutenants would call people on the telephone and tell them to leave. As he related, "Some grenades would drop out of my hands, and would fall into some Croatian houses." He took pride in this work, saying "thus I forced them out....[The town of] Slamkamen was thus cleansed very quickly."[6] Vojislav Šešelj's Chetniks were also active in Vojvodina, not only in the village of Hrtkovci, which drew considerable media attention at the time, but also throughout the province. On numerous occasions, his forces beat up, threatened and killed non-Serbs, and ultimately forced many out of the province.[7] Similarly, these Chetniks also intimidated the Croatian community in Janjevo, Kosovo, with the intent of forcing them to leave.[8]

Many paramilitary commanders had been prominent figures in Serbia's underworld, to which several subsequently returned. A significant proportion of the paramilitary groups' rank-and-file also had surfaced from the criminal underworld: according to a survey conducted in 1991, some twenty per cent had previous police records.[9] The activities of the paramilitary groups, in fact, served the domestic interests of Slobodan Milošević, while enabling him to maintain the fiction that the government was not involved. For instance, Vojislav Šešelj's policy at the time reinforced and ran parallel to official actions which included political intimidation as well as forced recruitment into the army, both of which worked to encourage non-Serbs to leave Vojvodina.[10] Mirko Jović's group of White Eagles from Nova Pazova also assisted Milošević in consolidating control over Vojvodina by violently intimidating the domestic opposition, such as when he helped overthrow the provincial authorities in street rallies in Vojvodina in 1989. In some cases, Milošević's government even abetted and indirectly legitimized such actions by insisting in public that non-Serbs were leaving Vojvodina "voluntarily," thus ignoring the continuing intimidation by the paramilitary groups of the population in the province. In fact, it appears that as a reward to Jović for services rendered, Vojvodina's police received instructions from Belgrade to allow Jović to form a "society," which he later transformed into a political party.[11] Like Jović, one of Šešelj's erstwhile vice presidents, Jovan Glamocanin, had also served Milošević earlier in toppling his opponents. As head of the "Solidarity Council," he claimed that he "made a great contribution to the return of Vojvodina and Kosovo-Metohija to Serbia's structure. There was cooperation at that time," he said, "and I went for discussions with Slobodan Milošević three times."[12]

In conjunction with their violent activities against non-Serbs, the commanders of paramilitary units also publicly expressed their views on the need to purge large swaths of the former Yugoslavia of non-Serbs. Virtually all of the new political parties attached to the paramilitary organizations made expanding Serbia's territory a pivotal tenet of their program, with these parties and their paramilitary commanders showing no reticence about creating an atmosphere of fear and violence to achieve their goals.[13] For instance, Mirko Jović had declared in June 1990, "We are not only interested in Serbia, but in a Christian, Orthodox Serbia, with no mosques or unbelievers."[14] In similar vein, Vojislav Šešelj announced his intentions in Parliament: "You can be sure that when Serbia's government changes, we will expel all of you [non-Serbs]."[15] Even in private, paramilitary commanders would repeat the same message to Serbian officials. For example, paramilitary leader and Parliament Deputy Milan Paroški told General Tomislav Simović, "My goal is not only to defend Serbianness but to cleanse territory, to have an ethnically clean state. You can have progress [only] within such a state." He had, Paroški added, "informed Radmilo Bogdanović [Serbia's Minister for Internal Affairs] about all of that."[16]

Clearly, following the siege of Vukovar and the Vukovar hospital massacre during the war in Croatia, Slobodan Milošević and Serbian forces under his control knew full well that their paramilitary units were prone to committing atrocities and would likely do so in Bosnia, especially given that, according to the indictment issued by the Tribunal, the paramilitary units responsible for the atrocities committed in Vukovar did so upon the instruction of JNA officers.[17] Indeed, Milošević and the forces under his control were complicit with the activities of the paramilitary groups because Serbia had itself assisted the establishment of many of these groups which operated from their bases in the

Republic of Serbia. When asked how paramilitary groups such as Arkan's had been set up in Serbia, the former chief of the criminal police in Belgrade, explained rather coyly, "Sometimes there is secret approval. Or, their establishment can be initiated by some centers of power. Thirdly, there is the possibility that they can be, let us say, legitimated [verifikovano] by the establishment. You can have a combination of all three possibilities, or just one of them."[18] Radmilo Bogdanović, Serbia's Minister for Internal Affairs (which includes the police) during the crucial 1987–1991 period,[19] declared:

> In the meantime, our National Parliament passed the Law on National Defense, with an amendment according to which volunteer units could be organized, and be put under the command of the JNA or the Territorial Defense. Thus, Arkan got started. At first, with forty volunteers, later with some more. I oversaw [pratio] that initially as president of the Security Council, then it was taken over by [Serbia's Minister of Defense] General Simović and other generals. Other volunteers, not only Arkan, were set up that way, that is as a component of the JNA or of the Territorial Defense on that territory.[20]

According to one report, the head of Serbia's State Security Service, Jovica Stanišić, was instrumental in organizing the Serb uprising in Croatia and served as Serbia's liaison to Milan Martić.[21]

Serbian authorities also facilitated recruitment for Arkan's Tigers by promoting his activities on state-run television, allowing recruitment advertisements to be published, and expediting the transit of foreign mercenaries on their way to join his paramilitary group. Russian mercenaries, for example, routinely came through Belgrade and encountered no problems with Serbian officials, even though they had no baggage and were clearly on their way to join the war. Several Russian mercenaries who were enrolled in the SDG have given such accounts.[22] It became an open secret within Serbia's defense and security establishment that its members were Arkan's patrons. According to the administrative assistant of Serbia's minister of defense, when Arkan appeared on television in 1991 and was asked to name his commander, everyone in the Ministry of Defense was afraid that Arkan would reveal the linkage. She stated, "In the office, there was a hush and all of us expected Arkan...to say in front of the whole world, 'General Simovic'. [But he said publicly instead], 'Patriarch

Pavle [of the Serbian Orthodox Church]'. Everyone began to laugh. That was done frivolously, in his manner."[23] On General Simović's staff, there was a discussion as to how best to portray Arkan if UN forces deployed to Croatia, and it was decided that "Arkan [could] not be looked upon as a citizen of Serbia in Croatia, but rather as temporary help to the Serbian people in Croatia."[24] But General Simović's staff was disappointed when the general, who was supposed to appear on television with "volunteers" from the front, was ordered not to do so. Instead, his deputy spoke, but failed to mention the role played by General Simović's office, "as if we were not the ones who were supporting all the volunteers and party armies which, according to legal rulings, are subordinate to the JNA and the Territorial Defense."[25]

The Serbian government was also instrumental in establishing and supporting local Serb paramilitary groups in Croatia and Bosnia-Herzegovina. One particularly notorious paramilitary unit was headed by Milan Martić. It operated both in Croatia and Bosnia and eventually became the Serb Krajina Republic's police force. According to Radmilo Bogdanović:

> Thus we had ties with [Milan] Martić, who was first the commander of the [Krajina] police and then Minister for Internal Affairs [in Krajina]. We extended help to enable them to…begin from nothing. It was the same way when people from the present-day Serb Republic [of Bosnia], the then-Bosnia-Herzegovina, turned to us.…We did our utmost to carry out, follow up, and provide [the help] they sought and for that which Serbia and the Serbian people offered. There, that is what the [police] Service did.[26]

According to the former Minister of Information in the Krajina, Milan Martić received support directly from several ministers and SPS officials in the government of the Republic of Serbia.[27] By late 1991, Bosnian Serbs were also visiting General Tomislav Simović, Serbia's Defense Minister, to seek and secure advice and aid.[28] A number of paramilitary commanders have confirmed the central role that Slobodan Milošević or his direct political appointees personally played in establishing the paramilitary groups. For instance, in a television interview, paramilitary leader Vojislav Šešelj stated:

> Milošević was a leading nationalist and patriot in '91 and '92. At that time, we cooperated closely. When 30,000 Serbian volunteers were

sent to the front, he was the one supplying the arms, the ammunition, the clothes, and the food. He supplied transportation. He allowed us to use military facilities, etc.[29]

Another paramilitary leader, Captain Dragan (Daniel Sneden), declared, "All that I was able to do successfully in the Krajina was while Mr. Radmilo Bogdanović was [Serbia's] Minister of Internal Affairs."[30] Elsewhere, referring to his collaboration with Bogdanović, Captain Dragan added, "I am looking only at operational problems in a detached manner. That is a great success on the part of the [Serbian] police. I cannot tell you too much about that because it is still going on, but Radmilo Bogdanović contributed a lot so that I could carry out my part of the task."[31] Gajic-Glišić notes that Captain Dragan had returned to Yugoslavia at the behest of the State Security Service and that he worked for both Radmilo Bogdanović and Jovica Stanišić (the Director of Serbia's Secret Service). The trainers for Captain Dragan's force were all personnel from special units of Serbia's Ministry of Internal Affairs.[32]

Once the paramilitary units were established, the Republic of Serbia systematized the relationship by designating specific paramilitary personnel to perform liaison functions with the Serbian government. Thus, for the SRS Chetniks, one of Šešelj's former lieutenants, Slobodan Jović, notes that he was responsible for liaison duties with Serbia's police.[33] In cases in which paramilitary units fell out of favor with Slobodan Milošević, their resources and support were cut off by the Serbian government. After Šešelj broke with Milošević, one of Šešelj's former lieutenants noted, "without the [Serbian] government's support, clearly, there are also no [more] volunteers."[34]

Having established their paramilitary units, the forces and agencies of the Republic of Serbia continued to aid and abet the commission of war crimes by the paramilitaries by providing them with substantial financial resources. Such funding was crucial to their continued survival as war booty by itself was not a sustainable source of income. On the whole, the most important forms of financial support to the paramilitary organizations from the Republic of Serbia were cash subsidies. In addition, the Republic of Serbia sanctioned paid leave from state-sector jobs for individuals who served in the ranks of paramilitary units; provided medical care for the wounded; and disbursed bonuses and pensions to the families of those who died while on duty.

According to Tomislav Nikolić, vice president of the SRS, after Vojislav Šešelj had broken with Slobodan Milošević as part of a power struggle, "The government's stance toward our volunteers changed drastically in May 1993. That is when significant problems began with medical care for our wounded, with permission for paid leaves of absence [from state-sector jobs], and soon to an end to paying the funeral costs to the families of the fallen."[35] Earlier, wounded members of paramilitary units had been sent back for treatment at the Yugoslav Army's medical facilities in Belgrade.[36] In some instances, Serbian authorities provided office space from which to operate. For example, as long as Mirko Jović's White Eagles maintained a working relationship with the Milošević government, he was provided with an entire floor in a building in Belgrade to serve as his paramilitary group's headquarters.[37] Ljubiša Petković, Vojislav Šešelj's liaison with the police, was also given an apartment, a car and free gasoline by the police.[38]

On a number of occasions, the Milošević government funneled financial assistance to paramilitary units through more circuitous routes, with agencies such as Serbia's Ministry of Defense using funds obtained from state-owned and private firms and individuals to equip and pay the paramilitary groups. According to the defense minister's administrative assistant, in the early period, "it was necessary to obtain clothing, arms and basic equipment for those deploying as volunteers. It was not possible. There was little money, there were no arms imports, and production capacities are small. What could we use?" Therefore, Jezdimir Vasiljević, a private entrepreneur, came to help and provided money and equipment through his companies and bank.[39] Vasiljević confirms that he "cooperated nicely" with two of Serbia's Ministers of Defense, Rear Admiral Miodrag Jokić (in that post until July 1991) and General Tomislav Simović.[40] In return, Vasiljević asked that his bank be allowed to function in the same way as state-owned companies and banks operated—in other words, that he be permitted to buy foreign currency from individuals.[41] Vasiljević also provided funds to Arkan's Tigers directly, including bonuses to the wounded and to the families of those who died in action, while other Serb businessmen made contributions to other paramilitary groups for similar purposes.[42] In one specific instance, the director of the Dafiment Bank claimed, "I financed most of the 'Captain Dragan' Fund."[43]

The Dafiment Bank also had financial dealings with Arkan, either in the form of contributions or joint investments.[44] According to Arkan's deputy, "There are many firms which help the Guard, but which do not want that to be known."[45] As an acknowledgement of support, Arkan gave medals to those who helped his paramilitary group, as, for example, to Dragan Tomić, the president of Serbia's Parliament, because he had provided oil to the SDG.[46] The cost of Arkan's extensive organization, in particular, must have been considerable. Not surprisingly, Arkan's spokesmen have been vague about the sources of the Tigers' funding. For instance, it appears that Italian-British businessman Giovanni Di Stefano, who has commercial interests in Serbia, also was a major contributor to Arkan, with the apparent blessing of the highest levels of the government of the Republic of Serbia. Giovanni Di Stefano acknowledged, for example, that he had contributed $1 million to Arkan's unsuccessful run for Parliament in 1993, as well as even more money to Slobodan Milošević directly. Indicative of official tolerance, if not support, is the fact that Di Stefano boasted a Yugoslav passport with Slobodan Milošević's home address listed as his reference. According to Di Stefano, "Well, maybe the president just thinks, for reasons of his own, that I'm worth it."[47]

Part of the funding also came from Arkan's own shadowy economic enterprises, such as his black and grey market oil import and sales, which received, at least, official benevolence in order to prosper. Arkan, for example, sold gasoline—which had to be smuggled in—for hard currency.[48] Pelević, one of Arkan's associates claimed that, "The Army of the Republic of the Serbian Krajina participates in funding the Tigers, since it is within the [their] organizational structure."[49] This was highly doubtful, however, since only the small eastern Slavonija area remained then under the control of the Krajina, which itself was virtually completely dependent on Slobodan Milošević for its finances. Pelević himself acknowledged that with regard to obtaining arms, "We have help from the Republic of the Serbian Krajina, and I suppose that the Republic of the Serbian Krajina gets help from Yugoslavia.[50] The Krajina relied almost entirely on Belgrade for its financial survival. According to Radmilo Bogdanović, at times, Serbia's financial support to the Krajina and to the Bosnian Serbs had amounted to one-fourth of Belgrade's total budget.[51]

In addition to funding, the provision of arms and training was crucial in enabling the Serbian paramilitary groups to carry out their criminal activities. It was alleged, for instance, that Serbia's Minister of Defense was a primary supplier, as he obtained weapons from various sources and turned them over to Serbia's Territorial Defense officials for distribution to the paramilitary units.[52] A number of paramilitary groups acknowledged receiving arms from Serbia. According to Vojislav Šešelj, for example, "we would not have been able to carry out the war during the first days by ourselves had we not received arms from them. How could we have?"[53] Elsewhere, Šešelj stated, "We received arms from him [Mihalj Kertes, then Serbia's Deputy Federal Minister of Internal Affairs, head of the Secret Service, and vice president of Serbia's Presidency] for our volunteers." Asked who else, specifically, had given him arms, Šešelj replied, "Serbia's leaders...gave some arms...old weapons...[United States-made] Thompson and [Soviet-made] Shpagni sub-machine guns....The [Serbian] police provided that from its stocks, and from the stocks of [Serbia's] Territorial Defense, since the Territorial Defense was under the authority of the Republic [of Serbia], rather than under the Federal Government [of Yugoslavia]."[54] On another occasion, Šešelj said, "We received arms from [the Serbian police]. Of course, we also received [arms] from the army, but many more from the police."[55] Another Serb Territorial Defense commander in Croatia also noted that the 300 Chetniks serving under him received their arms from Serbia, "at first from the Territorial Defense in Vojvodina and, later, also from the Šumadija region [of Serbia proper]."[56] Colonel Vojislav Šljivancanin, who served as chief of JNA security on the Vukovar front and who has been indicted by the Tribunal, adds, "Serbia's MUP [Ministry of Internal Affairs] provided the complete arsenal of the 'White Eagles,' 'Tigers,' and Šešelj's Radical Party."[57]

Another paramilitary commander, Branislav Vakić, stated that, in addition to the receipt of weapons, his forces also received extensive training by Serbian police forces:

> While the war was going on, our volunteers received arms and equipment from the [Yugoslav] Army and the [Serbian] police. Of course, appropriate receipts exist for that. Three hundred people were stationed in the MUP [Ministry of Internal Affairs] Personnel Training Center in Tara. We also received uniforms from the MUP.[58]

Vakić also noted in another interview that Šešelj's paramilitary group was armed both by the JNA and by the MUP of Serbia.[59] Ljubiša Petković, a former vice president of the SRS, likewise noted that they "received arms for the Serbian volunteers from the Yugoslav Army, and other forms of help from many [Serbian] government agencies."[60] For his part, Vojin Vucković, the commander of the Yellow Wasps paramilitary group stated that, when he had deployed from Serbia to Bosnia, he "arrived in Zvornik [Bosnia] already armed."[61] Likewise, hard-line Serbian rebel leader Šimo Dubajić from Croatia claimed that he coordinated the supply of weapons with Serbian officials such as Radmilo Bogdanović, Mihalj Kertes, and Jovica Stanišić (Director of Serbia's State Secret Service) and that he had received rifles from the state-owned "Crvena Zastava" (Red Flag) enterprise in Kragujevac, Serbia, even before fighting broke out in Croatia.[62]

In many instances, the transfer of these weapons and the provision of training was the direct result of Milošević's personal involvement. According to Šešelj, "Thanks to the cooperation and alliance with Milošević, our impact on this war was exceptionally great....We received from him weapons, uniforms, buses, and a barracks in Bubanj Potok [near Belgrade] where we trained our volunteers."[63] The central role played by Milošević is supported by the extensive involvement of various Serbian governmental agencies, which could only be coordinated and directed from Serbia's presidency and which clearly points to the central role played by Milošević. For instance, not only did the paramilitary groups receive weapons and training from the Serbian police force and Territorial Defense units, but they were also then permitted by the Serbian MUP border control forces and federal customs officers to transport those weapons across the border to Croatia and Bosnia. Thus when businessman Jezdimir Vasiljević imported military equipment for the paramilitary group's use, through Serbia's Ministry of Defense, it had to come in through international entry points and, apparently, did so without any obstruction.[64]

Once fully operational and deployed in Croatia and Bosnia, the paramilitary units then needed the assistance of the Republic of Serbia in facilitating the expulsion of Muslim civilians from Bosnia, and in illegally expropriating and transporting Bosnian civilian property to Serbia. (It should be noted here that, in three separate instances, the Tribunal indicted persons on the basis of direct responsibility for plunder and on the basis of command responsibility for plunder by forces under their control.)[65] A former official of Serbia's Border Police described the process by which Serbia aided and abetted Arkan's Tigers in carrying out the expulsions of non-Serbs from Bosnia to Hungary through Serbia:

> I spoke with Petar Duiković, who at the time was the Director of [Serbia's] Border Police. He confirmed to me that group [being expelled] had been transported across the territory of Yugoslavia, and quite simply: the border police in Sremska Raca had been informed that a bus with twenty-three people would be crossing Serbia's territory, and they did so.[66]

In fact, the Serbian authorities also allowed Serbian paramilitary groups based in Bosnia to operate on the Republic of Serbia's territory against the Muslim community in the Sandžak province, where they abducted people and raided villages.[67]

Serbian forces and agencies aided and abetted the looting that accompanied the paramilitary units' operations in Croatia and Bosnia by allowing the paramilitary personnel to keep and dispose of their booty in Serbia. In some instances, the plunder consisted of considerable quantities of cars, appliances, cash and other valuables, necessitating entire truck convoys to transport it to Serbia.[68] Šešelj accused Arkan of bringing back even a fire engine from Bijeljina to sell.[69] The former director of Belgrade's Museum of Modern Art estimated that Serbian paramilitary groups had brought back as 'booty' thousands of works of art, many of which were sold on the Belgrade market, with Arkan being the single biggest culprit.[70] The "booty" included such highly visible items as yachts taken from the Dubrovnik area and transported by road to Serbia.[71] Without a policy of tolerance-if not connivance-by the Serbian authorities, this would have been impossible to carry out, especially on a continuous basis and on such a large scale.

To cite just one example, the Serbian authorities who were in control of the bridges spanning the Drina and Sava Rivers separating Bosnia and Serbia allowed Arkan's SDG, Captain Dragan's men, and others to extort money from fleeing non-Serbs as they crossed the bridges into Serbia in transit to refuge abroad. One of the sites included the bridge over the Sava River at Bosanska Rača, located 20 kilometers north of Bijeljina, where Arkan's men demanded payment of 500 to 800 German marks for each Bosnian who wanted to cross the bridge to Serbia. In addition, these forces operated small boats and charged departing Muslims up to 1000 German marks for the crossing. As a U.S. Department of State report concluded, "Under the guise of aiding the voluntary resettlement of the Muslims, Serbs robbed them of their last coin."[72]

Serbian police would also regularly monitor the expropriated property and issue specific written permission to facilitate the paramilitary units' illegal transfer of this property when they crossed back into Serbia. In one notable case, a paramilitary commander, Branislav Vakić, published a permit he received in 1993 from the Serbian Police's section for Special Operations listing the items that "were taken as war booty" and that he was allowed to bring back to Serbia from Bosnia.[73]

In some instances, even Serbia's government-run agencies engaged directly in the looting. For example, when personnel from the Novi Sad station of Serbia's state-run television accompanied the JNA during operations in Eastern Croatia, they removed broadcast equipment from the occupied territories and shipped it back to Novi Sad, much to the chagrin of local Serbs who wanted to keep the equipment for their own use.[74] Such expropriation of property is a violation of both the laws of war and the Geneva Conventions of 1949.

In addition to the forces and agencies of the Republic of Serbia, Yugoslav federal forces also engaged in joint operations with paramilitary groups operating in Bosnia and Croatia that had the effect of aiding and abetting the commission of war crimes. According to the indictment of Mile Mrkšić, Miroslav Radić and Veselin Šljivancanin for war crimes committed during and after the siege of Vukovar, the Yugoslav federal forces participated in and in some instances ordered the commission of war crimes by paramilitary groups.[75] Without the overwhelming presence of the JNA in Croatia, it is unlikely that the siege of Vukovar would have been successful, and, without the subsequent control of the city by the JNA, it is unlikely that the paramilitary groups would have been able to successfully carry out their program of mass killings.

In the case of the siege and subsequent massacre at Prijedor in May 1992, Arkan's Tigers and other Serb paramilitary groups carried out their war crimes with JNA support. According to press reports, "During that time...JNA transport helicopters and Gazelles [attack helicopters] ferried arms and ammunition to the Serbian forces, while the JNA had distributed arms to Serb villages, such as Maricka, Tomašić, and Rakelić even before the war."[76] The negotiations, which led to the uncontested handover of the city and which were intended to guarantee the civilian population's safety, included Velibor Arsić, a colonel in the JNA.[77] When Arkan committed war crimes in Zvornik, the United Nations Commission of Experts noted that Arkan's forces were free to operate in the city center while the Yugoslav army forces secured the surrounding area.[78] Had paramilitary forces been left to their own devices, even the fledgling Croatian and Bosnian government forces would probably have been able to deal with them and could have prevented most of the atrocities. Even the paramilitary commanders recognized their need for support from the conventional army. As Branislav Lainović, field commander of the SPO's Serbian Guard, noted, "For us, it is not hard to take a position, but it is hard to hold on to it; in addition to light arms, one also needs heavy artillery in order to defend a position."[79]

Speaking about Arkan's operations in Croatia in 1991, Colonel Veselin Šljivancanin (himself indicted by the International Tribunal), then a JNA major at the front, noted, "Without the support of the JNA, he [Arkan] was nothing, because the JNA had tanks, artillery, medical support, logistics, and so on."[80] JNA generals made similar assessments; for example, after the end of the 1991 Serbo-Croatian War, Colonel General Života Avramović, at the time Yugoslavia's Deputy Minister of Defense, belittled the impact of paramilitary forces and ridiculed those in Serbia who "attributed military successes to various volunteer and other units." Continuing in this vein, he concluded, "I must say that the contribution made by [such] small-sized units cannot be compared to the operational-strategic achievements of the JNA's units....In reality, without the JNA, not a single 'guard' [paramilitary group] would be able to defend the Serbs successfully from the Ustaše knife and even less so to hold on to the front dividing [our] people from the enemy."[81]

Apart from the wide-ranging aid provided to Serbian paramilitary groups, the Republic of Serbia and Yugoslav Army also gave extensive support to the Bosnian Serb Army and the Army of the Republic of the Serbian Krajina enabling them to operate and commit extensive war crimes on territory under their control. Although the habitual commission of war crimes by the Bosnian Serb Army has been documented above, it is more telling to note that the Tribunal has indicted both the political Commander in Chief and the military commander of the Bosnian Serb Army for ordering and attempting to carry out the genocide of the Muslim population of Bosnia.[82] Without the Yugoslav Army's support, the operational effectiveness of the Bosnian Serb Army and the Army of the Republic of the Serbian Krajina would have been seriously degraded, and its capacity to conduct genocide would have been significantly circumscribed.

While publicly denying any involvement by the government of the Republic of Serbia with military operations beyond Serbia's borders, Serbian officials sometimes candidly acknowledged their country's role in aiding and abetting those military operations as they sought to claim credit for their policy. Thus, Borisav Jović, a vice president of the SPS, then Serbia's ruling party, boasted to a convention of Serbia's Young Socialists that although "the war was conducted far from Serbia's borders," its leadership still managed to "liberate" the Serbian population in what "Serbs until recently did not even know were Serb territories."[83] In a similar vein, the SPS's spokesman, Ivica Dacić, declared, "It would be difficult for any citizen of the Republika Srpska [Bosnian Serb

Republic] or the Republic of the Serbian Krajina to be able to show you a single inch (pedalj) of Serbian land which they have liberated."[84] According to then-Federal Yugoslav President Zoran Lilić, without the leaders of the Republic of Serbia and of the federal state of Yugoslavia, "it is certain, there would never have been a Republika Srpska."[85] Milošević also stressed that "Serbia ha[d] helped the Serbs of Bosnia a great deal, a very great deal. Thanks to that help, they were able to achieve most of what they wanted to achieve."[86]

In operational terms, the Yugoslav Army's involvement and support included sustained direct cross-border military operations from Serbia in conjunction with the attacks by the Bosnian Serb Army on civilian populations clustered in "safe areas." For instance, the takeover of Srebrenica in July 1995 was reportedly spearheaded by Yugoslav Army forces deployed from Serbia for that purpose.[87] As an eyewitness described the Yugoslav Army's earlier large-scale attack in January 1993:

> Just from the direction of Bajina Bašta [a border town within Serbia, on the way from the Yugoslav Army headquarters of the Užice Corps]...we watched 280 tanks, armored personnel carriers, self-propelled artillery, multiple rocket launchers, and missiles. The earth and sky were ablaze. We could not sleep. There were dozens of flights by helicopters and [fixed-wing] aircraft.[88]

Again, the attack against Goražde, a UN-designated safe zone, in April 1994, reportedly, was led by a mechanized infantry brigade and three batteries of artillery deployed from the Yugoslav Army's Užice Corps, as well as a battalion of "Specijalci," special forces.[89] On occasion, even the state-controlled Serbian press reported some of the operations that the Yugoslav Army conducted directly in Bosnia.[90] At times, Yugoslav Army veterans also wrote about their service in Bosnia, as was the case of a member of the Yugoslav Army's special forces who published excerpts of a diary of his unit's operations in the Srebrenica area in February–March 1993.[91] The Bosnian Serb police also retained close ties with the Republic of Serbia's police throughout the war, and Bosnian Serb police personnel trained in Serbia. A reporter on the scene in Northern Bosnia in late 1995 noted that "Members of the police, as well as of the State Security, from the homeland [i.e., Serbia] can be seen everywhere. The official explanation is that they are all under the command of the Republika Srpska's Ministry of Internal Affairs, since it was the latter which had invited them to come and help. The people of Banja Luka, however, say that these lads behave very arrogantly and that their presence is equivalent to a silent occupation by Serbia."[92]

According to Major-General Mladjen Mandić, Director of the Bosnian Serbs' Personnel Training Center for the Ministry of the Interior [Centar za obrazovanje kadrova MUP-a] in Banja Luka, "Cooperation with the Police Academy in Zemun [Vojvodina, Serbia] and the intermediary [police] school in Kamenica is wonderful. Cooperation with Yugoslavia was never interrupted, whatever the political circumstances were."[93] The Yugoslav Army also provided training to the Bosnian Serb Army and the Army of Krajina. According to the Bosnian Serb Army's later Chief of Staff, General Manojlo Milovanović, his personnel were still being trained in Yugoslavia, "since Yugoslavia provides that for free, and since the origin of the equipment is the same both here and in Yugoslavia." And, he added, "we have a center within the Main Staff of the Yugoslav Army, and some of our officers are in that center. They are for all intents and purposes seconded there. This is all according to the 1992 Agreement, which is still in force."[94]

The Bosnian Serb forces and the Army of the Republic of the Serbian Krajina, it needs to be remembered, were the creation of the JNA. Therefore, not only did the Yugoslav Army (the renamed and reconstituted JNA), engage in joint operations with these armies, it aided and abetted the commission of war crimes by supplying them with substantial amounts of material support. The Bosnian Serb Army received significant help with logistics, training, intelligence, and planning, including crucial supplies of fuel, spare parts, raw materials for military production, replacements for lost arms, and ammunition. (There are numerous captured official documents in the Bosnian Archives detailing the supply of military materiel from Serbia to the Bosnian Serbs.) Reacting to this support, the international community demanded an end to all such assistance.[95] As a result of this pressure, in August 1994, Slobodan Milošević announced that he would be halting military aid to the Bosnian Serb Army in order to force the Bosnian Serbs to be more flexible on the Contact Group peace plan. Unwilling actually to enforce such an embargo, however, he permitted only 135 foreign civilian observers with a restricted mandate instead of the 1,500–2,000 military observers that were thought necessary by the international community. He also significantly increased the number of helicopter supply flights into Serb-held areas of Bosnia.[96]

The overwhelming dependence of the Bosnian Serb Army was illustrated when its fuel supplies were temporarily cut off. This resulted in the Bosnian

Serb forces' defeat in several engagements in central Bosnia, with the army abandoning some of its tanks when it ran out of fuel.[97] In November 1994, the Bosnian Serb Army was under significant military pressure from the Bosnian Army. The Yugoslav Army proceeded to resupply the Bosnian Serb forces, providing key fuel, air defense systems, and even military personnel. Because of this assistance, the Bosnian Serb Army was able to sustain its assault in the Bihac area in late 1994.[98] This cooperation then remained in place-as demonstrated, for example, when an American aircraft was shot down in 1995 and it became public that the Bosnian Serb Army's air defense system was integrated into the headquarters in Belgrade, which directed operations. In a hearing before the U.S. Senate Armed Services Committe (13 July 1995), Walter B. Slocombe, Under Secretary of Defense for Policy, was asked by a Senator "Are the Serbian Serbs supplying the Bosnian Serbs, do we believe, with either intelligence or equipment?"

Slocombe replied: "We do believe that, sir. Once again, this is a Secret information issue here....As I have said repeatedly, we understand that the border is in the first place inherently porous; and second, that there is a certain amount of collusion reaching into senior levels in the Belgrade Government."[99] Also according to Slocombe, "I mentioned the third SA-6 [surface-to-air missile] battery that appeared in the eastern part of Bosnia-Herzegovina in May 1994. We do not know precisely where it came from... We have assumed that it came from Serbia."[100] The Yugoslav Army also provided intelligence to the BSA. According to then-Yugoslav Army Chief of Staff General Momcilo Perišić, "We knew exactly also when the NATO attack would occur against the Republika Srpska and passed on all the information about that. We informed the people and the Army of the Republika Srpska when the air strikes would occur."[101]

The Yugoslav federal forces also aided and abetted the commission of war crimes by the Bosnian Serb Army and the Army of the Republic of the Serbian Krajina through substantial financial assistance and the loan of a significant number of officers and front-line personnel.[102] According to General Ratko Mladić, "I participated in some significant decisions at the level of the then [JNA] Main Staff, where clear directions were given for all officers (career officers above all) who were born on this territory [Bosnia], and even for those who were not born [here], to place themselves at the defense of their people [in Bosnia]."[103] Colonel General Momcilo Perišić, later to become Chief of the Yugoslav Army General Staff, noted that he had stayed on in Bosnia beyond the announced date for the JNA's withdrawal in early May 1992: "After the withdrawal of the JNA [from Bosnia], I stayed for a month and a half longer until the Herzegovinians were trained on the equipment which we left behind."[104]

Djordje Djukic—who was indicted by the Tribunal for war crimes committed in Bosnia—resided in Belgrade and concurrently held the rank of lieutenant general in the Yugoslav Army and in the Bosnian Serb Army, in which he served as Assistant Commander for Logistics for Ratko Mladić.[105] Upon his release from the custody of the Tribunal for reasons of ill health, Djordje Djukić was treated for his illness at the Belgrade military hospital, where he subsequently died. In fact, according to other Western intelligence assessments made in late 1992, "The [Yugoslav Army] general staff in Belgrade is obedient to Milošević. Belgrade doesn't plan only the movement of Serbian forces....In B[osnia]-H[erzegovina], [BSA General Ratko] Mladić has multichannel communications to both his subordinate commanders and to the [Belgrade] general staff and Milošević."[106]

According to Richard Holbrooke, Milošević had a direct communication link to General Ratko Mladić, the Commander of the BSA's General Staff, and even the commander of the BSA's Romanija Corps responded to Milošević's orders.[107] General Mladić would also go to see Milošević in person. According to Vojislav Šešelj, "We [*i.e.*, Šešelj and Mladic] never met on the battlefield, only two or three times in Slobodan Milošević's office."[108] Well-placed Serb sources confirmed the continuing authority of the Yugoslav Army over the Serb armed forces in Croatia and Bosnia. According to Milan Martić, one-time President of the Serbian Krajina, "Yugoslav officers commanded the armies of the Krajina and of Republika Srpska."[109] Likewise, according to Vojislav Šešelj, "Until this year people did not understand how much power Milošević had over both the armies of Republika Srpska and of the Republic of the Serbian Krajina. He is their commander."[110]

In the case of the Krajina, Milan Babić, erstwhile president of the Serb government there, claimed that, "the [Krajina] police gets its pay and orders from Slobodan Miloševic" and that the Krajina's army "is under the control of the supreme command [the Yugoslav Ministry of Defense] and of the General Staff [of the Yugoslav Army]."[111] The Yugoslav Army supplied personnel, especially active-duty officers, to the Republic of the Serbian Krajina forces. Staff officers in the remnant of the Krajina acknowledged this:

When officers from the Yugoslav Army came from the parts of the Krajina which we lost [in 1995]...there was an abyss between the reserve officers and the active-duty Yugoslav officers . . .Now we are getting professional Yugoslav Army officers...I believe that it is a mistake to differentiate officers between active-duty-Yugoslav Army-and reserve-local-ones. All of us are part of the Yugoslav Army.[112]

At times, this relationship was unexpectedly transparent. In May 1995, for example, the Assistant Commander of the Yugoslav Army General Staff and Commander of the Yugoslav Army's Special Purpose Corps, Mile Mrkšić (subsequently indicted by the Tribunal), was simply shifted to become the Commander of the Republic of Serbian Krajina Army as the replacement of the existing commander after the latter's defeat in Western Slavonija.[113]

To conclude, a review of available information clearly provides the basis for the indictment of Slobodan Milošević for individual responsibility in the commission of war crimes in the territory of the former Yugoslavia. There is, thus, substantial evidence that Serbian forces and agencies under his official and actual control aided and abetted the widespread and systematic commission of war crimes by Serbian paramilitary groups. Specifically, this evidence indicates that, based on the previous public statements and activities of the paramilitary groups, Milošević had actual notice that the paramilitary groups would commit atrocities in Croatia and Bosnia if they were provided weapons, supplies, and access to the areas of conflict. With this knowledge, the forces and agencies of the Republic of Serbia, under the power, influence and control of Milošević, proceeded to organize Serbian paramilitary units; provided them with financial and other necessary resources, including weapons; and then facilitated the expulsion of non-Serbs from Bosnia and the illegal expropriation of Bosnian property which was transferred to Serbia. Ultimately, it is implausible that Milošević was not aware that his initial decision to craft and implement a policy of "all Serbs in a single state" would not ineluctably lead to systematic and widespread violence and the inevitability of destroying communities in order to secure the desired territorial contiguity inherent in such a policy.

The Yugoslav federal forces, also under the power, influence and control of Slobodan Milošević, similarly aided and abetted the commission of war crimes by the Bosnian Serb Army and the Army of the Republic of Serbian Krajina. In particular, the Yugoslav federal forces engaged in joint operations with the Bosnian Serb Army and the Army of the Republic of Serbian Krajina and provided them substantial material and personnel support, including the loan of senior officers. This collaboration and assistance resulted in the commission of war crimes.

NOTES

1. As noted above in section IV, this form of direct responsibility is more linear than command responsibility, which will be discussed below, as it infers that the Republic of Serbia forces and agencies which aided and abetted the commission of war crimes did so upon the instruction of Slobodan Milošević.

2. Press Release, General Djukić Indicted, 1 March 1996, p. 1, and Indictment of Djordje Djukić.

3. Indictment of Radovan Karadžić and Ratko Mladić #1, para 41, p. 16.

4. Indictment of Slobodan Miljković, Blagoje Simić, Milan Simić, Miroslav Tadić, Stevan Todorović, and Šimo Žarić, para 5, p. 1.

5. It is unlikely that the act of permitting others to commit a war crimes properly falls under command responsibility and not aiding and abetting, since it does not appear that those indicted actually exercised authority and control over the forces and individuals which were permitted to enter the detention sites and commit war crimes. Similarly, it does not properly fall within complicity-based responsibility for genocide as the crime of genocide was not alleged in the Simić indictment.

6. Interview with Ulemek, "I am a Serb and Proud of It," p. 19. Arkan played a similar role again when he bused in his supporters, in the guise of sports fans, to a soccer match in the Sandžak in 1993 to intimidate the Muslim community there. T. Vuković, "Poslanik po izboru 'Delja'" [Deputy Chosen by the "Tough Guys"], Vesti, 20 October 1993, p. 7.

7. Helsinki Watch, *War Crimes in Bosnia-Hercegovina*, vol. I, pp. 82–84.

8. Vladan Vasilijević, "Zlocin po meri vlasti" [Crime According to a Government Yardstick], Vreme, 15 November 1993, p. 29. Vojislav Šešelj was also useful at the strategic level to Slobodan Milošević, who used him to oust Milan Panić and Dobrica Cosić from office. Djukić, *Between Glory and Anathema*, pp. 254-55, 266, 277-78.

9. Quoted in Branka Andjelković and Batić Bacević, "Tigrovi odlaze?" [Are the Tigers Leaving?], *NIN*, 21 April 1995, p. 11.

10. Helsinki Watch, *War Crimes in Bosnia-Hercegovina*, vol. I, pp. 82–84.

11. See Slobodan Savić, "Nova epidemija vlasti" [New Epidemic of Power], *Intervju*, 28 September 1994, p. 26.

12. Quoted in Milivoje Glišić, "Jogurt i vlast" [Yogurt and Power], *NIN*, 9 February 1996, p. 23.

13. The party toughs who were the embryo of the future paramilitary organizations had already created an atmosphere of violence toward non-Serbs even before the war in Croatia. For example, in October 1990, when Gypsy musicians tried to perform on Belgrade's trendy pedestrian mall, a well-known venue for local artists and musicians, toughs in Chetnik uniforms drove them away, with the justification that there is "no place for Gypsy music here" and that the mall was located on a "Serbian Chetnik street." "Ko to tamo svira" [Who Plays the Tune There?], Borba (Belgrade), 30 October 1990, p. 12. Šešelj was personally involved in numerous acts of violence against political opponents throughout 1990. Moreover, it was not only figures like Šešelj and Jović who built up a reputation early for threatening non-Serbs. Vuk Drašković, likewise, known for his calls to expel the Albanians, stated, "The desire of the Albanian fifth column in Serbia to live in Albania is natural, and the Serbian state does not have the right to force anyone whose fatherland is on the other side of the Prokletija [Mountain] to stay [in Kosovo]." Speech of 2 April 1989 given in Zrenjanin, "Kako voditi i dobiti boj na Kosovu" [How to Conduct and Win the Battle in Kosovo], reprinted in *Koekude Srbijo* [Quo vadis Serbia?] (Belgrade: Nova Knjiga, 1990), p. 126. This goal was made an integral part of the SNO's January 1990 political

program, which Drašković drafted: "All those Shiptars [a derogatory Serbian term for Albanians] who desire to do so must of necessity be guaranteed the freedom to emigrate to Albania, or anywhere else outside of Serbia, with all the property they leave behind and all their other expenses to be reimbursed fairly." Ibid. p. 138.

14. Interview with Mirko Jović, "Novoosnovani, a ne opozicija" [Newly Established, But Not the Opposition], *Danas* (Zagreb), 19 June 1990, p. 16.

15. Quoted in Mirjana Bobic-Mojsilović, "Fašista sam, tim se dicim" [I Am a Fascist, and Proud of It], *NIN*, 10 April 1992, p. 24.

16. Gajic-Glišić, Srpska vojska, p. 178.

17. Indictment of Mile Mrkšić, Miroslav Radić, and Veselin Šljivancanin, para 26, p. 9.

18. Interview with Marko Nicović by Dragan Bujošević, "Sportski život 'Sive lisice'" [The Sporting Life of the "Gray Fox"], *NIN*, 12 April 1996, p. 17.

19. Radmilo Bogdanović later held other senior positions in Serbia's government, including deputy in the Serbian Parliament for the ruling SPS party, president of the Council for the Serbs Outside of Serbia (a Serbian government agency dealing with affairs of Serbs outside of Serbia), and member of the Supreme and Executive Council of the SPS, and president of the Security Council of the Federal Yugoslav Parliament.

20. Interview with Radmilo Bogdanović by Nenad Stefanović, "Logistika službe za volju naroda" [The Logistics of Service for the People's Will], *Duga*, 7-20 January 1995, p. 22. In another example, when one of the paramilitary leaders, Milan Paroški, was having difficulties in dealing with a Serbian official, General Tomislav Simović matter-of-factly suggested that he go directly to Serbia's new Minister of Internal Affairs, Zoran Sokolović, to resolve them. Gajic-Glišić, *Srpska vojska*, p. 179.

21. Marko Lopušina, "Kraj ratnog lobija" [The End of the War Lobby], *Intervju*, 5 August 1994, p. 13.

22. See Snežana Aleksendrić, "Nikad više preko Drine" [Never Again Across the Drina], Vesti, 2 July 1993, p. 8; and Vostrukhov, "To Die in Yugoslavia," p. 3. Wounded Russian volunteers were treated in hospitals in Serbia, as was the case with five wounded personnel in the Užice hospital. "Kozaci krunski svedoci" [The Cossacks: Crown Witnesses], *Evropske Novosti*, 19 January 1993, p. 10. According to one Russian volunteer, he obtained a regular visa immediately from the Yugoslav Embassy in Moscow despite the fact that he told officials there his purpose for going was to fight in Bosnia, A. A. Skobennikov, "Rasskaz dobrovol'tsa" [Tale of a Volunteer], *Russkiy dom* (Moscow), June 1999, online edition at www.rusk.ru/Rus_magazine/ Rus_home/Home6_15.htm

23. Gajic-Glišić, *Srpska vojska*, p. 60.

24. Ibid., p. 53.

25. As related by Gajic-Glišić, *Srpska vojska*, p. 60.

26. Interview with Bogdanović, "The Logistics of Service for the People's Will," p. 21. Radmilo Bogdanović, then Serbia's Minister of Internal Affairs, in fact, had to use his influence to rescue paramilitary leaders Milan Paroški and Mirko Jović when the Croatians had arrested them. Interview with Radmilo Bogdanović, "Uloga Radmila Bogdanovica u poslednjem ratu" [Radmilo Bogdanović's Role in the Last War], *Profil*, 12 January 1998, online edition at www./suc.org/news/profil/archive/15/tema.html.

27. Interview with Milena Tanjga by Dragan Radić, "Tudjman me je molio da pitam Milana Babica da li želi da pregovara, a ovaj je to arogantno odbio!" [Tudjman Requested That I Ask Milan Babić Whether He Wanted to Negotiate, But the Latter Refused Arrogantly!], *Svet*, 1 September 1995, p. 15.

28. Gajic-Glišić, *Srpska vojska*, p. 258.

29. *Rights & Wrongs*, television program hosted by Charlayne Hunter-Gault, 31 May 1995, "Yellow Wasps," part 1, Globalvision.

30. Interview with Captain Dragan by S. K., "Niko ne priznaje greške" [No One Admits His Errors], *Intervju*, 17 April 1992, p. 48. Captain Dragan had linkages with both the Republic of Serbia police and with the Territorial Defense, and he defended these training relationships by saying "If Milan Babić [President of the Krajina] can have thirteen posts, then I can probably have two." Branka Mitrović, "Knindže iz Bubanj potoka" [Knindžas from Bubanj Potok], *Borba*, 8 November 1991, p. 13.

31. Interview with Captain Dragan, "I Am Not a Rebel," p. 28.

32. Gajic-Glišić, *Srpska vojska*, pp. 101-102, 106. Another paramilitary agent leader, Milan Paroški, also coordinated with Radmilo Bogdanović when the latter was Minister for Serbs Outside of Serbia, p. 178.

33. Interview with Slobodan Jović by Predrag Popović, "Sve misteriozne smrti Šešeljevih saradnika" [All the Mysterious Deaths of Šešelj's Collaborators], *Svet*, 7 July 1995, p. 14.

34. Interview with Branislav Vakić, "Postponed Knock-out," p. 15.

35. Quoted in Branka Andjelković and Batić Bacević, "Tigrovi odlaze?" [Are the Tigers Leaving?], *NIN*, 21 April 1995, p. 11.

36 This was the case, for example, with the SDG. Interview with Ulemek, "I Am a Serb and Proud of It," p. 22.

37. Nenad Stefanović, *Tajni život srpske opozicije; Pokrštavanje petokrake* [The Secret Life of the Serbian Opposition; The Christianization of the Five-Pointed Star], Belgrade: BIGZ, [1994], p. 210.

38. Ibid., p. 69.

39. Gajic-Glišić, *Srpska vojska*, pp. 20, 21-28

40. Interview with Jezdimir Vasiljević by Blagica Stojanović, "Moj puc nije uspio" [My Coup Did Not Succeed], *Srpska rec*, 18 July 1994, p. 26.

41. Gajic-Glišić, *Srpska vojska* p. 27. One source claims that Serbia's secret service was involved in deals with these private banks in order to raise funds for the paramilitary groups. Lopušina, "The End of the War Lobby," pp. 13-14.

42. Gajic-Glišić, *Srpska vojska*, p. 22; and "Finansijski slomovi" [Financial Collapses], *Vreme*, 5 April 1993, p. 15. Vanja Bulić, "Legitimisanje Gazda Jezde" [The Legitimization of Boss Jezda], *Intervju*, 5 August 1994, p. 56. This allegation was reinforced by the fact that the credits taken out for that purpose by Vasiljević's bank were transferred to another private bank, the Dafiment Bank, when his bank collapsed and he fled the country. Dafina Milanović's bank, allegedly in return for kick-backs and other services to government officials, was allowed to deal in hard currencies domestically before its collapse amid accusations of shady pyramid schemes in which many ordinary depositors lost their life-savings. According to Gajic-Glišić, Jezdimir Vasiljević provided enough equipment for 2,000 personnel. *Srpska vojska*, p. 283.

43. Interview with Dafina Milanović by Vladan Dinić, "Sitne pare, krupan problem" [Small Amounts of Money, Big Problem], *Evropske Novosti*, 7 July 1993, p. 7. Gajic-Glišić claims that the Captain Dragan Fund remained under "public" [društveni, government] control. Captain Dragan also noted that his organization had received financial help from "individuals, directors of some state companies." Interview with Captain Dragan by Borić Gajić, "Ako u Srbiji krene gradjanski rat, bice krvaviji od svih dosadašnjih" [If a Civil War Breaks Out in Serbia, It Will Be Bloodier Than All the Wars Up to Now], *Nezavisne novine* (Banja Luka), 8 March 2000, at www.nnbl.co.yu/akou.htm.

44. Gajic-Glišić, *Srpska vojska*, p. 108. Ulemek reported that, for example, Arkan's Erdut-based caft-gas station complex was a joint company owned together with Dafina Milanović. "I Am a Serb and Proud of It," p. 18.

45. Interview with Pelević, "I Do Not Recognize Capitulation," p. 59.

46. Pavlović, 'Why Arkan's "Tigers' Pulled in Their Claws," p. 12. See also Vladan Vasiljević, "Nemocni pridikuju mocnima" [The Powerless Preach to the Powerful], *Srpska rec,* 11 May 1992, p. 29.

47. Bella Stumbo, "Slobo and Mira," *Vanity Fair*, June 1994, p. 171.

48. R. Stević, "Martić ispunio obecanje'" [Martić Fulfilled His Promise], *Evropske Novosti*, 29 March 1994, p. 19; and "Lik i delo: Željko Ražnatović Arkan" [Personality and Work: Željko Ražnatović Arkan], *Vreme*, 27 February 1995, p. 40.

49. Interview with Pelević, "I Do Not Recognize Capitulation," p. 59. Milošević was also personally involved in providing other forms of assistance to the Bosnian Serb authorities, such as with electronic media for propaganda and communications. According to Ilija Guzina, then Director of Bosnian Serb Radio and Television, when the 1995 NATO air strikes in Bosnia-Herzegovina damaged the Bosnian Serbs' broadcasting facilities, and the latter asked their counterparts in Serbia for help in using one of Serbia's own transmission relays, they were told that a political decision was necessary. Bosnian Serb leaders Radovan Karadžić and Momcilo Krajišnik then raised the issue directly with Slobodan Milošević who told them that "there [was] no reason not to permit that," and they got what they wanted. Interview with Ilija Guzina by Lidija Soldo, "Imali smo snimke zarobljenih francuskih pilota" [We Had Photos of the Captured French Pilots], *Telegraf international* (Belgrade), 27 February 1996, p. 41.

50. Interview with Pelević, "I Do Not Recognize Capitulation," p. 59.

51. Interview by Vladan Dinić and Slavko Curuvija, 'Knin je mogao da se brani barem dva meseca' [Knin Could Have Defended Itself for at Least Two Months], *Telegraf* (Belgrade), 23 August 1995, p. 8; all references are to the international edition. According to Yugoslav government sources, between 1991 and late 1994, Belgrade had provided $4.73 billion in aid to the Bosnian Serbs and to the Serb-held territories in Croatia. D. Dimitrovska and A. Vasin, "Drugi dinar preko Drine" [A Second Dinar across the Drina], *Evropske Novosti*, 5 August 1994, p. 5. As Borisav Jović assessed the Krajina's dependence on Belgrade, "They [the Krajina] are relatively too underdeveloped to maintain on their own such a large state and army." Interview with Borisav Jović by Milomir Marić, "Nikoga nismo terali da ostane" [We Did Not Force Anyone to Stay], *Intervju*, 19 August 1994, p. 6. Borislav Mikelić, the Krajina's Premier and Milošević's client, reports that "He [*i.e.*, Milošević] extended a great deal of help at a time when they attacked me the most in Croatia. He helped especially Gavrilović [*i.e.*, the food company run by Mikelic] by using Geneks [*i.e.*, the state-run Serbian trading firm], Belgrade banks, and trading firms." Borislav Mikelić, "Moj prvi susret sa Miloševicem" [My First Meeting with Milosevic], Svet, 2 October 1995, p. 20. General Perišić estimates that between $80-100 million were channeled from Serbia through the Gavrilović firm as aid. Quoted in Djuro Zagorac, "The Serbian Sadness in the Eyes Is Too Great," *Profil*, number 32 [no date], 2001.

52. Dobrila Gajic-Glišić, "Meler nije pucista" [Meler Is Not a Coup-Maker], *NIN*, 5 August 1994, p. 29.

53. Interview with Vojislav Šešelj by Blagica Stojanović, "Ako budete od Negotina do Knina" [If You Want to Stretch from Negotin to Knin], *Srpska rec*, 17 January 1995, p. 27.

54. Interview with Vojislav Šešelj by Mirjana Bobic-Mojsilović, "Milošević i ja" [Milošević and I], *Duga*, 28 May-10 June 1994, pp. 90 and 93.

55. Interview with Šešelj "I Am Ready, Awaiting Arrest," p. 15.

56. Quoted in Srdjan Stanišić, "Drvo za Djilasa" [Lumber for Djilas], *Pogledi*, 27 March 1992, p. 24.

57. Interview with Colonel Šljivancanin, "The Order Came from Dedinje," p. 20.

58. Interview with Vakić, "Postponed Knock-out." p. 15.

59. Interview with Vakić by Zorica Miladinović "General Perišić Gave Us Uniforms, the Army Gave Us Weapons, and Special Troops of the Ministry of Internal Affairs of Serbia Trained Us," *Telegraf*, 28 September 1994, pp. 6-7, in *FBIS-EEU-94-195*, 7 October 1994, p. 72.

60. Interview with Ljubiša Petković, "Šešelj lažno optužuje" [Šešelj Is Accusing Falsely], *Srpska Stvarnost* (Santa Monica, California, USA), 20 November 1993, p. 20.

61. Bogdanović, "Repić and the Tails," p. 23.

62. Interview with Šimo Dubajić by Predrag Popović, "Trebalo je da slušamo Tudjmana" [We Ought to Have Listened to Tudjman], *Intervju*, 10 March 1995, p. 53.

63. Interview with Šešelj "I Would Suggest to All Serbs from Croatia to Leave," p. 51.

64. Gajic-Glišić, "Meler Is Not a Coup-Maker," p. 29.

65. Indictment of Zejnil Delalić, Zdravko Mucić and Hazim Delić, para 37, p. 14; Indictment of Goran Jelišić and Ranko Cesić, para 42, p. 14; and Indictment of Nikolić, para 21, pp. 11-12.

66. Nataša Kandić, the Director of the Human Rights Fund, Belgrade, "Naš tužilac u Hagu" [Our Prosecutor in the Hague], *Intervju*, 24 March 1995, p. 9.

67. Human Rights Watch, *Former Yugoslavia: War Crimes Trials in the Former Yugoslavia*, pp. 39-40.

68. See Blaine Harden, "Serbia's Treacherous Gang of Three," *Washington Post*, 7 February 1993, p. C4.

69. Interview with Vojislav Šešelj by Coban, "They No Longer Accuse Me of War Crimes," p. 6.

70. Quoted in Gordana Igrić, "Tajna arkanskih depoa" [The Secret of Arkan's Warehouses], *NIN*, 10 February 1995, p. 29.

71. Uroš Komlenović, "Kralo se kapom i šapkom" [The Theft Was Open-Ended], *Vreme*, 13 December 1993, p. 41.

72. U.S. Department of State, *Eighth Report on War Crimes in Former Yugoslavia. Supplemental United States Submission of Information to UN Security Council in Accordance with Paragraph 5 of Resolution 771 (1992) and Paragraph 1 of Resolution 780 (1992)*, 16 June 1993.

73. Interview with Vakić, "How Frenki and I Conquered Srebrenica," p. 7.

74. P. Stanivuković, "Vukovar piše žalbe" [Vukovar Submits Complaints], Vecernje Novosti (Belgrade), 7 July 1992, p. 26.

75. Indictment of Mile Mrkšić, Miroslav Radić and Veselin Šljivancanin, para 26, p. 9.

76. Filip Švarm, "Pred strašni sud" [Facing Judgment Day], *Vreme*, 5 April 1993, p. 32.

77. Ibid., p. 31. The JNA role was confirmed by the *Final Report of the United Nations Commission of Experts Established Pursuant to Security Council Resolution 780 (1992); Annex V; The Prijedor Report*, paras 159, 182, and 183.

78. *Final Report of the United Nations Commission of Experts; Annex III. A; Special Forces*, para 49.

79. Branislav Lainović, "Neko je ginuo, neko šetao" [While Some Died Others Strolled], *Srpska rec*, 30 September 1991, p. 23.

80 Interview with Veselin Šljivancanin by Momcilo Petrović, "Ko sam, šta sam i šta sam radio u ratu" [Who I Am, What I Am, and What I Did During the War], Intervju, 29 March 1996, p. 20. See also Human Rights Watch, *Helsinki, War Crimes in Bosnia-Hercegovina:*

Bosanski Šamac, New York: Vol. 6, No. 5, April 1994, p. 6; Human Rights Watch, *Yugoslavia: Human Rights Abuses in the Croatian Conflict*, New York: Vol. 3, No. 14, September 1991, p. 15; and the letter which the U.S. Helsinki Watch Committee, New York, dated 21 January 1992, sent to Slobodan Milošević. Likewise, Chetnik warlord Oliver Bareta undertook joint operations with the JNA in Western Herzegovina. Z. V. Luković, "Sudbina na pragu" [Fate at the Doorstep], *Evropske Novosti*, 2 September 1994, p. 9.

81. Interview with General Avramović "Uspostavlja se moderan sistem komuniciranja armije s javnošcu" [A Modern System of Communications between the Army and the Public Is Being Set Up], *Narodna armija* (Belgrade), 12 March 1992, p. 7. *Narodna armija* was the JNA's official organ.

82. See Indictment of Radovan Karadžić and Ratko Mladić #1, paras 17-33, pp. 4-12; and Indictment of Radovan Karadžić and Ratko Mladić #2, paras 47-51, pp. 10-11.

83. Speech reported by D. Stevanović, 'Jović: *JNA je korišcena za zažtitu Srba*' [Jović: The JNA Was Used to Defend the Serbs], *Politika*, 4 March 1992, p. 1. As Radmilo Bogdanović later concluded, "O.K., we made mistakes. We thought that we would set up three Serbian states which would at some point then join Mother Serbia." Interview with Radmilo Bogdanović, "Uloga Radmila Bogdanovica u poslednjem ratu" [Radmilo Bogdanović's Role in the Last War], Profil (Belgrade), 12 January 1998, online edition at www.suc.org/news/profil/archive/15/tema.html

84. Interview with Ivica Dacić by Mirjana Bobic-Mojsilović, '*Partija koja seli srca u glavu*' [The Party Which Moves Hearts to the Head], *Duga*, 21 January-3 February 1995, p. 23.

85. Interview with Zoran Lilić, "Lilić: Verujem u buducnost SR Jugoslavije" [Lilić: I Believe in the Future of the Federal Republic of Yugoslavia], *Politika*, 27 September 1996, p. 14. Beginning with the 1991 meeting at Karadjordjevo, Slobodan Milošević, then and in subsequent years, continued to negotiate with Croatia's President Franjo Tudjman on the partition of Bosnia-Herzegovina. Tudjman's negotiator, Hrvoje Sarinić, has left an account of his talks with Milošević to divide and even trade territories in Bosnia-Herzegovina. Hrvoje Šarinić, *Svi moji tajni pregovori sa Slobodanom Miloševicem* [All My Secret Negotiations with Slobodan Miloševic]. (Zagreb: Globus International, 1999).

86. Interview with Slobodan Milošević by the Director of Tanjug, Slobodan Jovanović, "Kraj ratu" [An End to the War], in *Evropske Novosti* (European edition of the Belgrade daily *Vecernje Novosti*, published in Frankfurt, Germany), 13 May 1993, p. 5.

87. Michael Dobbs and R. Jeffrey Smith, "U.S. Gives Investigators New Evidence of Bosnian Serb War Crimes," *Washington Post*, 29 October 1995, p. A36.

88. Danica Drašković, a member of the Supreme Council of the SPO, "U Srebrenici je gorela zemlja" [In Srebrenica the Earth Was Ablaze], *Srpska rec*, 10 May 1993, p. 23.

89. Karlo Jeger, "Oklopno-mehanizirana brigada Užickog korpusa napada Goražde iz Srbije" [A Mechanized Infantry Brigade from the Užice Corps is Attacking Goražde from Serbia], *Globus*, 15 April 1994, pp. 7-8. Western press reports also confirmed that the commander of the Yugoslav Army's Special Forces, General Mile Mrkšić, was present when his forces took part in the April 1994 assault on Goražde, Pomfret, op. cit., p. A1. Special UN Reporter Tadeusz Mazowiecki also notes "the direct involvement of the Yugoslav armed forces" in Bosnia, *Sixth Periodic Report, Special Rapporteur of the Commission on Human Rights Pursuant to Paragraph 32 of Commission Resolution 1993/7 of 23 February 1993*, E/CN.4/1994/110, 21 February 1994, para 154.

90. "Gori Drina" [The Drina Is Burning], *Evropske Novosti,* 23 January 1993, p. 4.

91. "Akcija Srebrenica" [The Srebrenica Operation], *Duga*, 15-28 March 1997, pp. 76-78.

92. Violeta Marcetić, "Banjaluka: sve smo mogli mi" [Banja Luka: We Were Able to Do It All], *NIN*, 20 October 1995, p. 16.

93. Mandić quoted in Ljiljana Begenišić, "Iz rova-u patrolu" [From the Trenches to Patrols], *Javnost*, 16 September 1995, p. 29. Police from Serbia were reported present in Banja Luka in 1995, Ksenija Janković, "Drzava od suza" [State of Tears], Srpska rec, 23 October 1995, p. 10. *Javnost*, the official Bosnian Serb journal, also reported that police from Serbia had departed from Mrkonjic-Grad just three days before the 1995 attack on that city by Croatian and Bosnian government forces. Jovan Janjić, "Krajina nakraj sveta" [The Krajina at the End of the World], *Javnost*, 21 October 1995, p. 14.

94 Interview with General Manojlo Milovanović by Mirha Dedić, "Pokošaju li me silom odvesti u Haag, pružicu otpor" [If They Try to Take Me Away to the Hague, I Will Resist], *Slobodna Bosna* (Sarajevo), 13 April 2000, online edition at www.slobodna-bosna.ba/novi_broj/text3.htm. Recruits from the Republic of the Serbian Krajina were also trained by the Yugoslav Army until 1994, when the program was abandoned due to a lack of interest from the recruits and their frequent desertion once in Serbia. Sekulić, *Knin Fell in Belgrade*, pp. 146-47.

95 Prager, "Message from Serbia," pp. 26-27. Another veteran of the 63rd Niš Paratroop Brigade reported that, as early as 1990, his unit had delivered arms to rebels in Croatia and then operated in Srebrenica in Bosnia in 1993 and in the Krajina in 1995. Quoted in Miroslav Miletić, "Predsednik Milošević sada pere ruke od nas ali neka-zvace on kada bukne Kosovo" [President Milošević Is Now Washing His Hands of Us-Let Him; He Will Call Us When Kosovo Erupts], *Nedeljni telegraf*, 24 December 1997, online edition at www.suc.org/news/nedeljni_telegraf/1.htm

96. See Jonathan C. Randal, "Civilian Inspectors to Verify Blockade of Bosnian Serbs," *Washington Post*, 16 September 1994, p. A35; "John Pomfret 'Serbia Still Aiding War Effort,'" *Washington Post*, 4 July 1995, pp. A1, A18; and Vulliamy, "Serbian Lies World Chose to Believe," *The Guardian*, 29 February 1996, p. 12. A senior Milošević official, Dragan Tomić (president of Serbia's parliament), in fact, assured the public at the time that, "we have not cut back help to the Serbs across the Drina," although he insisted that nothing would be sent which would prolong the war. Interview by Rado Brajović and Ivan Lovrić, "Bracu nismo izdali" [We Have Not Betrayed Our Brothers], *Evropske Novosti*, 29 November 1994, pp. 2-3.

97. This was reported by the Bosnian Serbs' official representative in Belgrade. Interview with Momcilo Mandić by Vanja Bulić, "Ispali smo iz kengurove torbe" [We Have Fallen Out of the Kangaroo's Pouch], *Duga*, 12-25 November 1994, p. 87. In early 1995, Bosnian Serb economic specialists advised Slobodan Milošević that the Bosnian Serbs' economic situation would collapse in two or three months without Serbia's support. Dragan Cicić and Branko Perić, "Drmanje Karadžica" [Karadžic's Shaking], *NIN*, 10 February 1995, p. 11. There was also little illusion about the Bosnian Serbs' dependence on Belgrade. As the Bosnian Serbs' representative in Belgrade acknowledged, "Be assured that our people, both Karadžić and the entire leadership, are convinced that we cannot live without Serbia... [It would be] as if a seriously wounded individual had his oxygen cut off. That is, all that we have had and have, and what we get now by various means, has been from Serbia." Interview with Momcilo Mandić, "We Have Fallen Out of the Kangaroo's Pouch,"p. 16.

98. John Pomfret, "Serbs Gain New Leverage Over Bosnian Peace Plan," *Washington Post*, 2 December 1994, p. A39; and John Pomfret, "Serbia Suspected of Aiding Bosnian Allies," *Washington Post*, 9 December 1994, pp. A37-38.

99. *Briefing on the F-16 Shootdown in Bosnia and Current Operations, Hearing before the Committee on Armed Services, United States Senate, first session, July 13, 1995,* (Washington,

DC: U.S. Government Printing Office, 1996). p. 30. On the linkages between the Yugoslav Army and the BSA as revealed by this incident, also see Kenneth H. Bacon (Assistant to the Secretary of Defense for Public Affairs), Department of Defense News Briefing, 7 September 1995; Roy Gutman, "Yugoslav Link to Pilot Downing," *Newsday*, 11 June 1995, p. 2; interview of General Anton Tus, the fomer commander of the JNA Air Force and Air Defense, by Davor Alborghetti, "Uništenjem radara na Jahorini NATO je onesposobio protužracni sustav SRJ" [By Destroying the Radar on Jahorina NATO Has Disabled the Air Defense System of the Federal Republic of Yugoslavia], *Globus*, 8 September 1995, p. 7; and Albert Wohlstetter, "Relentless Diplomacy and Mass Murder," *Wall Street Journal*, 5 September 1995, p. A14.

100. Ibid., p. 45. Other unidentified "Western officials" added that "the SA-6 site and all other antiaircraft batteries in Serb-held territory throughout the former Yugoslav republics are part of an integrated air defense system that is headquartered in Belgrade and is under the command of the chief of staff of the Yugoslav army." John Pomfret, "Serbia Seen Still Aiding War Effort; Milosević Role Cited as Contradicting Peacemaking Pledge," *Washington Post*, 4 July 1995, p. A1.

101. "Treci svetski rat je vec završen" [The Third World War Has Already Finished], *Profil* (Belgrade), 22 December 1997, electronic edition at www.suc.org/news/profil/2.html.

102. Prager, "Message from Serbia," pp. 26-27. Personnel serving in the Yugoslav Army were pressured to "volunteer" to join the Bosnian Serb Army. See the account of one such soldier, Filip Švarm, "Generalske smijene" [General-Officer Changes], *Vreme*, 10 May 1993, p. 23.

103. Interview with General Ratko Mladić, "One Must Not Tell the People What They Want to Hear," p. 11.

104. Interview with Colonel General Perišić "Commander of Life and Death," p. 18.

105. Indictment of Djordje Djukić, para 1, p. 1.

106. Prager, "Message from Serbia," p. 29. Notably Bosnian Serb Army officers continued to be paid by Belgrade. Vulliamy, "Serbian Lies World Chose to Believe," p. 12. The Bosnian Serb Army's journal, *Srpska Vojska* (whose editorial office was listed as "Sarajevo") continued to be printed in Belgrade, at the state-owned "Stamparija Politika," 29 Makedonska Street, the same printer as for the Yugoslav Army's journal *Vojska*.

107. To End a War. (New York: Random House 1998), p. 6 and p. 158

108. Interview with Vojislav Šešelj by Snčžana Rakocevic-Novaković, "Pobedicu vec u prvom krugu" [I Will Win Already in the First Round], *Intervju*, 20 June 1997, p. 9.

109. Interview with Milan Martić, "Planiram povratak u Knin" [I Am Planning My Return to Knin], *Intervju*, 6 September 1996, p. 26.

110. Interview with Vojislav Šešelj by Ljilja Jorgovanović, "Branili smo Muslimane od Arkana!" [We Protected the Muslims from Arkan], *Srpska rec*, 11 September 1995, p. 41. According to Zvonimir Trajković, one of Milosević's advisers from 1991 to 1992, "All the commanders and generals Mladić, Gvero, Tolimir all of them are generals of the Yugoslav Army, who are originally from Bosnia...Only had command over them." Interview with Zvonimir Trajković by Ljubiša Stavrić, "Milosević: mit i stvarnost" [Milosević: Myth and Reality], *NIN*, 25 May 2000, p. 52. As Milan Martić, President of the Krajina, added on the corresponding situation the latter, ""Contrary to my orders to General Celeketić that the Slavonija-Baranija Corps of the Army of the Krajina move to the attack, [Milošević] prevented that... Unfortunately, according to that system, 'He who pays is your boss.' It was Slobodan Milošević who sent and paid General Mrkšić, and the latter obeyed his orders, not mine... The Corps commander received orders directly from Slobodan Milosevic" Interview with Milan Martić by Slobodan Nagradić, "Ucenjeni Mrksicem" [Blackmailed Using Mrkšic], *Vreme International*, 10 August

1996, pp. 48-49. When the Krajina was reduced to territories in Eastern Slavonija, Milan Milanović the Krajina's Deputy Minister of Defense, noted that "We have continuous contacts with Belgrade, since we do not do anything without Belgrade's approval." Interview with Milan Milanović by Momir Ilić, "Svi se boje Srbije" [Everyone Is Afraid of Serbia], *Intervju*, 22 September 1995, p. 7.

111. Interview with Milan Babić by Blagica Stopanović, "Milošević trguje Srbima" [Milošević Is Trading the Serbs], *Srpska rec*, 16 March 1992, p. 49.

112. Interview with Majors Dragomir Lilić and Jovica Krešović by Djoko Kesić and Zoran Lukić, "Spremni smo da sacekamo i razbijemo prvi udar hrvatske operacije" [We are Ready to Wait for and Smash the First Strike of the Croatian Operation], *Telegraf*, 30 August 1995, p. 14.

113. Srdjan Radulović, "Mile Cetvrti" [Mile the Fourth], *NIN*, 19 May 1995, p. 13. Krajina leaders were acutely aware of their dependence on Belgrade. As Borislav Mikelić, the Krajina's Premier, noted: "War is hard for the Krajina, since the Krajina is neither so large nor so strong, nor is it a military power, so that it could...The Krajina really does need a hinterland and an absolute link with Yugoslavia. If we do not have that, the Krajina could not bear the burden of a war." Interview with Borislav Mikelić, "Ljubav s predumišljajem" [Interested Love], *Vreme*, 5 June 1995, p. 16.

VI

UNDER INTERNATIONAL LAW AN INDIVIDUAL IS LIABLE FOR WAR crimes by virtue of his *command responsibility* if it is established that he failed to prevent or to punish the perpetration of those crimes by persons under his control. In addition, to establish that the accused failed to prevent the commission of war crimes, it must be demonstrated that the persons committing the war crimes were subject to his authority or control; he had either actual, constructive or imputed notice of the commission of the war crimes; and he failed to take such appropriate measures as were within his power to prevent or punish the commission of the war crimes.

As the preceding sections show, there is substantial evidence of the commission of war crimes by Serbian forces and Serbian paramilitary groups that were under Slobodan Milošević's power, influence, or control. It has also been established that the persons committing certain war crimes were under Slobodan Milošević's overall control, insofar as he had the authority to issue orders to his subordinate agencies to prevent those agencies themselves, or their paramilitary units that were committing illegal acts, from doing so. Moreover, Milošević had the authority and power to see that offenders were punished. In sum, we have established that the first element of command responsibility ("evidence of war crimes") and part of the second ("superior authority") apply to the case of Slobodan Milošević. In the pages that follow we shall argue that there is evidence that fulfills all the remaining conditions for the indictment of Milošević on the basis of command responsibility.

The Tribunal did indict a number of persons for war crimes in the former Yugoslavia on the basis of command responsibility.[1] However, in this series of indictments alleging command responsibility, the Tribunal did not elaborate on its basis for determining that the accused had either actual, constructive, or imputed notice of the commission of the war crimes, or that the accused failed to take such appropriate measures as were within his power to prevent or punish the commission of the war crimes. We were therefore unable to rely on the Tribunal's command responsibility indictments to elaborate on the criteria necessary to establish these elements of command responsibility.

The evidence available in the public domain shows that Slobodan Milošević had both actual and constructive notice that Yugoslav and Serbian forces and agencies under his control were engaged in the widespread commission of war crimes in the territory of the former Yugoslavia and that he not only failed to take appropriate measures—as were within his power—to prevent or punish those responsible, but that, in some instances, he actually rewarded the individuals responsible for war crimes.

Milošević had *actual notice* of the commission of war crimes in the territory of the former Yugoslavia as a result of reports made to him by the U.S. Helsinki Watch Committee and from indictments of JNA officers under his control as forwarded to his office by the Tribunal. He had further *constructive* and *imputed* notice by virtue of the fact that the involvement of forces under his authority and control was widespread, reported within official chains of command, and widely reported in the Serbian media.

The letter from Helsinki Watch, dated 21 January 1992, was addressed to Slobodan Milošević and catalogued, in over 25 pages, the extensive atrocities that had been committed in the territory of the former Yugoslavia by JNA forces and their paramilitary groups.[2] This letter detailed the activities of para-military groups active in Croatia, including Arkan's Tigers, Vojislav Šešelj's Chetniks, and Miro Jović's White Eagles, and explicitly described the support provided to these paramilitary units, including the supply of military and finan-cial assistance, by the government of the Republic of Serbia.[3] The letter further detailed the participation of JNA forces and their paramilitary units in the sum-mary executions of prisoners and civilians, provided extensive listings of names of victims and locations where the atrocities were committed, and highlighted the massacre at Vukovar hospital.[4] The letter then chronicled the unlawful detention of civilians in concentration camps held in Croatia, Bosnia, and Ser-bia itself, and provided locations of the camps and descriptions of the inhuman treatment of their detainees.[5] Finally, the letter cited ample evidence of indis-criminate and disproportionate attacks against civilians and civilian targets, including the destruction of cities, hospitals and churches, and the forced dis-placement and resettlement of civilians.[6]

Milošević not only acknowledged receiving the letter, but also acknowl-edged reading its contents as he chose to respond to the letter and deny its alle-gations.[7] If there were any need to verify these reports, Milošević could have raised the issue in his frequent meetings with Milan Paroški, Vojislav Šešelj, and other individuals who directly carried out the alleged war crimes.[8] Šešelj, in his political role, was Slobodan Milošević's coalition partner for a time and met with him in the latter's office and at his home.[9]

Milošević additionally received *actual* notice of the war crimes committed by forces under his authority and control when he received the indictments of Mile Mrkšić, Miroslav Radić and Veselin Šljivancanin on 7 November 1995 for the crimes that they committed in the Vukovar massacre.[10] As a controlling member of the Supreme Defense Council, which has official and actual author-ity over the Yugoslav Army, Milošević had the ability to punish these individ-uals for the commission of war crimes that were brought to his notice by the indictment. By failing to take such action or, alternatively, to transfer these indi-viduals to the custody of the Tribunal, Milošević became individually responsi-ble, by virtue of his command responsibility, for the commission of their war crimes.

Further evidence that Milošević had *actual* notice was provided by his extensive attempts to deny the commission of atrocities by forces under his authority and control, and, in some instances, to deny even the existence of such forces.[11] The basic presumption is that, unless Slobodan Milošević had notice of the possible commission of atrocities, he would not be in a position to deny the commission of those atrocities. For instance, as early as 1991, he declared, "As is known, there are no paramilitary formations in Serbia; they are forbidden."[12] Milošević has also attempted to shift the blame for war crimes to rivals within the Serbian community. When negotiating with the Bosnian Serb leadership in October 1995, for example, he placed all blame for the war on what he called "nationalist gang leaders."[13] In the same vein, an editorial in the government-controlled *Politika*, which accompanied attacks in the same issue by Milošević and other senior officials against the Bosnian Serb leadership, complained: "What has wounded us most as a people is that we have all been identified with a small group of criminals for whom war serves to give vent to their baser instincts and to plunder." Blaming Bosnian Serb "war leaders" for not having condemned the "crimes against humanity," the editorialist protested that the people of Serbia had not been consulted about such issues as the shelling of Sarajevo or the Serbian attack against the "safe area" of Goražde.[14] Milošević's wife, Mira Marković, also has sought to distance her husband's government from responsibility for any war crimes by blaming either unnamed perpetrators or, specifically, Vojislav Šešelj after he fell out of favor:

> All along we knew that some Serbs were burning down Croatian and Muslim houses. They were raping Croatian and Muslim women, and were killing Croatian and Muslim children, were plundering Croatian and Muslim families, and were ceaselessly provoking hate against all Croatians and Muslims, and even against anyone who is not a Serb....They are, simply put, criminals....Never in their history had the Serbs committed such abominations....For the first time they have done so on a massive scale, openly, and without being made to answer. That is why I hope that they will not escape being made to answer, not in some far away future but now, while the criminals are alive.[15]

One can conclude reasonably that Milošević had the capability to follow military events closely, as he has confirmed for the war in Kosovo: "I had the opportunity to follow [Chief of the General Staff of the Yugoslav Army] General Ojdanic's activity every day of the war in the command post of the Supreme Command, likewise the activity of [Third Army Commander] General Pavković, at times directly at others indirectly, and by means of reports, but in any case completely."[16]

There also is evidence that Slobodan Milošević had *constructive* and *imputed* notice of the commission of war crimes by those under his superior authority by virtue of the fact that frequent and regular public reports were made of the activities of those responsible for war crimes. Actual notice was thus augmented by constructive and imputed notice to Milošević that forces under his authority and control were responsible for the commission of war crimes, as these activities were reported routinely in a timely fashion both publicly and privately to the government of the Republic of Serbia.

With respect to official reporting of war crimes, the JNA high command and, presumably, the Supreme Military Council and the Supreme Defense Council received weekly after-action reports from the Yugoslav forces operating in Croatia and Bosnia. In one instance, a weekly after-action report (dated 23 October 1991) that was submitted to higher headquarters by a JNA lieutenant colonel operating in Croatia, and that criticized offenses by paramilitary units, appeared in a Belgrade weekly. This report stated, in part:

In zone b/d 1.pgmd there are several groups of paramilitary formations from Serbia, including the Chetniks, the 'Dušan the Terrible' units, and other self-styled volunteers whose main goal is not to fight against the enemy but to plunder people's property and to do their worst against the innocent ethnically-Croatian population.[17]

Information about the activities of paramilitary units in the field was also regularly provided to the highest levels of the Serbian government. As General Tomislav Simović, Minister of the Serbian Ministry of Defense, told Croatian Serb rebel leader Goran Hadžić, "Every day we had various information. The 'Dušan Silni' [Dušan the Terrible], 'Beli orlovi' [White Eagles], 'Srpske dobrovoljacke jedinice' [Serbian Volunteer Units], and JNA units were operating in that area...Various information came about their behavior."[18] General Simović's office was also interested in actively following the paramilitary groups' progress. For example, when Arkan and a group of his men found themselves in an encirclement in Croatia, after a joint operation with the JNA, General Simović and his staff spent the entire night in direct contact with the Yugoslav Air Force and followed the situation to see if the Air Force could intervene to rescue Arkan.[19] JNA officers who visited General Tomislav Simović also informed him of the activities of the paramilitary formations, as did journalists.[20] Their communication included specific reports such as "We know that

127

you [General Simovic] support Arkan, but we must tell you that Arkan does not always behave out there in the field."[21] In public, however, General Simović denied any knowledge that war crimes were occurring. Asked in an interview whether he had done anything to prevent war crimes, he answered the interviewer cynically, "From that question one can conclude that you know those who committed crimes. As a citizen, according to our laws, you are obligated to report that. Otherwise, you are an accomplice!"[22] Even unsolicited communications, such as reports to Radmilo Bogdanović and General Tomislav Simović from Šimo Dubajić who commanded a hard-line paramilitary unit in the Knin area, were sent to Serbian officials.[23]

The commission of atrocities was also widely reported in the Serbian press. For instance, Colonel Milorad Vucić, commander of a JNA Mechanized Infantry Brigade, which was operating in Croatia, noted in an interview in the official military press that in December 1991:

> Negative occurrences happened, particularly in relation to the treatment of the population, the treatment of their property, and their personal security. Personnel from some of [our] brigade's subordinate units protested to me with vehemence when they witnessed first-hand the criminal behavior by some individuals from various [paramilitary] groups, and sought earnestly that a stop be put to that. They simply do not want to die for such things.[24]

These official and public reports were amplified by regular meetings between the commanders of the paramilitary groups responsible for the commission of war crimes and senior officials from the Republic of Serbia, who then reported on these meetings to Milošević. Serbia's State Security Service, for instance, was in direct contact with Dragoslav Bokan, field commander of the White Eagles, and Vuk Drašković's field commanders. Paramilitary commanders also routinely visited General Simović's office; Vojislav Šešelj personally, and frequently, attended meetings in the headquarters of the State Security Services of Serbia's Ministry of Internal Affairs, and he made no attempt to hide his visits.[25] Bokan speaks of "all those talks [that] took place in the Federal Police buildings, in Sarajevo Street [Belgrade], and in the [Republic of Serbia] Police Building, on 29 November Street," while Milan Paroški received personal advice in coordinating his activities.[26] General Simović "assured him that his people could come as volunteers, and be entered on the rolls of the Territorial Defense and even proposed a meeting with [Krajina rebel leader] Goran Hadžić." General Simović also advised Paroški to coordinate with Serbia's police chief, Zoran Sokolović, and not to act independently.[27] Arkan also visited General Simović's office, on one occasion fresh from the Vukovar front.[28]

One of the purposes for the meetings was, in fact, to organize the operation of paramilitary units. Thus, most contacts with the paramilitary commanders were handled through Slobodan Milošević's direct subordinates, who had abundant information about the behavior of the paramilitary units that they supported. They would then coordinate their activities related to these groups with Serbia's Ministry of Defense.[29] For example, all dealings involving money and arms obtained for the paramilitary groups by Serbia's Minister of Defense through the banker Jezdimir Vasiljević were routinely reported to the civilian and military security agencies during the weekly meetings held at the Ministry of Defense. The Defense Minister, General Simović, then "personally informed President Slobodan Milošević" of the arrangements.[30]

Finally, *imputed* notice of the existence and activities of Serbian paramilitary units is established by the fact that they operated quite openly in the Republic of Serbia where they carried out their organization and recruitment. Indeed, paramilitary groups were set up and functioned, as noted earlier, with the participation of the government. Their members were recruited publicly and systematically within Serbia. When Mirko Jović set up his paramilitary agent, for example, he said that, "We informed all the national organizations in our country and abroad that we had formed our volunteer units."[31] Similarly, in the summer of 1991, Vuk Drašković widely publicized the establishment of the Serbian Guard as the paramilitary unit for his party. He noted that, "Lists of members of the Serbian Guard are being compiled in all local, district, and regional councils of the SPO. The future Guardists are already receiving their Guard membership cards...Over the next few days, the Guard will receive its code of conduct."[32] There was considerable publicity as paramilitary organizations sought to attract followers and training sometimes was conducted quite openly, as in the case of the Serbian Guard, with public relations in mind. Serbia's police were usually present at such venues to keep an eye on the situation.[33]

Thus, although Slobodan Milošević at various times denied any knowledge of the very existence of paramilitary groups or the atrocities committed by them and other forces under his authority or within his control, it is implausible that someone in his position would have been unaware of the existence and activities of the paramilitary groups, or of their presence in Serbia, and of their extensive relations with official agencies of the government of Serbia. This studied ignorance on his part was part of a consistent pattern of denial. He expressed shocked surprise over the existence of concentration camps in Bosnia. As he claimed, "I was astonished when I heard information that such camps existed there," but at the same time he sought to question the validity of such reports by casting doubt on the sources: "I cannot be sure....I cannot even be sure that those who inform me about it have the right information."[34] He also assured journalist Peter Maass that talk of his own responsibility for the atrocities was "dirty accusations without any evidence."[35] When asked by a U.S. State Department official in 1992 about Arkan, while the campaign of "ethnic cleansing" in Bosnia was in full swing, Milošević had responded that he had never even heard of Arkan.[36]

It was well within his power to prevent and punish the commission of war crimes because of the substantial authority and control that he exercised over both Yugoslav federal forces and the forces and agencies of the Republic of Serbia. His ability to do so was reinforced by the fact that the forces and agencies responsible for the commission of war crimes, including Serbian paramilitary groups, operated from the territory of the Republic of Serbia. Instead, not only did Milošević fail to prevent and punish the commission of war crimes, in many instances he also facilitated and rewarded the commission of war crimes by his forces. There is significant evidence to indicate that Milošević had ample opportunity to prevent the paramilitary groups' operation and their consequent commission of war crimes. He could do so because the Republic of Serbia's material support was vital to the operations of the paramilitary groups, including its assistance in transporting them to Croatia and Bosnia. The degree of control that he could exercise over the paramilitary groups was illustrated by subsequent events, when the Serbian authorities, usually as a result of domestic political rivalry, limited and, in some cases, eliminated completely the offending paramilitary unit's ability to function.

The ability of paramilitary units based in Serbia to obtain access to Croatia and Bosnia was an important element of their operations, and their dependence on Serbian agencies for such access was a key means of control over their activities. While individuals or small groups might reach a destination on their own, ensuring that larger groups did so—especially with the necessary speed and accompanying arms and logistic support—was a more complicated matter that required planning and often the use of state-controlled transportation and communications assets.

As one member of the SRS Chetniks' paramilitary group noted, he had been recruited in Sarajevo, had been instructed to go to Belgrade to join up, and from there had left for the Croatian front in 1991 in a convoy of nine buses.[37] In many instances, Serbian police were present when paramilitary units transited through Serbia to Croatia or Bosnia. In the case of the SPO's Serbian Guard, for example, Serbia's police did not seek to stop it from deploying to Croatia when this supported official objectives; rather, according to a commander of the SPO's paramilitary agent, the police provided the necessary security for the "Niš Iron Battalion" when they gathered in Belgrade to prepare to set off for Croatia.[38] Similarly, the Republic of Serbia provided a police escort for Arkan's forces as they traveled in a convoy across Serbia on their way to Bosnia.[39]

When for domestic political reasons, Milošević decided to restrict the transit of paramilitary units from Serbia, it was well within his power to do so. For example, paramilitary units deployed near the Danube in 1991 were not allowed by Serbia's police to travel to Slovenia, as Serbia sought to limit its involvement in a military situation that had gone badly for its forces.[40] A Serbian Guard veteran stated that the Serbian police on one occasion had orders, which it enforced, not to allow his unit to cross the Danube into Slavonija, while an official of Slobodan Milošević's ruling party was sent there to inform them that the police were empowered to shoot if need be.[41] Again, in May 1995, when Croatia moved against Western Slavonija, Milošević apparently preferred to see the situation end as quickly as possible in order to minimize the possibility of being drawn into a war and therefore did not want any paramilitary intervention that might prolong the fighting. As a result, the Serbian authorities prevented paramilitary units led by Vojislav Šešelj and Arkan from reaching the area. The methods used were relatively simple. According to Šešelj, in his case, Milošević directed that bus companies cancel the charter arrangements that Šešelj had made for transportation.[42]

Even when a paramilitary unit had its own transport, as in the case of Arkan's SDG, it was simply stopped by the Serbian police at the border and told to turn back because, as the Serbian police at the border pointed out, its members were citizens of Serbia.[43] The decisive influence that Serbia's officials could have in shutting down paramilitary operations was in evidence when Captain Dragan—seen as an uncooperative competitor by the Milošević government— was effectively neutralized. As Captain Dragan summed it up, "After him [Minister of Internal Affairs Radmilo Bogdanovic], in the area of defense there was no longer any room for me."[44] In an incident unrelated to war crimes, it is telling to note that Serbian police detained Milan Panic-after he had resigned as Premier-when he sought to reenter the country in the company of an economic delegation. Dobrica Cosić, who held the office of the President of Yugoslavia, had been obliged to request Slobodan Milošević to get Panić released.[45]

Beyond restricting transportation across Serbia and into Croatia or Bosnia, Milošević could, and did, restrict, and even quash paramilitary units, when they lost their utility. Vojislav Šešelj, for example, had already been arrested once in August 1990, prior to his rapprochement with Milošević. Subsequently, when relations between the two soured in the wake of a bitter political clash in 1993, Šešelj was again arrested and jailed for short periods, and his followers were dissuaded from any type of organized activity. As a result, his party and paramilitary group lost much of their influence.[46] As noted by Tomislav Nikolić, vice president of Vojislav Šešelj's SRS, "everything has changed significantly [since 1993]. Formerly, they ferried us to the battlefield in Republic [of Serbia] police and army helicopters," now the paramilitary group was obliged to hire private transportation.[47] Likewise, the Serbian police arrested Vuk Drašković in June 1993 in the wake of anti-Milošević demonstrations and Drašković's Serbian Guard, unable to operate any longer, was disbanded in late 1994.

There have been many indications that Serbian agencies were not only passive but active instruments in providing and facilitating access by Serbian paramilitary groups to Croatia and Bosnia and that, in many instances, they provided the actual element of transportation for those forces. Serbia's Ministry of Defense, typically, provided buses to take paramilitary groups to the front.[48] According to Branislav Vakić, an SRS Member of the Yugoslav Federal Parliament and formerly commander of one of Šešelj's units operating in Croatia and Bosnia, "When it was necessary to deploy seventy personnel quickly to Srebrenica [in 1992], Mile Ilić, the president of the local SPS [Milošević's party], supplied the bus at my request."[49] When Serbian agencies did not have the appropriate transport readily available, they helped coordinate alternative arrangements with the Yugoslav Army on behalf of the paramilitary units, as was the case when Vojislav Šešelj requested a helicopter from the Serbian Ministry of Defense to inspect his paramilitary forces deployed in Croatia. According to Dobrila Gajic-Glišić, "One day, [Šešelj] requested that Simović provide him with a helicopter to inspect 'his people' on the ground." General Simović did not have any helicopters, and his assistant suggested that he instead contact

JNA General Blagoje Adžić, who provided the helicopter. "When Šešelj needed to get a helicopter to return in order to attend a session of Parliament, we went about it the same way."[50] In another example, according to the field commander of SPO's Serbian Guard, when a contingent of fifty Guard members deployed from Serbia to Borovo Selo, Croatia, in 1991, Serbian police at the border cooperated in facilitating their crossing.[51]

In a related activity, forces and agencies of the Republic of Serbia also assisted Serbian paramilitary groups in expelling non-Serbs from Bosnia via Serbia to other countries. For example, according to eyewitnesses, such as Serbian journalist Jovan Dulović and American journalist Roy Gutman, who were at the state-owned railroad station in Belgrade when the state-owned chartered trains arrived, Muslims were deported from Kozluk by train through Serbia.[52] The level of systematic coordination in carrying out such expulsion was illustrated by one of Arkan's subordinates, Major Vojkan Djurković, who was in charge of expelling non-Serbs from Bijeljina. He described a process involving his "Commission," the Bosnian Serb authorities, and the Republic of Serbia in a three-sided cooperative effort. According to his account:

> That travel [expulsion] was undertaken in the following manner: the State Commission for the Free Transfer of the Civilian Population had as its duty to inform the State Security Service of the Serbian Republic [of Bosnia] (Republika Srpska) of that travel. The latter, by fax, would then pass that on to that ministry in the Republic of Serbia which has jurisdiction. The transit [on to Hungary] would occur in broad daylight, at noon.[53]

Not only did Slobodan Milošević fail to take action to prevent the commission of war crimes by forces and agencies under his authority and control, he also failed to punish those responsible when it was within his power to do so; in fact, he permitted agencies under his official control to take actions that legitimized individuals responsible for the commission of war crimes. In some instances, these individuals were even rewarded with promotions. Since he adopted a policy of not punishing those responsible, these offenders continue to operate openly in the Republic of Serbia or the territory controlled by the Republic of Serbia.

In almost all instances, as knowledge of and access to the location of paramilitary groups was easily obtainable, Slobodan Milošević had ample opportunity to arrest those responsible for the commission of war crimes. For instance, Arkan's principal operational base was in Erdut, in eastern Slavonija, an area then under Serbia's effective control. His highly visible, residence-cum-organizational headquarters were located in the same exclusive Belgrade suburb where Milošević and many of Serbia's top officials themselves resided. The complex's existence was well known and it was easily accessible. The Serbian press had reported on more than one occasion on his headquarters, which carried plainly his party's name over the doorway, and published photographs of it.[54] During the SDG's operations in Bosnia in 1995, Arkan was in Belgrade, where he passed down orders to his subordinates in the field. As Arkan's deputy noted, he had to ask Arkan for permission to engage his forces in Prijedor and called Arkan on his cellular phone with that request. Subsequently, at the height of the operation, Arkan himself, apparently unhindered by Serbian security or border controls, went to Bosnia from Belgrade to oversee operations.[55] On a number of occasions, Arkan's personnel performed public tasks in Belgrade itself.[56] In fact, Arkan had publicly cooperated with Slobodan Milošević within Serbia on Serbian security matters. During the summer of 1995, for example, joint patrols composed of Serbian police and Arkan's Tigers rounded up Serb refugees, originally from Bosnia and Croatia, and forced them to return home to join the army.[57] Notably, those arrested were taken by Serbia's police to Arkan's base in Erdut for processing and training. (According to Colonel Ulemek, "All we do is take them off the bus and shave their heads.")[58]

Arkan and his men thus remained immune from the law. As Marko Nicović, formerly chief of the Criminal Division in the Belgrade Police, when asked about the status of Arkan and his Tigers, stated, "Well, with such people who have proven their patriotism on the battlefield one must deal in a different manner. Those people have put the state in their debt. They must get special treatment, irrespective of whether or not they have a criminal record....They have succeeded in achieving the title of hero."[59] As a result of this immunity, despite the notoriety he enjoyed in human rights circles and the international community, Arkan was very much a public figure in Serbia and was accepted even in official quarters.[60] When Arkan married in 1995, his lavish wedding was the social event of the year in Belgrade and was attended by official representatives of the Slobodan Milošević government and other national institutions, such as the state-run media and the Serbian Orthodox Church. The ruling SPS party spokesman Ivica Dacić and the Minister for Sport both attended.[61] He sat as a deputy in the Serbian Parliament, and his Serbian Unity Party [*Stranka srp-*

skog jedinstva], which styled itself as a "centrist party," openly ran a slate of candidates in the 1993 national elections under the slogan "Cherishing the Best Traditions of the Serbian Nation." In March 1996 he announced the decision of his Serbian Unity Party to take part in the upcoming parliamentary elections in Serbia, Montenegro, and the Bosnian Serb Republic.

Arkan was no stranger to the social scene and before his assassination in 1999 maintained a high profile in public. For example, he attended the televised gala premiere of a new movie in June 1995, on which occasion he reportedly was seen talking to many of the leading political figures, such as the Federal President, Zoran Lilić, the mayor of Belgrade, Nebojša Ćović, and Yugoslavia's foreign minister, Vladislav Jovanović.[62] Arkan also lunched at the "Writers Club" at 7 Francuska Street, in Belgrade, where United Nations officials, who also dine there, had been introduced to him.[63] Even after the Dayton Accords, Arkan was still highly visible in Belgrade society, including at public dinners with Hadži Dragan Antić, the editor of the state-run daily *Politika* and a close ally of Slobodan Milošević.[64]

Through all his years in power, Milošević declined to detain indicted war criminals who came within his jurisdiction. For example, in July 1997, General Ratko Mladić visited Belgrade, where he appeared at public functions and then vacationed at the beach in Montenegro. By that time, Milošević, as the newly minted President of Yugoslavia, had authority in both republics. In the limited number of cases where he sought to punish those responsible for the commission of war crimes, he did so only when political differences had broken the compact between a paramilitary group and the government (as in the case of Vojislav Šešelj), or when a paramilitary group had lost its utility and became expendable. Such action led, for example, to the sentencing of several individuals from rival movements or free-lancers for ethnically-motivated killings committed within Serbia.[65] But he did not put key Serbian paramilitary leaders on trial or transfer them to the custody of the Tribunal. In large part, this reluctance was based on the concern that these individuals might seriously incriminate Milošević himself.

A case in point is the late 1994 trial of the Vucković brothers, the commanders of the "Yellow Wasps" paramilitary agent, who were charged with the commission of atrocities in Bosnia. There was widespread local media coverage of the opening of the trial, and the intent may have been to show that the government was serious about prosecuting war crimes. The accused admitted, *inter alia*, that they had cut the ear off one Muslim and had shot civilians near

Zvornik. The indictment was relatively mild, and read, "In the former Bosnia-Herzegovina in 1992 there was civil war, and D. Vuković and his older brother Vojin set off to the former Bosnia-Herzegovina in order to help the Serbian people to hold on to their territory."[66] The trial stalled, however, as one of the accused stubbornly maintained that he had been acting as an operative of Serbia's Security Service and claimed that the Security Service now wanted him to plead insanity and had assured him that he would then no longer be bothered. The defendant began to name names and sought to have police officials testify at the trial. The trial was postponed repeatedly because the witnesses, according to the government, could not be made available. According to an observer present at the trial, the prosecution had been described as being blatantly perfunctory in any event.[67] Although, two former Bosnian Serb Army soldiers who participated in the Srebrenica massacre were handed over after international pressure was exerted, they very likely had little personal knowledge of Milošević's role in the commission of war crimes.

The tolerance and often active support that his government extended to the paramilitary groups and other subordinates lent the war criminals a certain legitimacy and legal standing in the eyes of public opinion without which it would have been considerably harder for the paramilitary groups to recruit and operate or for Serbia's officials to aid and abet such actions. It was also the Serbian government that authorized, or, at least, allowed, activities such as Jezda Vasiljević's and Dafina Milanović's fraudulent banking schemes to help finance and equip the various paramilitary formations. For example, Dafina Milanović claimed that she had had the personal support of Slobodan Milošević for her activities and that he had asked her to "carry on."[68] The favorable coverage provided to paramilitary commanders in the state-run media, praise from government officials, and exemption from prosecution, all created an aura of acceptability and approval around the activities of the paramilitary units. A glossy training film on behalf of Arkan's SDG was shown on state-run Belgrade TV, while, both Arkan and Šešelj were given wide coverage on television during their operations in Croatia and Bosnia.[69] The latter included Arkan's account of how he had "liberated" the Zvornik area in Bosnia.[70] The state-run press also continued to give organizations affiliated with paramilitary commanders, such as the "Captain Dragan Fund," favorable publicity when their activities coincided with official policy.[71] Similarly, before Vojislav Šešelj fell out with Milošević in 1993, his activities continued to be covered favorably and he was frequently interviewed by the media. When Stevan Mirković, a former JNA general and senior official of the SK-PJ, suggested to Mira Marković, Milošević's wife and the leader of the SK-PJ, that they should condemn Vojislav Šešelj, she responded, "Let's not [attack] him; he is one of ours."[72] Slobodan Milošević himself had said of Šešelj that of all the opposition leaders "I value Šešelj the most....since he is consistent in expressing his political views."[73] Some paramilitary groups even received certificates of appreciation from Serbia's government agencies. Šešelj's lieutenant Vakić reported that the paramilitary force had been given "a letter of thanks from the Serbia Ministry of Internal Affairs' Unit for Special Operations, signed by its commander, Obrad Stefanović."[74]

Within the government itself, rather than punishing subordinates involved directly in or aiding and abetting the commission of war crimes, Slobodan Milošević was known to reward them. Thus for services rendered, in March 1996 the Republic of Serbia Presidential Council promoted Radovan Stojcić Badža (Deputy Minister of Internal Affairs and Head of the Department of Public Security) to Colonel-General—the highest rank in the Republic of Serbia's uniformed police force.[75] Similarly, subsequent to his participation in the siege of Vukovar and the execution of the Vukovar hospital captives, Colonel Mile Mrkšić was promoted to the rank of general in the Yugoslav Army. Later, he assumed a position in the army of the Republic of Serbian Krajina. Major Veselin Šljivancanin was promoted to the rank of lieutenant colonel in the Yugoslav Army.[76] Following his indictment by the Tribunal, Veselin Šljivancanin was given yet another promotion in February 1996. As a member of the Supreme Defense Council, Milošević would have had authority and control over these promotions.

In sum, the evidence presented in the preceding pages provides sufficient grounds to establish Slobodan Milošević's *command responsibility* for the commission of war crimes in the territory of the former Yugoslavia on the basis that Yugoslav federal forces, the forces and agencies of the Republic of Serbia, and Serbian paramilitary units subject to his superior authority were responsible for the widespread and systematic commission of war crimes. Not only did Slobodan Milošević fail to take appropriate measures to prevent or punish the commission of these crimes, but also he frequently aided and abetted their commission and rewarded those individuals responsible for committing the war crimes.[77]

There also is sufficient evidence to hold Slobodan Milošević criminally responsible for the commission of war crimes in Croatia and Bosnia. He was individually responsible, by virtue of *direct responsibility*, for ordering, planning, and instigating the commission of war crimes in the territory of the former Yugoslavia by Yugoslav federal forces and the forces and agencies of the Republic of Serbia. He was responsible for ordering, planning, and instigating the commission of war crimes in the territory of the former Yugoslavia by Serbian paramilitary groups based out of the Republic of Serbia. He was responsible for ordering Yugoslav federal forces and the forces and agencies of the Republic of Serbia to aid and abet the commission of war crimes by Serbian paramilitary units. He was responsible for aiding and abetting the commission of war crimes by Serbian paramilitary groups in the territory of the former Yugoslavia. He was responsible for aiding and abetting the commission of war crimes by the Bosnian Serb Army and the Army of the Republic of Serbian Krajina. He was responsible for complicity in the commission of genocide.

By virtue of *command responsibility*, Milošević was responsible for failing to prevent or punish the commission of war crimes in the territory of the former Yugoslavia by Yugoslav federal forces, including the Yugoslav People's Army (JNA) and the Yugoslav Army. He was responsible for failing to prevent or punish the commission of war crimes in the territory of the former Yugoslavia by the forces and agencies of the Republic of Serbia. He was responsible for failing to prevent or punish the forces and agencies of the Republic of Serbia, in particular forces under the control of the Serbian Ministry of Defense and Ministry of Internal Affairs, when they were aiding and abetting the commission of war crimes by Serbian paramilitary groups. He was responsible for failing to prevent or punish the commission of war crimes in the territory of the former Yugoslavia by Serbian paramilitary groups such as Arkan's Tigers, Vojislav Šešelj's Chetniks, and Mirko Jović's White Eagles.

Therefore, it is the conclusion of this study that there is a firm basis in international law for the indictment of Slobodan Milošević for war crimes committed in Bosnia-Herzegovina and Croatia that preceded by almost a decade his responsibility for actions in Kosovo. Accordingly, it was imperative to broaden the indictment against Milošević and other responsible figures in the Milošević regime, and to have them brought to trial before the International Criminal Tribunal for the Former Yugoslavia for their individual responsibility in the war crimes of the Balkan Wars.

NOTES

1. For a review of the individuals indicted on the basis of command responsibility, see Indictment of Radovan Karadžić and Ratko Mladić #1; Indictment of Radovan Karadžić and Ratko Mladić #2; Indictment of Milan Martić; Indictment of Ivica Rajić; Indictment of Mile Mrkšić, Miroslav Radić, and Veselin Šljivancanin; Indictment of Duško Šikirica, Damir Došen, Dragan Fuštar, and Dragan Kulundžija; Indictment of Željko Meakić; Indictment of Miroslav Kvocka, Dragoljub Prcac, Mladen Radić, Momcilo Gruban; Indictment of Dragan Nikolić; Indictment of Blagoje Simić; Indictment of Dario Kordić, Tihomir Blaškić, Mario Cerkez, Ivan Šantić, Pero Skopljak, and Zlatko Aleksovski; and Indictment of Zejnil Delalić, Zdravko Mucić and Hazim Delić.

2. Letter from the U.S. Helsinki Watch Committee to Slobodan Milošević, New York, dated 21 January 1992.

3. Ibid., p. 2.

4. Ibid., pp. 2-11, 13-15.

5. In his response, Slobodan Milosević claimed that he was not responsible because the alleged crimes had been committed outside of Serbia. However, he also promised to investigate and punish anyone who guilty, confirming his authority (see Document xx).

6. Ibid., pp. 15-19.

7. In his response, Slobodan Milošević claimed, "on the territory of Serbia, and even less so on the territory of Croatia, the Serbian government did not set up paramilitary agents. On the contrary, from the very beginning of the armed clashes it opposed the setting up of party and national armies." The response also denied the existence of any concentration camps in Serbia or the killing of the wounded captured in the hospital when Vukovar fell. Reported in D. Glišić, "Unapred doneta presuda" [Verdict Formulated in Advance], *Narodna armija*, 9 April 1992, p. 8. Milošević continued to make sweeping denials about any involvement beyond Serbia's borders. As he told a French newspaper: "There is not a single soldier from the Yugoslav federal army in Bosnia-Herzegovina now. Serbia is not involved in that conflict in any way, it is a civil war." Interview with Slobodan Milošević by Eric Laurent, *Le Figaro* (Paris), 20 July 1992, p. 4, in *FBIS-EEU-92-141*, 22 July 1992, p. 26.

8. Milan Paroški gave a short account of a meeting in 1991 in "Ljudi i vreme" [Time and People], *Vreme*, 13 September 1993, p. 55.

9. Interview with Vojislav Šešelj, "Kad Vuka hapse to je demokratija, kad mene hapse to je diktatura" [When They Arrest Vuk, That Is Democracy; When They Arrest Me, That Is Dictatorship], *Srpska rec*, 15 January 1996, p. 17. Šešelj claimed to have met with Milošević on a monthly basis and also to have sent his deputy, Toma Nikolić, to such meetings; interview with Šešelj, "Milošević and I," p. 91.

10. Indictment of Mile Mrkšić, Miroslav Radić, and Veselin Šljivancanin.

11. Moreover, there are indications that there was sufficient sensitivity within official circles about the nature of the activities of paramilitary units and about international concern to seek to conceal the presence of paramilitary forces in the field as time went on. Branislav Gavrilović, a Chetnik commander who had served in Western Slavonia and was then active in the Sarajevo area, for example, compared his unit's situation thus: "Unlike in Slavonia, where it was not hidden that there were Chetniks, here [in Bosnia] this is being hidden because of official policy and international pressure." Quoted in Kolja Besarović, "Pobedom do mira" [Peace through Victory], *Pogledi*, 15 May 1992, p. 22. Thus, as Arkan stepped up his activity in northern Bosnia in late 1995, official circles in Belgrade remained adamant that they had no

connection with any paramilitary forces. For example, as the editor of the semi-official *Politika* insisted, "What U.S. officials have to know is that Belgrade is not behind any paramilitary formation." Editorial by Hadži Dragan Antić, "Shots at Conference," *Politika*, 23 October 1995, p.2., in *FBIS-EEU-95-208*, 27 October 1995, p. 44.

12. Reported in Djukić, *Between Glory and Anathema*, p. 201. Zoran Lilić, then Federal President, also claimed that, "Party-based and other paramilitary formations, groups, and individuals are forbidden in the Federal Republic of Yugoslavia according to the Constitution and the law.... We are opposed to paramilitary groups relying on a party or any other basis.... That [disarming and neutralizing paramilitary groups] presumes that the competent organs of the Ministry of Internal Affairs and of the Yugoslav Army are to maintain complete control over all border crossings, the strict honoring of procedures at the border, and the prevention of movement by individuals in uniform and with arms who are not part of the army or of the Internal Affairs forces. The republic and federal Ministry of Internal Affairs must strengthen that activity." Interview with Zoran Lilić by Colonel Stanoje Jovanović, Lieutenant-Colonel Milorad Pantelić and Nikola Ostojić, "Država ce uciniti sve za uspešno delovanje Vojske" [The State Will Do Everything for a Successful Functioning of the Army], *Vojska*, 18 November 1993, p. 8. The Yugoslav Army Chief of the General Staff, Colonel General Života Panić, too, had denied the existence of any paramilitary agents in Serbia: "Quite simply, the emphasis on the existence of paramilitary formations on the Serbian side represented a vulgar forgery and a form of systematic manipulation of the truth." Interview with Colonel General Života Panić, "Bili smo u ratu" [We Were at War], *Vojska*, 15 July 1993, p. 5.

13. Janjić, "The Machine Is Broken," p. 17. Even when acknowledging that crimes did occur, Milošević typically sought to transfer responsibility to others. Thus, when asked why he had not tried to stop Bosnian Serb leader Radovan Karadžic's "policy of rape and concentration camps," Milošević had replied: "When we first heard about it, Karadžić assured us that this was by no means true. We trusted him. Let me give you an example: A Muslim girl who became pregnant after a rape gave birth to a black child. There are no black Serbs." Interview with Slobodan Milošević, Secret Winner, *News* (Vienna), 20 July 1995, p. 43, in *FBIS-EEU-95-140*, 21 July 1995, p. 42.

14. Zorana Suvaković, "Ceo narod-jedan žeton" [The Entire Nation In a Single Basket], *Politika*, 6 August 1994, p. 2. Press sources list a number of daily intelligence reports from a variety of military and civilian intelligence agencies. See "Crveni bilten ostaje kod Miloševica 24 sata, a onda se stavlja na microfilm i unistava" [Milošević Keeps the Red Book for Twenty-Four Hours, after Which It Is Microfilmed and Destroyed], *Nedeljni telegraf*, 21 May 1997, p. 6.

15. Mira Marković, "Ko je moj brat" [Who Is My Brother?], *Duga*, 1-14 October 1994, p. 4. Elsewhere, she expressed indignation with Šešelj, "That extremism, that brutality, that cruelty, that is not *us*.... Šešelj does not express the interests of the Serbian nation since he does not belong to it. I am not thinking, of course, in terms of genes or ancestry. I will not go into that, that is whether he is of Croatian or Muslim origin.... But Šešelj does not belong to the Serbian nation spiritually.... He is a foreigner, but a primitive, aggressive, and greedy fellow.... [N]othing remains except the dark satisfaction of having caused harm, of having injured and caused evil to others" (emphasis in the original). Mira Marković, "Prošlost kao buducnost, ali, nece" [The Past Like the Present, But No], *Duga*, 28 May-10 June 1994, p. 9. In an interview first published in *Borba*, Mira Marković noted of Šešelj that, "He is a person who compromises Serbian national interests and who, in general, compromises policy.... I also am critical of the fact that they [members of the ruling SPS] not only reacted late [to Šešelj], but that they entered into any cooperation at all with him.... That vision [Šešelj's] is so dangerous and so possible that it should unite

all citizens and all political figures in a struggle to ensure that vision is never made real." Interview reprinted in Mira Marković, *Odgovor*, pp. 259-260.

16. Speech by Slobodan Milošević as he presented medals to Yugoslav Army officers, "Rat koji smo vodili bio je najneravnopravnoj rat za koji se do sada zna" [The War We Fought Was the Most Uneven War Known Up to Now], *Politika*, 27-30 November 1999, at www.politika.co.yu/politika/01_01.htm. Press sources list a number of daily intelligence reports from a variety of military and civilian intelligence agencies. See "Crveni bilten ostaje kod Miloševica 24 sata, a onda se stavlja na microfilm i unistava" [Milošević Keeps the Red Book for Twenty-Four Hours, after Which It Is Microfilmed and Destroyed], *Nedeljni telegraf*, 21 May 1997, p. 6.

17. *Vreme* published a photocopy of this report, 24 February 1992, p. 13.

18. Gajic-Glišić, *Srpska vojska*, p. 144. "From the Office," part 5, 15 May 1992, p. 53.

19. *Srpska vojska*, p. 58.

20. *Srpska vojska*, pp. 42-43.

21. *Srpska vojska*, p. 43.

22. *Srpska vojska*, p. 91.

23. Šimo Dubajić, "Srpska garda mora da postoji" [The Serbian Guard Must Exist], *Srpska rec*, 2 March 1992, p. 69.

24. Interview with Colonel Milorad Vucić, conducted by Lieutenant Colonel General Dušan Dozet (Ret.), Lieutenant Colonel Nikola Ostojić and Pero Damjanov, "Ti divni ljudi, mladi ratnici (2)" [Those Wonderful People, Young Soldiers, Part 2], *Narodna armija*, 25 December 1991, p. 13.

25. Vasić and Švarm, "Chetnik Watergate," p. 25.

26. Interview with Dragoslav Bokan by Slavica Jovović, "Hteli su da zaboravim da sam Srbin" [They Wanted Me to Forget That I Am a Serb], *Intervju*, 2 September 1994, p. 31. On Drašković's contacts, see Gajic-Glišić, *Srpska vojska*, p. 93.

27. Gajic-Glišić, *Srpska vojska*, p. 179. Vuk Drašković's representative, Bogoljub Pejcić, also visited. *Srpska vojska*, pp. 92, 96-97.

28. *Srpska vojska*, p. 58.

29. In relation to attempts to secure funding from private sources for the paramilitary agents, for example, one source involved in the dealings notes that "All security agencies were informed routinely." Gajic-Glišić, Srpska vojska, p. 22.

30. This was outlined in a report submitted in January 1992 by the Minister's administrative assistant. Gajic-Glišić, "Meler Is Not a Coup-Maker," p. 29. As Mrs. Gajic-Glišić noted elsewhere regarding dealings with businessman Jezdimir Vasiljević, "[Vojvodina's representative on the SFRY Presidency Dragutin] Zelenović and President Milošević were informed of Vasiljević's good will," and "everything proceeded in a legal manner." In the Minister's office, records were kept by a Colonel Kovacevié of all the contributions that Vasiljević made. *Srpska vojska*, pp. 21–22.

31. Interview with Mirko Jović by Aleksandar Popović, "Osveceni Jasenovac" [Jasenovac Avenged], *Pogledi*, 29 November 1991, p. 34.

32. Vuk Drašković, "Srpska garda" [The Serbian Guard], Srpska rec, 8 July 1991, p. 13. As Radmilo Bogdanović, then Minister of Internal Affairs, noted, "From the very beginning we endeavored by secret means to achieve a complete oversight into the activities of the SPO. Above all, into those activities which bordered on the law and which represented an attack on Serbia's constitutional order." Interview with Radmilo Bogdanović, "Radmilo Bogdanović's Role in the Last War," 12 January 1998.

33. See Vanja Bulić, "Gišne gliste, sokolovi i crveni džokeri" [Giska's Earthworms, Falcons, and Red Jokers], *Duga*, 4-18 January 1992, p. 34.

34. Interview with Slobodan Milošević on Radio-TV Belgrade Television Network, 28 August 1992, in *FBIS-EEU-92-169*, 31 August 1992, p.

35. "Will Killers Go Free?" *The Washington Post*, 25 February 1996, p. C1.

36 Reported in Laura Silber and Alan Little, *The Death of Yugoslavia* (London: Penguin 1995), p. 248. When Arkan was engaged in campaign of ethnic cleansing in Northern Bosnia in 1995, U.S. envoy Richard Holbrooke stated that he had brought the matter to Milošević's notice: "I raised this point the last three times I met with President Milošević, with specific reference to the activities of a man who calls himself Arkan... also operating in Eastern Slavonia." U.S. Department of State briefing by Assistant Secretary of State Richard Holbrooke, 12 October 1995.

37. Quoted in Jevrić, "The Guilty Ones with the Blue-Red-Gray Sleeves," p. 25.

38. Reported in Aleksandar Cotrić, "Dobrovoljci srpske garde krecu u Gospic" [The Volunteers of the Serbian Guard Are Deploying to Gospic], *Srpska rec*, 28 October 1991, p. 44.

39. Serbian journalists tracking the movement even registered the escorting Republic of Serbia police vehicle's license plate. Dejan Anastasijević, "Tigrovska posla" [Tiger Jobs], *Vreme*, 16 October 1995, p. 11.

40. See Vanja Bulić, "Krvna osveta u krugu dvojke" [Blood Feud in Runs of Two], *Duga*, 10-23 December 1994, p. 37.

41. Interview with Milan Janković by Vanja Bulić, "Slike sa iskljucenog televizora" [Images from a Turned-Off Television Set], *Duga*, 29 March-11 April 1992, p. 13. The Serbian authorities, however, did allow the Serbian Guard to deploy to Gospić instead. See Bulić, "Giška's Earthworms," p. 34.

42. "The government gave us arms and buses [earlier].... [In 1995] They did not stop us anywhere [on our way to fight in Western Slavonia]; rather they prevented us here, in Belgrade, from chartering buses.... We know that Slobodan Milošević is behind that. For example, we chartered buses through some travel agencies, but they canceled the following day." Interview with Šešelj, "I Would Suggest to All Serbs from Croatia That They Leave," p. 12. On at least one occasion, the Republic of Serbia police banned paramilitary elements from crossing through certain zones of Serbia while armed and in uniform as they deployed to and from Bosnia and obliged them to carry official documents. D. Pilcević, "'Beli orlovi' proterani sa Zlatibora" [The "White Eagles" Expelled from Zlatibor], *Borba* (Belgrade), 28 July 1992, p. 5. Again, in 1997, Milošević's Serbian security prevented several hundred of Šešelj's followers from crossing into Bosnia from Serbia as they sought to go and support hardline Serb elements in Bosnia, Ivan Djordjević, "Pukovnici i pokojnici" [Colonels and the Departed], *Nezavisna svetlost* (Kragujevac), 18 September 1997, online edition at www/svetlost.co.yu/arhiva/97/103/103-dop.html

43. Interview with Ulemek, "I Am a Serb and Proud of It," p. 20.

44. Interview with Captain Dragan "No One Admits His Mistakes," p. 48.

45. Djukić, *Between Glory and Anathema*, p. 268.

46. The first arrest occurred in 1994, after a brawl in parliament, when Šešelj spat on the Premier, Radoman Božović, a close Slobodan Milošević ally. The rivalry had been exacerbated by public insults that Šešelj had directed at Milošević. These included the charge that Milošević's wife was the boss in the family. Šešelj was arrested again in 1995 after organizing a political rally in Gnjilane, Kosovo as the latest venue for a string of protest meetings that were held throughout the country and that were meant to embarrass Slobodan Milošević. See Petar Ignja, "Uloga državnog neprijatelja" [The Role of an Enemy of the State], *NIN*, 9 June 1995, pp. 20-21; and Batić Bacević, "Radikalski bluz" [Radical Blues], *NIN*, 16 June 1995, pp. 16-18.

47. Quoted in Andjelković and Bacević, "Are the Tigers Leaving?", 21 April 1995, p. 11.

48. Gajic-Glišić, *Srpska vojska*, p. 61.

49. In Bogdanović, "Postponed Knock-out," p. 15.

50. Gajic-Glišić, *Srpska vojska*, pp. 16-17.

51. According to the interview with Djordje Božović Giška by Slavica Lazić, "Bicemo vojska moderne i humane Srbije," [We Will Be the Army of a Modern and Humane Serbia], *Srpska rec*, 5 August 1991, p. 17.

52. Jovan Dulović and Roy Gutman, interviewed on Rights & Wrongs, Yellow Wasps," part 1, Globalvision, 31 May 1995; and Roy Gutman, *A Witness to Genocide* (New York: Macmillan 1993), pp. 20-23.

53. Interview with Vojkan Djurković by Slavica Jovović, "Kako je Bijeljina zaista ocišcena od Muslimana" [How Bijeljina Was Really Cleansed of Muslims], *Intervju*, 17 April 1995, p. 16.

54. See, for example, Aleksandra Bilanović, "Tajna Arkanovog zamka" [The Secret of Arkan's Castle], *NIN*, 9 September 1994, p. 29. At least one other paramilitary agent commander, Siniša Vucinić, commander of the United Royalist Youth [*Udružena Rojalisticka omladina*] also lives on Dedinje Hill. Stefanović, *Tajni život srpske opozicije*, p. 220.

55. Interview with Ulemek, "I Am a Serb and Proud of It," p. 22.

56. Tasks included providing crowd control for a concert in Belgrade given by Arkan's wife, a popular pop-singer, on 23 November 1995. A photograph of the uniformed SDG personnel at the concert was published in *Vreme*, 4 December 1995, p. 27. A Tiger honor guard in uniform, likewise, fired their rifles at Arkan's funeral in full view of the government's law enforcement authorities. The Belgrade daily *Danas*, among others, carried an account and a photograph of the event, Nataša Rašić "Posao za policiju i tuzilaštvo" [A Matter for the Police and the Courts], *Danas*, 26 January 2000, at www.danas.co.yu/20000126/tema.htm#3

57. Dejan Anastasijević, Jelena Grujić and Filip Švarm, "Danak u krvi" [Blood Tribute], Vreme, 26 June 1995, p. 14.

58. Interview with Ulemek, "I Am a Serb and Proud of It," p. 21.

59. Interview with Marko Nicović by Borivoje Soleša, "Sto pedeset Specijalaca sredilo bi kriminal u Srbijii" [One Hundred Fifty Special Forces Would Take Care of Crime in Serbia], *Duga*, 23 December 1995-5 January 1996, p. 98.

60. Tracy Wilkinson, "Acceptance of Warlord Sends Mixed Signals," *The Los Angeles Times*, 1 December 1995, p. 1. In 1994 a state-run Belgrade newspaper still described Arkan's men as "fighters who achieved glory in many battles. Stević, "Martić Fulfilled His Promise," p. 19. Arkan also apparently was able to travel abroad. Interview with Pelević, 'I Do Not Recognize Capitulation,' p. 59.

61. Milivoje Glišić, "Vatreno vencanje" [Fiery Wedding], *NIN*, 24 February 1995, p. 23; and Roger Cohen, "Serbia Dazzles Itself; Terror Suspect Weds Singer," *The New York Times*, 20 February 1995, p. A3. A government-controlled newspaper, writing about Arkan's wedding, identified him as "a successful businessman." M. Aksić, "Ceca kao Skarlet" [Ceca As Scarlett], *Evropske Novosti*,18 February 1995, p. 11.

62. M. Mirkov, "Ma sedi, Rado, gdc hoceš, ovo sam i onako sve ja platio" [Come On, Rada, Sit Anywhere You Want, Since in Any Case I Paid For Everything], *Telegraf*, 5 July 1995, p. 2.

63. See the interview with Susan Manuel, the American-born United Nations spokesperson in Belgrade, by Snežana Rakocevic-Novaković, "Arkanova poznanica iz Ohaja" [Arkan's Acquaintance from Ohio], *Intervju*, 19 April 1996, p. 16.

64. Tracy Wilkinson, "Acceptance of Warlord Sends Mixed Signals," *The Los Angeles Times,* 1 December 1995, p. 1.

65 For example, in May 1996, Milan Nikolić Djeneral and Goran Vuković, minor paramilitary figures who seem not to have belonged to any political party, were sentenced for killing several Croatians and Slovaks in Vojvodina. See *OMRI Daily Digest* (Prague), 29 April 1996, citing a *Vecernje Novosti* report of 28 April 1996. Background on the Vuković group is found in Gordana Jovanović, "Ubistva sa prigušivacem" [Killing with a Silencer], *Intervju*, 21 July 1995, pp. 21-23; and Dragoljub Petrović, "Sudjenje Djeneralovoj grupi" [The Trial of the "Djeneral Group"], *Svet*, 8 January 1996, pp. 6 and 38.

66. Jovan Dulović, "Sudjenje za ratni zlocin: Šabacka posla" [Trial for War Crimes: The Šabac Business], *Vreme*, 2 January 1995, p. 19.

67. See M. M. "Witness in Hiding," *Politika Ekspres*, 16 January 1996, in *FBIS-EEU-96-011*, 17 January 1996, p. 83. *Human Rights Watch, Former Yugoslavia; War Crimes Trials in the Former Yugoslavia*, (New York: June 1995), pp. 43-44. The convictions and sentences eventually meted out, but without investigations of higher-level linkages, confirmed the responsibility that Serbia had for such crimes and its ability to punish.

68. Dimitrije Boarov and Ivan Radovanović, "Srpska majka ili maceha" [Serbian Mother or Step-mother], *Vreme*, 25 April 1994, pp. 15-17. Admissions by Dafina Milanović and published receipts indicate that many government officials - as well as paramilitary agents such as Arkan, Vojislav Šešelj, and Captain Dragan - had profitable, if suspect, transactions with her bank and that Mrs. Milanović also contributed large sums of money directly to government projects. See Ljiljana Habjanovic-Djurović, "Klošara su nova kategorija stediša" [Tramps Are a New Category of Depositors], *Duga*, 4-17 February 1994, p. 9; Ljiljana Habjanovic-Djurović, "S kim je Dafina bila fina?" [To Whom Was Dafina Nice?], *Duga*, 30 April-13 May 1994, pp. 19-24; Ljiljana Habjanovic-Djurić, "Tražimo istinu o našim parama" [We Are Seeking the Truth about Our Money], *Duga*, 30 April-14 May 1994, pp. 25-30; and Zoran Marković, "Istina sa kamatom umrtvljene banke" [The Truth with Interest of the Comatose Bank], *Duga*, 14-27 October 1995, pp. 24-26. Furthermore, the National Bank of Yugoslavia has released a report on the Dafiment Bank, which is based on the National Bank's internal documents. The report reveals that not only did Dafina Milanović coordinate her activities with the government, but also allegedly had the support of government officials. Narodna banka Jugoslavije; Istvestaj o poslovanju piramidalnih banaka: Dafiment Banka [Report on the Activity of Pyramid Bankers].

69. Radovan Pavlović, "Mnogo vojske pod jednom komandom" [Many Armies under One Command], *Politika*, 11 November 1993, p. 9.

70. United Nations Security Council, *Final Report of the United Nations Commission of Experts Established Pursuant to Security Council Resolution 780 (1992); Annex III. A; Special Forces*, document *S/1994/674/Add.* 2, 28 December 1994, para 97. Slobodan Milošević had established effective control over the state-run media already in the early days of his consolidation of power and has long used it skillfully for political ends. See Djukić, *Between Glory and Anathema*, pp. 70-72, 90.

71. The Fund was covered favorably on Belgrade TV, 13 September 1992 news broadcast, for example. See also Vesna Pantelić, "Ogranak Fonda Kapetan Dragan u Šapcu; Hrana za Benkovac" [The Branch of the "Captain Dragan Fund" in Šabac; Food for Benkovac], *Evropske Novosti*, 19 July 1994, p. 15.

72. Stevan Mirković, in "Ljudi i vreme" [People and Times], Vreme, 5 July 1993, p. 73. General Mirković amplified later that he had complained to Mira Marković about the government's cooperation with Šešelj, but that she had replied: "Don't [go after] Šešelj now, Stevo; we need him now in order to break Vuk [Draškovic], and once we break Vuk, then we'll see." See the interview with General Stevan Mirković by Novka Ilić, "Vojska nije izgubila ugled"

[The Army Has Not Lost Its Reputation], *Užicke Vesti* (Užice, Serbia), 11 March 2000, at www.vesti.co.yu/mirković.html

73. Interview with Slobodan Milošević, "Kakvi su bili marksisti, takvi ce biti biznismeni" [As They Were Marxists, So Shall They Be Businessmen], *Ilustrovana Politika*, 23 March 1992, p. 2.

74. Vakić, "Postponed Knock-out," p. 15. A copy of the certificate was published along with the article.

75. D. Petrović, "Badža u prvom izvlacenju dobio najviši moguci cin" [Badža on His First Try Achieved the Highest Possible Rank], *Naša Borba*, 1 April 1996.

76. Indictment of Mile Mrkšić, Miroslav Radić and Veselin Šljivancanin, paras 15 and 17, p. 8.

77. See section V, supra.

DOCUMENTS

"Sarajevo will always be, everything else will pass...", says a song, one of the many composed in this capital city of war-ravaged Bosnia during the first year of its siege....*The wounds are so horrible, so deep, that thinking about the future of Sarajevo—will it ever be the same?—I reach for a simple, affirmative answer and know that to find it will require a tremendous leap of optimism and imagination. Every day in this city of half a million souls, without food, milk, vegetables or fruit to buy, it is a struggle to survive. Every day without electricity, without running water, without heat in destroyed, windowless apartments under constant shelling and sniping, it is a struggle to stay alive. And yet with all the terrible memories...(I am writing in mid-February 1993) I still believe in the song-writer's prediction: "Sarajevo will always be, everything else will pass...."*

Kemal Kurspahić
"Letter From Sarajevo: Is There A Future?"
Why Bosnia? Writings on the Balkan War

The cumulative effect of the number of civilian casualties, the destruction of non-military structures, attacks upon and destruction of protected targets, such as hospitals, cultural property and other impermissible targets, evidence a consistent and repeated pattern of grave breaches of the Geneva Conventions and other violations of international humanitarian law. The length of time over which these violations took place and their recurrence clearly establish that, in at least a large number of incidents, those ordering and carrying out these actions committed such violations.

The Battle & Siege of Sarajevo
Final Report of the Commission of Experts

I

THE BATTLE AND SIEGE OF SARAJEVO

This document is drawn from the *Final Report of the Commission of Experts* established pursuant to Security Council resolution 780 (1992) to present its findings to the Secretary General of the United Nations on grave breaches of the Geneva Conventions and other violations of international humanitarian law in the territories of the former Yugoslavia. For the full text of the Report, see U.N. Doc. S/1994/674.

THE BATTLE AND SIEGE OF SARAJEVO

FINAL REPORT OF THE COMMISSION OF EXPERTS ESTABLISHED PURSUANT TO SECURITY COUNCIL RESOLUTION 780 (1992)

The battle and siege of Sarajevo began on 5 April 1992, the eve of European Community recognition of Bosnia and Herzegovina as an independent State. On that date, thousands of people took to the streets in spontaneous peace marches. The largest body of demonstrators headed towards the Parliament building and other buildings reportedly seized by Serb forces. Unidentified gunmen were then reported to have fired into the crowd. One protestor was confirmed dead. Since that date, the siege and relentless bombardment from the hills surrounding Sarajevo has taken a tremendous physical toll on the city and its inhabitants.

1. **Structure and location of forces in and around the city**
    Since the beginning of the siege, the first Corps Sarajevo has served as the defensive force of the Bosnian Government in and around Sarajevo. Most assessments characterize the first Corps Sarajevo as superior in infantry numbers as compared to the besieging forces, but clearly deficient in firepower. The first Corps Sarajevo headquarters is located at Sarajevo. The Croatian Defence Council and the first Corps forces fought together in defence of the city throughout much of the siege despite opposing one another in Mostar and in other parts of Bosnia and Herzegovina. However, on 10 November 1993, the Croatian Defence Council Brigade was disbanded and part of its personnel joined a new Croatian brigade of the first Corps.

    The Sarajevo Romanija Corps is the Bosnian-Serb force of the Bosnian-Serbian Army. The Corps has surrounded the city since the beginning of the siege.[1] It is the successor of the unit of JNA that occupied the same positions until May 1992. The Romanija Corps headquarters are located overlooking the city at Lukavica. The command structure has for the most part remained the same throughout the siege. Three succeeding Generals have commanded that Corp since 1992.

    Although the Serbian forces surrounding the city have superior firepower, it has been observed that it is unlikely that they could effectively take control of the city. This observation is based, in part, on the fact that the Bosnian forces have more combatants. In addition, controlling the city and its numerous buildings and streets could prove an overwhelming task for the Serb forces. The Serb forces have, therefore, concentrated their efforts on weakening the city through constant bombardment from the surrounding hillsides. A possible explanation for the shifting of firing sites from the mountainous areas surrounding Sarajevo may be that artillery personnel move from one emplacement to the other. Another explanation for this phenomenon could be the pattern of delivery of munitions. There were, however, no apparent munitions shortages.

2. Location and nature of the artillery

Many reports in the chronology described shelling as generally coming from artillery, mortars and tanks located in the hills surrounding the city. Some reports described various Serb-held areas and deployment of forces. Reports of the besieging artillery and other heavy-to-medium weapons employed in the siege vary from 600 to 1,100 pieces, but no verified account is available. These estimates do not include tanks. Some of the weapons were in fixed emplacements such as bunkers in the wooded hills and mountains surrounding Sarajevo and its suburbs. On account of the dense foliage, the emplacements were hard to detect from the air, particularly in the summer. Although the bunkers were difficult to see from the roads, the direction from which artillery and heavy mortar shells were fired revealed their emplacement. However, it was difficult to determine whether the bunkers also had snipers with rifles or personnel with small arms.

3. Frequency of shelling

UNPROFOR and city officials indicate that the daily shelling of the city ranges from 200 to 300 impacts on a quiet day to 800 to 1,000 shell impacts on an active day. The chronology confirms that the city has been relentlessly shelled. On the days where a total shelling count was documented, Sarajevo was hit by an average of 329 shell impacts per day. The range of shelling activity on these days varied from a low of two impacts on both 17 and 18 May 1993 to a high of 3,777 impacts on 22 July 1993.

4. Systematic shelling of specific targets

An examination of the range of destruction in Sarajevo reveals a pattern of specific targeting. The following targets were documented in the chronology as being among the most frequently targeted sites in the city: the Koševo Hospital; the Sarajevo radio and television stations; the Oslobodjenje Newspaper building, which is still in operation; the public transportation system; the Presidency and Parliament buildings; the main city brewery; the flour mill; the main bakery; the Olympic complex; the industrial area of Alipašin Most near the railway station and main television tower; the Jewish cemetery; the Lion Cemetery; the city airport; the tobacco factory; the Dobrinja apartment complex; the central district; Baščaršija (the old quarter of mosques); the Stari Grad Section; New Sarajevo; the main thoroughfare on Marshal Tito Street; and the shopping district at Vase Miškina.

The chronology confirms that certain areas of the city have also been systematically shelled throughout the course of the siege, particularly cultural and religious structures and public utilities. The city centre, the airport and southwestern suburbs had consistently been the most often targeted areas. The historic old town area had also been heavily shelled.

5. **Patterns of random shelling**

A review of the incidents in the chronology also indicates a random process of shelling throughout the civilian areas of the city. The shelling, which occurs at different times of the day without any apparent pattern or specific target, has a terror- inspiring effect on the civilian population. It is particularly telling that deaths, injuries and destruction have occurred in various parts of the city and in such well-known non-military settings as schools, open streets, public parks, football and athletic fields, cemeteries, hospitals, and even bread, water and relief lines in the city.

6. **Link between shelling activity and political events**

A review of the incidents in the chronology reveals a pattern of heavy shelling prior to and during the various peace conferences, and other negotiations, suggesting a political link to the attacks.[2] There are also indications that shell fire has increased or decreased in reaction to statements by local and international political leaders and Governments.[3]

On 5 February 1994, at least 68 persons were killed and 200 others were wounded in the shelling of a market in the city centre. In reaction to that attack, NATO issued an ultimatum on 9 February which gave Bosnian Serb and Bosnian forces 10 days, starting on 11 February, to withdraw their heavy weapons from a designated exclusion zone or face heavy airstrikes. Very little progress was made with regard to the ultimatum until 17 February, when the Russian Federation announced that it was sending a contingent of 400 troops to the city, and persuaded Bosnian Serb forces to comply with the NATO ultimatum. On 20 February, NATO announced that there had been virtual compliance with the ultimatum and that there was no need for airstrikes "at this stage". Since that date, artillery fire has substantially decreased in Sarajevo.

The cumulative effect of the number of civilian casualties, the destruction of non-military structures, attacks upon and destruction of protected targets, such as hospitals, cultural property and other impermissible targets, evidence a consistent and repeated pattern of grave breaches of the Geneva Conventions and other violations of international humanitarian law. The length of time over which these violations took place and their recurrence clearly establish that, in at least a large number of incidents, those ordering and carrying out these actions committed such violations. Command responsibility also clearly exists.

SARAJEVO INVESTIGATION

From 20 June to 9 July 1993, the Commission sent an investigative mission to Sarajevo, then under siege, to undertake a law-of-war study of a specific incident in the battle of Sarajevo and an analytical law-of-war survey of the battle of Sarajevo. The mission included a group of Canadian military lawyers and police investigators. The mission participants met with a wide range of local officials, including the Bosnian State War Crimes Commission, city officials, medical officials and military officers.

The objective of the incident study was to analyse in depth a specific incident which occurred during the siege of Sarajevo, to identify specific violations of the law of war (particularly violations in which civilian casualties have occurred) to analyse the circumstances of the incident and to assess the feasibility of identifying and prosecuting alleged offenders (particularly the military commanders). The report is based on information that could be obtained in and around Sarajevo.

No incident was chosen prior to arrival in Sarajevo. Criteria to be considered in selecting an incident included: number of casualties, number of projectiles fired, sources and, to a lesser extent, time elapsed since the incident. It was hoped that it would be possible to get information from Bosnian, UNPROFOR and Serbian sources. The rationale for preferring an incident in which more than one projectile was fired was that multiple projectiles would give a stronger indication of intent to commit an offence.

Bosnian State War Crimes Commission authorities were requested to provide evidence concerning six incidents of their choice, on the understanding that those incidents would be considered, but not necessarily chosen, for in-depth investigation. The evidence could not be compiled by the Commission within a short period of time and, as a result, an alternative approach was decided upon. Bosnian authorities suggested six incidents about which they believed a reasonable amount of information would be available. Two of these incidents, the shelling of a soccer game on 1 June 1993 and the shelling of a funeral in mid-June 1993, were selected for the possible in-depth investigation. Preliminary investigation indicated information on the shelling of the funeral would only be available from one source, as heavy rains the day after had washed away the evidence which UNPROFOR had intended to gather.

The incident finally selected for in-depth investigation was the mortar shelling of a soccer game in the Dobrinja suburb of Sarajevo on 1 June 1993. The investigators interviewed several witnesses on the Bosnian side, and also reviewed the crater analysis produced by UNPROFOR. Investigators were unable to interview witnesses on the Serbian side.

On the basis of the investigation it is reasonable to conclude that:

a. Two mortar shells landed at the soccer tournament at approximately 10.30 a.m. on 1 June 1993;

b. Thirteen persons were killed and 133 injured by the shells;

c. The shells were fired from the Serbian side, approximately 300 m south of Lukavica barracks;

d. The weather was clear and sunny with good visibility;

e.   The area where the shelling occurred was exclusively residential;

f.   The game site could not be seen from the Serbian side because it was surrounded by apartment buildings, but the cheering could be heard at the front line;

g.   No projectiles had landed in the area for several months.

On the basis of the above factors, it is reasonable to conclude that a prima facie case exists that persons on the Serbian side deliberately attacked civilians and, therefore, committed a war crime. With the information available, it is not possible to identify the probable offenders at present.

In connection with the analytical law-of-war survey and of the battle of Sarajevo, the study team visited several incident sites in Sarajevo. The shelling and sniping precluded an in-depth survey of property damage. The team, however, met with a wide range of officials of the Bosnian Government and UNPROFOR officers and obtained documentary material from them. The team was unable to meet with Serbian officials in Pale, even though it attempted to do so.

The report prepared by the investigation team is a non-exhaustive survey of law of armed conflict issues arising during the siege of Sarajevo. The team did not have an opportunity to visit the Bosnian Serb Army forces during the investigation and received no allegations of Bosnian Government misconduct during the siege except for allegations from UNPROFOR sources concerning positioning of and firing by Bosnian Government forces. The report focuses on combat-related offences, unlawful targeting and the use of unlawful means and methods of warfare. It concluded that it is unlikely that weapons that are illegal per se were used during the siege, or that there was unauthorized use by personnel of the Bosnian Serb Army of vehicles carrying United Nations markings—which could be viewed as perfidious conduct. If persons were killed or wounded as a result of perfidious action, a grave breach of Protocol I would be established. Somewhat similarly, it would have to be established that named individuals attacked or authorized attacks on United Nations forces for these persons to be charged with violating the laws or customs of war, as set out in article 3 of the statute of the International Tribunal, in that they would be committing a grave breach of article 85, paragraph 3 (a), of Protocol I by making the civilian population or individual civilians the object of attack. In the Sarajevo context, United Nations peace-keepers are non-combatants and entitled to be treated as civilians. The tendency of both sides to control food, water and electricity for publicity purposes, the intermingling of military forces and the civilian population and the fact that no one appears to have died during the siege from starvation, dehydration or freezing, combine to make difficult the establishment of a solid case that starvation is being used as a method of warfare. The conduct of this matter has been deplorable, but its criminality is debatable.

Most of the war crimes committed in Sarajevo have involved attacks on civilian persons and objects and destruction of cultural property. An accurate list of persons killed and seriously injured during the siege of Sarajevo needs to be established. It will also have to be determined if, at the time of death, they were combatants or non-combatants and when, where and how they were killed or injured. Once this information is available, it will be possible to distinguish military and civilian casualties. It may also be possible to determine where the projectiles causing casualties came from in such a way that one can establish that they were caused by a particular unit. It will also be possible to determine how many of the civilian casualties were caused by some form of sniper fire. Irrespective of the rule of proportionality, it is reasonable to presume that civilian casualties caused by sniper fire are the result of deliberate attacks on civilians and not the result of indiscriminate attacks, as may be the case in shelling.

The compilation of a chronological and quantitative survey of damage to civilian objects in Sarajevo was not attempted by the study team. Its preliminary observations follow. It is obvious that damage has been caused to certain religious, cultural and medical buildings. There is a strong possibility that there has been a deliberate attempt to target certain types of objects. For example, a detailed study of the shelling of the Koševo medical facility or of the National Library would probably indicate these objects had been deliberately targeted. There is also a strong possibility that a deliberate effort has been made to target religious facilities. The concealment of Bosnian Government forces among civilian property may have caused the attraction of fire from the Bosnian Serb Army which may have resulted in legitimate collateral damage. There is enough apparent damage to civilian objects in Sarajevo to conclude that either civilian objects have been deliberately targeted or they have been indiscriminately attacked.

There have been incidents in the past where substantial civilian casualties have been caused and substantial military advantage gained by a particular military action. In those cases, one might attempt to quantify both military advantage and civilian losses and apply the somewhat subjective rule of proportionality. As a general statement, however, the rule of proportionality is not relevant to the sniping activities of the Bosnian Serb Army forces, and it is of questionable relevance to many of the artillery bombardments. The Bosnian Serb Army forces are deliberately targeting the civilian population of Sarajevo, either as a measure of retaliation or to weaken their political resolve. Attacking the civilian population is a war crime.

It will probably be very difficult to link particular individuals to specific incidents in which civilians or civilian objects have been deliberately attacked or subjected to indiscriminate attacks. However, it may be less difficult to identify specific units. It may be possible to localize incidents in such a way that it is clear that a certain unit under a particular commander was the cause of a number of incidents. Whether or not it is possible to develop a firm case against individual soldiers or unit commanding officers, it should be quite practicable to develop a prima facie case against the officer or officers responsible for the Bosnian Serb Army forces that have been surrounding Sarajevo from the beginning of the siege.

It is the view of the Commission that:

a.   The study of a specific incident in the battle of Sarajevo established with a reasonable degree of certainty that the civilian population had been deliberately targeted, but it was not practicable to identify the perpetrators;

b.   The general study on the law of armed conflict and the battle of Sarajevo assessed a range of information sources and, relying on the doctrine of command responsibility, provided support for the suggestion that it would be possible to develop a prima facie case against the commander of the Bosnian-Serb forces surrounding Sarajevo for deliberately attacking the civilian population

NOTES

1. There are indications that early in the siege and until late May 1992, the Yugoslav Army (JNA) was involved in the fighting in Sarajevo. Bosnian officials frequently charged that JNA tanks joined Bosnian-Serb forces in barrages, and that the JNA provided the Bosnian-Serb forces with logistical support and protection. In April 1992, the Government of Bosnia and Herzegovina requested the withdrawal of all JNA forces from its soil. The Government of the Federal Republic of Yugoslavia announced that it would withdraw from Bosnia and Herzegovina troops that were not residents of the Republic. Since most of the JNA troops in Bosnia and Herzegovina were Bosnian Serbs, the withdrawal of other troops had limited impact on the Serbian forces, as an estimated 80,000 Yugoslav soldiers were transferred with their equipment to the "Serb Republic of Bosnia".

2. It has been observed that the besieging forces have often increased their artillery attacks on Bosnian Government-controlled areas of the city prior to and during international peace conferences or other negotiations. One explanation for this increased shelling activity is that the besieging forces are using the siege of Sarajevo presumably as a means to politically pressure the Government of Bosnia and Herzegovina to agree to terms which are important to the Bosnian-Serbs.

3. It has been observed that the besieging forces have on many occasions increased shell fire in reaction to statements made by local political leaders. It has also been observed that the besieging forces seem to calculate events and the risks that they can take in relation to threats by third-party Governments and organizations. In this regard, when threats by third-party Governments or organizations are not perceived as immediate, the besieging forces increase or continue their shelling of the city. For example, Sarajevo was hit with a siege-high 3,777 shells on 22 July 1993 after the United States ruled out direct intervention to prevent the shelling of the city. The opposite behaviour was observed in August 1993, when President Clinton warned that the United States would consider bombing Serbian forces if the shelling of Sarajevo continued. When this threat appeared immediate, the attacks on Sarajevo diminished and Serbian troops were withdrawn from the surrounding mountains to the south-west. Likewise in reaction to the ultimatum by the North Atlantic Treaty Organization (NATO) on 9 February 1994, which gave Bosnian Serb forces 10 days to withdraw their heavy weapons or face heavy airstrikes, the besieging forces substantially complied and curtailed their shelling of the city. This behaviour suggests that there is a centralized command and control of the besieging forces and that when there is pressure for the shelling to stop, it does.

What actually is the crime in Bosnia, the practice known in the West as "ethnic cleansing"? Undoubtedly it has been anything but a coincidence: the key component of a grand greater state project, and conducted through all political, psychological, and military means. The aim is not only to expel the ethnically "unclean" population from the desired territory but also to destroy all possibilities of their return—completely to dismantle the spiritual and material structure of the civilization....The authentic reality of Bosnia before the war and the supposedly inevitable reality after ethnic cleansing are completely different. From the pre-war perspective, any idea of division was nonsense, because the regions, towns, streets, flats, and beds were so mixed....

Opposing division meant, in the first point, simply recognizing that reality. With the Bosnia of today, however, it is possible to think of the idea of division. After ethnic cleansing, Bosnia is like a blank piece of paper. The existing structure has been all but erased, and theoretically could be replaced by any other. "Realities" are created, and the present one would never have happened peacefully.

Tihomir Loža
"A Civilization Destroyed" Balkan War Report, July 1993
Quoted in *Why Bosnia? Writings on the Balkan War*

The investigations conducted by the Boltzmann Institute of Human Rights showed that from April to June 1992 the following measures and practices were undertaken against the resident Muslim civilian population in the Zvornik region: mass and single murders, arbitrary mass and individual executions, tortures, physical and psychological mistreatment, rape, kidnapping, arbitrary arrest and detention, acts of terror in the form of threats, military attacks on the civilian population and civilian objects, looting, wanton destruction of property, forcible expropriations, forceful transfer of real property, as well as mass deportations and mass expulsions.

The totality of these measures and practices as well as the systematic and consequent manner in which the deportations and expulsions were carried out indicate that their purpose was to prevent the Muslim population from returning.

Ludwig Boltzmann Institute of Human Rights

II

"ETHNIC CLEANSING OPERATIONS" IN THE NORTHEAST CITY OF ZVORNIK

This document is an abridged version of the fuller report. See Tretter/Muller/Schwankel/ Angeli/Richter, *Ethnic Cleansing Operations* in the northeast Bosnian city of Zvornik from April through June 1992, Ludwig Boltzmann Institute of Human Rights (BIM), Vienna, 1994. Also see UN Doc. S/1994/674/add. 2 (vol. 1), December 1994.

"ETHNIC CLEANSING OPERATIONS"
IN THE NORTHEAST-BOSNIAN CITY OF ZVORNIK
FROM APRIL THROUGH JUNE 1992

Ludwig Boltzmann Institute of Human Rights

PREFACE

This report was established within the framework of the project "Human Rights Violations in Bosnia-Herzegovina and Chances for Repatriation and Integration of Bosnian
Refugees," conducted by the Vienna-based Ludwig Boltzmann Institute for Human Rights.
It was encouraged by the UN Commission of Experts... [and] was handed over to the UN
Experts Commission on April 6. In its final report (UN Doc. S/1994/674) presented May
27, 1994, the Commission cited this report as an exemplary study on "ethnic cleansing
operations," and published it as an annex (UN Doc. S/1994/674/add.2 (vol.I) December
1994). The present report is an extended and revised version of the report for the Commission of Experts ....

1. INTRODUCTION

This report sets out to reconstruct the genesis and pattern of the process leading to the
irrevocable expulsion ("ethnic cleansing") of the non-Serbian population of the town of
Zvornik. It was our objective to evaluate events in exact chronological order. At the same
time the investigation focused primarily on the identification of those responsible for the
military operations, for the war crimes, and for committing serious human rights violations. The study furthermore seeks to identify a likely structure or even a distinct system
of operations which characterized events from the time of the attack (on the city) to the
expulsion of the Muslim population.

The present analysis relies on information obtained by the Ludwig Boltzmann Institute for Human Rights (BIM) in the course of an inquiry of 887 expellees from the Zvornik
area....

2. SOCIO-DEMOGRAPHIC DATA

According to the 1991 census, the district of Zvornik had a population of 81,111. Of them, 48,208 were ethnic Bosnians (Muslims 59.4%), 30,839 were Serb nationals (38.0%). A total of 14,660 people lived in the city of Zvornik, 8,942 (61,0%) of them were Bosnian, 4,281 or 29.2% Serbian nationals, 74 (0.5%) were Croatians, and 1,363 (9.3%) were defined as "others" (mostly Roma).

The following additional municipalities are relevant to the study:

The municipality of Jardan north of Zvornik, which includes the towns of Jardan and Lipovac, had a population of 2,503, with a 53.1% share of ethnic Serbs, and a 46% share of Bosnians. These towns are located close to the industrial area of Karakaj, where JNA units had been stationed already prior to the attack. Later, the "headquarters" of both the "Serbian militia" and of the JNA units were moved there, and several camps were established. The municipality of Ćelopek (pop. 1,894) is situated north of Jardan; its population consisted of 93.1% ethnic Serbs and 6.3% Bosnians. Well before the attack, units of the former JNA were stationed in Ćelopek.

In 1981, a total of 27,695 (38.5%) people held jobs, 9,487 of them in the farming and forestry sectors, 18,208 in non-agrarian occupations. The total number of self-employed was 2,202. The "Birač" company in the Karakaj industrial zone was the biggest and most important local employer. It manufactured precursor material for the production of aluminum.

3. STRATEGIC SITUATION OF ZVORNIK

Being a border town situated directly at the Bosnian-Serb border river Drina, Zvornik's location was strategically important. This is where Bosnia-Herzegovina and Serbia are linked not only via a car bridge in the city itself and in the Karakaj industrial zone north of Zvornik, but also via a railroad bridge between Karakaj and the town of Ćelopek. This fact lent the city particular strategic importance. After all, Zvornik represented an important link on the Belgrade-Sarajevo line, as well as on the Belgrade-Tuzla line.

Having control of Zvornik meant that any future movements of troops or logistic material from Serbian territory toward Tuzla or Sarajevo could be accomplished without any obstacles. The early deployment of units of the former JNA clearly indicated the objective to secure control over the two corridors of Belgrade-Tuzla and Belgrade-Sarajevo by taking control of Zvornik....

4. MILITARY SITUATION
4.1. *Yugoslav National Army (JNA)*

There was no official garrison of the former JNA in the district of Zvornik. The Zvornik region was under the command of the 17th Corps Tuzla. Up to the fall of 1991, the 17th Corps consisted of three brigades and one partisan brigade. It belonged to the 1st Military District of Belgrade. After the reorganization of the JNA in spring 1992, it was formally incorporated into the 2nd Military District of Sarajevo. However, it apparently remained under the command of the 1st Military District of Belgrade.

At the turn of the year 1991/92, the first tank units (apparently from the abandoned Jastrebarsko garrison in Croatia) were stationed near Zvornik (i.e. on the Bosnian side of the Drina river). In February/March 1992 (at the time of the referendum for independence), additional troops of the former JNA—tank, artillery and anti-aircraft units—were stationed there. Initially, the tanks still carried the emblems of the JNA. It was only later that they sported the Serbian flag and badges showing the coat-of-arms. At the same time, the members of the units—officers and soldiers alike—had been wearing Serb badges on their uniforms from the very beginning. Since the beginning of that year, various tank positions could be identified on the Serbian side of the Drina river bank as well. Later, artillery positions and anti-aircraft weaponry were added.

4.1.1. *Units participating in the attack*

According to witness accounts, former JNA troops from the following garrisons participated in the course of the attack:

- Tuzla (Bosnia-Herzegovina): some of the tanks used in Zvornik formed part of the units which were transferred from Jastrebarsko/Croatia to Tuzla.
- Bijeljina (Bosnia-Herzegovina): the infantry divisions of the former JNA were reserve units of the Bijeljina mobilization base, the Bijeljina garrison belonged to the 17th Corps Tuzla.

The units from Šabac, Sremska Mitrovica and Valjevo, all of which belonged to the 1st Military District, were all organized as readily deployable troops up until the fall of 1991. Prior to the attack, these units were partly stationed on the Serbian and partly on the Bosnian side of the Drina river bank. They also participated in the attack on Zvornik, operating from Serbian territory....

Niš (Serbia): Up until the reorganization of the former JNA, the 21st Corps stationed in Niš was under the authority of the 3rd Military District of Skopje. Later a separate 3rd Military District was established. There is some indication that a specialized unit originating in Niš participated in the attack on Zvornik and, later, on Kulagrad. It was reportedly composed of the 63rd airborne brigade Niš of the "Corps for Special Tasks Belgrade". It was especially trained to handle matters of internal security.

Infantry divisions which had been withdrawn from the Croatian (Vukovar) war theater and which had participated in the attack on Zvornik could not be identified in more detail.

4.1.2. *Commander*

General Janković was garrison commander in Tuzla and is said to have repeatedly visited the troops from Tuzla stationed in and around Zvornik prior to the attack. In the course of the restructuring of the JNA in May 1992—when "pro-Yugoslav" officers were replaced by "pro-Serb" officers—he was forced to retire.

General Milutin Kukanjac was commander of the 2nd Military District of Sarajevo. After the reorganization of the JNA, he was responsible for the Zvornik area during the time of the attack. In a TV interview following the attack on Zvornik, Kukanjac reportedly said: "If the people of Zvornik return their weapons, the army will protect them. This should serve as an example for other towns."

Lieutenant Colonel Pejić was the commander of the troops participating in the attack on Zvornik and commander-in-chief until April 26. During the Croatian War Pejić was head of the operations division at the 32nd Corps Varaždin. In the course of the reorganization of the JNA he was moved to Sarajevo. It is, therefore, believed that his responsibilities in Zvornik also included the preparation and execution of the attack—a task which was indeed attributed to him by many of the respondents.

Colonel Marko Pavlović belonged to a unit in Croatia until December 1991; he was commander of the 622nd motorized brigade Petrinja, which belonged to the 10th Corps Zagreb. Later, he was detached to the 2nd Military District of Sarajevo. Following Pejić, Pavlović is said to have taken over the command of the troops after the fall of Kulagrad on April 26. According to witness accounts, he is believed to have been responsible for the ethnic cleansing operations. After the fall of Zvornik he apparently assumed administrative tasks. Formally, however,—at least by mid-June or by the end of June—he no longer acted as a member of the JNA, but as "commander of the Zvornik territorial defense," which is the title attributed to him in a newspaper interview with the Serbian publication "Borba".

Lieutenant Radovan Tičić reportedly commanded the tank-unit from Tuzla.

4.1.3. Armaments

Using photographic evidence, the following armaments could be identified in the course of the research by the Institute:

Infantry
Automatic rifles/carabines and M 52, M 59, M65, M66, M70A, M70B, M72 and "Kalashnikov" machine guns, bajonettes, hand grenades, "Soja" anti-tank grenade launchers, portable grenade launchers.

Tanks
Battle tanks T 344, T 54, T 55, T 72 and T 84; "Marda(er)" armored personnel carriers with machine canons; "Samohodka" wheeled tanks.

Artillery
Howitzers as well as 122mm and 130mm canons; 60mm, 80 mm, and 120 mm mortars; anti-aircraft artillery.

Air force
MIG 21 and MIG 29 fighter bombers; "Jastreb" training and ground fighter planes with

machine guns and missiles; "Galeb" training and ground fighter planes; "Eagle" reconnaissance planes; MI 8, MI 9 and "Gazella" helicopters.

4.2. Paramilitary Units
4.2.1. General Remarks

During the entire period studied the supreme military command was held by the JNA officers Pejić and Pavlović. Except for the "Arkanovci," the para-military groups accepted the command of the JNA when conducting military operations. From the time after the attack until the final "ethnic expulsion," a considerable number of para-military groups stayed in the city. They included "organized" partisan groups as well as so-called "week-end Chetniks," especially from Serbia. Almost all groups exerted some form of terror over the city population. They are being held responsible for murders, rapes, lootings and tortures in the camps. They seemed to be under nobody's command or control. The most important "organized" para-military units were the "Arkanovci," the so-called "territorial defense" (TO), the "Šešeljevci," and the "Beli Orlovi."

It proved impossible to distinguish the last three units mentioned above explicitly from each other, nor was it possible to identify them as separate from the infantry units of the former JNA. There is considerable evidence that infantry units not only included regular members of the former JNA and reserve soldiers called to arms, but of "volunteers" as well....

4.2.2. "Territorial Defense" (TO)

Shortly after the dissolution of the regular territorial defense in Bosnia-Herzegovina in fall 1991, SDS leaders in Zvornik began recruiting, equipping and obviously also training a new "Serbian territorial defense." Many of them came from predominantly Serb-populated towns such as Ćelopek or Šemlija near Zvornik, or from various districts of Zvornik (Lisišnjak).... Like all other para-military units, the territorial defense, too, cooperated with the JNA and operated under its command. Being from the area themselves, its members are said to have been under special orders to act as informants for the military; later, they reportedly identified many wealthy and prominent Muslims who were subsequently robbed and arrested (many of them handed over to the "Arkanovci" as prisoners). During the attack, they came into the city in a second wave directly in the wake of the "Arkanovci".

4.2.3. Arkanovci, ("Srpska dobrovoljačka garda"/ "Serb Volunteer Guard")

The Arkanovci as well as "Arkan" himself are unanimously being described as the decisive personalities of the attack. During the attack proper, Arkan's responsibilities as leader not only went beyond those of the commanders of the former JNA, they also surpassed those of the leading personalities of the local SDS. During the attack, Arkan himself held the supreme command over the Arkanovci....

...Reportedly, it was the Arkanovci in particular who, accompanied by local Serbs, were systematically involved in house searches, killings, rapes, and lootings. The "right to be the first to loot," which they apparently enjoyed, was obviously part of their "remuneration."

Arkan himself is said to have arrived in Zvornik on April 7.... Members of the Arkanovci wearing civil clothes are said to have been present in the city since the end of March. Their participation in the fighting began on April 8 with mortar fire and attacks by snipers located in Mali Zvornik. They conquered the city and assumed control of it on April 9, having taken control of the most important facilities (hospital, radio station) as well as of strategic points.

The Arkanovci were supported all along by JNA artillery and logistics. Apparently, strategic planning and command structures had been uniform. Later other groups (Šešeljevci, Beli Orlovi, the "territorial defense," and "volunteers" from neighboring towns in Serbia assumed the task of securing the city (militarily). After the occupation of the city (April 10/11), the core troops apparently left Zvornik.

The Arkanovci were highly mobile and had many vehicles from private owners. Apart from their "military tasks," the Arkanovci were responsible for many of the atrocities and lootings. Arkan himself purportedly ordered Muslims and hospital patients to the execution sites. His people murdered several men in the house of Salim Donjić and committed massacres in the city districts Zamlaš and Hrid....Their arms included: automatic rifles M 70A, M 70B and U.S. rifles, "Škorpion" rifles, hand grenades, anti-tank grenades and launching grenades; ropes for choking people, long "Rambo-style" knives, clubs; they wore bullet-proof jackets for their own security.

4.2.4. Šešeljevci

The Šešeljevci were described as "bearded" men. They wore Serbian military berets with the Serbian flag or a skull on the front side, or black fur hats ("Šapka") with Serbian cockade. The cross-shaped ammunition belts worn across the breast and the handgrenades on the belt were another identification mark....

Prior to the attack, members of the Šešeljevci were already present as civilians. They participated in the attack as early as April 9 and stayed involved throughout the entire period of the occupation until the conquest of Kulagrad. They assumed control of various parts of the city and were responsible for lootings wherever they went. They always cooperated with the JNA, both with regard to strategy and command structure. Their weapons included: automatic rifles M 59, M 66, M 70A, M 70B, long, curved knives, hand grenades.

4.2.5. Beli Orlovi (White Eagles)

They were reportedly sloppily dressed, wearing all sorts of uniforms from various JNA stock, or civilian clothes. They wore a badge on the cap and the upper arm depicting a white, two-headed eagle. They came for the most part from near-by towns in Serbia

(Lojnica, Valjevo, etc.). Their leaders were, alternately, Mirko Jović, Dragoslav Bokan, and Vojislav Šešelj....

Like the Šešeljevci, they, too, participated only in the second wave of the attack. Their "task" was to assist in the fighting and to secure strategic positions. They participated in the shelling, siege, and occupation of the city, as well as in the attack on Kulagrad.

Their prime responsibility appears to have been the military securement of the deportations; they patrolled intersections and streets (frequently in a drunk and provocative manner), routinely arrested "suspects," and customarily looted. White eagles were painted on homes and warehouses. It was forbidden for the locals to remove them. They operated under the command of the JNA. Their weapons included light armaments (no detailed information was available).

4.2.6. *Draganovci*

Another important unit was that of the Draganovci of "Kapetan Dragan" (Vasijković Dragan). While they did not participate in the attack, they did take part in the occupation of Zvornik. Its members wore red berets and camouflage uniforms. Kapetan Dragan himself reportedly wore civilian clothes only....

5. CHRONOLOGY
....5.1. The time prior to the attack

As pointed out in the study by the "BIM", the climate of co-existence of the various ethnic groups progressively deteriorated in the course of the months preceding the attack. While the relationship between the various ethnic groups prior to the war in Croatia could be characterized as good—after all, only 4 percent of the Muslim persons interviewed said they had no friends among the Serbs—this situation apparently deteriorated already with the escalation of the war in Croatia in the summer of 1991. Tensions emerged at the workplace, in schools, and in the neighborhood. The individual ethnic groups increasingly began to isolate themselves. This was paralleled by a growing militarization of the society. According to the persons interviewed, the Serbian side was well informed about all imminent actions.

There is considerable evidence that the attack and the expulsion of the Muslim population was pre-planned: Around the turn of the year 1991/1992, troops of the JNA were for the first time assembled in the region of Zvornik. About 2–3 months prior to the attack, military training exercises lasting up to 2 weeks were conducted in Osmaci near Kalesija (about 30 kilometers north of Zvornik) and in other places. They were organized by the JNA and only Serbs were invited, under the pretext that the territorial defense was being trained. Already during the weeks prior to the attack, members of all ethnic groups procured arms. According to the interviewees, the Serb population of Zvornik received their weapons largely through the SDS or the JNA, while the Muslim population arranged for its weapons supply through "private" channels—a fact which is also supported by the BIM study.

According to statements by 31 interviewees, many Serb citizens of Zvornik left the town during the month of March prior to the attack for a weekend, but returned to work the following Monday. These observations have once again been confirmed by the results of the BIM study. It is hard to ascertain whether this was an SDS-organized trial evacuation in the event of an attack on Zvornik—as claimed by one of the respondents. Nevertheless, there is evidence that this was an organized action since it was, after all, the overwhelming part of Serb families that had left the city for the weekend. At the time of the attack, women and children of Serb nationality had left the city already. Some of the interviewees recounted that in the days prior to the attack they had been advised by Serb friends or colleagues to leave the town soon. This serves as evidence in support of the statements by many of the respondents, according to which the Serb population of Zvornik had at least been informed shortly before the attack about the attack.

During the weekend prior to the attack (April 4/5), Serbs erected a barricade at the Meterize part of the city using trucks of the "Boksit" company (a bauxite mine in Milici, 20 km south of Zvornik). This separated the town from the industrial area of Karakaj. On the following Monday, April 6, Muslims were barred from going to work. School children from the Technical School Center in Karakaj, too, were told to turn back at the barricades. The developments during the last few days and fear of a military confrontation prompted many Muslim families to leave the city via the "Old Bridge" in the city center.

In reaction to the Serb barricade, the Muslims, too, put up barricades with trucks at the same site which was guarded by the "Muslim" police and by armed volunteers. Initially, only some verbal exchanges took place at the barricades. On April 6/7, the barricades became the site of demonstrations for a peaceful coexistence, and members of all ethnic groups participated.

Also on April 6th, the local police units were separated. The headquarters of the police in Zvornik were vacated by Serb police; weapons, equipment and cars were moved to the Karakaj industrial zone north of Zvornik. During the weeks prior to the attack, patrols in the city and on the bridges had still been conducted by ethnically mixed police forces in order to demonstrate the unity of all ethnic groups.

On April 7, a large part of the Muslim population fled from Lipovac and Karakaj to Zvornik. On the evening of April 7, one day prior to the attack, Belgrade TV justified the heavy presence of JNA units by claiming that an attack by "Muslim extremists" hiding in Kulagrad was imminent.

On April 8, negotiations took place in Mali Zvornik which were attended by representatives of the SDS from Zvornik, delegates of the Party of the Democratic Action (SDA) from Zvornik, and by Arkan. The talks were reportedly aimed at a "peaceful surrender of the city", i.e. at a "capitulation by the Muslim population." Moreover, the two representatives from Zvornik apparently reached an "agreement" which aimed at dividing the city. The center of the city of Zvornik was to remain "Muslim," while the northern parts, including the Karakaj industrial zone, were to be "awarded" to the Serbs. According to one respondent who had briefly talked to the chief negotiator of the SDA shortly after the meeting, the SDS and the SDA had agreed to this scenario; However, the SDA representative reportedly still feared an attack, since Arkan was said to have been dissatisfied with this meeting and reportedly announced that he would "take charge of things from now on". According to similar reports, Arkan even attacked the two other individuals. In the morning of April 9, another round of negotiations took place—albeit without results.

5.2. *The attack on Zvornik*

The military attack on Zvornik lasted from April 8 through April 10/11, 1992. Thereafter, only sporadic military operations were carried out, involving units of the former JNA which cooperated with para-military troops. These operations focused primarily on the medieval fortress of Kulagrad, which is situated to the north of Zvornik, because some resistance fighters (about 100 to 300 persons) were holding out there. Still, the fortress was conquered in a concerted attack by former JNA troops and para-military units relying on air support on April 26, 1992.

Immediately after the fall of Kulagrad, the town of Divič, situated south of Zvornik, was attacked. Divič, a predominantly Muslim settlement, is located near the hydro-electric power plant serving the city. Since Divič could also be controlled from Kulagrad, the aggressors believed a decisive attack on Divič was not possible until after the conquest of Kulagrad. Moreover, Divič was considered a "Muslim stronghold" from which strong resistance was to be expected. It was also assumed that the plant's dam had been mined. The attack was carried out both from the Serbian side and from Bosnian territory, using tanks, artillery, and infantry units with portable mortars. JNA units and para-military units worked hand in hand. The "Arkanovci" operated from front-line positions, conquering the city. Their core troops left the city after the successful attack in order to prepare a raid on the next town (Bratunac).

Following sporadic rifle fire, the actual attack on the city began in the late morning hours of April 8. The Bukovik and Meterize city districts as well as the Muslim-held defense positions on the Debelo Brdo hill were attacked by mortar fire from artillery positions in Karakaj, from the Bosnian river bank before Meterize, and from Mali Zvornik (Serbia). This attack was mainly carried out by JNA units using heavy artillery and tanks. Reports further mention Arkanovci snipers firing from Mali Zvornik on the opposite Bosnian river bank, as well as snipers shooting from high-rise buildings within Zvornik on the citizens. The Muslim position on Debelo Brdo was conquered on the same day and occupied by the aggressors.

During the following night the city was heavily bombed. The following morning, negotiations were conducted once again. They resulted in an ultimatum according to which the weapons were to be handed over and the city was to be surrendered by 8 p.m. of that day. In reaction, the Bosnians sent desperate messages to the crisis committee of the Bosnian Government in Tuzla, to Radio Tuzla, Radio Zenica, and to Sarajevo TV and Radio. The call for help was aired by all media, but had no effect.

At 8 a.m. mortar fire resumed. Thereafter, the conquest of the city by infantry units began. The Arkanovci assumed the leading role in the conquest of the city, coming from the north via the Bukovik and Meterize city districts to take control of the city center, facing hardly any resistance. By noon, the Arkanovci had occupied the hospital, and, by the afternoon, the radio station. In addition, infantry units of the JNA cooperated with "Serb volunteers" (Šešeljevci, Beli Orlovi, "Territorial Defense") in the conquest of the city. They approached the city in a second wave primarily from the west, from Šemlije and Lisišnjak. Massacres, killings, deportations and rapes reportedly happened in the camps already during the first weeks, but continued throughout the weeks that followed. Units of the Arkanovci, Šešeljevci, Beli Orlovi, and the "territorial defense" participated in those atrocities. On April 10/11, Zvornik was fully conquered. The Kulagrad fortress north of Zvornik and the town of Divič bordering on Zvornik to the south had not yet been occupied.

5.3. The attack on Kulagrad and Divič

Kulagrad is a settlement in the vicinity of a medieval fortress on the Kula hill, located on the southern outskirts of Zvornik. In view of the geographical location of Zvornik and the strategic position of the attacking units, there were only two escape routes open to the population after the beginning of the artillery fire: either towards the east across the "Old Bridge" to Serbia in the direction of Mali Zvornik or Loznica or in a south-western direction via Kulagrad and Liplje to Tuzla. Kulagrad and Liplje were each only used as short stopovers and, during the period after the attack, had to accommodate highly fluctuating numbers of refugees.

On April 9, an artillery assault on Kulagrad started since the attacking units were expecting major Muslim resistence forces. Already before the attack, the Serbian media reported that "several thousand Muslim extremists" were hiding in Kulagrad. In fact, there were probably no more than 30 to 100 armed Muslims under the command of Kapetan Almir, a former JNA officer, who had spontaneously started to organize a resistance movement with light equipment (small arms) (30).

From April 11 onward, there were almost daily attempts by small combat groups composed of various paramilitary units to capture the fortress. These attempts failed, however, despite the fact that Kulagrad was constantly under fire from mortars, anti-aircraft guns and tanks. The reason for this failure might be that there was both an apparent lack of coordination of the attacks and deficiencies in the training of the involved infantry units.

On April 25, Colonel Pavlović presented an ultimatum to the inhabitants of Divič to turn in their arms. The defenders of Kulagrad were given a number of ultimatums since the beginning of the attack on April 11, the last one on April 26, the day of the decisive attack on Kulagrad.

In the morning of April 26, the villages around Kulagrad were the first to fall in the wake of a concerted attack. At the same time, Kulagrad and Divič were attacked by heavy artillery fire from the Serbian bank of the Drina river. This enabled the attackers, who this time had coordinated their actions, to capture Kulagrad. For one, because the units were able to approach the fortress from all directions, including the power station in the south.

For another, because the attack was conducted more effectively. Some respondents stated that members of the 63rd Niš parachute brigade were involved in the decisive attack and the seizure of Kulagrad.

The Muslims remaining in Kulagrad left the town at approx. 10:30 a.m. together with the rest of the inhabitants and the refugees accommodated in Kulagrad (approx. 100 persons) via Liplje in the direction of Tuzla. In Liplje, they were only able to stay very briefly as later that afternoon this village was also taken by the Serbs without any resistance. On the same afternoon, paramilitary units marched into Divič, and pillages were reported. Some time later, Divič was also occupied by the JNA.

6. CIVIL DEVELOPMENT IN ZVORNIK AFTER THE ATTACK
6.1. *From the aftermath of the attack on Zvornik until the fall of Kulagrad*

Control over the "civil administration" was first in the hands of the so-called "crisis committee" which above all included members of the local SDS and the militia. Some of these persons were also integrated into the so-called "territorial defense". On the basis of one document it is clear that the "crisis committee" did not come into existence until April 8 but had by that time already taken a "decision to introduce a general obligation to work" in the so-called "Serbian Community of Zvornik" . However, already in the early days of the aggression (around April 10) a "Provisional Government" of the "Serbian Community of Zvornik" was founded. Its most important members were Branko Grujić (baker and president of the "Serbian Community"), Radosav Perić (elementary school teacher) and Stevo Radić (jurist, municipal secretary). Other important members of the SDS and the "Serbian Community" were: Sveto Popović (postal employee), Zoran Jovanovič, Boško Ceranić, Dragan Spasojević and Zoran Pazin.

Already shortly after the occupation (approx. April 10/11) a proclamation was broadcast by Radio Zvornik, appealing to the refugees to return to their workplaces. This appeal was however hardly complied with, as there were still numerous paramilitary troops in town who were looting and terrorizing the locals. Therefore, the appeal was broadcast once more a few days later (approx. April 15/16). However, the overall response to these appeals was rather poor. And the experiences of those who did follow the appeal to return to the workplace showed that the true purpose of this appeal—and of others that followed—was to monitor the male Muslim population.

Also immediately after the occupation of the town, a nocturnal curfew was imposed which remained in force until the "ethnic cleansing" was completed. During the day, men were allowed to move around only with a pass issued by the Zvornik Serbian police department. Many of the men who went to Karakaj (or later to the police department in Zvornik) in order to apply for a "pass" were suddenly deported into one of the camps in the industrial district of Karakaj. There they were subjected to severe torture and murder, in particular by members of the para-military troops whose quarters were partly in the same buildings as those in which the prisoners were detained. The detainees were entirely at the mercy of their torturers. Many of the men therefore did not dare to pick up their passes themselves and remained in hiding in their houses. But even persons with a pass were not safe from random aggressions by the numerous para-military units in town. It was reported by some witnesses that they had their passes taken away or torn into pieces by members of a para-military group immediately upon leaving the police station. Some of them were even physically attacked and deported into camps.

Everyday life was dominated by the fact that marauding para-military troops, who were not controlled by any authority, terrorized the Muslim population of Zvornik. While male Muslims were required to carry a day-time pass with them, women were permitted to leave the house for shopping during the day. In order to do so, however, they had to cross the old bridge to Mali Zvornik (Serbia) as the stores in Zvornik had already been looted. At the check-points on the bridge, the women were frequently molested. There were also several reports of rape.

From the onset of the occupation, Muslims were prohibited from working unless they held jobs which were indispensible for the aggressors (e.g. hospital employees, who were not released until May 19).

There are only few established data on the behavior of the local Serb population as the respondents were almost exclusively Muslims, and also because there were only few Serbs left in Zvornik at the time of the attack.... Apart from that, local Serbs also took part, as members of para-military groups and units of police and SDS, in numerous acts of violence committed in the town.

Apparently it was disadvantageous for local Serbs to talk to the Muslim inhabitants. However there were also reports of clandestine assistance including food supplies. Serbs who stood up against the atrocities inflicted on the Muslim population also fell victim to the Serbian guerilla. One case which was confirmed by several respondents was that of a young Serbian woman whose throat was cut through by guerilla fighters when she tried to protect her Muslim friends.

6.2. After the fall of Kulagrad

There is agreement that after the fall of Kulagrad on April 26, 1992, the situation in Zvornik was less strained for a while. Many members of the para-military units as well as parts of the troops of the former JNA were reported to have left town by the end of April. Many of the local Serbs who had also fled from Zvornik came back into town. The SDS started to organize a local administration in the new "Serbian Community of Zvornik" with Branko Grujić as its "president".

At the end of April, the "Serbian Community of Zvornik" issued another appeal for the Muslim refugees to return to Zvornik. Relying on a large number of consistent reports, one could summarize the message of the appeal as follows: The situation in town was now back to normal and everybody would be able to come back unharmed. Any personal property would have to be registered with the Zvornik police by May 15 as all unregistered property would otherwise fall to the "Serbian Community of Zvornik". This appeal to return was broadcast daily for a period of approximately two weeks by Radio Zvornik, Radio Loznica and, most likely, also by the Belgrade TV station in a variety of versions. This appeal was more successful with the refugees than an earlier appeal to return to the workplace. In addition to the fear of losing their property, the situation in town, which, on the surface, had indeed "returned to normal", seemed to have been the decisive reason for an astonishingly large number of persons to come back. However, their return had grave consequences for the Muslim inhabitants. For only now was it possible for the aggressors to prepare and actually carry out the "ethnic cleansing" procedure. Therefore, it was not until the fall of Kulagrad that one could actually speak of an organized expulsion of the Muslim population.

Consequently, after a relatively short time, around May 10, the situation for the Muslim inhabitants began to deteriorate again. New para-military units came into town. Attempts to instil terror in the civilian population began to increase and men were more frequently deported in the camps at Karakaj. In particular, former members of the SDA fell victim to such deportations into the camps in Karakaj or Batković near Bijeljina. The militia and other local Serbs who were frequently referred to as members of the SDS appear to have been regularly involved in these aggressions. It was hardly possible anymore to leave the town at that point of time due to the fact that check points had been erected on all exit roads. There seems to have been a further exacerbation of the situation around end-May/early June. This is seen by some respondents as being linked to the arrival of the Draganovci in town.

7. EXPULSION AND DEPORTATION

After the "unorganized" expulsion of the Muslim inhabitants through a reign of terror, the next stage was their expulsion by means of administrative measures. The first step had already been the above-mentioned appeal to return. The registration of property that was mandatory for all inhabitants including the Serbs served above all the purpose of registering the male Muslim population. For this reason, only men were eligible for registration, which had to be done before the "Serbian municipality" or the "Serbian militia", even if a property was registered under the wife's name. These registrations also led to arrests and deportations into camps, apparently on the basis of a pre-established list.

Furthermore, an "agency for the exchange of houses" was set up, to which the Muslim inhabitants were to transfer their houses. In return, the Muslims were promised houses belonging to Bosnian Serbs (e.g. in the Tuzla region) who supposedly had also assigned their homes to the agency. In order to make this "offer to exchange houses" appear more attractive, Serbian radio stations broadcast reports about the successful exchange of houses by prominent Muslim inhabitants, which in many cases however turned out to be false or to only have been brought about under coercion. Muslims were only allowed to leave the town on the condition that they renounced their property and transferred it to the "Serbian Community of Zvornik". This forced transfer of property was executed by the "Serbian Community of Zvornik" in cooperation with the police and the Draganovci.

....The forced transfer of property to the "Serbian Community of Zvornik" made the former house-owners eligible for obtaining an official stamp on their ID-card indicating a change of domicile. This stamp was an indispensable prerequisite for being allowed to leave town later on. Some of the deportees, especially men, also had to prove that they had "donated blood". Documents required in order to be allowed to leave town included:

- an ID card which guaranteed the holder the freedom of movement on the territory of the Serbian Community of Zvornik,
- a slip certifying the "change of address",
- a personal ID card in which the date of the notice of change of address was entered by the authority.

From the end of May to the beginning of June, there were days on which the Muslim populations of entire municipal districts or neighboring villages were deported. These organized deportations were reportedly carried out with vehicles provided by the "Drina-trans" company, which brought the deportees to Mali Zvornik, and from there via Loznica to Subotica or onto the Bosnian territory of Tuzla. The deportees were only permitted to take with them a very limited number of personal belongings. Quite frequently, though, even these were taken away from them at the check-points...

10. SUMMARY OF ANALYSES

On the basis of the available data it can be concluded that the attack on the northeastern Bosnian city of Zvornik had been prepared according to military rules quite some time ahead and was executed with the massive participation of JNA units and paramilitary combat and terror units. The dimensions and systematic conduct of the operation suggest that these units were under the command of a superior military and political authority. Many circumstances also substantiate the assumption that the expulsion of the Muslim inhabitants was not only desired, prepared and carried out by the local Serb authorities, but that this "ethnic cleansing" procedure was at least conducted with the understanding and permission of these superior instances.

Judging from the reports submitted by our respondents, genocide has been committed against the Muslim population in the city of Zvornik in that members of this ethnic group were killed and subjected to physical and mental harm. Such acts as the arbitrary detention of numerous members of this group in camps where they were tortured, or the deportation of the majority of the Muslim inhabitants of Zvornik, also appear to have inflicted on the group conditions of life calculated within the meaning of the Genocide Convention "to lead to their physical destruction in whole or in part".

The occurrences established on the basis of the questionnaire, including murder, deportation, arbitrary arrests, torture and rape, can also be rated as crimes against humanity within the meaning of international humanitarian law.

We therefore recommend to interpret the "ethnic cleansing" operations per se in such a way as to qualify them as acts of genocide and as crimes against humanity within the meaning of international humanitarian law.

No one laments more than we the failure of the international community to take decisive action to halt the suffering and end a war that had produced so many victims. Srebrenica crystallized a truth understood only too late by the United Nations and the world at large: that Bosnia was as much a moral cause as a military conflict. The tragedy of Srebrenica will haunt our history forever.

....The body of this report sets out in meticulous, systematic, exhaustive and ultimately harrowing detail the descent of Srebrenica into a horror without parallel since the Second World War. I urge all concerned to study this report carefully, and to let the facts speak for themselves. The men who have been charged with this crime against humanity reminded the world, and in particular, the United Nations, that evil exists in the world. They taught us also that the United Nations' global commitment to ending conflict does not preclude moral judgements, but makes them necessary.

Kofi Annan
Secretary General of the United Nations

In April 1993, as Srebrenica was about to be overrun [the first time], twelve State Department officials specializing in the Balkans condemned American policy in a letter to the Secretary of State. By August, three officials—Marshall Harris, Jon Western, and Stephen Walker—had resigned from the Department....American pressure on the Bosnian government to accept the ethnic partition of their state had placed the imprimatur of the United States on the irreversibility of Serbia's "ethnic cleansing." In his letter of resignation Harris [the desk officer for Bosnia] said he could not be a party to the ongoing "pressure on the Bosnian government to agree to partition....I can no longer serve in a Department of State that accepts the forceful dismemberment of a European state and that will not act against genocide." Explaining the depth of disaffection in the State Department, George Kenney, the desk officer for Yugoslavia who resigned during the Bush Administration, stated that "virtually all the staff working on these issues agree that our Balkan policy is a total failure" and "that American policy borders on complicity in genocide."

Introduction: "In Plain View"
Why Bosnia? Writings on the Balkan War

III

THE FALL OF SREBRENICA

This document reproduces the Introduction (paragraphs 1–7) and Chapter XI, the concluding section (paragraphs 467-506) of the Report of the Secretary-General on the fate of the "protected enclave" of Srebrenica. For full text of the Report, see UN Doc. A/54/549 (15 November 1999). The Report also may be read on the web at www.un.org/News/ossg/srebrenica.pdf

THE FALL OF SREBRENICA

REPORT OF THE SECRETARY GENERAL [KOFI ANNAN]
PURSUANT TO GENERAL ASSEMBLY RESOLUTION 53/35 (1998)

INTRODUCTION

This report is submitted pursuant to paragraph 18 of General Assembly resolution 53/35 of November 30, 1998. In that paragraph, the General Assembly requested:

"A comprehensive report, including an assessment, on the events dating from the establishment of the safe area of Srebrenica on 16 April 1993 under Security Council resolution 819 (1993) of 16 April 1993, which was followed by the establishment of other safe areas, until the endorsement of the Peace Agreement by the Security Council under resolution 1031 (1995) of 15 December 1995, bearing in mind the relevant decisions of the Security Council and the proceedings of the International Tribunal in this respect,"

and encourages Member States and others concerned to provide relevant information.

On November 16, 1995, the International Criminal Tribunal for the Former Yugoslavia (ICTY) indicted Radovan Karadžić ("President of the Republika Srpska") and Ratko Mladić (Commander of the Bosnian Serb Army) for their alleged direct responsibility for the atrocities committed in July 1995 against the Bosnian Muslim population of the United Nations-designated safe area of Srebrenica. After a review of the evidence submitted by the Prosecutor, Judge Riad confirmed the indictment, stating that:

"After Srebrenica fell to besieging Serbian forces in July 1995, a truly terrible massacre of the Muslim population appears to have taken place. The evidence tendered by the Prosecutor describes scenes of unimaginable savagery: thousands of men executed and buried in mass graves, hundreds of men buried alive, men and women mutilated and slaughtered, children killed before their mothers' eyes, a grandfather forced to eat the liver of his own grandson. These are truly scenes from hell, written on the darkest pages of human history."[1]

The United Nations had a mandate to "deter attacks" on Srebrenica and five other "safe areas" in Bosnia and Herzegovina. Despite that mandate, up to 20,000 people, overwhelmingly from the Bosnian Muslim community, were killed in and around the safe areas. In addition, a majority of the 117 members of UNPROFOR who lost their lives in Bosnia and Herzegovina died in or around the safe areas. In requesting the submission of the present report, the General Assembly has afforded me the opportunity to explain why the United Nations failed to deter the Serb attack on Srebrenica and the appalling events that followed...

In reviewing these events, I have in no way sought to deflect criticism directed at the United Nations Secretariat. Having served as Under-Secretary-General for Peacekeeping Operations during much of the period under review, I am fully cognizant of the mandate entrusted to the United Nations and only too painfully aware of the Organization's failures in implementing that mandate. Rather, my purpose in going over the background of the failure of the safe area policy has been to illuminate the process by which the United Nations found itself, in July 1995, confronted with these shocking events. There is an issue of responsibility, and we in the United Nations share in that responsibility, as the assessment at the end of this report records. Equally important, there are lessons to be drawn by all of those involved in the formulation and implementation of international responses to events such as the war in Bosnia and Herzegovina. There are lessons for the Secretariat, and there are lessons for the Member States that shaped the international response to the collapse of the former Yugoslavia.

Before beginning with the account of the events in question, it is important to recall that much of the history of the war in Bosnia and Herzegovina will not be touched upon at all in the body of this report. The war began on 6 April 6, 1992. Most of the territory captured by the Serbs was secured by them within the first 60 days of the war, before UNPROFOR had any significant presence in Bosnia and Herzegovina. During those 60 days, approximately one million people were displaced from their homes. Several tens of thousands of people, most of them Bosnian Muslims, were killed. The accompanying scenes of barbarity were, in general, not witnessed by UNPROFOR or by other representatives of the international community, and do not form a part of this report. In addition, the war in Bosnia and Herzegovina included nine months of open warfare between the mainly Muslim forces of the Bosnian Government and the mainly Croat forces of the Croatian Defense Council (HVO). This fighting, although important to understanding the conflict in Bosnia and Herzegovina, did not generally involve the safe areas that are the central focus of this report. The record of that conflict, therefore, does not appear in this document.

At the outset, I wish to point out that certain sections of this report may bear similarity to accounts of the fall of Srebrenica that have already appeared in a number of incisive books, journal articles, and press reports on the subject. Those secondary accounts were not used as a source of information for this report. The questions and account of events which they present, however, were independently revisited and examined from the United Nations' perspective. I hope that the confirmation or clarification of those accounts contributes to the historical record on this subject. I also wish to point out that I have not been able to answer all the hitherto unanswered questions about the fall of Srebrenica, despite a sincere effort to do so.

This report has been prepared on the basis of archival research within the United Nations system, as well as on the basis of interviews with individuals who, in one capacity or another, participated in, or had knowledge of the events in question. In the interest of gaining a clearer understanding of these events, I have taken the exceptional step of entering into the public record information from the classified files of the United Nations... All of these exceptional measures that I have taken in preparing this report reflect the importance which I attach to shedding light on what Judge Riad described as the "darkest pages of human history"....

* * * * * *

XI. THE FALL OF SREBRENICA: AN ASSESSMENT

The tragedy that took place following the fall of Srebrenica is shocking for two reasons. It is shocking, first and foremost, for the magnitude of the crimes committed. Not since the horrors of World War II had Europe witnessed massacres on this scale. The mortal remains of close to 2,500 men and boys have been found on the surface, in mass grave sites and in secondary burial sites. Several thousand more men are still missing, and there is every reason to believe that additional burial sites, many of which have been probed but not exhumed, will reveal the bodies of thousands more men and boys. The great majority of those who were killed were not killed in combat: the exhumed bodies of the victims show large numbers had their hands bound, or were blindfolded, or were shot in the back or the back of the head. Numerous eyewitness accounts, now well corroborated by forensic evidence, attest to scenes of mass slaughter of unarmed victims.

The fall of Srebrenica is also shocking because the enclave's inhabitants believed that the authority of the United Nations Security Council, the presence of UNPROFOR peacekeepers, and the might of NATO air power, would ensure their safety. Instead, the Serb forces ignored the Security Council, pushed aside the UNPROFOR troops, and assessed correctly that air power would not be used to stop them. They overran the safe area of Srebrenica with ease, and then proceeded to depopulate the territory within 48 hours. Their leaders then engaged in high-level negotiations with representatives of the international community while their forceson the ground executed and buried thousands of men and boys within a matter of days.

Questions must be answered, and foremost among these are the following: how can this have been allowed to happen? And how will the United Nations ensure that no future peacekeeping operation witnesses such a calamity on its watch? In this assessment, factors ranging from the most proximate to the more over-arching will be discussed, in order to provide the most comprehensive analysis possible of the preceding narrative.

A. *Role of the United Nations Protection Force in Bosnia*

In the effort to assign responsibility for the appalling events that took place in Srebrenica, many observers have been quick to point to the soldiers of the UNPROFOR Dutch battalion as the most immediate culprits. They blame them for not attempting to stop the Serb attack, and they blame them for not protecting the thousands of people who sought refuge in their compound.

As concerns the first criticism, the commander of the Dutch battalion believed that the Bosniaks could not defend Srebrenica by themselves and that his own forces could not be effective without substantial air support. Air support was, in his view, the most effective resource at his disposal to respond to the Serb attack. Accordingly, he requested air support on a number of occasions, even after many of his own troops had been taken hostage and faced potential Serb reprisal. These requests were unheeded by his superiors at various levels, and some of them may not have been received at all, illustrating the command-and-control problems from which UNPROFOR suffered throughout its history. However, having been told that the risk of confrontation with the Serbs was to be avoided, and that the execution of the mandate was secondary to the security of his personnel, the Dutch battalion withdrew from Observation Posts under direct attack.

It is true that the Dutch UNPROFOR troops in Srebrenica never fired at the attacking Serbs. They fired warning shots over the Serbs' heads and their mortars fired flares, but they never directly fired on any Serb units. Had they engaged the attacking Serbs directly it is possible that events would have unfolded differently. At the same time, it must be recognized that the 150 fighting men of the Dutch battalion were lightly armed and in indefensible positions, and were faced with 2,000 Serbs advancing with the support of armour and artillery.

As concerns the second criticism, it is easy to say with the benefit of hindsight and the knowledge of what followed that the Dutch battalion did not do enough to protect those who sought refuge in their compound. Perhaps they should have allowed everyone into the compound and then offered themselves as human shields to protect them. This may have slowed down the Serbs and bought time for higher level negotiations to take effect. At the same time, it is also possible that the Serb forces would then have shelled the compound, killing thousands in the process, as they had threatened to do. Ultimately, it is not possible to say with any certainty that stronger actions by the Dutch would have saved lives, and it is even possible that such efforts could have done more harm than good. Faced with this prospect and unaware that the Serbs would proceed to execute thousands of men and boys, the Dutch avoided armed confrontation and appealed in the process for support at the highest levels.

It is harder to explain why the Dutch battalion did not report more fully the scenes that were unfolding around them following the enclaves fall. Although they did not witness mass killing, they were aware of some sinister indications. It is possible that if the members of the Dutch battalion had immediately reported in detail those sinister indications to the United Nations chain of command, the international community may have been compelled to respond more robustly and more quickly, and that some lives might have been saved. This failure of intelligence-sharing was also not limited to the fall of Sre-brenica, but an endemic weakness throughout the conflict, both within the peacekeeping mission, and between the mission and Member States.

B. *Role of the Bosniak forces on the ground*

Criticisms have also been leveled at the Bosniaks in Srebrenica: among them that they did not fully demilitarize and that they did not do enough to defend the enclave. To a degree, these criticisms appear to be contradictory. Concerning the first criticism, it is right to note that the Bosnian Government had entered into demilitarization agreements with the Serbs. They did this with the encouragement of the United Nations. And while it is true that the Bosniak fighters in Srebrenica did not fully demilitarize, they demilitarized enough for UNPROFOR to issue a press release, on 21 April 1993, saying that the process had been a success. Specific instructions from United Nations Headquarters in New York stated that UNPROFOR should not be too zealous in searching for Bosniak weapons and, later, that the Serbs should withdraw their heavy weapons before the Bosniaks gave up their weapons. The Serbs never did withdraw their heavy weapons.

Concerning the accusation that the Bosniaks did not do enough to defend Srebrenica, military experts consulted in connection with this report were largely in agreement that the Bosniaks could not have defended Srebrenica for long in the face of a concerted attack sup-ported by armour and artillery. The defenders were an undisciplined, untrained, poorly armed, totally isolated force, lying prone in the crowded valley of Srebrenica. They were ill-equipped even to train themselves in the use of the few heavier weapons that had been smuggled to them by their authorities. After over three years of siege, the population was demoralized, afraid and often hungry. The only leader of stature was absent when the attack occurred. Surrounding them, controlling all the high ground, handsomely equipped with the heavy weapons and logistical train of the Yugoslav army, were the Bosnian Serbs. There was no contest.

Despite the odds against them, the Bosniaks requested UNPROFOR to return to them the weapons they had surrendered under the demilitarization agreements of 1993. They requested those weapons at the beginning of the Serb offensive, but the request was rejected by UNPROFOR because, as one commander explained, "it was our responsibil-ity to defend the enclave, not theirs." Given the limited number and poor quality of the Bosniak weapons held by UNPROFOR, it seems unlikely that releasing those weapons to the Bosniaks would have made a significant difference to the outcome of the battle; but the Bosniaks were under attack at that point, they wanted to resist with whatever means they could muster, and UNPROFOR denied them access to some of their own weapons. With the benefit of hindsight, this decision seems to have been particularly ill-advised, given UNPROFOR's own unwillingness consistently to advocate force as a means of deterring attacks on the enclave.

Many have accused the Bosniak forces of withdrawing from the enclave as the Serb forces advanced on the day of its fall. However, it must be remembered that on the eve of the final Serb assault the Dutch Commander urged the Bosniaks to withdraw from defensive positions south of Srebrenica town—the direction from which the Serbs were advancing. He did so because he believed that NATO aircraft would soon be launching widespread air strikes against the advancing Serbs.

There is also a third accusation levelled at the Bosniak defenders of Srebrenica, that they provoked the Serb offensive by attacking out of that safe area. Even though this accusation is often repeated by international sources, there is no credible evidence to support it. Dutchbat personnel on the ground at the time assessed that the few 'raids' the Bosniaks mounted out of Srebrenica were of little or no military significance. These raids were often organized in order to gather food, as the Serbs had refused access for humanitarian convoys into the enclave. Even Serb sources approached in the context of this report acknowledged that the Bosniak forces in Srebrenica posed no significant military threat to them.

The biggest attack the Bosniaks launched out of Srebrenica during the over two years during which it was designated as a safe area appears to have been the raid on the village of Visˇnjica, on 26 June 1995, in which several houses were burned, up to four Serbs were killed and approximately 100 sheep were stolen. In contrast, the Serbs overran the enclave two weeks later, driving tens of thousands from their homes, and summarily executing thousands of men and boys. The Serbs repeatedly exaggerated the extent of the "raids" out of Srebrenica as a pretext for the prosecution of a central war aim: to create a geographically contiguous and ethnically pure territory along the Drina, while freeing up their troops to fight in other parts of the country. The extent to which this pretext was accepted at face value by international actors and observers reflected the prism of "moral equivalency" through which the conflict in Bosnia was viewed by too many for too long.

C. *Role of air power*

The next question that must be asked is this: Why was NATO air power not brought to bear upon the Serbs before they entered the town of Srebrenica? Even in the most restrictive interpretation of the mandate the use of close air support against attacking Serb targets was clearly warranted. The Serbs were firing directly at Dutch Observation Posts with tank rounds as early as 5 days before the enclave fell.

Some have alleged that NATO air power was not authorized earlier, despite repeated requests from the Dutchbat Commander, because the Force Commander or someone else had renounced its use against the Serbs in return for the release of United Nations personnel taken hostage in May-June 1995. Nothing found in the course of the preparation of this report supports such a view.

What is clear is that my predecessor, his senior advisers (amongst whom I was included as Under-Secretary-General for Peacekeeping Operations), the SRSG and the Force Commander were all deeply reluctant to use air power against the Serbs for four main reasons. We believed that by using air power against the Serbs we would be perceived as having entered the war against them, something not authorized by the Security Council and potentially fatal for a peacekeeping operation. Second, we risked losing control over the process:

once the "key" was turned "on" we did not know if we would be able to turn it "off", with grave consequences for the safety of the troops entrusted to us by Member States. Third, we believed that the use of air power would disrupt the primary mission of UNPROFOR as we then saw it: the creation of an environment in which the humanitarian aid could be delivered to the civilian population of the country. And fourth, we feared Serb reprisal against our peacekeepers. Member States had placed thousands of their troops under United Nations command. We, and many of the troop contributing nations, considered the security of these troops to be of fundamental importance in the implementation of the mandate. That there was merit in our concerns was evidenced by the hostage crisis of May–June 1995.

At the same time, we were fully aware that the threat of NATO air power was all we had at our disposal to respond to an attack on the safe areas. The lightly armed forces in the enclaves would be no match for (and were not intended to resist) a Serb attack supported by infantry and armor. It was thus incumbent upon us, our concerns notwithstanding, to make full use of the air power deterrent, as we had done with some effect in response to Serb attacks upon Sarajevo and Gorazde in February and April 1994, respectively. For the reasons mentioned above, we did not use with full effectiveness this one instrument at our disposal to make the safe areas at least a little bit safer. We were, with hindsight, wrong to declare repeatedly and publicly that we did not want to use air power against the Serbs except as a last resort, and to accept the shelling of the safe areas as a daily occurrence. We believed there was no choice under the Security Council resolutions but to deploy more and more peacekeepers into harm's way. The Serbs knew this, and they timed their attack on Srebrenica well. The UNPROFOR Commander in Sarajevo at the time noted that the reluctance of his superiors and of key troop contributors to "escalate the use of force" in the wake of the hostage crisis would create the conditions in which we would then always be "stared down by the Serbs".

D. *Unanswered questions*

The above assessment leaves unanswered a number of questions often asked about the fall of Srebrenica and the failure of the safe area regime. Two of these questions, in particular, are matters of public controversy and need to be addressed, even if no definitive answer can be provided.

The first question concerns the possibility that the Bosnian Government and the Bosnian Serb party, possibly with the knowledge of one or more Contact Group states, had an understanding that Srebrenica would not be vigorously defended by the Bosniaks in return for an undertaking by the Serbs not to vigorously defend territory around Sarajevo. However, the Bosniaks tried to break out of Sarajevo and were repulsed by the Serbs before the Serbs attacked Srebrenica. This would appear to remove any incentive the Bosniak authorities might have had to let the Serbs take Srebrenica. There is no doubt that the capture of Srebrenica and Žepa by the Serbs made it easier for the Bosniaks and Serbs to agree on the territorial basis of a peace settlement: the Serbs, who felt that they needed to control the border with Serbia for strategic reasons, had the territory they wanted and would not trade it back; the Bosniaks, who felt that they needed to control Sarajevo and its approaches, were able to demand this in "exchange" for Srebrenica and Žepa. The fact that the result of the tragedy in Srebrenica contributed in some ways to the conclusion of a peace agreement—by galvanizing the will of the international community, by distracting the Serbs from the coming Croatian attack, by reducing the vulnerability of UNPROFOR personnel to hostage-taking, and by making certain territorial questions easier for the parties to resolve—is not evidence of a conspiracy. It is a tragic irony. No evidence reviewed in the process of assembling this report suggests that any party, Bosnian or international, engineered or acquiesced in the fall of Srebrenica, other than those who ordered and carried out the attack on it. My personal belief is that human and institutional failing, at many levels, rather than willful conspiracy, account for why the Serbs were not prevented from overrunning the safe area of Srebrenica.

A second question concerns the possibility that the United Nations, or one or more of its Member States, had intelligence indicating that a Serb attack on Srebrenica was being prepared. I can confirm that the United Nations, which relied on Member States for such intelligence, had no advance knowledge of the Serb offensive. Indeed, the absence of an intelligence-gathering capacity, coupled with the reluctance of Member States to share sensitive information with an organization as open, and from their perspective, as "insecure" as the United Nations, is one of the major operational constraints under which we labor in all our missions. As to whether any intelligence was available to Member States, I have no means of ascertaining this; in any case none was passed on to the United Nations by those Member States who might have been in a position to assist.

Had the United Nations been provided with intelligence that revealed the enormity of the Bosnian Serbs' goals, it is possible, though by no means certain, that the tragedy of Srebrenica might have been averted. But no such excuse can explain our failure in Žepa: before they began their advance into Žepa, the Serbs made a public announcement regarding their plans. Žepa was not overrun because of a lack of intelligence, but because the international community lacked the capacity to do anything other than to accept its fall as a fait accompli.

E. *Role of the Security Council and Member States*

With the benefit of hindsight, one can see that many of the errors the United Nations made flowed from a single and no-doubt well-intentioned effort: we tried to keep the peace and apply the rules of peacekeeping when there was no peace to keep. Knowing that any other course of action would jeopardize the lives of the troops, we tried to create—or imagine—an environment in which the tenets of peacekeeping—agreement between the parties, deployment by consent, and impartiality—could be upheld. We tried to stabilize the situation on the ground through ceasefire agreements, which brought us close to the Serbs, who controlled the larger proportion of the land. We tried to eschew the use of force except in self-defense, which brought us into conflict with the defenders of the safe areas, whose safety depended on our use of force.

In spite of the untenability of its position, UNPROFOR was able to assist in the humanitarian process, and to mitigate some—but, as Srebrenica tragically underscored, by no means all—the suffering inflicted by the war. There are people alive in Bosnia today who would not be alive had UNPROFOR not been deployed. To this extent, it can be said that the 117 young men who lost their lives in the service of UNPROFOR's mission in Bosnia and Herzegovina did not die in vain. Their sacrifice and the good work of many others, however, cannot fully redeem a policy that was, at best, a half-measure.

The community of nations decided to respond to the war in Bosnia and Herzegovina with an arms embargo, with humanitarian aid and with the deployment of a peacekeeping force. It must be clearly stated that these measures were poor substitutes for more decisive and forceful action to prevent the unfolding horror. The arms embargo did little more than freeze in place the military balance within the former Yugoslavia. It left the Serbs in a position of overwhelming military dominance and effectively deprived the Republic of Bosnia and Herzegovina of its right, under the Charter of the United Nations, to self-defense. It was not necessarily a mistake to impose an arms embargo, which after all had been done when Bosnia-Herzegovina was not yet a Member State of the United Nations. But having done so, there must surely have been some attendant duty to protect Bosnia and Herzegovina, after it became a Member State, from the tragedy that then befell it. Even as the Serb attacks on and strangulation of the "safe areas" continued in 1993 and 1994, all widely covered by the media and, presumably, by diplomatic and intelligence reports to their respective governments, the approach of the Members of the Security Council remained largely constant. The international community still could not find the political will to confront the menace defying it.

Nor was the provision of humanitarian aid a sufficient response to "ethnic cleansing" and to an attempted genocide. The provision of food and shelter to people who have neither is wholly admirable, and we must all recognize the extraordinary work done by UNHCR and its partners in circumstances of extreme adversity. But the provision of humanitarian assistance could never have been a solution to the problem in that country. The problem, which cried out for a political/ military solution, was that a Member State of the United Nations, left largely defenseless as a result of an arms embargo imposed upon it by the United Nations, was being dismembered by forces committed to its destruction. This was not a problem with a humanitarian solution.

Nor was the deployment of a peacekeeping force a coherent response to this problem. My predecessor openly told the Security Council that a United Nations peacekeeping force could not bring peace to Bosnia and Herzegovina. He said it often and he said it loudly, fearing that peacekeeping techniques inevitably would fail in a situation of war. None of the conditions for the deployment of peacekeepers had been met: there was no peace agreement—not even a functioning ceasefire—there was no clear will to peace and there was no clear consent by the belligerents. Nevertheless, faute de mieux, the Security Council decided that a United Nations peacekeeping force would be deployed. Lightly armed, highly visible in their white vehicles, scattered across the country in numerous indefensible observation posts, they were able to confirm the obvious: there was no peace to keep.

In so doing, the Council obviously expected that the "warring parties" on the ground would respect the authority of the United Nations and would not obstruct or attack its humanitarian operations. It soon became apparent that, with the end of the Cold War and the ascendancy of irregular forces—controlled or uncontrolled—the old rules of the game no longer held. Nor was it sufficiently appreciated that a systematic and ruthless campaign such as the one conducted by the Serbs would view a United Nations humanitarian operation, not as an obstacle, but as an instrument of its aims. In such an event, it is clear that the ability to adapt mandates to the reality on the ground is of critical importance to ensuring that the appropriate force under the appropriate structure is deployed. None of that flexibility was present in the management of UNPROFOR.

F. *Failure to fully comprehend the Serb war aims*

Even before the attack on Srebrenica began, it was clear to the Secretariat and Member States alike that the safe areas were not truly "safe". There was neither the will to use decisive air power against Serb attacks on the safe areas, nor the means on the ground to repulse them. In report after report the Secretariat accordingly and rightly pointed out these conceptual flaws in the safe area policy. We proposed changes: delineating the safe areas either by agreement between the parties or with a mandate from the Security Council; demilitarizing the safe areas; negotiating full freedom of movement. We also stressed the need to protect people rather than territory. In fact, however, these proposals were themselves inadequate. Two of the safe areas—Srebrenica and Žepa—were delineated from the beginning, and they were cited in our reports as relatively more successful examples of how the safe area concept could work. The same two safe areas were also demilitarized to a far greater extent than any of the others, though their demilitarization was by no means complete. In the end, however, the partial demilitarization of the enclaves did not enhance their security. To the contrary, it only made them easier targets for the Serbs.

Nonetheless, the key issue—politically, strategically and morally—underlying the security of the "safe areas" was the essential nature of "ethnic cleansing". As part of the larger ambition for a "Greater Serbia", the Serbs set out to occupy the territory of the enclaves; they wanted the territory for themselves. The civilian inhabitants of the enclaves were not the incidental victims of the attackers; their death or removal was the very purpose of the attacks upon them. The tactic of employing savage terror, primarily mass killings, rapes and brutalization of civilians, to expel populations was used to the greatest extent in Bosnia and Herzegovina, where it acquired the now-infamous euphemism of "ethnic cleansing". The Bosnian Muslim civilian population thus became the principal victim of brutally aggressive military and para-military Serb operations to depopulate coveted territories in order to allow them to be repopulated by Serbs.

The failure to fully comprehend the extent of the Serb war aims may explain in part why the Secretariat and the Peacekeeping Mission did not react more quickly and decisively when the Serbs initiated their attack on Srebrenica. In fact, rather than attempting to mobilize the international community to support the enclave's defence we gave the

Security Council the impression that the situation was under control, and many of us believed that to be the case. The day before Srebrenica fell we reported that the Serbs were not attacking when they were. We reported that the Bosniaks had fired on an UNPROFOR blocking position when it was the Serbs. We failed to mention urgent requests for air power. In some instances in which incomplete and inaccurate information was given to the Council, this can be attributed to problems with reporting from the field. In other instances, however, the reporting may have been illustrative of a more general tendency to assume that the parties were equally responsible for the transgressions that occurred. It is not clear in any event, that the provision of more fully accurate information to the Council—many of whose Members had independent sources of information on the ongoing events—would have led to appreciably different results.

In the end, these Bosnian Serb war aims were ultimately repulsed on the battlefield, and not at the negotiating table. Yet, the Secretariat had convinced itself early on that the broader use of force by the international community was beyond our mandate and anyway undesirable. A report of the Secretary-General to the Security Council spoke against a "culture of death", arguing that peace should be pursued only through non-military methods. And when, in June 1995, the international community provided UNPROFOR with a heavily armed Rapid Reaction Force, we argued against using it robustly to implement our mandate. When decisive action was finally taken by UNPROFOR in August and September 1995, it helped to bring the war to a conclusion.

G. *Lessons for the future*

The fall of Srebrenica is replete with lessons for this Organization and its Member States—lessons that must be learned if we are to expect the peoples of the world to place their faith in the United Nations. There are occasions when Member States cannot achieve consensus on a particular response to active military conflicts, or do not have the will to pursue what many might consider to be an appropriate course of action. The first of the general lessons is that when peacekeeping operations are used as a substitute for such political consensus they will likely fail. There is a role for peacekeeping—a proud role in a world still driven by conflict—and there is even a role for protected zones and safe havens in certain situations. But peacekeeping and war fighting are distinct activities which should not be mixed. Peacekeepers must never again be deployed into an environment in which there is no ceasefire or peace agreement. Peacekeepers must never again be told that they must use their peacekeeping tools—lightly armed soldiers in scattered positions—to impose the ill-defined wishes of the international community on one or another of the belligerents by military means. If the necessary resources are not provided—and the necessary political, military and moral judgments are not made—the job simply cannot be done.

Protected zones and safe areas can have a role in protecting civilians in armed conflict. But it is clear that they either must be demilitarized and established by the agreement of the belligerents, as with the "protected zones" and "safe havens" recognized by international humanitarian law, or they must be truly "safe areas", fully defended by a credible military deterrent. The two concepts are absolutely distinct and must not be confused. It is tempting for critics to blame the UNPROFOR units in Srebrenica for its fall, or to blame the United Nations hierarchy above those units. Certainly, errors of judgement were made—errors rooted in a philosophy of impartiality and non-violence wholly unsuited to the conflict in Bosnia—but this must not divert us from the more fundamental mistakes. The safe areas were established by the Security Council without the consent of the parties and without providing any credible military deterrent. They were neither protected areas nor "safe havens" in the sense of international humanitarian law, nor safe areas in any militarily meaningful sense. Several representatives on the Council, as well as the Secretariat, noted this problem at the time, warning that, in failing to provide a credible military deterrent, the safe area policy would be gravely damaging to the Council's reputation and, indeed, to the United Nations as a whole.

The approach by the United Nations Secretariat, the Security Council, the Contact Group and other involved Governments to the war in Bosnia and Herzegovina had certain consequences at both the political and the military level. At the political level, it entailed continuing negotiations with the architects of the Serb policies, principally, Mr. Milosevic and Dr. Karadžić. At the military level, it resulted in a process of negotiation with and reliance upon General Mladić, whose implacable commitment to clear Eastern Bosnia— and Sarajevo if possible—of Bosniaks was plainly obvious and led inexorably to Srebrenica. At various points during the war, these negotiations amounted to appeasement.

The international community as a whole must accept its share of responsibility for allowing this tragic course of events by its prolonged refusal to use force in the early stages of the war. This responsibility is shared by the Security Council, the Contact Group and other Governments which contributed to the delay in the use of force, as well as by the United Nations Secretariat and the Mission in the field. But clearly the primary and most direct responsibility lies with the architects and implementers of the attempted genocide in Bosnia. Radovan Karadžić and Ratko Mladić, along with their major collaborators, have been indicted by the International Criminal Tribunal for the Former Yugoslavia. To this day, they remain free men. They must be made to answer for the barbaric crimes with which they have been charged.

The cardinal lesson of Srebrenica is that a deliberate and systematic attempt to terrorize, expel or murder an entire people must be met decisively with all necessary means, and with the political will to carry the policy through to its logical conclusion. In the Balkans, in this decade, this lesson has had to be learned not once, but twice. In both instances, in Bosnia and in Kosovo, the international community tried to reach a negotiated settlement with an unscrupulous and murderous regime. In both instances it required the use of force to bring a halt to the planned and systematic killing and expulsion of civilians.

The United Nations experience in Bosnia was one of the most difficult and painful in our history. It is with the deepest regret and remorse that we have reviewed our own actions and decisions in the face of the assault on Srebrenica. Through error, misjudgement and an inability to recognize the scope of the evil confronting us, we failed to do our part to help save the people of Srebrenica from the Serb campaign of mass murder. No one regrets more than we the opportunities for achieving peace and justice that were missed. No one laments more than we the failure of the international community to take decisive action to halt the suffering and end a war that had produced so many victims. Srebrenica crystallized a truth understood only too late by the United Nations and the world at large: that Bosnia was as much a moral cause as a military conflict. The tragedy of Srebrenica will haunt our history forever.

In the end, the only meaningful and lasting amends we can make to the citizens of Bosnia and Herzegovina who put their faith in the international community is to do our utmost not to allow such horrors to recur. When the international community makes a solemn promise to safeguard and protect innocent civilians from massacre, then it must be willing to back its promise with the necessary means. Otherwise, it is surely better not to raise hopes and expectations in the first place, and not to impede whatever capability they may be able to muster in their own defense.

To ensure that we have fully learned the lessons of the tragic history detailed in this report, I wish to encourage Member States to engage in a process of reflection and analysis, focused on the key challenges the narrative uncovers. The aim of this process would be to clarify and to improve the capacity of the United Nations to respond to various forms of conflict. I have in mind addressing such issues as the gulf between mandate and means; the inadequacy of symbolic deterrence in the face of a systematic campaign of violence; the pervasive ambivalence within the United Nations regarding the role of force in the pursuit of peace; an institutional ideology of impartiality even when confronted with attempted genocide; and a range of doctrinal and institutional issues that go to the heart of the United Nations' ability to keep the peace and help protect civilian populations from armed conflict. The Secretariat is ready to join in such a process.

The body of this report sets out in meticulous, systematic, exhaustive and ultimately harrowing detail the descent of Srebrenica into a horror without parallel in the history of Europe since the Second World War. I urge all concerned to study this report carefully, and to let the facts speak for themselves. The men who have been charged with this crime against humanity reminded the world, and, in particular, the United Nations, that evil exists in the world. They taught us also that the United Nations' global commitment to ending conflict does not preclude moral judgments, but makes them necessary. It is in this spirit that I submit my report of the fall of Srebrenica to the General Assembly, and to the world.

NOTES

1. Press Release issued by ICTY (CC/PIO/026-E), 16 November 1995, The Hague.

It may seem that now the Serbian game is over, that the West "finally got it" and put the blame on the true culprit. The true desire of the West is nevertheless discernible in innumerable telltale details: the continuous compulsive search for stains also on the other side, with the aim to establish a kind of balance of guilt where "everybody is equally mad," where the equals sign is placed between the aggressor and its victim; the centering of attention on humanitarian problems (who will receive the flood of refugees?) which not only treats the conflict as if it were a kind of natural disaster, but also helps the Serbs in carrying out their program of "ethnic cleansing" in a more human way; the invention of ever new excuses against the military intervention (the Balkan countryside as the ideal ground for a prolonged guerrilla warfare; the ridiculous rejection of the desperate Bosnian plea to be allowed to buy arms and thus defend itself, characterized as "pouring oil on flames." Suffice it to quote Time: "Western weaponry would probably not be useful to Bosnians without special training..."—the blatant racism of it strikes the eye. How come Serbs in Bosnia can handle sophisticated weaponry, including MIG fighter planes? How come the same problem did not prevent the United States from arming anti-Communist rebels in Afghanistan?

Slavoj Žižek
"Caught in Another's Dream in Bosnia"
Why Bosnia? Writings on the Balkan War

After Srebrenica fell to besieging Serbian forces in July 1995, a truly terrible massacre of the Muslim population appears to have taken place. The evidence tendered by the Prosecutor describes scenes of unimaginable savagery: thousands of men executed and buried in mass graves, hundreds of men buried alive, men and women mutilated and slaughtered, children killed before their mothers' eyes, a grandfather forced to eat the liver of his own grandson. These are truly scenes from hell, written on the darkest pages of human history.

Judge Fouad Riad
International Criminal Court for the Former Yugoslavia

IV

UNITED STATES REPORTS TO
THE UNITED NATIONS SECURITY COUNCIL
ON WAR CRIMES IN THE FORMER YUGOSLAVIA

U.S. State Department War Crimes Commission, "War Crimes in the Former Yugoslavia," originally published in the U.S. *Department of State Dispatch* 3.39, 3.44, 3.52 (1992); 4.6, 4.15, 4.16, 4.30 (1993). These reports were edited, numbered, and indexed by Michael Sells and Aida Premilovac in 1993. The official name of the reports is "XXX (First, Second, Third etc) REPORT ON THE WAR CRIMES IN THE FORMER YUGOSLAVIA, "Submission of Information to the United Nations Security Council in Accordance With Paragraph 5 of Resolution 771 (1992)," September 22, 1992. Only excerpts from these reports have been used in this volume. Full text of the reports can be found at www.haverford.edu/relg/sells/reports.html#771

UNITED STATES REPORTS TO
THE UNITED NATIONS SECURITY COUNCIL
ON WAR CRIMES IN THE FORMER YUGOSLAVIA

Submission of Information to the United Nations Security Council
in Accordance With Paragraph 5 of Resolution 771 (1992),
September 22, 1992.

INTRODUCTION

In paragraph 5 of Resolution 771 (1992), the United Nations Security Council called upon States and international humanitarian organizations to collate substantiated information in their possession or submitted to them relating to the violation of humanitarian law, including grave breaches of the Geneva Conventions, being committed in the territory of the former Yugoslavia and to make this information available to the Council. This report is in response to that request....

WILLFUL KILLING

25 August 92:

At Manjaca prison camp, south of Banja Luka, 25 bodies of emaciated men, believed to be prisoners, were discovered with their throats cut. The camp was operated by the Serbian Army of Bosnia-Herzegovina under General Ratko Mladić. (Department of State)

24 August 92:

A resident of Pososje, Bosnia saw 24 men, 2 women, and 2 boys machine-gunned by Serbs in her neighbor's garden. (Reuters)

26 May 92:

About 200 Muslim refugees from Višegrad heading for Macedonia were turned back at the Mokra Gora border crossing into Serbia on May 26. An employee of the bus company that was transporting the refugees said that the group was stopped outside Bosanska Jagodina later that day by a group of armed men, and that he saw 17 male refugees taken from the buses and "liquidated." The killers were members of two Serbian "volunteer" groups operating in a local Serb "territorial defense" formation, which had been systematically abducting and murdering Muslims in the region. (Department of State)

26 May 92:

On May 26, the 200-year-old mosque of Prijedor was destroyed. (MAGYAR SZO)

April 92:

In a letter to the US Secretary of State dated May 1, Professor Muhamed Dreševljaković—the mayor of Sarajevo—wrote that militant parts of the Serbian Democratic Party had destroyed"... civil sections, vital economy and communal buildings, schools and nursery schools, monuments of culture, boards of health, sacred monuments." The mayor begged, "Don't let Sarajevo become a second Vukovar, Bosanski Brod or Foča—cities vanished from the face of the earth." (Department of State)

4 August 92:

Serbian Democratic Party (SDS) strategy is to expel Muslim Slavs from most of Bosnia, according to the US Embassy in Belgrade. The SDS campaign of ethnic cleansing is causing misery and death for large numbers of Bosnian Muslims. (Department of State)

24 June 92:

SDS/JNA forces drove non-Serbs—as well as Serbs married to Muslims or Croats, and Serbs who were "disloyal"—out of their homes. Those expelled were given as little as 30 minutes to gather their belongings. (Department of State)

9 June 92:

Serb paramilitaries who had taken control of the Muslim-majority districts of Zvornik, Srebrenica, Bratunac, and Vlasenica were systematically expelling Muslims. Muslims in the settlement of Grobnica, near Zvornik, were given a 24-hour ultimatum to leave, and were not being allowed to carry any possessions with them. The nearby town of Kozluk, whose population of 6,000 was predominantly Muslim, was under SDS occupation and "cleansed" as well. (Department of State)

[FIRST SUBMISSION]

27 August 92:

Bosnian Muslim forces killed at least 20 Serbians after ambushing a convoy of people flee-ing the outskirts of Goražde on August 27. One of the survivors, a 64 year-old Serbian who lost his left leg after he was wounded in the ambush, told a correspondent that about 15–20 Muslim guerrillas had opened fire with automatic weapons beside the road ust north of Kukavice. One witness, who lost his 11-year-old son during the ambush, claimed as many as 300 people were killed on the road. (The New York Times, The Daily Telegraph)

24 July 92:

Three male Bosnian Muslims witnessed and survived a mass slaughter at Keraterm camp on July 24, when guards opened fire with automatic rifles on a room packed with prisoners. About 150 men were killed or wounded in this one incident. According to these witnesses:

They were locked along with 200-300 men into a single room estimated to be about 80 square meters in size, with a small alcove in the right rear corner. The room had a sin-gle window high up in the front wall above a large sheet-metal "garage-type" door with a smaller opening in it.

Prisoners received little water or food. The temperature in the room was stifling, the conditions nearly unbearable.

On July 24, the prisoners in the room were given some water, but in the words of one of the witnesses, "they put something in the water" and the men "became crazy." Then something was shot through the window which produced smoke and gas. The prisoners began screaming and pounding on the doors; some began to hallucinate and fight each other. Others managed to force a hole in the sheet metal of a door and started to escape the room, but were then killed by guards standing outside.

After the disturbance in the room had gone on for some time, the soldiers opened fire with large machine guns. Those near the door were killed first. One of the witnesses sur-vived because he had been in the back alcove and out of direct line of fire. Another sur-vived when the body of another prisoner fell on him. An estimated 150 men were killed or wounded.

On the following day, July 25, soldiers came into the room and choose about 20 of the surviving prisoners, took them outside, lined them up against an outside wall of the room and shot them. (Department of State)

Another Bosnian Muslim from the Prijedor region, interviewed separately, also wit-nessed the July 24 massacre at Keraterm camp. He said that prisoners were kept in four rooms. He was in room two. Room three was where prisoners were most severely tortured and where the massacre occurred. From a window in room two, he witnessed the changes of the guards and automatic rifle fire.

On July 25, guards choose two prisoners each from rooms one and two to remove the dead. These prisoners counted 99 dead and 42 wounded. They were ordered to put the wounded on the same truck as the dead. The truck was labeled Prijedor Autotransport. Neither the wounded nor the driver [was] seen again.

Another witness believes the bodies were buried in the village of Tomašica, near Omarska, in an area called Depunija. The witness's uncle watched a truck unload many bodies into a very deep pit and cover them with a large layer of dirt. A few days later, the uncle saw trucks dump animal corpses into the same pit. Another layer of soil was put on top of the animal corpses. (Department of State)

May-August 92:

A 40-year-old Muslim from Prijedor, who was interned in Omarska camp from May 30 to August 3, described the final ordeal of a Muslim named Emir Karabašić. Emir, who had been tortured regularly, one day returned to the sleeping room with his back severely burned by a guard. Two days later, two Serbian brothers were let into the camp after 5 pm. They had often visited the camp at night.

These brothers entered the sleeping quarters carrying pistols and automatic rifles. They called for Emir, Jasmin, and Alić to come forward. The three were beaten with rifle butts and police batons in full view of the other prisoners, including this witness. The brothers forced Alić first to drink a glass of motor oil and then to drink the urine of the other two prisoners.

Alić was next beaten until he was unconscious and then revived with cold water. After further beatings, Alić was forced to take his pants off. The brothers then forced Emir and Jasmin to bite off Alić testicles. Alić died of his wounds that night. According to the witness, these crimes were committed on the shift of the shift leader under whom the most heinous tortures and beatings occurred. (Department of State)

May–June 92:

About 3,000 men, women, and children were killed during May and June at the Luka-Brčko camp, which held approximately 1,000 civilian internees at any one time. Some 95% were ethnic Muslims, and the remainder were Croatians. Approximately 95% were men. Until May, the bodies were dumped into the Sava River. Thereafter they were transported to and burned in both the old and new "kafilerija" factories located in the vicinity of Brčko.

All internees in the camp came from within a 14 kilometer radius of Brčko. The first hangar was occupied by Muslims from Brezovo Polje. The Serbian police appeared to have administrative control of the camp.

Upon arrival, all internees were questioned by one of three inspectors who decided their fate. For example, if a person was a member of the SDA or HDZ political parties, he was executed at the camp. Other questions included whether the person had foreign currency, gold, or weapons, or if the neighbor might have any of these items. Without a signature from either the police chief at the camp, or one of the military officers, a person could not be released. Approximately 1,000 people were released from the camp when Serbs vouched with their lives—and signed documents to that effect—that the internees would not leave Brčko, discuss politics, or own weapons. These people were all released within a 48-hour period; thereafter releases were not authorized. One example was an individual who had his ears cut off with a knife by a "Specijalci" soldier. As he grabbed for his ears in pain, a young woman cut off his genitalia with an instrument called a "spoon." As he fell forward and lay on the ground, he was shot in the head by a guard. In other instances, ears and noses were cut off and eyes gouged out. Knives were used to cut into the skin of internees all the way to the bone; some fingers were cut off entirely. All was done in front of other internees.

Beatings with clubs were common. A Specijalci soldier used a wooden club with metal protruding from it to kill several people. He forced internees to lick the blood from the metal studs. Another shot an individual in the back several times after he had carried a dead body behind the third hangar. In June, some 50–60 men had their genitalia removed.

Approximately 10–15 Chetniks, Yugoslav Federal Specijalci, and Serbian police were involved during the daily occurrences, but some participated on a more regular basis. Some were drunk. Internees were told to sing. Those who did not sing loud enough were shot point blank. After they had started singing, the men would come in and randomly start shooting. About 50 men, women, and children were killed in one case, allegedly in retaliation for the death of 12 Chetniks who had been killed on the front. This type of shooting occurred on a daily basis with anywhere form 15 to 50 victims.

There was also a torture room at Luka-Brčko camp. Those tortured were either killed immediately after being tortured or were left to bleed and, if they did not die in 2 to 4 days on their own, shot to death. They were left lying in their own blood in the living areas and other internees were not allowed to help in any way. People were beaten with clubs to the point that the bones in their faces caved in, and they died.

The internees were then "volunteered" by camp personnel to carry the dead bodies behind their living areas or to the camp garbage dump. During the movement of the bodies, additional internees were killed when a camp official took shots at them.

Another frequent occurrence was the shooting of internees with three bullets in the back of the head of each victim. This was done at a drain, and the blood was allowed to go down the drain that emptied into the Sava River. Internees carried victims, some still alive, and had to dump their bodies at the camp garbage dump. Internees were sent on a detail to clean the blood from the floor and dump dead bodies outside of a Serbian building in Brčko. A female internee was sexually assaulted by a soldier while her husband and other internees watched. One Chetnik sexually assaulted several women, some as young as 12, in front of internees as Specijalci soldiers held the women to the ground. The same man killed 80–100 people at the camp. Another Chetnik sexually assaulted women and killed internees, in some cases using an ax to the head.

The dead bodies of internees from the Brčko camp were burned at the old "kafilerija" factory. The trucks carrying bodies drove into a building that had three industrial-sized cooking vats with furnaces used ordinarily to make animal feed. The bodies were dumped inside the building with the three furnaces, then Chetniks dumped the dead bodies into the furnaces. Before the bodies were dumped, jewelry was removed from them and, in order to remove rings, fingers were cut off. Gold and silver teeth were removed from the bodies as well. Chetniks kicked the jaws of the corpses open to see if they had gold or silver fillings and, if so, removed them with pliers.

The transporting of the bodies to be burned began in mid-May. Trucks left every morning at about 4 am. On a typical morning, three trucks left together. One was a civilian refrigerator truck with the dead bodies and three Chetniks in the cabin, the second had 10–12 internees who unloaded the bodies at the factory, and the third had approximately 13 Chetnik guards.

After they arrived at the factory and had began unloading bodies, two or three more refrigerator trucks often arrived with approximately 20 dead bodies transported in each vehicle, perhaps from another location. All the trucks were Yugoslavian-made civilian trucks. (Department of State)

21 May 92:

A former employee of the Zvornik medical center reported that he was required to remain on duty in the center from April 8 until his dismissal on May 26. He said that the need for more hospital space for wounded Serbian soldiers eventually led to the mass murder of Muslim patients on May 21. At about 1 pm that day, he watched as 36 remaining Muslim adult patients were forced outside and shot on hospital grounds.

Shortly thereafter, uniformed and non-uniformed Serbian soldiers moved through the pediatric center breaking the necks and bones of the 27 remaining Muslim children, the only children left as patients in the hospital. Two soldiers forced him to watch for about 15 minutes, during which time 10 or 15 of the children were slaughtered. Some were infants. The oldest were about 5 years old.

The witness said that a Serbian surgeon, who also stood by helplessly, later went insane. (Department of State)

November 1991:

International observers on November 20, 1991, monitored the evacuation of about 420 Croatian patients and 25 hospital staff of the Vukovar hospital in Croatia. A JNA army colonel selected young, lightly-wounded hospitalized soldiers to get on three buses. Each bus had about 60 men aboard, for a total of about 180 men.

Two witnesses—both among the "selected"—described how the buses were taken first to JNA barracks for 2 or 3 hours, then taken to Ovčara, where the prisoners were offloaded and taken to a farming equipment storage building. Paramilitary soldiers beat the prisoners at this location with fists, iron bars, and batons as officers watched. Apparently, two men died there from the beatings they received.

At about 5 pm on November 20 after it was quite dark, the men were divided into groups of about 20 men, taken outside the barn, and put on a truck. The truck returned empty about every 15 minutes. The truck drove about 3 kilometers southeast of Ovčara towards Grabovo and turned left onto a dirt road. Knowing that this road led to an extremely isolated area, one of the witnesses jumped from the truck and eventually lived to give this account. A member of the team working with UNHRC Special Rapporteur Mazowiecki discovered evidence on October 18–19, 1992, of a mass grave in the area from which the witness had escaped. The Croatian government claims that 174 people—believed to be buried in this mass grave—have never been found. The team member found skeletons of young adult males in an area of recently disturbed earth and a skull with a gunshot wound exiting from the left temple. (Department of State)

[THIRD SUBMISSION]

TORTURE OF PRISONERS

May-October 92:

A 33-year-old Muslim doctor from Prijedor, who had been interned in **Trnopolje** camp from May 25 until his release to the Karlovac transit center for ex-detainees on October 1, described the operation of a medical clinic in Trnopolje camp—the only reported clinic in any of the camp in the Prijedor area.

Trnopolje is a small village within the municipality of **Kozarac**, about 6 kilometers away. It lies on the railroad track between Prijedor and Omarska. Most maps identify it as "Kozarac Station." Trains came often through Trnopolje traveling to Banja Luka. Women, children, boys under 16, men over 65, and the very sick were loaded on through trains; able bodied men remained in Trnopolje.

The witness said that Serbian soldiers wandered through Trnopolje camp nightly, brutally beating the male prisoners and randomly raping female prisoners. They did this with the knowledge and permission of camp guards stationed at several locations at Trnopolje. The witness examined some of the raped women but was not allowed to indicate on any documents that they had been raped. The doctors kept a log of patients for a few weeks, until they were stopped by the Serbs. The doctors were not allowed to indicate in the log that patient had been beaten or raped, but the witness and others used a code to indicate who had been beaten or raped. The witness smuggled these logs out of the camp and turned them over to the Muslim club of Kozarac in Zagreb.

Several times the employees of the clinic came under suspicion, and their lives were threatened. One of the female aides was a Serb, and she was repeatedly interrogated and told to stop working at the clinic, but she stayed. The witness believes the presence of this Serb saved the lives of the other staff many times. (Department of State)

August 92:

A 40-year-old woman described how followers of Serbian leader **Milan Martić** selected women from her city and put hundreds of them in a school in **Doboj**.

In front of a few hundred prisoners they raped and tortured women and girls for days. It was unbearable to watch girls being raped in front of their fathers.

I was raped and tortured too, because they knew that I am a wife of a leader of the Muslim party. In August, some prisoners were exchanged, including me and my sons. Many women and girls who were pregnant remained in the camp. They were transferred to a hospital and fed twice a day, because, as the Chetniks said, they had to bear their offspring. (The New York Times)

May-August 92:

A 39-year-old Bosnian Muslim from **Prijedor** was held in **Keraterm** camp from May 31 until August 5. Upon his arrival at Keraterm, one guard—whom he identified—used a knife to saw off the witness's left index finger at the first knuckle and chopped of the tip of his left ring finger.

During his detention, the witness saw four guards cut another prisoner across the face and torso with a knife. One of the guards cut off the bottom half of the man's left ear. After the beating they left him in the room without any medical care. The man survived his injuries, but, after a few days his wounds became infected, and the witness said he could see maggots moving around inside the open wounds. The witness believes the man remains in Prijedor.

The witness described another form of cruelty he saw in Keraterm. The Serbian guards gathered two-liter glass bottles from a nearby bottling plant. A bottle would be placed on the ground and a prisoner, trousers and underwear pulled down, would be forced to sit upon it. The guards would then push down on the prisoner's shoulders until the man's buttocks touched the ground, forcing the bottle all the way up the man's anus. Of the guards he said: "Whatever they imagined, they tried; if they liked the effect they would do it to other prisoners." (Department of State)

OTHER, INCLUDING MASS FORCIBLE EXPULSION AND DEPORTATION OF CIVILIANS

12 January 93:

As many as 35,000 men, women, and children risk death by illness and starvation in Žepa. Bosnian Serbs refuse to permit food, medicines, and other supplies into the town. To this date they are not allowing any UN humanitarian convoys into Žepa. (Department of State)

WILLFUL KILLING

June–September 92:

A 32-year-old Muslim had fled with some other men into the woods around his village of Čarakovo in early May 1992. On June 22, after nearly 2 months of hiding, Serbian soldiers captured him, the six men with whom he had been hiding, and around 22 men from the village.

An estimated 40 Serb soldiers wearing JNA [Yugoslav National Army] uniforms marched the men along the road to a spot called Poljski Put near the Sidro Kavana (Anchor Cafe), where they ordered the men to sit on the ground. The Serb soldiers then threw two pictures of Tito onto the ground in front of the men and told some of them to tear up the pictures and eat them. After this, the Serbs began to take the men one by one off to the side to beat them.

The witness saw them carve orthodox crosses into the chest of some of the men. After each prisoner was beaten, he was taken into a nearby shed and shot. The beatings and killings lasted about 2 hours, during which time the group's commander was in a nearby yard and did nothing to stop the violence.

As the soldiers tried to carve a cross into the 20th man in the group, the prisoner struggled free—his head covered with the blood and one eyeball hanging from its socket. A soldier then shot the man in the head and nearly shot one of his comrades in the process. At this point , the commander ordered the soldiers to stop the killings before they kill one of their own. Thus, nine men, including the witness, survived.

The nine survivors were loaded onto a bus for Keraterm camp. As the bus drove off, the witness saw the shed that held the corpses of 20 dead men engulfed in flames.

This witness was in Room Three at Keraterm on the night of July 24, 1992, when Serbian guards opened fire on the room with machine guns. He said 157 men were killed, and 57 wounded.

On September 3, 1992, the witness was transferred with about 1,000 other prisoners to Trnopolje camp, where he said security is lax, and the prisoners were allowed out of the camp to find food. After 19 days at Trnopolje, the witness escaped. (Department of State)

3 July 92:

A middle-aged Muslim woman described the attack on her village of Trosan, near Foča.

Local Serbs had surrounded Trosan from April 8 to July 3, 1992, prohibiting Muslims from entering or leaving. Every night, the villagers slept in the woods out of fear of being attacked. They returned by day for food.

On July 3, an 80-member band of local Serbs attacked the sleeping villagers in the woods. The band called themselves White Eagles and had White Eagle emblems on the shoulders of their camouflage uniforms. Their leader was a man from a neighboring village and known to the witness.

The band started the attack by opening fire on the group, immediately killing Edhem Barlov, Esad Čalovo, Selima Pekaz, and Faila Odobašić. At least four others were wounded and a woman was beaten until she fainted. Everyone was treated roughly. Eventually another local Serb approached the group and told them to leave the villagers alone.

The villagers were then separated—men in one group, women in another. When the approximately 35 women and children were led away about 20 meters, the Serbs opened automatic weapons fire on the men. The women and children, who were not allowed to bury the dead or see who was killed, were led around Trosan, through the woods and observed the burning of all 30 homes in the village. (Department of State)

June-July 92:

A 55-year-old Bosnian Muslim from Brčko stated that Serbian forces "stormed" into the suburb of Novo Brčko. Chetniks, including White Eagle forces, shot rifles into the windows of residences and drove people into the street. All residents were put into six trucks, which made about three trips to ferry the people to an area where three schools were co-located.

The residents of Novo Brčko were gathered onto the combined athletic fields of the schools. With megaphones, the captors directed Serbs to one part of the field, Croats to another and yet Muslim to another. Members of mixed marriages and children were not permitted to remain together. Along with the group of males aged 13 or older, the witness was among the first prisoners taken to Luka camp, where he was forced to sign documents "selling" his property in Novo Brčko at a low price to a Serb whom he identified.

During his first days at the camp, the captors called out names of prisoners from electoral rolls. All those who were members of SDA (a Bosnian, primarily Muslim, political party) or who had held positions of leadership in business or industry were killed. Shootings often occurred at 4 am. The witness estimates that, during his first week at Luka, more than 2,000 men were killed or thrown into the Sava River. (See section that includes mass graves.)

After four days of mass shootings, there was a lull. From the fifth day, prisoners who were ethnic Serbs and were accused of being disloyal to the Chetnik cause were taken for interrogation and beatings.

The witness was interrogated on the seventh day of his captivity. This was the stage where detainees with property or money were subjected to questioning and torture. The witness, who was affluent, would not describe his own beating. By this point all prisoners who have known to have been politically active have already been killed.

Following his second week in the Luka facility, the witness said guards torture or kill Serbs who had hidden or helped Muslims. The camp commander designated a Bosnian

Serb who had been a waiter at Brčko hotel to seek out specific ethnic Serb prisoners for interrogation because he knew most of the Brčko area residents by name.

After the witness had been interrogated, he was taken with other prisoners to Hangar Two of the loading dock, where they were forced to look at a pile of more than 200 corpses or torsos. Most of the body parts had been chopped off: hands, arms, and genitals. The prisoners standing outside the Hangar Two were told [that] they would end up like that if they told lies while being interrogated.

When the 13-year-old son of Raško Kartal tried to protect his father from the sight, one of the Chetniks hit the boy with a butt of a gun shattering his face. The guard killed the father with three shots when Raško went after the guard for crushing the boy's face.

Looking out the window during one of his interrogation, the witness saw the soldiers gang-rape a woman whom he had known since his school days and murder her husband. A Brčko school teacher among the guards, an ethnic Serb, was shot dead for refusing to join the torture and killing of this couple. The witness identified many of those responsible for the atrocities at Luka, including its second camp commander. This commander, according to the witness, showed serious concern over the fact that some guards carried out their "duties" with knives. Most other guards at Luka were also visibly afraid ofthe knife-wielding guards, who were regularly seen castrating male prisoners. (Department of State)

1 June 92:

A 62-year-old Bosnian Muslim witness the willful killing by ethnic Serb paramilitary forces of at least 53 men, women, and children in the village of Prhovo, Bosnia.

At about 3 PM on May 30, 1992, a large force of ethnic Serb paramilitary soldiers and three armored personnel carriers entered Prhovo, a village located about 7 kilometers northeast of Ključ. The village, which contained 45 houses grouped along the main road and several small streets, had more than 150 inhabitants.

The soldiers who wore stocking masks over their face, went from house to house searching for weapons. After finding some weapons, the soldiers proceeded to ransack the homes, break windows and doors, and pull the residents out into the streets. These men, women, and children were ordered to fold their hands behind their heads and were herded through the village to a point on the road where they were stopped and lined up.

Meanwhile the soldiers attempted to coax back into the village those residents who had run into the woods when the soldiers arrived. The soldiers announced through megaphones that the residents would not be harmed if they returned. When these people returned, the soldiers beat them severely; about 10 were beaten into unconsciousness.

The assembled villagers were then told that they were free, that they need not worry anymore, and that they must place white flags on their homes to indicate the village had surrender. During the nights of May 30–31, some people fled to the woods, while others slept in their cellars.

At about 6 PM on June 1, the soldiers returned and again used megaphones to call people in from the forest. They also went from house to house, pulling people out into the streets. The male residents were beaten severely. At about 7 PM, the soldiers began murdering the residents with automatic weapons. They fired single shots then long bursts of automatic gunfire.

After the shooting stopped and the soldiers had departed, the witness, who had fled to the woods when the shooting started, returned to the village. The murdered men, women, and the children lay in the streets. Houses were burning, and their roofs were collapsing. Some women and children who had hidden in basements began coming into the street crying and looking for their loved ones.

The following 53 people were killed in the massacre:

1. Ekrem HADŽIĆ, 32
2. Izet HADŽIĆ, 30
3. Suvad HADŽIĆ, 31
4. Zijad HADŽIĆ, 30, husband of No.5
5. Rubija HADŽIĆ, 32, wife of No.4
6. Amel HADŽIĆ, 14, son of Nos. 4 and 5
7. Amela HADŽIĆ, 9, daughter of Nos. 4 and 5
8. Hajro HADŽIĆ, 55
9. Hasim HADŽIĆ, 34, son of No.8
10. Senad HADŽIĆ, 17, grandson of No.8
11. Ilfad BRKOVIĆ, 45, husband of No.12
12. Rasema BRKOVIĆ, 45, wife of No.11
13. Nisveta BRKOVIĆ, 10, daughter of Nos. 11 and 12
14. Ćamil MEDANOVIĆ, 40
15. Enes MEDANOVIĆ, 21
16. Sulejman MEDANOVIĆ, 55
17. Ahmo MEDANOVIĆ, 59, brother of No.16
18. Vahid MEDANOVIĆ, 60
19. Suvad MEDANOVIĆ, 23, son of No.18
20. Safet MEDANOVIĆ, 32
21. Nasiha MEDANOVIĆ, 30
22. Enesa MEDANOVIĆ, 20
23. Fadila MEDANOVIĆ, 18
24. Hadžera MEDANOVIĆ, 65
25. Indira MEDANOVIĆ, 7
26. Hava MEDANOVIĆ, 30
27. Arif MEDANOVIĆ, 70
28. Šefik MEDANOVIĆ, 28
29. Teufik MEDANOVIĆ, 30
30. Fatima MEDANOVIĆ, 55
31. Midheta MEDANOVIĆ, 18
32. Hasan MEDANOVIĆ, 45

33. Halil MEDANOVIĆ, 22, son of No.32
34. Mujo MEDANOVIĆ, 15, son of No.32
35. Hilmo JUSIĆ
36. Nedžad JUSIĆ
37. Nermin JUSIĆ
38. Enisa JUSIĆ
39. Azemina JUSIĆ
40. Emira JUSIĆ
41. Samira JUSIĆ
42. Latif JUSIĆ
43. Ramiza JUSIĆ
44. Osme JUSIĆ
45. Isak MESIĆ
46. Ismet MESIĆ
47. Gane MESIĆ
48. Ismeta MESIĆ
49. Kamanfie OSMANOVIĆ
50. Tehvid OSMANOVIĆ
51. Rufad OSMANOVIĆ
52. Mehmed DEDIĆ
53. Hamdo ISLAMAGIĆ

Most of the survivors left Prhovo on June 2 to live with friends and relatives in nearby villages. The witness and few other Muslim men buried the dead on June 9. (Department of State)

[SEVENTH SUBMISSION]

1 Jun 93:

Bosnian Serb mortar crews shelled a soccer game in the Sarajevo suburb of Dobrinja where about 200 Bosnians, celebrating a Muslim holiday, were watching the game. The attack killed at least 11 people and wounded at least 80, about 25 of those with life-threatening injuries.

25 Apr 93:

A UN Security Council mission to Srebrenica called the Muslim enclave "an open jail" where Serbian forces were planning "slow-motion genocide." Serbian nationalist forces had cut off water and electricity supplies to Srebrenica, reportedly in retaliation for similar actions against Serbian villages earlier in the war, when the Muslims still controlled the source. (The New York Times)

12 Apr 93:

Serb nationalist forces shelled Srebrenica twice on April 12, once from 2:15 pm to 3:20 pm, and the second time from 3:50 pm to 4:10 pm. Most or all of the dead were civilians, including 15 children.

Rounds fell first at the north end of town and proceeded toward the south end of town. At least 14 children were found dead in the school yard, where they had been playing football.

During the next barrage of direct shelling, a child of about six years of age was decapitated. The UNHCR representative who witnessed these attacks said: "I will never be able to convey the sheer horror of the atrocity I witnessed on April 12. Suffice it to say that I did not look forward to closing my eyes at night for fear that I would relive the images of a nightmare that was not a dream."

As of April 13, total casualties in the town of Srebrenica were 56 dead and approximately 100 wounded. A senior UN official in Zagreb called the Srebrenica shelling a violation of international conventions prohibiting attacks on civilian targets. "It is an atrocity," he said. (Department of State, API, The Washington Post, The New York Times)

7 May 93:

Bosnian Serbs blew up the 1587 Ferhad-Paša mosque and the 1587 Arnaudija mosque, both located in Banja Luka. Yugoslav President Ćosić issued a statement calling the bombing an "act of barbarity" and "the final warning to all reasonable and responsible people on all warring sides to act resolutely, immediately and with all means at their disposal to stop the war and destruction." (The New York Times)

[EIGHTH SUBMISSION]

Serb officials explain that the towns were destroyed in "the war." But war is random, and in these villages nothing is random. Every house has been destroyed in exactly the same way—from within, by demolition squads. In fact, there's so little external damage that it's clear no battles were fought here at all.

There is no resentful subject population in the towns that the Serbs have seized, because there is no one left. One village remains in my mind long after this bus journey ends. The most beautiful long-stemmed yellow flowers are blooming everywhere. In this village not one house is left unburned. There is not one sign of human life—only those glorious yellow flowers. It's as though the flowers, in spectacular profusion, have moved in to fill the ecological niche once held by people.

T. D. Allman
"Serbia's Blood War"
Why Bosnia? Writings on the Balkan War

The expression "ethnic cleansing" is relatively new. Considered in the context of the conflicts in former Yugoslavia, 'ethnic cleansing' means rendering an area ethnically homogenous by using force or intimidation to remove persons of given groups from the area. 'Ethnic cleansing' is contrary to international law....The Commission confirms its earlier view that "ethnic cleansing" is a purposeful policy designed by one ethnic or religious group to remove by violent and terror-inspiring means the civilian population of another ethnic or religious group from certain geographic areas. To a large extent, it is carried out in the name of misguided nationalism, historic grievances and a powerful driving sense of revenge. This purpose appears to be the occupation of territory to the exclusion of the purged group or groups.

Final Report of the Commission of Experts

V

FINAL REPORT OF THE COMMISSION OF EXPERTS
TO THE SECRETARY GENERAL
OF THE UNITED NATIONS

This document consists of excerpts from the *Final Report of the Commission of Experts* established pursuant to Security Council resolution 780 (1992) to present its findings to the Secretary General of the United Nations on grave breaches of the Geneva Conventions and other violations of international humanitarian law in the territories of the former Yugoslavia. For full text of the Report, see U.N. Doc. S/1994/674 (1994).

FINAL REPORT OF THE COMMISSION OF EXPERTS
TO THE SECRETARY GENERAL OF THE UNITED NATIONS

On 6 October 1992 the Security Council adopted resolution 780 (1992), by which it requested the Secretary-General to establish a Commission of Experts to examine and analyse, inter alia, information submitted pursuant to Security Council resolutions 771 (1992) of 13 August 1992 and 780 (1992) of 6 October 1992, with a view to providing the Secretary-General with its conclusions on the evidence of grave breaches of the Geneva Conventions and other violations of international humanitarian law committed in the territory of the former Yugoslavia....

Having considered the recommendations in the interim report of the Commission of Experts (S/25274, annex I (hereinafter first interim report)), the Security Council decided in its resolution 808 (1993) of 22 February 1993 that an international tribunal should be established for the prosecution of persons responsible for serious violations of international humanitarian law committed in the territory of the former Yugoslavia since 1991. On 25 May 1993, the Council, by its resolution 827 (1993), acting under Chapter VII of the Charter of the United Nations, adopted the statute of the International Tribunal for the Prosecution of Persons Responsible for Serious Violations of International Humanitarian Law Committed in the Territory of the Former Yugoslavia since 1991 contained in the report of the Secretary-General (S/25704, annex). To this effect, the Council requested the Commission, pending the appointment of the Prosecutor of the International Tribunal, to continue on an urgent basis the collection of information relating to its mandate.

The Commission took note of references made to it by different organs and bodies of the United Nations system. Specifically, it took note of General Assembly resolution 47/147 of 18 December 1992, in which the Assembly reaffirmed that all persons who perpetrate or authorize crimes against humanity or other grave breaches of international humanitarian law are individually responsible for those breaches and that the international community would exert every effort to bring them to justice, and called upon all parties to provide all pertinent information to the Commission.

* * * * * *

APPLICABLE LAW

The Commission has chosen to comment on selected legal issues because of their particular significance for understanding the legal context related to violations of international humanitarian law committed in the territory of the former Yugoslavia. The Commission's mandate is to provide the Secretary-General with its conclusions on the evidence of such violations and not to provide an analysis of the legal issues. It will be for the International Tribunal to make legal findings in connection with particular cases.

A. International/non-international character of the conflict

Classification of the various conflicts in the former Yugoslavia as international or non-international depends on important factual and legal issues. If a conflict is classified as international, then the grave breaches of the Geneva Conventions, including Additional Protocol I, apply as well as violations of the laws and customs of war. The treaty and customary law applicable to international armed conflicts is well-established....

To date, the major conflicts in the territory of the former Yugoslavia have occurred in Croatia and in Bosnia and Herzegovina. Determining when these conflicts are internal and when they are international is a difficult task because the legally relevant facts are not yet generally agreed upon. This task is one which must be performed by the International Tribunal.

However, as indicated in paragraph 45 of its first interim report, the Commission is of the opinion that the character and complexity of the armed conflicts concerned, combined with the web of agreements on humanitarian law that the parties have concluded among themselves, justifies the Commission's approach in applying the law applicable in international armed conflicts to the entirety of the armed conflicts in the territory of the former Yugoslavia.

B. Grave breaches of the Geneva Conventions of 1949 and Protocols I and II

"Grave breaches" are specified major violations of international humanitarian law which may be punished by any State on the basis of universal jurisdiction....

Under all four Conventions, grave breaches prohibit, inter alia, willful killing, torture, rape or inhuman treatment of protected persons, including biological experiments, willfully causing great suffering or serious injury to body or health, and extensive destruction and appropriation of property, not justified by military necessity and carried out unlawfully and wantonly.

In the case of prisoners of war, it is also a grave breach to compel a prisoner of war to serve in the forces of the hostile power or to deprive him of his rights to a fair and regular trial. In the case of civilians in the hands of the adverse party, it is also a grave breach to:

a. Unlawfully deport or transfer a protected person;

b. Unlawfully confine a protected person;

c. Compel a protected person to serve in the forces of a hostile power;

d.   Willfully deprive a protected person of the rights of fair and regular trial prescribed;

e.   Take hostages.

Article 11 of Additional Protocol I makes a number of medical practices grave breaches of the Protocol.

Under article 85, paragraph 3, of Additional Protocol I, the following acts constitute grave breaches if committed willfully, in violation of the relevant provisions of the Protocol, and causing death or serious injury to body or health:

"(a) Making the civilian population or individual civilians the object of attack;

"(b) Launching an indiscriminate attack affecting the civilian population or civilian objects in the knowledge that such attack will cause excessive loss of life, injury to civilians or damage to civilian objects ...;

"(c) Launching an attack against works or installations containing dangerous forces in the knowledge that such attack will cause excessive loss of life, injury to civilians or damage to civilian objects ...;

"(d) Making non-defended localities and demilitarized zones the object of attack;

"(e) Making a person the object of attack in the knowledge that he is hors de combat;

"(f) The perfidious use ... of the distinctive emblem of the red cross, red crescent or red lion and sun or of other protective signs recognized by the Conventions or this Protocol."

Additional Protocol I also provides, in article 85, paragraph 4 that certain acts are grave breaches when committed willfully and in violation of the Conventions or Protocol, namely:

"(a) The transfer by an Occupying Power of parts of its own civilian population into occupied territory it occupies or the deportation or transfer of all or parts of the population of that territory within or out of this territory ...;

"(b) Unjustifiable delay in the repatriation of prisoners of war or civilians;

"(c) Practices of apartheid and other inhuman and degrading practices involving outrages upon personal dignity, based on racial discrimination;

"(d) Making the clearly-recognized historic monuments, works of art or places of worship which constitute the cultural or spiritual heritage of peoples and to which special protection has been given by special arrangement, ... the object of attack, causing as a result extensive destruction thereof, where there is no evidence of (prior use of such objects in support of the adverse party's military effort), and when such (places) are not located in the immediate proximity of military objectives;

"(e) Depriving any person protected by the Conventions (or the Protocol) of fair and regular trial."

It must be noted that the statute of the International Tribunal refers to grave breaches of the Geneva Conventions of 1949 in article 2 and to violations of the laws or customs of war in article 3. It does not refer explicitly to grave breaches of Additional Protocol I. Many of the grave breaches of Additional Protocol I also constitute violations of the laws and customs of war.

C. Customary international law of armed conflict

It is necessary to distinguish between customary international law applicable to international armed conflict and to internal armed conflict. The treaty-based law applicable to internal armed conflicts is relatively recent and is contained in common article 3 of the Geneva Conventions, Additional Protocol II, and article 19 of the 1954 Hague Convention on Cultural Property. It is unlikely that there is any body of customary international law applicable to internal armed conflict which does not find its root in these treaty provisions. It is probable that common article 3 would be viewed as a statement of customary international law, but unlikely that the other instruments would be so viewed. In particular, there does not appear to be a customary international law applicable to internal armed conflicts which includes the concept of war crimes.

The body of customary international law applicable to international armed conflicts includes the concept of war crimes, and a wide range of provisions also stated in Hague Convention IV of 1907, the Geneva Conventions of 1949 and, to some extent, the provisions of Additional Protocol I.

It must be observed that the violations of the laws or customs of war referred to in article 3 of the statute of the International Tribunal are offences when committed in international, but not in internal armed conflicts.

D. Command responsibility

The Commission addressed the matter of command responsibility in paragraphs 51 through 53 of its first interim report as follows:

"51. A person who gives the order to commit a war crime or crime against humanity is equally guilty of the offence with the person actually committing it. This principle, expressed already in the Geneva Conventions of 1949, applies to both the military superiors, whether of regular or irregular armed forces, and to civilian authorities.

"52. Superiors are moreover individually responsible for a war crime or crime against humanity committed by a subordinate if they knew, or had information which should have enabled them to conclude, in the circumstances at the time, that the subordinate was committing or was going to commit such an act and they did not take all feasible measures within their power to prevent or repress the act.

"53. Military commanders are under a special obligation, with respect to members of the armed forces under their command or other persons under their control, to prevent and, where necessary, to suppress such acts and to report them to competent authorities."

The Commission notes with satisfaction that article 7 of the statute of the International Tribunal uses an essentially similar formulation.

The doctrine of command responsibility is directed primarily at military commanders because such persons have a personal obligation to ensure the maintenance of discipline among troops under their command. Most legal cases in which the doctrine of command responsibility has been considered have involved military or paramilitary accused. Political leaders and public officials have also been held liable under this doctrine in certain circumstances.

It is the view of the Commission that the mental element necessary when the commander has not given the offending order is (a) actual knowledge, (b) such serious personal dereliction on the part of the commander as to constitute willful and wanton disregard of the possible consequences, or (c) an imputation of constructive knowledge, that is, despite pleas to the contrary, the commander, under the facts and circumstances of the particular case, must have known of the offences charged and acquiesced therein. To determine whether or not a commander must have known about the acts of his subordinates, one might consider a number of indices, including:

a. The number of illegal acts;
b. The type of illegal acts;
c. The scope of illegal acts;
d. The time during which the illegal acts occurred;
e. The number and type of troops involved;
f. The logistics involved, if any;
g. The geographical location of the acts;
h. The widespread occurrence of the acts;
i. The tactical tempo of operations;
j. The modus operandi of similar illegal acts;
k. The officers and staff involved;
l. The location of the commander at the time.

The military commander is not absolutely responsible for all offences committed by his subordinates. Isolated offences may be committed of which he has no knowledge or control whatsoever. As a fundamental aspect of command, however, a commander does have a duty to control his troops and to take all practicable measures to ensure that they comply with the law. The arguments that a commander has a weak personality or that the troops assigned to him are uncontrollable are invalid. In particular, a military commander who is assigned command and control over armed combatant groups who have engaged in war crimes in the past should refrain from employing such groups in combat, until they clearly demonstrate their intention and capability to comply with the law in the future. Thus, a commander has a duty to do everything reasonable and practicable to prevent violations of the law. Failure to carry out such a duty carries with it responsibility.

Lastly, a military commander has the duty to punish or discipline those under his command whom he knows or has reasonable grounds to know committed a violation.

E. Superior orders

In paragraph 54 of its first interim report, the Commission made the following statement:

"54. A subordinate who has carried out an order of a superior or acted under government instructions and thereby has committed a war crime or a crime against humanity, may raise the so-called defence of superior orders, claiming that he cannot be held criminally liable for an act he was ordered to commit. The Commission notes that the applicable treaties unfortunately are silent on the matter. The Commission's interpretation of the customary international law, particularly as stated in the Nuremberg principles, is that the fact that a person acted pursuant to an order of his Government or of a superior does not relieve him from responsibility under international law, provided a moral choice was in fact available to him."

The Commission notes with satisfaction that article 7, paragraph 4, of the statute of the International Tribunal adopts an essentially similar approach on this subject.

F. Reprisals

A reprisal must be distinguished from a simple act of retaliation or vengeance. An unlawful act committed under the guise of retaliation or vengeance remains unlawful, and the claim of retaliation or vengeance is no defence.

A reprisal is an otherwise illegal act resorted to after the adverse party has himself indulged in illegal acts and refused to desist therefrom after being called upon to do so. The purpose of a reprisal is to compel the adverse party to terminate its illegal activity. It must be proportionate to the original wrongdoing and must be terminated as soon as the original wrongdoer ceases his illegal actions. The proportionality is not strict, for if the reprisal is to be effective, it will often be greater than the original wrongdoing. Nevertheless, there must be a reasonable relationship between the original wrong and the reprisal measure.

However, reprisals against the following categories of persons and objects are specifically prohibited:

a. The wounded, sick, personnel, buildings or equipment protected by the First Geneva Convention (art. 46);
b. The wounded, sick and shipwrecked persons, the personnel, the vessels and equipment protected by the Second Geneva Convention (art. 47);
c. Prisoners of war (Third Geneva Convention, art. 13 and Additional Protocol I, art. 44);
d. Civilians in the hands of a party to the conflict of which they are not nationals, including inhabitants of occupied territory (Fourth Geneva Convention, art. 33 and Additional Protocol I, art.73);
e. Civilians (Additional Protocol I, art. 51, para. 6);
f. Civilian objects (Additional Protocol I, art. 52, para. 1);
g. Cultural objects and places of worship (Additional Protocol I, art. 53 (c));
h. Objects indispensable to the survival of the civilian population (Additional Protocol I, art. 54, para. 4);
i. The natural environment (Additional Protocol I, art. 55, para. 2);

j.   Works and installations containing dangerous forces (Additional Protocol I, art. 56, para. 4).

There is no ban on reprisals contained in common article 3 and Additional Protocol II applicable to internal armed conflict. In international armed conflicts to which the four Geneva Conventions and Additional Protocol I apply, lawful reprisals as defined above must be directed exclusively against combatants or other military objectives subject to the limitations contained in the Geneva Conventions, Protocol I and customary international law of armed conflicts. In international armed conflicts where Additional Protocol I does not apply, reprisals may be directed against a much wider category of persons and objects, but subject to the limitations of customary international law of armed conflicts.

G. Interference with humanitarian aid convoys

Interference with humanitarian aid convoys is a practice which has been all too prevalent in the various conflicts in the former Yugoslavia.

The Commission is of the view that, when and where the law relating to international armed conflicts applies, the provisions of article 54 of Additional Protocol I are also applicable. This article states in part:

"1.   Starvation of civilians as a method of warfare is prohibited.

"2.   It is prohibited to attack, destroy, remove or render useless objects indispensable to the survival of the civilian population, such as foodstuffs, agricultural areas for the production of foodstuffs, crops, livestock, drinking water installations and supplies and irrigation works, for the specific purpose of denying them for their sustenance value to the civilian population or to the adverse Party, whatever the motive, whether in order to starve out civilians, to cause them to move away or for any other motive."

The use of starvation as a method of war, regardless of the modalities used, is also contrary to the customary law applicable in international armed conflicts.

The Commission also considers article 70, paragraphs 2 to 4, of Additional Protocol I to apply:

"2.   The parties to the conflict and each High Contracting Party shall allow and facilitate rapid and unimpeded passage of all relief consignments, equipment and personnel provided in accordance with this Section, even if such assistance is destined for the civilian population of the adverse party.

"3.   The parties to the conflict and each High Contracting Party which allow the passage of relief consignments, equipment and personnel in accordance with paragraph 2:

"(a) Shall have the right to prescribe the technical arrangements, including search, under which such passage is permitted;

"(b) May make such permission conditional on the distribution of this assistance being made under the local supervision of a Protecting Power;

"(c) Shall, in no way whatsoever, divert relief consignments from the purpose for which they are intended nor delay their forwarding, except in cases of urgent necessity in the interest of the civilian population concerned.

"4. The parties to the conflict shall protect relief consignments and facilitate their rapid distribution."

The Commission deplores any acts taken to interfere with humanitarian aid convoys, as the safe and expeditious passage of these convoys is essential to the well-being of the civilian population.

H. Crimes against humanity

Article 5 of the statute of the International Tribunal affirms the competence of the International Tribunal to prosecute persons committing "crimes against humanity", which are defined as specified acts "committed in armed conflict, whether international or internal in character, and directed against any civilian population," such as national, political, ethnic, racial or religious groups.

The definition of "crimes against humanity" in article 5 of the statute codifies accepted principles of international law applicable erga omnes. As ascertained by the International Military Tribunal at Nuremberg, there are "elementary dictates of humanity" to be recognized under all circumstances. The General Assembly in its resolution 95 (I) of 11 December 1946 affirmed the principles of international law recognized by the Charter of the Nuremberg Tribunal and the judgement of the Tribunal.

The Nuremberg application of "crimes against humanity" was a response to the shortcoming in international law that many crimes committed during the Second World War could not technically be regarded as war crimes stricto sensu on account of one or several elements, which were of a different nature. It was, therefore, conceived to redress crimes of an equally serious character and on a vast scale, organized and systematic, and most ruthlessly carried out.

1. Armed conflict

Crimes against humanity apply to all contexts. They are not, therefore, confined to situations of international armed conflict, but also apply to all armed conflicts including internal ones—civil wars and insurrection—and whatever casus mixtus may arise in between internal and international armed conflict. Thus, it includes all armed conflicts, whether they are of an international or non-international character. However, not every act committed by force of arms is an armed conflict; a genuine armed conflict has to be distinguished from a mere act of banditry or an unorganized and short-lived insurrection. Crimes against humanity are also no longer dependent on their linkage to crimes against peace or war crimes.

Articles 2 and 3 of the statute of the International Tribunal for the Prosecution of Persons Responsible for Serious Violations of International Humanitarian Law Committed in the Territory of the Former Yugoslavia since 1991 address grave breaches of the Geneva

Conventions of 1949 and violations of the laws and customs of war. Article 5, which concerns crimes against humanity, contains minimum provisions which must be respected, a fortiori, whether or not articles 2 or 3 are applicable to a specific conflict.

2. Protected persons

Article 5 of the statute of the International Tribunal protects "any civilian population", which undoubtedly includes the whole of the populations of the area afflicted by the armed conflict, without any adverse distinction based, in particular, on race, nationality, religion or political opinion. Refugees are not different from other civilians, and as such are protected within the meaning of "civilian population". "Civilian population" is used in this context in contradistinction to combatants or members of armed forces.

It seems obvious that article 5 applies first and foremost to civilians, meaning people who are not combatants. This, however, should not lead to any quick conclusions concerning people who at one particular point in time did bear arms. One practical example: in the former Yugoslavia, large-scale arbitrary killings were one of the hallmarks of attacks by a given group. Information about such arbitrary killings was then used by the same group to instill fear and demand total subjugation of the other group in other areas as well. Many of the most barbarous onslaughts on villages started with heavy artillery bombardments followed by the villages being stormed by infantry in tandem, while paramilitary groups sought the inhabitants in each and every house. A head of family who under such circumstances tries to protect his family gun-in-hand does not thereby lose his status as a civilian. Maybe the same is the case for the sole policeman or local defence guard doing the same, even if they joined hands to try to prevent the cataclysm. Information of the overall circumstances is relevant for the interpretation of the provision in a spirit consistent with its purpose. Under such circumstances, the distinction between improvised self-defence and actual military defence may be subtle, but none the less important. This is no less so when the legitimate authorities in the area—as part and parcel of an overall plan of destruction—had previously been given an ultimatum to arm all the local defence guards.

The International Military Tribunal at Nuremberg stated the following concerning crimes against humanity and the importance of the overall circumstances:

> "The defendant contends that stealing the personal property of Jews and other concentration camp inmates is not a crime against humanity. But under the circumstances which we have here related (emphasis added), this plea is and must be rejected. What was done was done pursuant to a government policy, and the thefts were part of a program of extermination and were one of its objectives. It would be a strange doctrine indeed, if, where part of the plan and one of the objectives of murder was to obtain the property of the victim, even to the extent of using the hair from his head and the gold of his mouth, he who knowingly took part in disposing of the loot must be exonerated and held not guilty as a participant in the murder plan. Without doubt all such acts are crimes against humanity and he who participates or plays a consenting part therein is guilty of a crime against humanity."[1]

It is significant to note that Protocol II to the Geneva Conventions of 1949 Relating to the Protection of Victims of Non- International Armed Conflicts addresses "fundamental guarantees" in article 4 and includes in the protected group "all persons who do not take a direct part or who have ceased to take part in hostilities".

3. Acts constituting crimes against humanity

The different acts constituting crimes against humanity are enumerated in article 5 of the statute of the International Tribunal for the Prosecution of Persons Responsible for Serious Violations of International Humanitarian Law Committed in the Territory of the Former Yugoslavia since 1991. Such acts are: "murder, extermination, enslavement, deportation, imprisonment, torture, rape, persecutions on political, racial and religious grounds and other inhumane acts". "Other inhumane acts" covers serious crimes of a nature similar to the other crimes cited. It is not equally obvious if the eiusdem generis principle of interpretation will rule out a wider interpretation. It is necessary to ascertain that the acts included in the concept of "crimes against humanity" correspond to what is already considered part of international customary law.

In the context of crimes against humanity, it is relevant to observe that the same kind of prohibited acts listed in common article 3 (relevant to conflicts not of an international character) in the four Geneva Conventions of 1949, and in Protocol II to the Geneva Conventions are mere codification of elementary dictates of humanity. Article 3 prohibits "violence to life and person, in particular murder of all kinds, mutilation, cruel treatment and torture; taking of hostages; outrages upon personal dignity, in particular humiliating and degrading treatment; and the passing of sentences and the carrying out of executions without previous judgment pronounced by a regularly constituent court, affording all the judicial guarantees which are recognized as indispensable by civilized peoples". Article 4 bans "violence to the life, health and physical or mental well-being of persons, in particular murder, as well as cruel treatment such as torture, mutilation or any form of corporal punishment; collective punishment; taking of hostages; acts of terrorism; outrages upon personal dignity, in particular humiliating and degrading treatment, rape, enforced prostitution and any form of indecent assaults; slavery and the slave trade in all their forms; pillage; and threats to commit any of the foregoing acts". The former Yugoslavia signed Protocol II on 11 June 1979 and ratified it that same day, without reservations, declarations or objections.

Crimes against humanity are not confined to situations where there exists an intent to destroy, in whole or in part, a national, ethnical, racial or religious group, as such, which are preconditions for genocide. Crimes against humanity are, however, serious international violations directed against the protected persons, in contradistinction to a fate befalling them merely as a side-effect, for example, of a military operation dictated by military necessity.

4. Widespread and systematic nature of the acts

Isolated acts constituting offences, such as extra-judicial executions or other common crimes punishable under municipal law, do not qualify as crimes against humanity by themselves. The acts must be part of a policy of persecution or discrimination. In addition, the acts must be carried out in a systematic way or by means of a mass action. Thus, the number of victims and perpetrators are characteristically high. Because the perpetrators have a common plan containing the elements described above, they need not resort to the same means or acts against their victims. It is the systematic process of victimization against the protected group which is essential. For example, a number of interviewees reported that some persons had been crucified, but it is not necessary that all victims of the protected group be crucified or that this particular inhumane act be recognized in and of itself to be part of a crime against humanity. It is the overall context of large-scale victimization carried out as part of a common plan or design which goes to the element of systematicity.

It should be noted that the ensuing upsurge in crimes that follows a general breakdown of law and order does not qualify as crimes against humanity. However, a general breakdown in law and order may be a premeditated instrument, a situation carefully orchestrated to hide the true nature of the intended harm. Thus, it should not be accepted at face value that the perpetrators are merely uncontrolled elements, especially not if these elements target almost exclusively groups also otherwise discriminated against and persecuted. Unwillingness to manage, prosecute and punish uncontrolled elements may be another indication that these elements are, in reality, but a useful tool for the implementation of a policy of crime against humanity.

Crimes against humanity may also amount to extermination of national, ethnical, racial, religious or other groups, whether or not the intent that makes such crimes punishable as genocide can be proven. They may also, through inhumane acts, amount to large-scale human degradation. The scale and nature of such crimes become of special significance and of concern to the international community because of the abhorrent character of the overall policy, the means employed to carry out the policy and the number of victims it produces.

I. Genocide

The 1948 Convention on the Prevention and Punishment of the Crime of Genocide states that "genocide is a crime under international law, contrary to the spirit and aims of the United Nations and condemned by the civilized world", and that "at all periods of history genocide has inflicted great losses on humanity".[2]

The Convention was manifestly adopted for humanitarian and civilizing purposes. Its objectives are to safeguard the very existence of certain human groups and to affirm and emphasize the most elementary principles of humanity and morality. In view of the rights involved, the legal obligations to refrain from genocide are recognized as erga omnes.

When the Convention was drafted, it was already envisaged that it would apply not only to then existing forms of genocide, but also "to any method that might be evolved in the future with a view to destroying the physical existence of a group".[3] As emphasized in the preamble to the Convention, genocide has marred all periods of history, and it is this very tragic recognition that gives the concept its historical evolutionary nature.

The Convention must be interpreted in good faith, in accordance with the ordinary meaning of its terms, in their context, and in the light of its object and purpose. Moreover, the text of the Convention should be interpreted in such a way that a reason and a meaning can be attributed to every word. No word or provision may be disregarded or treated as superfluous, unless this is absolutely necessary to give effect to the terms read as a whole.

Genocide is a crime under international law regardless of "whether committed in time of peace or in time of war" (art. I). Thus, irrespective of the context in which it occurs (for example, peace time, internal strife, international armed conflict or whatever the general overall situation) genocide is a punishable international crime.

The acts specified in the Convention must be "committed with intent to destroy, in whole or in part, a national, ethnical, racial or religious group, as such" (art. II).

1. The extent of destruction of a group

Destruction of a group in whole or in part does not mean that the group in its entirety must be exterminated. The words "in whole or in part" were inserted in the text to make it clear that it is not necessary to aim at killing all the members of the group.

If essentially the total leadership of a group is targeted, it could also amount to genocide. Such leadership includes political and administrative leaders, religious leaders, academics and intellectuals, business leaders and others—the totality per se may be a strong indication of genocide regardless of the actual numbers killed. A corroborating argument will be the fate of the rest of the group. The character of the attack on the leadership must be viewed in the context of the fate or what happened to the rest of the group. If a group has its leadership exterminated, and at the same time or in the wake of that, has a relatively large number of the members of the group killed or subjected to other heinous acts, for example deported on a large scale or forced to flee, the cluster of violations ought to be considered in its entirety in order to interpret the provisions of the Convention in a spirit consistent with its purpose. Similarly, the extermination of a group's law enforcement and military personnel may be a significant section of a group in that it renders the group at large defenceless against other abuses of a similar or other nature, particularly if the leadership is being eliminated as well. Thus, the intent to destroy the fabric of a society through the extermination of its leadership, when accompanied by other acts of elimination of a segment of society, can also be deemed genocide.

2. The groups protected

National, ethnical, racial or religious groups are all protected. The different groups relevant to the conflict in the former Yugoslavia—the Serbs, the Croats, the Muslims, the Gypsies and others—all have status as ethnic groups, and may, at least in part, be characterized by religion, ethnicity and nationality. It is not a condition that the victim group be a minority, it might as well be a numerical majority.

If there are several or more than one victim groups, and each group as such is protected, it may be within the spirit and purpose of the Convention to consider all the victim groups as a larger entity. The case being, for example, that there is evidence that group A wants to destroy in whole or in part groups B, C and D, or rather everyone who does not belong to the national, ethnic, racial or religious group A. In a sense, group A has defined a pluralistic non-A group using national, ethnic, racial and religious criteria for the definition. It seems relevant to analyse the fate of the non-A group along similar lines as if the non-A group had been homogenous. This is important if, for example, group B and to a lesser degree group C have provided the non-A group with all its leaders. Group D, on the other hand, has a more marginal role in the non-A group community because of its small numbers or other reasons. Genocide, "an odious scourge" which the Convention intends "to liberate mankind from" (preamble), would as a legal concept be a weak or even useless instrument if the overall circumstances of mixed groups were not covered. The core of this reasoning is that in one-against-everyone-else cases the question of a significant number or a significant section of the group must be answered with reference to all the target groups as a larger whole.

3. Intent

It is the element of intent to destroy a designated group in whole or in part, which makes crimes of mass murder and crimes against humanity qualify as genocide. To be genocide within the meaning of the Convention, the crimes against a number of individuals must be directed at their collectivity or at them in their collective character or capacity. This can be deduced from the words "as such" stated in article II of the Convention (see para. 92). In most countries, penal codes do not regard motives, rather only intent, as the subjective or mental constituent element of a crime. Motive and intent may be closely linked, but motive is not mentioned in the Convention. The necessary element of intent may be inferred from sufficient facts. In certain cases, there will be evidence of actions or omissions of such a degree that the defendant may reasonably be assumed to have been aware of the consequences of his or her conduct, which goes to the establishment of intent, but not necessarily motive.

4. Acts constituting the crime of genocide

The different acts constituting the crime of genocide are enumerated in article II of the Convention. Such acts are: "killing members of a national, ethnical, racial or religious group, causing serious bodily or mental harm to members of the group, deliberately inflicting on the group conditions of life calculated to bring about its physical destruction in whole or in part, imposing measures intended to prevent births within the group and forcibly transferring children of the group to another group". Each of these categories of acts can constitute the crime of genocide, as could any combination of these acts.

5. Punishable acts

Article III of the Convention lists the punishable acts as being: "genocide, conspiracy to commit genocide, direct or public incitement to commit genocide, attempt to commit genocide and complicity in genocide". This enumeration indicates how far the crime needs to have advanced before it becomes punishable. For example, an attempt will suffice. Secondly, it describes what kind of involvement in actual genocide may result in penal responsibility under the Convention. Thus, criminal responsibility extends to those involved in incitement, conspiracy and attempt, as well as individuals actually executing the specific acts prohibited by the Convention. Political masterminds or propaganda people are no less responsible than the individuals who perform the actual carnage. There are, therefore, several legal bases for criminal responsibility of individuals who engage in or are part of the various aspects of genocide.

6. Culpability

It is explicitly stated in the Convention that people who have committed genocide shall be punished whether they are "constitutionally responsible rulers, public officials or private individuals" (art. IV). Public officials include both civilian and military personnel and everyone who holds (or held) a public office—be it legislative, administrative or judicial. To meet the aims of the Convention, people in the said categories must be treated equally irrespective of their de jure or de facto positions as decision-makers. As individuals, they are subject to prosecution like any other individual violator. They cannot hide behind any shield of immunity. The legal and moral responsibilities are the same and the need to prevent genocide no less clear because of the position of the violator.

7. The statute of the International Tribunal for the Prosecution of Persons Responsible for Serious Violations of International Humanitarian Law Committed in the Territory of the Former Yugoslavia since 1991

Article 4 of the statute of the International Tribunal affirms the competence of the International Tribunal to prosecute persons committing genocide. The definition of genocide in article 4 of the statute is identical to the provisions of the Genocide Convention.

J. Legal aspects of rape and other sexual assaults

Rape constitutes a crime under international humanitarian law as well as under the criminal laws of the various republics which constituted the former Yugoslavia. It is also part of the substantive applicable law of the statute of the International Tribunal where it is referred to in several articles.

Unlike most codified penal laws in the world, in international humanitarian law rape is not precisely defined. But on the basis of the contemporary criminal laws of the world's major criminal justice systems, the Commission considers rape to be a crime of violence of a sexual nature against the person. This characteristic of violence of a sexual nature also applies to other forms of sexual assault against women, men and children, when these activities are performed under coercion or threat of force and include sexual mutilation. It should be noted that irrespective of their definition, acts of sexual assault against women, men and children are prohibited by international humanitarian law through normative provisions prohibiting violence against the physical integrity and dignity of the person. Therefore, rape and other sexual assaults are covered in pari materia.

Even though sexual assaults imply the commission of the crime by a given perpetrator, persons who do not perform the act but are indirectly involved in the commission of this crime, like decision-makers and superiors, are also responsible under the Genocide Convention (art. III) and general norms of command responsibility (see paras. 55–60).

Violations of the laws and customs of war applicable to conflicts of an international character are contained in a number of international instruments. The Hague Convention (IV) Respecting the Laws and Customs of War on Land deals with the question of sexual assaults in article 46: "Family honour and rights, the lives of persons and private property, as well as religious convictions and practice, must be respected." The Fourth Geneva Convention explicitly prohibits rape in article 27. The Commission deems that article 147 of the same Convention on "grave breaches" includes rape and other sexual assaults as constituting "torture or inhumane treatment" and that they are also prohibited because they are among those acts "wilfully causing great suffering or serious injury to body or health". Furthermore, Protocol I to the Geneva Conventions contains in article 76 an express prohibition of rape and other sexual assaults. In addition, such practices which are based on racial discrimination also constitute "grave breaches" under article 85, paragraph 4 of Protocol I, which holds that "inhuman and degrading practices involving outrage upon personal dignity, based on racial discrimination" are prohibited. It is also considered that article 27 of the Fourth Geneva Convention constitutes part of customary international law, thus also establishing a basis for universal jurisdiction. Furthermore, it should be noted with respect to Protocol I, that the provisions of article 85, when violated on the basis of racial discrimination, also constitute a violation of customary international law. Under all of these provisions, a single act of rape or sexual assault constitutes a war crime. As a "grave breach", this type of violation falls under universal jurisdiction. The perpetrator, however, must be a person who is linked to one of the parties to the conflict and the victim must be linked to another party to the conflict or be a citizen of a neutral State. It is also held that article 76 of Protocol I is applicable to victims who are not protected by other provisions of the four Geneva Conventions.

With respect to provisions applicable to conflicts of a non-international character, common article 3 to the four Geneva Conventions applies, as does article 4, paragraph 2 of Protocol II. Both of these provisions include a prohibition against rape and other sexual assaults in so far as they constitute wilful injury to the person. A single act is enough to constitute such a violation when the perpetrator is linked to one of the parties to the conflict and the victim is linked to another party to the conflict or is a citizen of a neutral State. Under Protocol II, such prohibited acts constitute a violation when the conflict takes place "in the territory of a High Contracting Party between its armed forces and dissident forces or other organized groups which, under responsible command, exercise such control over a part of its territory as to enable them to carry out sustained and concerted military operations and to implement this Protocol" (art. 1, para. 1).

Two other sources of international humanitarian law apply to the prohibition of sexual assault and rape irrespective of the nature and characterization of the conflict. They are the conventional and customary law of "crimes against humanity" and the Genocide Convention. With respect to crimes against humanity, sexual assaults and rape fall within the meaning of other inhumane acts. However, the prohibited conduct must be part of an overall policy of persecution based on ethnic or religious grounds against a civilian population. Under the Genocide Convention, sexual assault and rape are included within the meaning of article II of the Convention, provided that the prohibited conduct is committed as part of an "intent to destroy, in whole or in part, a national, ethnical, racial or religious group". Under both crimes against humanity and the Genocide Convention, such prohibited acts are subject to universal jurisdiction. It is also well-established that both of these sources of international humanitarian law are considered part of jus cogens and are, therefore, binding under customary international law.

The parties to this conflict are bound by the four Geneva Conventions of 12 August 1949 and Additional Protocols I and II, both under State succession and by the parties' specific accession thereto. The parties are also bound by the Genocide Convention under State succession in so far as that convention has been ratified by the former Federal Republic of Yugoslavia. The parties are bound by that Convention under jus cogens and customary international law. The parties are also bound under jus cogens and customary international law by the obligations arising under crimes against humanity, as developed in conventional and customary international law.

The Commission concludes that there is no doubt about the prohibition of rape and sexual assault in the Geneva Conventions and other applicable sources of international humanitarian law. Furthermore, the Commission finds that the relevant provisions of the statute of the International Tribunal adequately and correctly state the applicable law to this crime.

III. GENERAL STUDIES

A. The military structure of the warring factions and the strategies and tactics they employ

The military conflicts in the former Yugoslavia must be examined on the basis of their evolution, which involved different parties at various times, operating in separate, though frequently interrelated, theatres of operation.

The first phase involved the conflict in Slovenia. The conflict began when that Republic declared its independence from the former Yugoslavia on 25 June 1991. That conflict involved the Yugoslav People's Army (JNA), Slovenia Territorial Defence Forces—Slovenian troops who left JNA to join the newly created Slovenian Army—and local Slovenian Police. This phase lasted for only a few weeks, in June and July 1991.

The second phase of the conflict, involving Croatia, started before that Republic officially declared its independence on 25 July 1991. On one side, that conflict involved JNA, Serb militia in Krajina and in eastern and western Slavonia, special forces from Serbia (with the participation of Serb expatriates and mercenaries), local special forces, and Serb police and armed civilians from the same areas. On the other side, the newly formed Croatian Army consisted of Croatian troops who left JNA, the Croatian National Guard, local militia; special forces consisting of expatriate Croats and mercenaries, and local Croatian police and armed civilians. After November 1991, JNA formally withdrew from Croatia, but continued to support the newly formed, self-proclaimed "Serb Republic of Krajina" army. Meanwhile, the newly established Republic of Croatia had formed its army, the Croatian Army, which, along with Croatian special forces and others, continued the armed conflict in what became the United Nations protected areas (UNPAs) in Croatia.

The third phase of the conflict began in Bosnia and Herzegovina following its declaration of independence on 6 March It simultaneously involved fighting between Croatian and Bosnian Government forces, Bosnian Government and Serbian forces, and Croatian and Serbian forces. The Croatian Defence Council forces in the Bosnian and Herzegovina are supported by the Croatian Army, local Croatian police, volunteer civilians and "special forces" like the military wing of the Croatian Party of Rights (HOS) (named after the former Ustashas of the Second World War, who also fought against the Serbs in the Krajina area). Other Croatian armed civilian forces operate essentially in local areas. At first, the Bosnian Government and JNA opposed each other. This lasted from April to June 1992, during which time the JNA troops from Serbia and Montenegro "officially" withdrew from Bosnia and Herzegovina, leaving behind JNA Serbian troops from Bosnia and their equipment. They were supplemented by "special forces" from Serbia which consisted of expatriate volunteers and mercenaries, Bosnian-Serb militia and police, and Serb volunteers.

At the early stages of the conflict, most of the combatants, including those in the regular army, did not wear distinctive uniforms, emblems or insignias of rank. As a result, officers freely moved from army to militia and from one unit to another. To further complicate matters, at the early stages of the conflict between: (a) Croatia and the Federal Republic of Yugoslavia and other Serb forces within Croatia, and (b) between Bosnia and Herzegovina and the Federal Republic of Yugoslavia and other forces within Bosnia and Herzegovina (in May 1992, JNA forces from the Federal Republic of Yugoslavia officially withdrew from Bosnia), the "order of battle" of almost all army and militia units was not clearly established. The chain of command was significantly blurred, even to insiders. Consequently, the organizations' "command and control" structures were seriously eroded, which resulted in much confusion. The confusion was more pronounced in Bosnia among Serb combatants, but seems to have been purposely kept that way for essentially political reasons.

When each of the three Republics of Slovenia, Croatia and Bosnia and Herzegovina respectively declared their independence, they did not have a separate army. Previously, the Yugoslavian People's Army (JNA), also referred to as the Yugoslavian National Army, was a single unitary army for all members of the former Yugoslavia. The armies of the "warring factions" consisted mainly of military personnel and equipment of the former JNA.

Each of these republics had local territorial defence forces (TDF) which were part of the total defence systems of the Federal Republic of Yugoslavia. The republics also had local police forces consisting of personnel from their respective republics.

Upon the successive declarations of independence of these three republics, some of the military personnel of JNA (who had been located in each of these republics) left JNA and reconstituted themselves as part of the newly created national armies of Slovenia, Croatia and Bosnia and Herzegovina.[4] JNA "officially" withdrew from Croatia in November 1991 and from the Bosnia and Herzegovina between May and June 1992. Throughout this period, JNA was reorganized several times by the Federal Republic of Yugoslavia. As of May 1992, JNA—now called the Yugoslav Army—consisted essentially of troops from the Republics of Serbia and Montenegro. These two Republics form the successor federal union to the former Yugoslavia.

In addition to the regular armies mentioned above, there are three additional armies: the Bosnian-Serb Army, which operates in Bosnia and Herzegovina; the Serbian Army of Croatia, which operates in Croatia; and the Croatian Defence Council, which operates primarily outside the border of the Republic of Croatia, and mostly in Bosnia and Herzegovina. The first two were at one time and may still be armed and supported by JNA (now the Yugoslav Army) and the third may have been armed and supported by the Croatian Army.

The territorial defence forces (TDFs) are known as militia. In the case of Croatia, TDFs were known as the Croatian National Guard. The TDFs have a separate command structure from the regular army. Nevertheless, they join in the armed conflict, frequently operating with the regular army and under regular army officers' command. They also operate independently in certain geographic areas, usually where most of the personnel in these units came from.

In addition, two other types of paramilitary groups and formations are also engaged in military operations. They consist of: (a) what are called "special forces", and (b) local police forces augmented by local armed civilians. All the warring factions make use of such forces among their combatants, but the lines of authority and the structure of command and control are confusing, even to the combatants.

There are 45 reported special forces, which usually operate under the command of a named individual and apparently with substantial autonomy, except when they are integrated into the regular army's plan of action. The special forces are supplied and often trained by the respective Governments that they serve. Many special forces answer only to senior political officials in the respective Governments. Such a relationship is frequently based on political allegiance and is not always publicly known. However, in time, information about the political sponsorship and support of these groups will become available. As these units usually operate independently and outside the apparent chain of command, their order of battle is not known. Notwithstanding the strong links between these units and the respective armies, the regular army failed to restrain them from the commission of grave breaches of the Geneva Conventions and other violations of international humanitarian law. Among the most notorious of the special forces are Arkan's "Tigers" and Šešelj's "White Eagles" (also referred to as "Chetniks").[5] Lastly, many of these units operate throughout the territory of the former Yugoslavia. Thus, the Serbian units operate in Bosnia and Herzegovina and Croatia, and the Croatian units in Bosnia and Herzegovina. These special forces have committed some of the worst violations of international humanitarian law (see paras. 129–150, 236–237, and 216–231).

Some towns and villages formed paramilitary units, which are not to be confused with the special forces mentioned above. These local forces operate in the areas of their towns and villages. Occasionally, they also lend support to similar groups and other combatants in the same opština (county) and neighbouring areas. Their command and control is local, and the chain of command difficult to establish, though characteristically these groups, like the special forces, have an identifiable leader. Frequently, the unit or group is called by the leader's name. Otherwise, the unit or group uses a politically significant name or the name of their town, village or area. The leadership is local, mostly consisting of political figures. These units, particularly among Serbs in Bosnia and Herzegovina and Croats in Krajina, have, like the special forces, committed many violations of international humanitarian law (see paras. 129–150). The police, augmented by "volunteer" armed civilians, also participate in military activities. These forces operate within a given municipality. They are nominally under the overall control of the Ministry of Interior. Furthermore, the respective ministries of interior also have national and regional police units, which usually operate outside the boundaries of local municipalities. The relationship between national, regional and local police is not always clear and varies in each country, and sometimes within the regions of each country. During the early stages of the conflicts in Croatia and in Bosnia and Herzegovina, the police, augmented by "volunteer" armed civilians, operated without apparent command and control from the army. Their leadership was local and included many political figures. These forces acted with almost complete autonomy in their respective areas. They also share responsibility with the special forces described above.

The situation consists of a multiplicity of combatant forces (for example, regular armies, militias, special forces, police and armed civilians) operating within different structures or outside any structure. These forces sometimes operate under no command and control. They may be without uniforms, emblems or insignias. Frequently, these forces merge or combine in connection with certain operations. Probably the only factor common to all of these forces is their receipt of military equipment, ammunition and supplies from their respective armies and other governmental sources.

The outcome of such a structure and the strategies and tactics employed help to blur the chain of command and conceal responsibility. This concealment may well be intended by some of the parties to provide a shield of plausible deniability.

All parties to the conflict have specifically adhered to the Geneva Conventions of 12 August 1949 and Additional Protocols I and II thereto. Furthermore, the Federal Republic of Yugoslavia is a signatory to these Conventions, and all of the parties to the conflict concede that they are also bound by these obligations under the international law of State succession.

The Federal Criminal Code of the former Yugoslavia embodied the international rules of armed conflict. JNA military personnel were instructed accordingly. Thus, grave breaches of the Geneva Conventions and other violations of international humanitarian law are part of the applicable national laws of all warring factions.

All of the combatant forces, in significantly different degrees, have committed grave breaches of the Geneva Conventions.

The grave breaches of the Geneva Conventions and other violations of international humanitarian law occurring in this conflict are, in part, the product of the military structure that results in a lack of effective command and control. The violations are also the result of the strategies and tactics employed by the warring factions.

B. "Ethnic cleansing"

In its first interim report (S/25274), the Commission stated:

> "55. The expression 'ethnic cleansing' is relatively new. Considered in the context of the conflicts in the former Yugoslavia, 'ethnic cleansing' means rendering an area ethnically homogenous by using force or intimidation to remove persons of given groups from the area. 'Ethnic cleansing' is contrary to international law.

> "56. Based on the many reports describing the policy and practices conducted in the former Yugoslavia, 'ethnic cleansing' has been carried out by means of murder, torture, arbitrary arrest and detention, extra-judicial executions, rape and sexual assaults, confinement of civilian population in ghetto areas, forcible removal, displacement and deportation of civilian population, deliberate military attacks or threats of attacks on civilians and civilian areas, and wanton destruction of property. Those practices constitute crimes against humanity and can be assimilated to specific war crimes. Furthermore, such acts could also fall within the meaning of the Genocide Convention.

> "57. The Commission is mindful of these considerations in the examination of reported allegations."

Upon examination of reported information, specific studies and investigations, the Commission confirms its earlier view that "ethnic cleansing" is a purposeful policy designed by one ethnic or religious group to remove by violent and terror-inspiring means the civilian population of another ethnic or religious group from certain geographic areas. To a large extent, it is carried out in the name of misguided nationalism, historic grievances and a powerful driving sense of revenge. This purpose appears to be the occupation of territory to the exclusion of the purged group or groups. This policy and the practices of warring factions are described separately in the following paragraphs.

With respect to the practices by Serbs in Bosnia and Herzegovina and Croatia, "ethnic cleansing" is commonly used as a term to describe a policy conducted in furtherance of political doctrines relating to "Greater Serbia". The policy is put into practice by Serbs in Bosnia and Herzegovina and Croatia and their supporters in the Federal Republic of Yugoslavia. The political doctrine consists of a complex mixture of historical claims, grievances and fears and nationalistic aspirations and expectations, as well as religious and psychological elements. The doctrine is essentially based on ethnic and religious exclusivity and the dominance of Serbs over other groups in certain historically claimed areas. These views contrast with ethnic and religious pluralism. This doctrine breeds intolerance and suspicion of other ethnic and religious groups and is conducive to violence when it is politically manipulated, as has been the case.

It should be emphasized that this policy and the manner in which it is carried out is supported only by some Serbs. In addition, the Commission emphasizes that responsibility for criminal conduct must be determined on an individual basis.[6]

The manner in which the policy of "ethnic cleansing" is carried out by Serbs in Bosnia is consistent throughout a certain geographic area represented by an arc ranging from northern Bosnia and covering areas in eastern and western Bosnia adjoining the Serb Krajina area in Croatia. The practice of "ethnic cleansing" is carried out in strategic areas linking Serbia proper with Serb-inhabited areas in Bosnia and Croatia. This strategic factor is significantly relevant to understanding why the policy has been carried out in certain areas and not in others.

The coercive means used to remove the civilian population from the above-mentioned strategic areas include: mass murder, torture, rape and other forms of sexual assault; severe physical injury to civilians; mistreatment of civilian prisoners and prisoners of war; use of civilians as human shields; destruction of personal, public and cultural property; looting, theft and robbery of personal property; forced expropriation of real property; forceful displacement of civilian population; and attacks on hospitals, medical personnel and locations marked with the Red Cross/Red Crescent emblem.

Many of these acts of violence are carried out with extreme brutality and savagery in a manner designed to instill terror in the civilian population, in order to cause them to flee and never to return. This is evidenced by the large number of purposeful and indiscriminate killings, rape and sexual assaults, and other forms of torture committed against civilians and prisoners of war, both inside and outside detention facilities. These acts are also highly publicized by the perpetrators in order to achieve a terror-inspiring effect on others and cause them to flee.

Other noteworthy practices are widespread destruction of villages by systematically burning them to the ground and blowing up all the houses and structures in a given area. This includes cultural and religious monuments and symbols. The purpose of this destruction is to eradicate cultural, social and religious traces that identify the ethnic and religious groups. In the cases where the practices described above do not occur, these groups are forced to leave under duress by reason of a well-founded fear for their personal security.

Another recurring practice is to force civilian inhabitants to sign over their property as a condition of their departure or removal to other areas. Mayors and public officials, including the police, are frequently involved in this practice.[7]

Two additional factors also indicate the existence of a policy of "ethnic cleansing": (a) the wholesale and surreptitious departure of the Serbian population living in certain areas, which are to be "ethnically cleansed", before the acts described above take place;[8] and (b) the practices reported occur under the supervision of a "crisis committee" (Krizni Štab), comprised of local political leaders, police and others, which made such decisions with the direct or indirect involvement and support of the Bosnian-Serb Army.

Special forces (see paras. 121–122) frequently carry out "ethnic cleansing". These forces clearly seem to be supported, equipped and supplied by the Governments they serve and are allowed to operate without control by the authorities in charge. Two particular groups of special forces that have committed the largest number of reported violations are Arkan's Tigers and Šešelj's White Eagles (see para. 121).

The study of the Prijedor district described in paragraphs 151 to 182 below, reveals the extent of the policy of "ethnic cleansing" and the manner in which it was systematically carried out together with the local and regional authorities. The same patterns and practices described in the study on the district of Prijedor repeatedly occurred in many opštinas, such as Banja Luka, Brčko, Foča and Zvornik, about which the Commission received significant information supporting the above conclusions.

Three additional observations are noteworthy:

f.   JNA and the Army of the so-called "Bosnian Serb Republic" have been involved in carrying out and facilitating the policy and practices of "ethnic cleansing" in certain parts of the territory;

g.   The practices implementing the policy, particularly in certain parts of Bosnia, have been carried out to a large extent by the most marginal social elements of that society;

h.   The leaders of Bosnian Serbs influenced, encouraged, facilitated and condoned these social elements to carry out the crimes described above. The combination of these factors, stimulated by misguided nationalism, fanned by historical grievances and fuelled by reciprocal violence and revenge, has led to tragic consequences.

There is sufficient evidence to conclude that the practices of "ethnic cleansing" were not coincidental, sporadic or carried out by disorganized groups or bands of civilians who could not be controlled by the Bosnian-Serb leadership. Indeed, the patterns of conduct, the manner in which these acts were carried out, the length of time over which they took place and the areas in which they occurred combine to reveal a purpose, systematicity and some planning and coordination from higher authorities. Furthermore, these practices are carried out by persons from all segments of the Serbian population in the areas described: members of the army, militias, special forces, the police and civilians. Lastly, the Commission notes that these unlawful acts are often heralded by the perpetrators as positive, patriotic accomplishments.

The above-mentioned factors and others indicate the existence of an element of superior direction. At the very least, they indicate a purposeful failure by superiors to prevent and punish the perpetrators once their crimes become known to the responsible commanders.[9]

Lastly, it should be noted that there was initially a link between local activities and activities of Serbs from the Federal Republic of Yugoslavia in Bosnia and Herzegovina and in Krajina, Croatia, and also involvement by JNA. This linkage existed until 2 January 1992, the date of the cease-fire between Serbs in Krajina and JNA and the Federal Republic of Yugoslavia, and is evident in many ways. In fact, these links are not denied by the Federal Republic of Yugoslavia. This is supported by the use of JNA in Croatia and Bosnia and Herzegovina before the conversion of some of these forces into the army of the so-called "Serbian Republic of Bosnia".[10] Furthermore, there is a strong political, diplomatic and military influence on the part of the Federal Republic of Yugoslavia over a wide range of decisions of the "Bosnian Serb Republic" and the "Serb Republic of Krajina".

Similar policies and practices of "ethnic cleansing" have occurred in the Serb-Krajina area and in eastern and western Slavonia in Croatia by Serbs against Croats and also by Croats against Serbs, as discussed below.[11] The patterns and practices of "ethnic cleansing" described above are the same in separate theatres of operation. This further substantiates the existence of a Serbian policy. One significant instance where this policy was carried out in Croatia is the destruction of the city of Vukovar in 1991.[12]

Manifestations of "ethnic cleansing" have occurred throughout the territory of the former Yugoslavia, and similar practices have been committed at certain times and places by Croatian warring factions, as discussed in paragraph 147.

"Ethnic cleansing" practices committed by Bosnian Croats with support from the Republic of Croatia against Bosnian Muslims in Herzegovina are politically related.[13] Furthermore, Croatian forces also engage in these practices against Serbs in the Krajina area and in eastern and western Slavonia. The violence committed against Serbs in these areas appears, however, to have the more defined political aim of removing them from the areas. Croats have used the Croatian Defence Council, police, armed civilians and local special forces to carry out these acts in the areas mentioned above. They have committed grave breaches of the Geneva Conventions, including the destruction of Serbian villages and churches, killing of innocent civilians, torture and forceful removal of the civilian population. In the Krajina area and in eastern and western Slavonia, the cycle of violence between Serbs and Croats started in the early part of 1991, before the war formally began. The violence continued well beyond the end of that war. Similar practices were also, on occasion, carried out by Croats against Muslims in Bosnia and Herzegovina. But, the Croatian authorities have publicly deplored these practices and sought to stop them, thereby indicating that it is not part of the Government's policy.

Bosnian Government forces have also committed the same type of grave breaches of the Geneva Conventions against Serbs and Croats, but not as part of a policy of "ethnic cleansing". The number of these violations, as reported, is significantly less than the reported violations allegedly committed by the other warring factions.

The Commission is unable to determine the amount of harm and the exact number of violations committed by each of the warring factions. Nevertheless, it is clear that there is no factual basis for arguing that there is a "moral equivalence" between the warring factions.

It should be noted in unequivocal terms, however, that reprisals, retribution and revenge do not constitute a valid legal justification or excuse for committing grave breaches of the Geneva Conventions and other violations of international humanitarian law (see paras. 63 - 66). The Commission emphasizes that in addition to the individual criminal responsibility of perpetrators who commit violations, military and political leaders who participate in the making, execution and carrying out of this policy are also susceptible to charges of genocide and crimes against humanity, in addition to grave breaches of the Geneva Conventions and other violations of international humanitarian law.

* * * * * *

F. Rape and other forms of sexual assault

Throughout the various phases of the armed conflicts in the former Yugoslavia, there have been numerous reports of widespread and systematic rape and other forms of sexual assault. The Commission, concerned about these reported crimes, undertook several means of research and investigation to ascertain the facts.

The Commission sought particularly to examine the relationship between "ethnic cleansing" and rape and other forms of sexual assault.

Owing to the social stigma attached—even in times of peace—rape is among the least reported crimes. For this reason, it is very difficult to make any general assessment of actual numbers of rape victims. In the former Yugoslavia, there appears to have been very little, if any, difference between the ethnic groups in the reluctance to report rape. The over-all reluctance to report rape is aggravated by war, especially if the perpetrators are soldiers and also where there is a general condition of chaos and a breakdown in law and order. The victims may have little confidence in finding justice. The strong fear of reprisal during wartime adds to the silencing of victims. The perpetrators have a strong belief that they can get away with their crimes.

Men are also subject to sexual assault. They are forced to rape women and to perform sex acts on guards or each other. They have also been subjected to castration, circumcision or other sexual mutilation.

1. Rape and sexual assaults study: the Commission's database
The reports contained in the Commission's database identify close to 800 victims by name or number. An additional 1,673 victims are referred to, but not named in reports of vic-tims who indicate that they have witnessed or know of other similar victims. Additionally, there are some 500 reported cases which refer to an unspecified number of victims. The victims' ages, as reported, range from 5 to 81 years old, with the majority of victims below 35 years old. The reported cases identify some 600 alleged perpetrators by name. In other cases, victims refer to a specific number of perpetrators, but do not identify them by name. In those cases of unidentified perpetrators, about 900 perpetrators are referred to. Of all the reports received, about 800 contain general information, identifying some perpetrators as soldiers, police, paramilitary, special forces, etc. The alleged perpetrators include mili-tary personnel, special forces, local police and civilians. About 80 per cent of the reported cases specify that they occurred in settings where the victims were held in custody.

The reported cases of rape and sexual assault contained in the database occurred between the fall of 1991 and the end of 1993. The majority of the rapes occurred from April to November 1992; fewer occurred in the following five months. In the same time period, the number of media reports increased from a few in March 1992 to a high of 535 news stories in January 1993 and 529 in February 1993. This correlation could indicate that the media attention caused the decline. In that case, it would indicate that command-ers could control the alleged perpetrators if they wanted to. This could lead to the conclu-sion that there was an overriding policy advocating the use of rape as a method of "ethnic cleansing", rather than a policy of omission, tolerating the widespread commission of rape.

....In the following paragraphs, the patterns of rape and sexual assault identified through the database are outlined, while illustrations are given which are drawn from among the interviews [conducted by the Commission].

Five patterns emerge from the reported cases, regardless of the ethnicity of the perpetrators or the victims (see also para. 229 for a description of rape practices in custodial settings).

The first pattern involves individuals or small groups committing sexual assault in conjunction with looting and intimidation of the target ethnic group. This is before any widespread or generalized fighting breaks out in the region. Tensions in an area grow and members of the ethnic group controlling the regional government begin to terrorize their neighbours. Two or more men break into a house, intimidate the residents, steal their property, beat them and often rape the females. Some of the reported rapes are singular and some multiple. In either case, there is often a gang atmosphere where the abuses are part of the same event and all the attackers participate, even if they do not sexually assault the victims. One of the women interviewed was gang-raped by eight soldiers in front of her six-year-old sister and her five-month-old daughter. One of the men was forced at gunpoint to rape the victim, "as she was an Ustasha". When she reported the crimes to local authorities, they said they could do nothing as "she was a Croat".

The second pattern of rape involves individuals or small groups committing sexual assaults in conjunction with fighting in an area, often including the rape of women in public. When forces attack a town or village, the population is rounded up and divided by sex and age. Some women are raped in their homes as the attacking forces secure the area. Others are selected after the roundup and raped publicly. The population of the village is then transported to camps. One victim-witness interviewed saw an elderly woman and others raped in front of a group of 100 detained villagers. The witness was herself threatened with rape and she saw a number of men from the group having their throats cut.

The third pattern of rape involves individuals or groups sexually assaulting people in detention because they have access to the people. Once the population of a town or village has been rounded up, men are either executed or sent off to camps, while women are generally sent off to separate camps. Soldiers, camp guards, paramilitaries and even civilians may be allowed to enter the camp, pick out women, take them away, rape them and then either kill them or return them to the site. Reports frequently refer to gang rape, while beatings and torture accompany most of the reported rapes. Survivors report that some women are taken out alone, and some are taken out in groups. Though this is the general pattern, there are also many allegations that women are raped in front of other internees, or that other internees are forced to sexually abuse each other. In camps where men are detained, they are also subjected to sexual abuse. During the Commission's interviewing process 15 people were interviewed whose major allegations related to the same detention camp. Some witnesses were men, and all of the women victims had been raped. The women were sometimes gang raped by, or in the presence of, the camp commander. Guards from the external ring of security around the camp (who apparently did not enter the camp in the course of their work) and soldiers who were strangers to the camp would be allowed access to the camp for rape. One of the victim-witnesses interviewed saw a woman die after being in a coma for a week as a result of about 100 sadistic rapes by guards. Sexual assaults were also practised against men: one witness saw prisoners forced to bite another prisoner's genitals.

In addition, 10 of those interviewed had witnessed deaths by torture and seven of the group had survived or witnessed mass executions (there or in other camps). Another incident related in an interview involved prisoners lined up naked while Serb women from outside undressed in front of the male prisoners. If any prisoner had an erection, his penis was cut off. The witness saw a named Serb woman thus castrate a prisoner. Another ex-detainee told of suffering electric shocks to the scrotum and of seeing a father and son who shared his cell forced by guards to perform sex acts with each other.

The fourth pattern of rape involves individuals or groups committing sexual assaults against women for the purpose of terrorizing and humiliating them often as part of the policy of "ethnic cleansing". Survivors of some camps report that they believe they were detained for the purpose of rape. In those camps, all of the women are raped quite frequently, often in front of other internees, and usually accompanied by beatings and torture. Some captors also state that they are trying to impregnate the women. Pregnant women are detained until it is too late for them to obtain an abortion. One woman was detained by her neighbour (who was a soldier) near her village for six months. She was raped almost daily by three or four soldiers. She was told that she would give birth to a chetnik boy who would kill Muslims when he grew up. They repeatedly said their President had ordered them to do this. One woman's home was taken by Serbian neighbours and used as a detention centre for interrogations over several months. She was raped almost daily and beaten for several months; two other women were raped there too. She saw several killings and torture.

The fifth pattern of rape involves detention of women in hotels or similar facilities for the sole purpose of sexually entertaining soldiers, rather than causing a reaction in the women. These women are reportedly more often killed than exchanged, unlike women in other camps. One woman interviewed was detained in a private house with a number of other women for six months. The women were of mixed ethnicity. All the women were raped when soldiers returned from the front line every 15 days. The witness was told that the women had to do this because the women in another camp (which the witness named and which has been documented by other information gatherers) were exhausted.

Common threads run through the cases reported whether within or outside of a detention context:

i.   Rapes seem to occur in conjunction with efforts to displace the targeted ethnic group from the region. This may involve heightened shame and humiliation by raping victims in front of adult and minor family members, in front of other detainees or in public places, or by forcing family members to rape each other. Young women and virgins are targeted for rape, along with prominent members of the community and educated women;

j.   Many reports state that perpetrators said they were ordered to rape, or that the aim was to ensure that the victims and their families would never want to return to the area. Perpetrators tell female victims that they will bear children of the perpetrator's ethnicity, that they must become pregnant, and then hold them in custody until it is too late for the victims to get an abortion. Victims are threatened that if they ever tell anyone, or anyone discovers what has happened, the perpetrators will hunt them down and kill them;

k. Large groups of perpetrators subject victims to multiple rapes and sexual assault. In detention, perpetrators go through the detention centres with flashlights at night selecting women and return them the next morning, while camp commanders often know about, and sometimes participate in, the sexual assaults;

l. Victims may be sexually abused with foreign objects like broken glass bottles, guns and truncheons. Castrations are performed through crude means such as forcing other internees to bite off a prisoner's testicles.

Rape has been reported to have been committed by all sides to the conflict. However, the largest number of reported victims have been Bosnian Muslims, and the largest number of alleged perpetrators have been Bosnian Serbs. There are few reports of rape and sexual assault between members of the same ethnic group.

In Bosnia, some of the reported rape and sexual assault cases committed by Serbs, mostly against Muslims, are clearly the result of individual or small group conduct without evidence of command direction or an overall policy. However, many more seem to be a part of an overall pattern whose characteristics include: similarities among practices in non-contiguous geographic areas; simultaneous commission of other international humanitarian law violations; simultaneous military activity; simultaneous activity to displace civilian populations; common elements in the commission of rape, maximizing shame and humiliation to not only the victim, but also the victim's community; and the timing of rapes. One factor in particular that leads to this conclusion is the large number of rapes which occurred in places of detention. These rapes in detention do not appear to be random, and they indicate at least a policy of encouraging rape supported by the deliberate failure of camp commanders and local authorities to exercise command and control over the personnel under their authority.

These patterns strongly suggest that a systematic rape policy existed in certain areas, but it remains to be proven whether such an overall policy existed which was to apply to all non-Serbs. It is clear that some level of organization and group activity was required to carry out many of the alleged rapes. Furthermore, rape and sexual assault should be examined in the context of the practice of "ethnic cleansing", which is discussed in paragraphs 129 to 150 and the practices in detention camps discussed in paragraph 230. When viewed in these contexts, it is clear that grave breaches of the Geneva Conventions occurred, as did other violations of international humanitarian law. [14]

* * * * * *

V. GENERAL CONCLUSIONS AND RECOMMENDATIONS

The disintegration of a federal State, as in the case of the former Yugoslavia, is often at first a civil conflict. However, as the respective States of Slovenia, Croatia and Bosnia and Herzegovina declared their independence, received international recognition and were admitted to membership in the United Nations, the conflict with respect to each of these States became an international conflict. The first interim report stated:

"45. The Commission is of the opinion, however, that the character and complexity of the armed conflicts concerned, combined with the web of agreements on humanitarian issues the parties have concluded among themselves, justify an approach whereby it applies the law applicable in international armed conflicts to the entirety of the armed conflicts in the territory of the former Yugoslavia."

....This is the case irrespective of whether the conflict is determined to be of an international or non-international character.

....Reports received and investigations conducted by the Commission indicate that the level of victimization in this conflict has been high. The crimes committed have been particularly brutal and ferocious in their execution. The Commission has not been able to verify each report; however, the magnitude of victimization is clearly enormous.[15]

The Commission finds significant evidence of and information about the commission of grave breaches of the Geneva Conventions and other violations of international humanitarian law which have been communicated to the Office of the Prosecutor of the International Tribunal.

Some of the conclusions relative to these violations are reflected in the present report, but for obvious reasons information and evidence of a prosecutorial nature are not described herein.

The practices of "ethnic cleansing" (see paras. 129 - 150), sexual assault and rape (see paras. 232 - 253 and 230) have been carried out by some of the parties so systematically that they strongly appear to be the product of a policy. The consistent failure to prevent the commission of such crimes and the consistent failure to prosecute and punish the perpetrators of these crimes, clearly evidences the existence of a policy by omission. The consequence of this conclusion is that command responsibility can be established.

Knowledge of these grave breaches and violations of international humanitarian law can reasonably be inferred from consistent and repeated practices.

The domestic criminal laws of the former Socialist Federal Republic of Yugoslavia and the criminal codes of all the republics formerly comprising it contain prohibitions against the violations that have taken place. Therefore, there should be no doubt in anyone's mind that such acts as murder, torture, rape, robbery and theft constitute crimes.

The observations set forth in paragraphs 110 to 127 on the military structure of the warring factions and the strategies and tactics they employ may reveal an initial state of confusion, reducing the effectiveness of command and control. This apparent confused state of affairs continued well beyond the initial stages of the respective conflicts. This leads to the conclusion that the existence of separate military structures and the multiplicity of units may well have been intended by some of the parties. The confusion may be intended to permit senior military and political leaders to argue lack of knowledge of what was happening and inability to control such unlawful conduct.

Notwithstanding the strong feelings of the warring factions concerning their victimization, both historical and contemporary arguments concerning reprisals (see paras.

63–66) and superior orders (see paras. 61 and 62) do not constitute a defence under the well-established law of international armed conflict and under the national laws of the parties to the conflict.

The type, range and duration of the violations described in the present report strongly imply command responsibility by commission and omission and also indicate that the absolute defence of obedience to superior orders is invalid and unfounded (ibid.). This is particularly evident in view of the loose command and control structure where unlawful orders could have been disobeyed without individuals risking personal harm. Indeed, some did. A moral choice usually existed. Individual cases, however, will have to be judged on their respective merits in accordance with the statute of the International Tribunal.

The Commission is shocked by the high level of victimization and the manner in which these crimes were committed, as are the populations of all the parties to the conflict. The difference is that each side sees only its own victimization, and not what their side has done to others.

It is particularly striking to note the victims' high expectations that this Commission will establish the truth and that the International Tribunal will provide justice. All sides expect this. Thus, the conclusion is inescapable that peace in the future requires justice, and that justice starts with establishing the truth.[16] The Commission would be remiss if it did not emphasize the high expectation of justice conveyed by the parties to the conflict, as well as by victims, intergovernmental organizations, non-governmental organizations, the media and world public opinion. Consequently, the International Tribunal must be given the necessary resources and support to meet these expectations and accomplish its task. Furthermore, popular expectations of a new world order based on the international rule of law require no less than effective and permanent institutions of international justice. The International Tribunal for the Prosecution of Persons Responsible for Serious Violation of International Humanitarian Law Committed in the Territory of the Former Yugoslavia since 1991 must, therefore, be given the opportunity to produce the momentum for this future evolution.

The Commission requests the Secretary-General to publish this report and its annexes in their entirety and to give them the widest possible dissemination in order to inform Member States and the interested public.

NOTES

1. U.S. v. von Weizsaecker (Ministries Case), 14 Trials of War Criminals before the Nuremberg Military Tribunals under Control Council Law No. 10 at 611 (1949) (the Green Series). See also International Military Tribunal sitting at Nuremberg, reported in Trial of the Major War Criminals before the International Military Tribunal (1949).

2. General Assembly resolution 260 (III) of 9 December 1948, annex, second and third preambular paragraphs.

3. From a statement made by Mr. Morozov, representative of the Union of Soviet Socialist Republics, on 19 April 1948 during the debate in the Ad Hoc Committee on Genocide (E/AC.25/SR.12).

4. It should be noted that the Army of Bosnia and Herzegovina includes among its ranks Croatian and Serbian personnel. Also, Croatian Defence Council units have on occasion either been part of Bosnian Government operations or have fought alongside the Bosnian Government Forces against the Bosnian Serb Army.

5. ...Like Arkan's Tigers, Šešelj's White Eagles committed the crimes referred to above and in other parts of this report. The group seems to have been armed and supported by JNA. Moreover, since mid-1993, the group is believed to have been under the direct control of JNA....

6. Several reports indicate that individual Serbs acted with courage and generosity in helping persons of other ethnic or religious groups to flee to safety or shield such persons from certain harm. But, in almost all these reports, it is clear that those concerned persons did so surreptitiously, thus emphasizing the overall climate of fear and even terror inspired by those in control.

7. However, even the involvement of public officials is frequently insufficient to ensure the safety of the forcefully removed civilian population. Some of those evicted were forced to walk across minefields, which resulted in many deaths and severe injuries. Additionally, troops along the confrontation lines opened fire on the civilians who were pushed across the lines.

8. This is due to the fact that the Serb population is notified in advance of an attack. In some areas, this "ethnic cleansing" is done by "special forces" but frequently, it is the very civilian population which lives alongside the Bosnian Muslims in the areas described above who carry out or share in carrying out the criminal practices referred to elsewhere in this report, particularly the Prijedor study, paras. 151–182.

9. Command responsibility by commission and by omission exists (see paras. 55 - 60), even though the policy of "ethnic cleansing" is carried out in a way which tends to conceal the responsibility of superiors in the political and military hierarchy through a structural separation of army, militia, police and special forces (discussed in paras. 110–128). Considering, however, the extent of these violations, the vast areas over which they occurred and the length of time over which they took place, it is difficult to conceive how responsible commanders can claim ignorance of the violations that have occurred.

10. This conversion kept local JNA military personnel in Bosnia and Herzegovina, using substantially the same equipment of the former JNA, and thereafter receiving support from Serbia across the Drina River.

11. Serbs have inhabited the Krajina area and eastern and western Slavonia since the late 1300s and have had a particular historic presence since 1578. But during the Second World War, the Ustasha regime killed a large number of Serbs, whose numbers ranged from a low of 200,000 to a high of 700,000 most of them from these regions. The memory of this tragedy looms large over the apprehensions of Serbs and is a factor in the spiral of violence that took place in the region.

12. Most of Vukovar was razed to the ground. One incident, in particular, will forever symbolize this terrible battle. It is the mass grave at Ovčara, where some 200 plus Croats are believed to have been taken by Serbs from the Vukovar Hospital and summarily executed and then left in a shallow mass grave. The Commission conducted several reconnaissance missions to the areas, discovered the existence of a large number of bodies, collected some evidence and started to exhume the bodies in October 1993. Representatives of the "local Serbian administration" prevented the Commission from continuing its work. The Commission could not undertake the Ovčara and other mass graves investigations. However, before it was obliged to terminate its work, all of the relevant evidence was communicated to the Office of the Prosecutor of the International Tribunal. (For more detail see paras. 265–276 and annexes X, X.A and X.B.)

13. This is evidenced by the Croatian Defence Council and Croatian police attacks on the villages of Ahmići-Vitez and Stupni Do in 1993. These attacks would be characterized as repre-

senting a certain policy. The first was investigated by the European Community Monitoring Mission and Mr. Mazowiecki, the Special Rapporteur of the Commission on Human Rights. The second was investigated by UNPROFOR. All evidence was delivered to the Office of the Prosecutor of the International Tribunal.

14. It should be noted that several victims have reported acts of courage and generosity by Serbs who tried and at times succeeded in saving and sparing victims from death, torture and rape. Such acts should be acknowledged and recognized.

15. The territory over which most of the victimization occurred had a population base of an estimated 6 million persons, of whom 1.5 to 2 million are now refugees in more than 20 countries. Most of them were deported or forced to leave and are unable to return. The civilian and military casualties among all warring factions are reported to exceed 200,000. The number of reported mass graves, 150, discussed in paras. 254–264, tends to support the estimates of the number of casualties. Over 700 prison camps and detention facilities are reported to have existed (see paras. 216–231). The number of detainees and reports on mistreated prisoners, in for example, the Prijedor area alone exceeds 6,000 (see paras. 151–182). As stated in paragraph 153 concerning the Prijedor area, "the total number of killed and deported persons as of June 1993 is 52,811". The rape and sexual assault study and investigation discussed in paragraphs 232–253 suggests a very high number of rapes and sexual assaults in custodial and non- custodial settings (see also para. 229). Thus, the earlier projection of 20,000 rapes made by other sources are not unreasonable considering the number of actual reported cases.

16. Establishing the truth is the best method of enhancing deterrence. In fact, early investigation of the facts, in any context of criminal activity, increases the effectiveness of future prosecution. The combination of investigation and prosecution makes deterrence more effective, thereby reducing possible violations in the future. Without effective investigations and prosecutions, the converse is true.

One cannot speak about the protection of human rights with credibility when one is confronted with the lack of consistency and courage displayed by the international community and its leaders. The reality of the human rights situation today is illustrated by the tragedy of the people of Srebrenica and Žepa. I would like to believe that the present moment will be a turning point in the relationship between Europe and the world towards Bosnia. The very stability of international order and the principle of civilization is at stake over the question of Bosnia. I am not convinced that the turning point hoped for will happen and cannot continue to participate in the pretence of the protection of human rights.

Letter of Resignation by Tadeusz Mazowiecki
Special Raporteur to the UN Commission on Human Rights

"Another safari?" an acquaintance asked me when I arrived in the city [of Sarajevo] in late winter. "What do you hope to see this time, more corpses, more destruction? We should charge you admission".... A lot of dreams have died there in the past year—dreams that the world has a conscience, that Europe is a civilized place, that there is justice in human affairs as well as sorrow. It should be no surprise that the old millenarian dream that knowledge and truth would set us free would die there as well. Reality, it turns out, is better apprehended in the Lion Cemetery [in Sarajevo] than in the Palais des Nations in Geneva or the United Nations in New York, much as we might wish otherwise.

David Rieff
"On Your Knees with the Dying"
Why Bosnia? Writings on the Balkan War

VI

**LETTER OF RESIGNATION
AND LIST OF PERIODIC REPORTS
SUBMITTED BY
TADEUSZ MAZOWIECKI
SPECIAL RAPPORTEUR TO THE UNITED NATIONS
COMMISSION ON HUMAN RIGHTS**

On 14 August 1992 the United Nations Commission on Human Rights adopted resolution 1992/S-1/1 in which it asked its Chairman to appoint a special rapporteur to investigate first hand the human rights situation in the territory of the former Yugoslavia. On 1 December 1992, the Commission asked the Special Rapporteur, Mr. Tadeusz Mazowiecki, "to continue his efforts, especially by carrying out such further missions to the former Yugoslavia as he deemed necessary...".

Mr. Mazowiecki submitted seventeen reports to the Commission over the next three years. On 27 July 1995, he submitted his letter of resignation. This letter as well as a list of the reports submitted to the Commission formed Annex I and II, respectively, to the seventeenth and final report. See the Special Rapporteur's final periodic report, 22 August 1995, E/CN.4/1996/9. The full text of this and other reports is available on the Commission's website at www.unchr.ch.

LETTER OF RESIGNATION AND LIST OF PERIODIC REPORTS SUBMITTED BY TADEUSZ MAZOWIECKI SPECIAL RAPPORTEUR TO THE UNITED NATIONS COMMISSION ON HUMAN RIGHTS

Annex I

Letter dated 27 July 1995 addressed by Mr. Tadeusz Mazowiecki to the Chairman of the Commission on Human Rights.

Dear Mr. Chairman,

Events in recent weeks in Bosnia and Herzegovina, and above all the fact that the United Nations has allowed Srebrenica and Žepa to fall, along with the horrendous tragedy which has beset the population of those "safe havens" guaranteed by international agreements, oblige me to state that I do not see any possibility of continuing the mandate of Special Rapporteur entrusted to me by the Commission on Human Rights.

On accepting the mandate which was given to me for the first time in August 1992, I declared unequivocally that my goal would not simply be writing reports but helping the people themselves. The creation of "safe havens" was from the very beginning a central recommendation in my reports. The recent decisions of the London conference which accepted the fall of Srebrenica and resigned itself to the fate of Žepa are unacceptable to me. Those decisions did not create the conditions necessary for the defence of all "safe havens".

These events constitute a turning point in the development of the situation in Bosnia. At one and the same time, we are dealing with the struggle of a State, a member of the United Nations, for its survival and multi-ethnic character, and with the endeavour to protect principles of international order. One cannot speak about the protection of human rights with credibility when one is confronted with the lack of consistency and courage displayed by the international community and its leaders. The reality of the human rights situation today is illustrated by the tragedy of the people of Srebrenica and Žepa.

Human rights violations continue blatantly. There are constant blockades of the delivery of humanitarian aid. The civilian population is shelled remorselessly and the "blue helmets" and representatives of humanitarian organizations are dying. Crimes have been committed with swiftness and brutality and by contrast the response of the international community has been slow and ineffectual.

The character of my mandate only allows me to further describe crimes and violations of human rights. But the present critical moment forces us to realize the true character of those crimes and the responsibility of Europe and the international community for their own helplessness in addressing them. We have been fighting in Poland against a totalitarian system with a vision for the Europe of tomorrow. How can we believe in a Europe of tomorrow created by children of people who are abandoned today?

I would like to believe that the present moment will be a turning point in the relationship between Europe and the world towards Bosnia. The very stability of international order and the principle of civilization is at stake over the question of Bosnia. I am not convinced that the turning point hoped for will happen and cannot continue to participate in the pretence of the protection of human rights.

Mr. Chairman, please understand the motives behind my decision and convey them to the members of the Commission on Human Rights. I will submit my final eighteenth report based on my recent mission to Tuzla to the Commission in the near future.

Please accept, Excellency, the assurances of my highest consideration.

Yours sincerely,

Tadeusz Mazowiecki

Special Rapporteur on the situation of human rights
in the territory of the former Yugoslavia

Annex II

List of all periodic reports on the situation of human rights in the territory of the former Yugoslavia submitted by Mr. Tadeusz Mazowiecki, Special Rapporteur of the Commission on Human Rights

1. E/CN.4/1992/S-1/9, (28 August 1992)

Covers the policy of ethnic cleansing as regards Bosnia and Herzegovina, Croatia, Serbia and Montenegro. Also concerns detention, executions, disappearances, factors contributing to the violations of human rights, and difficulties affecting the functioning of humanitarian organizations.

2. E/CN.4/1992/S-1/10, (27 October 1992)

Second visit to the former Yugoslavia. Annex I: programme of second visit; Annex II: Statement of Clyde Snow concerning mass graves.

3. A/47/666-S/24809 (17 November 1992)

Covers the general situation in Bosnia and Herzegovina, Croatia, and Serbia with specific reference to destruction of religious sites and rape as a feature of "ethnic cleansing"; other war crimes, and the humanitarian crisis.

4. E/CN.4/1993/50 (10 February 1993)

Covers whole territory of former Yugoslavia with specific reference in Bosnia and Herzegovina to executions, arbitrary detentions, rape, and the situation of children, forced transfer of populations, attacks on non-military targets, and the humanitarian crisis; annexes refer to extra judicial, summary or arbitrary executions and report of team of experts on their mission to investigate rape.

5. E/CN.4/1994/3 (5 May 1993)

Covers "ethnic cleansing" of eastern enclaves, allegations regarding the government offensive of December/January1993, forcibly displaced in east, forced recruitment, situation of Serbs in Tuzla.

6. E/CN.4/1994/4 (19 May 1993)

Covers "ethnic cleansing" by Bosnian Croat forces and arbitrary executions by Bosnia and Herzegovina Government forces in the Vitez area.

7. E/CN.4/1994/6 (26 August 1993)

Covers the general situation in Sarajevo including the use of basic utilities as a weapon of war, the blocking of humanitarian aid, victimization of those in need of special respect and protection, and the rapid disintegration of the rule of law.

8. E/CN.4/1994/8 (6 September 1993)

Covers the situation in Mostar including "ethnic cleansing", arbitrary arrest and detentions, and civilians as targets of military attacks.

9. E/CN.4/1994/47 (17 November 1993)

Covers the situation in Bosnia and Herzegovina, Croatia, the Federal Republic of Yugoslavia, with specific reference to arbitrary executions and "ethnic cleansing," arbitrary detention, citizenship, evictions, destruction of property, the situation of the media, etc.

10. E/CN.4/1994/110 (21 February 1994)

Covers the whole territory of former Yugoslavia, with special reference to the problem of disappearances, the situation of children, previous recommendations and their follow-up.

11. E/CN.4/1995/4 (10 June 1994)

Covers the situation in Goražde.

12. E/CN.4/1995/10 (4 August 1994)

Covers the situation in central Bosnia and the Mostar area, Sarajevo, Mostar, Bihać, activities of international agencies and organizations, areas under the control of Bosnian Serb forces, and the Former Yugoslav Republic of Macedonia.

13. A/49/641-S/1994/1252 (4 November 1994)

Covers the general situation in Bosnia and Herzegovina, Croatia, the Federal Republic of Yugoslavia, and The Former Yugoslav Republic of Macedonia.

14. E/CN.4/1995/54 (13 December 1994)

Covers Bosnia and Herzegovina, Croatia, Federal Republic of Yugoslavia, and the Former Yugoslav Republic of Macedonia, with specific reference to international activities. Special report on the media.

15. E/CN.4/1995/57 (9 January 1995)

Covers Bosnia and Herzegovina, Croatia, the Federal Republic of Yugoslavia, the Former Yugoslav Republic of Macedonia, with special reference to disappearances and field operations.

16. E/CN.4/1996/3 (21 April 1995)

Covers the situation in Banja Luka with specific reference to developments prior to and immediately following February 1995, including forced labour and departure procedures.

17. E/CN.4/1996/6 (5 July 1995)

Covers the situation in Western Slavonia following the 1 May 1995 Croatian offensive and the situation in Bosnia and Herzegovina, with specific reference to Sarajevo, violations occurring in safe areas, Banja Luka, central Bosnia and Herzegovina and Mostar.

Other enemies [through the ages] have burnt [Bosnia's] fields, have put her villages to the knife or sword and slaughtered her flocks. And yet, fields can be sown again, the blackened plum tree puts forth new shoots, the massacre's cowed survivors come down from their caves and build shacks from the rubble.

But the new overlords are not content with conquest, with subjugation. They mean to obliterate a people; and they know full well that the most effective obliteration comes from within, by setting neighbor against neighbor. To wipe out a people, it is not enough to harry, to burn, and to kill. Memory itself must be cleansed—the memory that there ever was such a land, a land where the living was good, a land that all its people knew as home.

Francis R. Jones
"Return"
Why Bosnia? Writings on the Balkan War

Bosnia matters, because it has chosen to defend not just its own self-determination but the values of multicultural, long-evolved, and mutually fruitful cohabitation. Not since Andalusia has Europe owed so much to a synthesis, which also stands as a perfect rebuke to the cynical collusion between the apparently "warring" fanatics. If Sarajevo goes under, then all who care for such things will have lost something precious, and will curse themselves because they never knew its value while they still had it.

Christopher Hitchens
"Why Bosnia Matters"
Why Bosnia? Writings on the Balkan War

VII

INDICTMENTS ISSUED BY
THE INTERNATIONAL CRIMINAL TRIBUNAL
FOR THE FORMER YUGOSLAVIA
AT THE HAGUE

INDICTMENT I

RATKO MLADIĆ AND RADOVAN KARADŽIĆ

(BOSNIA-HERZEGOVINA)

International Criminal Tribunal for the former Yugoslavia, Indictments and Proceedings, Case No. IT-95-5, 24 July 1995, www.un.org/icty/ind-e.htm. While this is the full text of the Indictment, for Schedules or Annexures appended to the indictments see the ICTY documents on the web.

THE INTERNATIONAL CRIMINAL TRIBUNAL
FOR THE FORMER YUGOSLAVIA

THE PROSECUTOR OF THE TRIBUNAL
AGAINST
RADOVAN KARADŽIĆ
RATKO MLADIĆ

INDICTMENT

Richard J. Goldstone, Prosecutor of the International Criminal Tribunal for the Former Yugoslavia, pursuant to his authority under Article 18 of the Statute of the International Criminal Tribunal for the Former Yugoslavia ("The Statute of the Tribunal"), charges:

THE ACCUSED

1. **RADOVAN KARADŽIĆ** was born on 19 June 1945 in the municipality of Savnik of the Republic of Montenegro. From on or about 13 May 1992 to the present, he has been president of the Bosnian Serb administration in Pale.

2. **RATKO MLADIĆ** was born on 12 March 1943 in the municipality of Kalinovik of the Republic of Bosnia and Herzegovina. He is a career military officer and holds the rank of general in the Bosnian Serb armed forces. From on or about 14 May 1992 to the present, he has been the commander of the army of the Bosnian Serb administration.

SUPERIOR AUTHORITY

RADOVAN KARADŽIĆ

3. **RADOVAN KARADŽIĆ** was a founding member and president of the Serbian Democratic Party (SDS) of what was then the Socialist Republic of Bosnia and Herzegovina. The SDS was the main political party among the Serbs in Bosnia and Herzegovina. As president of the SDS, he was and is the most powerful official in the party. His duties as president include representing the party, co-ordinating the work of party organs and ensuring the realisation of the programmatic tasks and goals of the party. He continues to hold this post.

4. **RADOVAN KARADŽIĆ** became the first president of the Bosnian Serb administration in Pale on or about 13 May 1992. At the time he assumed this position, his *de jure* powers,

as described in the constitution of the Bosnian Serb administration, included, but were not limited to, commanding the army on the Bosnian Serb administration in times of war and peace and having the authority to appoint, promote and discharge officers of the army.

5. In addition to his powers described in the constitution, **RADOVAN KARADŽIĆ'S** powers as president of the Bosnian Serb administration are augmented by Article 6 of the Bosnian Serb Act on People's Defence which vested in him, among other powers, the authority to supervise the Territorial Defence both in peace and war and the authority to issue orders for the utilisation of the police in case of war, immediate threat and other emergencies. Article 39 of the same Act empowered him, in cases of imminent threat of war and other emergencies, to deploy Territorial Defence units for the maintenance of law and order.

6. **RADOVAN KARADŽIĆ'S** powers are further augmented by Article 33 of the Bosnian Serb Act on Internal Affairs, which authorised him to activate reserve police in emergency situations.

7. **RADOVAN KARADŽIĆ** has exercised the powers described above and has acted and been dealt with internationally as the president of the Bosnian Serb administration in Pale. In that capacity, he has, *inter alia*, participated in international negotiations and has personally made agreements on such matters as cease-fires and humanitarian relief that have been implemented.

RATKO MLADIĆ

8. **RATKO MLADIĆ** was, in 1991, appointed commander of the 9th Corps of the Yugoslav People's Army (JNA) in Knin in the Republic of Croatia. Subsequently, in May 1992, he assumed command of the forces of the Second Military District of the JNA which then effectively became the Bosnian Serb army. He holds the rank of general and from about 14 May 1992 to the present, has been the commander of the army of the Bosnian Serb administration.

9. **RATKO MLADIĆ** has demonstrated his control in military matters by negotiating, *inter alia*, cease-fire and prisoner exchange agreements; agreements relating to the opening of Sarajevo airport; agreements relating to access for humanitarian aid convoys; and anti-sniping agreements, all of which have been implemented.

GENERAL ALLEGATIONS

10. At all times relevant to this indictment, a state of armed conflict and partial occupation existed in the Republic of Bosnia and Herzegovina in the territory of the former Yugoslavia.

11. All acts or omissions herein set forth as grave breaches of the Geneva Conventions of 1949 (hereafter "grave breaches") recognised by Article 2 of the Statute of the Tribunal occurred during that armed conflict and partial occupation.

12. In each paragraph charging crimes against humanity, crimes recognised by Article 5 of the Statute of the Tribunal, the alleged acts or omissions were part of a widespread, systematic or large-scale attack directed against a civilian population.

13. The term "UN peacekeepers" used throughout this indictment includes UN military observers of the United Nations.

14. The UN peacekeepers and civilians referred to in this indictment were, at all relevant times, persons protected by the Geneva Conventions of 1949.

15. The accused in this indictment were required to abide by the laws and customs governing the conduct of war, including the Geneva Conventions of 1949.

CHARGES

16. The charges set forth in this indictment are in three parts:

Part I of the indictment, Counts 1 to 9, charges a crime of genocide, crimes against humanity and crimes that were perpetrated against the civilian population and against places of worship throughout the territory of the Republic of Bosnia and Herzegovina.

Part II of the indictment, Counts 10 to 12, charges crimes relating to the sniping campaign against civilians in Sarajevo.

Part III of the indictment, Counts 13 to 16, charges crimes relating to the taking of UN peacekeepers as hostages.

PART I

COUNTS 1–2
(GENOCIDE)
(CRIME AGAINST HUMANITY)

17. **RADOVAN KARADŽIĆ** and **RATKO MLADIĆ**, from April 1992, in the territory of the Republic of Bosnia and Herzegovina, by their acts and omissions, committed genocide.

18. Bosnian Muslim and Bosnian Croat civilians were persecuted on national, political and religious grounds throughout the Republic of Bosnia and Herzegovina. Thousands of them

were interned in detention facilities where they were subjected to widespread acts of physical and psychological abuse and to inhumane conditions. Detention facility personnel who ran and operated the Omarska, Keraterm and Luka detention facilities, among others, including, but not limited to Željko Meakić (Omarska), Duško Sikirica (Keraterm) and Goran Jelisić (Luka), intended to destroy Bosnian Muslim and Bosnian Croat people as national, ethnic, or religious groups and killed, seriously injured and deliberately inflicted upon them conditions intended to bring about their physical destruction. The conditions in the detention facilities, which are described in paragraphs 20–22 hereunder, are incorporated in full herein.

19. **RADOVAN KARADŽIĆ** and **RATKO MLADIĆ**, between April 1992 and July 1995, in the territory of the Republic of Bosnia and Herzegovina, by their acts and omissions, and in concert with others, committed a crime against humanity by persecuting Bosnian Muslim and Bosnian Croat civilians on national, political and religious grounds. As set forth below, they are criminally responsible for the unlawful confinement, murder, rape, sexual assault, torture, beating, robbery and inhumane treatment of civilians; the targeting of political leaders, intellectuals and professionals; the unlawful deportation and transfer of civilians; the unlawful shelling of civilians; the unlawful appropriation and plunder of real and personal property; the destruction of homes and businesses; and the destruction of places of worship.

DETENTION FACILITIES

20. As soon as military forces from Bosnia and elsewhere in the former Yugoslavia began to attack towns and villages in the Republic of Bosnia and Herzegovina, thousands of Bosnian Muslim and Bosnian Croat civilians were systematically selected and rounded up on national, ethnic, political or religious grounds and interned in detention facilities throughout the territory occupied by the Bosnian Serbs. These facilities include, but are not limited to:

Detention Facility	Dates of existence
Omarska:	May–August 1992
Keraterm:	May–August 1992
Trnopolje:	May–December 1992
Luka	May–July 1992
Manjača:	Summer 1991–December 1992
Sušica:	June 1992 –September 1992
KP Dom Foča:	April–mid-1993

21. Many of these detention facilities were staffed and operated by military and police personnel and their agents, under the control of **RADOVAN KARADŽIĆ** and **RATKO MLADIĆ**. In addition, Bosnian Serb police and military interrogators had unfettered access to all of the detention facilities and operated in conjunction with the personnel in control of these detention facilities. These facilities and personnel include, but are not limited to:

Detention Facility	Commander	Guards
Omarska	Željko Meakić (police)	police/military
Keraterm	Duško Sikirica (police)	police/military
Trnopolje	Slobodon Kuruzović (military)	police/military
Luka	Goran Jelisić (police)	paramilitary
Manjača	Božidar Popović (military)	military
Sušica	Dragan Nikolić (military)	military
KP Dom Foča	Milorad Krnojelac	military

22. Thousands of Bosnian Muslim and Bosnian Croat civilians, including women, children and elderly persons, were detained in these facilities for protracted periods of time. They were not afforded judicial process and their internment was not justified by military necessity. They were detained, in large measure, because of their national, religious and political identity. The conditions in the detention facilities were inhumane and brutal. Bosnian Serb military and police personnel in charge of these facilities, including Dragan Nikolić (Sušica), Željko Meakić (Omarska), Duško Sikirica (Keraterm) and other persons over whom they had control, subjected the civilian detainees to physical and psychological abuse, intimidation and maltreatment. Detention facility personnel, intending to destroy Bosnian Muslim and Bosnian Croat people as national, ethnic or religious groups, killed, seriously injured and deliberately inflicted upon them conditions intended to bring about their physical destruction. Detainees were repeatedly subjected to and/or witnessed inhumane acts, including murder, rape, sexual assault, torture, beatings, robbery as well as other forms of mental and physical abuse. In many instances, women and girls who were detained were raped at the camps or taken from the detention centres and raped or otherwise sexually abused at other locations. Daily food rations provided to detainees were inadequate and often amounted to starvation rations. Medical care for the detainees was insufficient or non-existent and the general hygienic conditions were grossly inadequate.

TARGETING OF POLITICAL LEADERS, INTELLECTUALS AND PROFESSIONALS

23. Particularly singled out for persecution by the Bosnian Serb military, Bosnian Serb police and their agents, under the direction and control of **RADOVAN KARADŽIĆ** and **RATKO MLADIĆ**, were civilian political leaders and members of the primary Bosnian Muslim political party, the Party for Democratic Action (SDA), and the principal Bosnian Croat political party, the Croatian Democratic Union (HDZ), from the cities of Prijedor, Vlasenica, Bosanski Šamac and Foča, amongst others. In many instances, lists identifying leaders of the SDA and the HDZ were provided by the SDS to personnel of the Bosnian Serb military, police and their agents. Using these lists, Bosnian Muslim and Bosnian Croat political leaders were arrested, interned, physically abused and, in many instances, murdered. Some local SDA leaders who were persecuted because of their political beliefs

include, but are not limited to, Muhamed Čehajić (Prijedor), Sulejman Tihić (Bosanski Šamac), and Ahmet Hadžić (Brčko).

24. In addition to persecutions of Bosnian Muslim and Bosnian Croat political leaders, the Bosnian Serb military, police and their agents systematically targeted for persecution on national or religious grounds, Bosnian Muslim and Bosnian Croat intellectuals and professionals in many towns and villages including Prijedor, Vlasenica, Bosanski Šamac and Foča, among others. Individuals who were persecuted include, but are not limited to Abdulah Puškar (academic), Žiko Crnalić (businessman) and Esad Mehmedalija (attorney) from Prijedor; Osman Vatić (attorney) from Brčko.

DEPORTATION

25. Thousands of Bosnian Muslims and Bosnian Croats from the areas of Vlasenica, Prijedor, Bosanski Šamac, Brčko and Foča, among others, were systematically arrested and interned in detention facilities established and maintained by the Bosnian Serb military, police and their agents and thereafter unlawfully deported or transferred to locations inside and outside of the Republic of Bosnia and Herzegovina. In addition, Bosnian Muslim and Bosnian Croat civilians, including women, children and elderly persons, were taken directly from their homes and eventually used in prisoner exchanges by Bosnian Serb military and police and their agents under the control and direction of **RADOVAN KARADŽIĆ** and **RATKO MLADIĆ**. These deportations and others were not conducted as evacuations for safety, military necessity or for any other lawful purpose and have, in conjunction with other actions directed against Bosnian Muslim and Bosnian Croat civilians, resulted in a significant reduction or elimination of Bosnian Muslims and Bosnian Croats in certain occupied regions.

SHELLING OF CIVILIAN GATHERINGS

26. Beginning in July 1992 and continuing through to July 1995, Bosnian Serb military forces, under the direction and control of **RADOVAN KARADŽIĆ** and **RATKO MLADIĆ**, unlawfully fired on civilian gatherings that were of no military significance in order to kill, terrorise and demoralise the Bosnian Muslim and Bosnian Croat civilian population. These incidents include, but are not limited to the following:

Location/Type of Municipality	Date	Casualties	Civilian Gathering
Sarajevo (picnic) Sarajevo	03/07/92	10	
Sarajevo (airport) Sarajevo	11/02/93	4	
Srebrenica (playground) Srebrenica	12/4/93	15	
Dobrinja (soccer game) Sarajevo	01/06/93	146	
Dobrinja (water line) Sarajevo	12/07/93	27	
Sarajevo (residential street) Sarajevo	28/11/93	11	

Ciglane Market (fruit market) Sarajevo	06/12/93	20	
Alipašino Polje (children) Sarajevo	22/01/94	10	(playing)
Cetinjska St (children) Sarajevo	26/10/94	7	(playing)
Sarajevo (Livanjska Street) Sarajevo	08/11/94	7	
Sarajevo (flea market) Sarajevo	22/12/94	9	
Tuzla (plaža) Tuzla	24/05/95	195	

APPROPRIATION AND PLUNDER OF PROPERTY

27. Shortly after armed hostilities broke out in the Republic of Bosnia and Herzegovina, Bosnian Serb forces quickly suppressed armed resistance in most villages and cities. During and after the course of consolidating their gains, Bosnian Serb military and police personnel, and other agents of the Bosnian Serb administration, under the direction and control of **RADOVAN KARADŽIĆ** and **RATKO MLADIĆ**, systematically and wantonly appropriated and looted the real and personal property of Bosnian Muslim and Bosnian Croat civilians. The appropriation of property was extensive and not justified by military necessity. It occurred from April 1992 to January 1993 in the municipalities of Prijedor, Vlasenica, and Bosanski Šamac, among others.

28. The appropriation and looting of said property was accomplished in the following manner and by the following means, among others:

A. Thousands of Bosnian Muslim and Bosnian Croat civilians were forced into detention facilities where they remained for protracted periods of time. Upon entering these internment facilities, the personnel who ran the internment facilities systematically stole the personal property of the detainees, including jewellery, watches, money and other valuables. The detainees were rarely provided receipts for the property taken from them or given their property back upon their release.

B. Civilians interned in these camps witnessed and/or were subjected to physical and psychological abuse. After witnessing or experiencing serious abuse, thousands of internees were forcibly transferred from these camps to locations inside and outside the Republic of Bosnia and Herzegovina. Before being forcibly transferred, many detainees were compelled to sign official Bosnian Serb documents wherein they "voluntarily" relinquished to the Bosnian Serb administration title to and possession of their real and personal property.

C. In many instances, Bosnian Muslim and Bosnian Croat civilian detainees were taken from internment camps to their homes and businesses and forced to turn over to their escorts money and other valuables. In other instances, they were used as labourers to load property from Bosnian Muslim and Bosnian Croat homes and businesses onto trucks for transportation to parts unknown. This occurred with the consent and approval of those in control of the detention facilities.

D. Many Bosnian Muslim and Bosnian Croat civilians who were not interned in camps were forced to stay in their communities where they were subjected to physical and psychological abuse from Bosnian Serb military and police and their agents, paramilitary forces and lawless elements of the Bosnian Serb community. Conditions for many became intolerable and they left. Before leaving, many civilians were compelled to sign official Bosnian Serb documents wherein they "voluntarily" relinquished to the Bosnian Serb administration their rights to their real and personal property. In some cases, Bosnian Muslim and Bosnian Croat civilians who left their communities were permitted to take with them limited amounts of personal property and money, but even that property was stolen from them at Bosnian Serb checkpoints or at other locations.

E. In many instances during and after the Bosnian Serb military take-over of towns and villages, Bosnian Serb military, police and their agents, entered the homes of non-Serb civilians and plundered the personal property of non-Serb civilians.

DESTRUCTION OF PROPERTY

29. Persecution throughout the occupied territory by Bosnian Serb military, police and their agents, or third parties with their acquiescence, involved the systematic destruction of Bosnian Muslim and Bosnian Croat homes and businesses. These homes and businesses were singled out and systematically destroyed in areas where hostilities had ceased or had not taken place. The purpose of this unlawful destruction was to ensure that the inhabitants could not and would not return to their homes and communities. The cities, villages and towns, or Bosnian Muslim and Bosnian Croat portions thereof, where extensive destruction of property occurred include, but are not limited to the following:

Town/Village	Municipality	Approximate dates of destruction
Grebnice	Bosanski Šamac	19-22 April 1992
Hrvatska Tišina	Bosanski Šamac	19-22 April 1992
Hasići	Bosanski Šamac	19-22 April 1992
Derventa	Derventa	4 April 1992
Vijaka	Derventa	4 April 1992
Bosanski Brod	Bosanski Brod	3 March 1992
Odžak	Odžak	July 1992
Modriča	Modriča	Late April 1992
Vidovice	Orašje	29 April and 4 May 1992
Gradačac	Gradačac	mid-1992
Piskavice	Vlasenica	22 April 1992
Gobelje	Vlasenica	28 April 1992
Turalići	Vlasenica	28 April 1992
Djile	Vlasenica	1-3 May 1992

Pomol	Vlasenica	1 May 1992
Gaj	Vlasenica	1 May 1992
Bešići	Vlasenica	1 May 1992
Nurići	Vlasenica	1 May 1992
Vrsinje	Vlasenica	1 May 1992
Džamdžići	Vlasenica	8 May 1992
Pivići	Vlasenica	11 May 1992
Hambarine	Prijedor	23 May 1992
Ljubija	Prijedor	23 May 1992
Kozarac	Prijedor	24 May 1992
Bišćani	Prijedor	20 July 1992
Čarakovo	Prijedor	20 July 1992
Rizvanovići	Prijedor	20 July 1992
Sredice	Prijedor	20 July 1992
Žikovi	Prijedor	20 July 1992

DESTRUCTION OF SACRED SITES

30. Muslim and Catholic places of worship were systematically damaged and/or destroyed by Bosnian Serb military forces and others. In many instances, where no military action had taken place or had ceased, these sacred sites were also damaged and/or destroyed. These places of worship include, but are not limited to those mentioned in paragraph 37 of this indictment. Bosnian Serb military and police forces failed to take reasonable and necessary measures to ensure that these religious sites would be protected.

31. The events described above were directed against Bosnian Muslim and Bosnian Croat civilians. Individually and collectively, these actions taken by or on behalf of the Bosnian Serb administration, have been on such a large scale and implemented in such a systematic way that they have destroyed, traumatised or dehumanised most aspects of Bosnian Muslim and Bosnian Croat life in those areas where the Bosnian Serb administration has taken control.

32. **RADOVAN KARADŽIĆ** and **RATKO MLADIĆ** knew or had reason to know that subordinates in detention facilities were about to kill or cause serious physical or mental harm to Bosnian Muslims and Bosnian Croats with the intent to destroy them, in whole or in part, as national, ethnic or religious groups or had done so and failed to take necessary and reasonable measures to prevent such acts or to punish the perpetrators thereof.

33. **RADOVAN KARADŽIĆ** and **RATKO MLADIĆ** individually and in concert with others planned, instigated, ordered or otherwise aided and abetted in the planning, preparation or execution of persecutions on political and religious grounds or knew or had reason to know that subordinates were about to do the same or had done so and failed to

take necessary and reasonable measures to prevent such acts or to punish the perpetrators thereof.

By these acts and omissions, **RADOVAN KARADŽIĆ** and **RATKO MLADIĆ** committed:
> **Count 1:** GENOCIDE as recognised by Articles 4(2)(a),(b),(c) and 7(3) of the Statute of the Tribunal.
>
> **Count 2:** a CRIME AGAINST HUMANITY as recognised by Articles 5(h) and 7(1) and 7(3) of the Statute of the Tribunal.

COUNTS 3-4
(UNLAWFUL CONFINEMENT OF CIVILIANS)

34. From the outset of hostilities in the Republic of Bosnia and Herzegovina, thousands of Bosnian Muslim and Bosnian Croat civilians were unlawfully interned in detention facilities. Many of these facilities were established and operated by the Bosnian Serb military, police and their agents under the direction and control of **RADOVAN KARADŽIĆ** and **RATKO MLADIĆ**. As described in paragraphs 18 and 20-22 of this indictment and incorporated in full herein, the conditions in these facilities were inhumane. Countless civilians were abused and many perished in these internment facilities.

35. **RADOVAN KARADŽIĆ** and **RATKO MLADIĆ** individually and in concert with others planned, ordered, instigated or otherwise aided and abetted in the planning and preparation or execution of the unlawful detention of civilians or knew or had reason to know that subordinates were unlawfully detaining civilians and failed to take necessary and reasonable measures to prevent such acts or to punish the perpetrators thereof.

By these acts and omissions, **RADOVAN KARADŽIĆ** and **RATKO MLADIĆ** committed:
> **Count 3:** a GRAVE BREACH as recognised by Articles 2(g) (unlawful confinement of civilians), 7(1) and 7(3) of the Statute of the Tribunal.
>
> **Count 4:** a VIOLATION OF THE LAWS OR CUSTOMS OF WAR (outrages upon personal dignity) as recognised by Articles 3, 7(1) and 7(3) of the Statute of the Tribunal.

COUNT 5
(SHELLING OF CIVILIAN GATHERINGS)

36. As described in paragraph 26 of this indictment, which is incorporated in full herein, Bosnian Serb military forces fired upon civilian gatherings that were of no military significance, thereby causing injury and death to hundreds of civilians. **RADOVAN KARADŽIĆ** and **RATKO MLADIĆ**, individually and in concert with others planned, instigated,

ordered or otherwise aided and abetted in the planning, preparation or execution of unlawful attacks against the civilian population and individual civilians with area fire weapons such as mortars, rockets and artillery or knew or had reason to know that the Bosnian Serb military forces were about to unlawfully attack the civilian population and individual civilians, or had already done so, and failed to take the necessary and reasonable steps to prevent such shelling or to punish the perpetrators thereof.

By these acts and omissions, **RADOVAN KARADŽIĆ** and **RATKO MLADIĆ** committed:

Count 5: a **VIOLATION OF THE LAWS OR CUSTOMS OF WAR** (deliberate attack on the civilian population and individual civilians) as recognised by Articles 3, 7(1) and 7(3) of the Statute of the Tribunal.

COUNT 6
(DESTRUCTION OF SACRED SITES)

37. Since April 1992 to the end of May 1995, in territory of the Republic of Bosnia and Herzegovina controlled by the Bosnian Serb military and police, including areas where no military conflict was ongoing, there has been widespread and systematic damage to and destruction of Muslim and Roman Catholic sacred sites. In areas such as Banja Luka, the near total obliteration of these religious sites has occurred. The sites in the Banja Luka area include the following:

MUSLIM SACRED SITES

Name of Mosque	Location	Date of Destruction or Damage
Sefer-Beg Mosque	Banja Luka	09.04.93
Ferhadija Mosque	Banja Luka	07.05.93
Arnaudija Mosque	Banja Luka	07.05.93
Mosque in Vrbanja	Banja Luka	11.05.93
Zulfikar Mosque	Banja Luka	15.05.93
Behram-Efendija Mosque	Banja Luka	26.05.93
Mehidibeg Mosque	Banja Luka	04.06.93
Sufi Mehmed-Paša Mosque	Banja Luka	04.06.93
Hadži-Begzade Mosque	Banja Luka	04.06.93
Gazanferija Mosque	Banja Luka	04.06.93
Hadži-Seben Mosque	Banja Luka	14.06.93
Hadži-Kurt Mosque	Banja Luka	14.06.93
Hadži-Pervis Mosque	Banja Luka	06.09.93
Hadži-Osmanija Mosque	Banja Luka	08.09.93
Hadži-Omer Mosque	Banja Luka	09.09.93
Hadži-Salihija Mosque	Banja Luka	09.09.93

ROMAN CATHOLIC SACRED SITES

Name of Church	City	Date of Destruction or Damage
Church of St. Joseph at Trno	Banja Luka	24.10.91
Parish Church	Banja Luka	00.12.91
St. Bonaventura Cathedral	Banja Luka	31.12.91
St. Vincent Monastery	Banja Luka	00.12.92
Village Church	Vujnovići	05.05.95
Parish Church	Petričevac	06.05.95
St. Anthony of Padua Church and Franciscan Monastery	Banja Luka	07.05.95
Parish Church	Šargovac	07.05.95
Village Church	Majdan	08.05.95
Parish Church	Presnace	12.05.95

38. In other areas, damage and destruction to places of worship has been widespread These sites include, but are not limited to the Aladža Mosque (Foča); the Sultan Selim Mosque (Doboj); the Church of St. Peter and St. Paul, the Obri Chapel and the Sevri-Hadži Mosque (Mostar); the parish church (Novi Šeher) and the Čršijska Mosque (Konjic). Bosnian Serb military and police forces failed to take reasonable and necessary measures to ensure that these religious sites were protected.

39. **RADOVAN KARADŽIĆ** and **RATKO MLADIĆ**, individually and in concert with others planned, instigated, ordered or otherwise aided and abetted in the planning, preparation or execution of the destruction of sacred sites or knew or had reason to know that subordinates were about to damage or destroy these sites or had done so and failed to take necessary and reasonable measures to prevent them from doing so or to punish the perpetrators thereof.

By these acts and omissions, **RADOVAN KARADŽIĆ** and **RATKO MLADIĆ** committed:
  Count 6: a **VIOLATION OF THE LAWS OR CUSTOMS OF WAR** (destruction or wilful damage to institutions dedicated to religion) as recognised by Articles 3(d), 7(1) and 7(3) of the Statute of the Tribunal.

COUNT 7
(EXTENSIVE DESTRUCTION OF PROPERTY)

40. After the take-over of Foča (8 April 1992), Bosanski Šamac (17 April 1992), Vlasenica (21 April 1992), Prijedor (30 April 1992), Brčko (30 April 1992) and other municipalities in the Republic of Bosnia and Herzegovina, Bosnian Serb military and police forces and other elements over whom they had control, under the direction and control of

RADOVAN KARADŽIĆ and **RATKO MLADIĆ**, systematically destroyed, or permitted others to destroy, for no justifiable military reasons, Bosnian Muslim and Bosnian Croat businesses and residences in occupied cities and villages. The areas where extensive destruction occurred include those areas described in paragraph 29 of this indictment, which is incorporated in full herein.

41. **RADOVAN KARADŽIĆ** and **RATKO MLADIĆ**, individually and in concert with others planned, instigated, ordered or otherwise aided and abetted in the planning, preparation or execution of the extensive, wanton and unlawful destruction of Bosnian Muslim and Bosnian Croat property, not justified by military necessity or knew or had reason to know that subordinates were about to destroy or permit others to destroy the property of Bosnian Muslim or Bosnian Croat civilians or had done so and failed to take necessary and reasonable measures to prevent this destruction or to punish the perpetrators thereof.

By these acts and omissions, **RADOVAN KARADŽIĆ** and **RATKO MLADIĆ** committed:

> **Count 7:** a **GRAVE BREACH** as recognised by Articles 2(d) (destruction of property), 7(1) and 7(3) of the Statute of the Tribunal.

COUNTS 8-9
(APPROPRIATION AND PLUNDER OF PROPERTY)

42. As described in paragraphs 27-28 of this indictment, which are incorporated in full herein, Bosnian Serb military and police personnel and other agents of the Bosnian Serb administration, under the direction and control of **RADOVAN KARADŽIĆ** and **RATKO MLADIĆ**, systematically appropriated and looted the real and personal property of Bosnian Muslim and Bosnian Croat civilians.

43. **RADOVAN KARADŽIĆ** and **RATKO MLADIĆ**, individually and in concert with others planned, instigated, ordered or otherwise aided and abetted in the planning, preparation or execution of the extensive, wanton and unlawful appropriation of real and personal property owned by Bosnian Muslim and Bosnian Croat civilians or knew or had reason to know that subordinates were about to appropriate real and personal property of Bosnian Muslim and Bosnian Croat civilians or had done so and failed to take necessary and reasonable measures to prevent this appropriation or to punish the perpetrators thereof.

By these acts and omissions, **RADOVAN KARADŽIĆ** and **RATKO MLADIĆ** committed:

> **Count 8:** a **GRAVE BREACH** as recognised by Articles 2(d) (appropriation of property), 7(1) and 7(3) of the Statute of the Tribunal.
>
> **Count 9:** a **VIOLATION OF THE LAWS OR CUSTOMS OF WAR** (plunder of public or private property) as recognised by Articles 3(e), 7(1) and 7(3) of the Statute of the Tribunal.

PART II

COUNTS 10-12
(SARAJEVO SNIPING)

44. Since 5 April 1992, the City of Sarajevo has been besieged by forces of the Bosnian Serb army. Throughout this siege, there has been a systematic campaign of deliberate targeting of civilians by snipers of the Bosnian Serb military and their agents. The sniping campaign has terrorised the civilian population of Sarajevo and has resulted in a substantial number of civilian casualties, killed and wounded, including women, children and elderly. Between 5 May 1992 and 31 May 1995, snipers have systematically, unlawfully and wilfully killed and wounded civilians in the area of Sarajevo, including but not limited to the following individuals:

KILLED

Children
Elma Jakupović, age 2, at Jukićeva Street, No 17, on 20 July 1993
Elvedina Čolić, age 4, at Kobilja Glava on 8 August 1993
Adnan Kasapović, age 16, at Dj.A.Kuna Street on 24 October 1994
Nermina Omerović, age 11, at Djure Daničića Street on 8 November 1994

Women
Almasa Konjhodžić, age 56, at the intersection of Kranjčevića and Brodska Streets on 27 June 1993
Sevda Kustura, age 50, at Špicasta Stijena on 5 August 1993
Sada Pohara, age 19, at Žarka Zgonjanina Street, No 13, on 30 August 1993
Saliha Čomaga, age 38, at Mujkića Brdo, Ugorsko, on 8 September 1993
Edina Trto, age 25, at Ivana Krndelja Street on 26 September 1993
Hatema Mukanović, age 38, at Obala 27 July 89 Street on 11 January 1994
Radmila Plainović, age 51, at Vojvode Putnika Street on 7 February 1994
Lejla Bajramović, age 24, at B. Boris Kidrić Street, No 3, on 8 December 1994

Elderly
Hajrija Dizdarević, age 66, at Ivo Kranjčević Street 11 on 17 July 1993
Marko Stupar, age 64, at Zmaja od Bosne No 64 Street on 12 January 1994
Fadil Zuko, age 63, at Stara Cesta Street, bb on 2 February 1994
Dragomir Čulibrk, aged 61, at Prvomajska BB on 16 June 1994

Men
Adnan Mesihović, age 34, at Hasana Brkića Street on 3 September 1993
Junuz Čampara, age 59, at Milutin Djurašković Street on 6 September 1993

Augustin Vučić, age 57, at Ante Babića Street on 13th March 1994

Jasmin Podžo, age 23, at Mala Berkuša Street 10 on 4 March 1995

WOUNDED

Children

Boy, age 2, at Stara Cesta Street on 26 June 1993

Boy, age 12, at Kupališta swimming pool on 5 August 1993

Girl, age 9, at Kobilja Glava on 8 August 1993

Boy, age 14, at Džemal Bijedić Street on 3 September 1993

Girl, age 8, at Ivana Krndelja Street on 3 September 1993

Boy, age 15, at X transverzale Street bb on 4 October 1993

Boy, age 13, at Donji Hotonj II Street on 10 November 1993

Boy, age 12, at Petra Drapšina Street on 28 November 1993

Boy, age 17, at Džemala Bijedića Street on 10 January 1994

Boy, age 5, at Zmaja od Bosne Street on 19 June 1994

Girl, age 16, at Senada Mandića-Dende Street on 26 June 1994

Boy, age 13, at Miljenka Cvitkoviča Street on 22 July 1994

Boy, age 7, at Zmaja od Bosne Street on 18 November 1994

Girl, age 13, at the cross-roads of Rogina and Sedrenik Streets on 22 November 1994

Boy, age 14, at Sedrenik Street on 6 March 1995

Women

Female, age 20, at Hotonj on 5 August 1993

Female, age 52, at Franca Rožmana Street on 6 August 1993

Female, age 55, at Španskih Boraca Street on 30 August 1993

Female, age 35, at Ivana Krndelja Street on 3 September 1993

Female, age 32, at Nikola Demonja/ Grada Bakua Street area on 6 January 1994

Female, age 46, at Olimpijska Street, No 15, on 18 January 1994

Female, age 42, at 21 Maj Street on 9 May 1994

Female, age 50, and female, age 62, at Nikole Demonje Street on 25 May 1994

Female, age 45, at Mojmilo- Dobrinja Road on 13 June 1994

Female, age 46, at Zaim Imamović Street, No 15 on 20 July 1994

Female, age 54, at Baruthana Street on 8 November 1994

Female, age 28, at Zmaja od Bosne Street on 9 November 1994

Female, age 28, at Zmaja od Bosne Street on 18 November 1994

Female, age 24, at Franca Lehara Street, No 3 on 8 December 1994

Female, age 49, at Sedrenik Street on 10 December 1994

Elderly

Female, age 71, at "Ciglane" Market on 17 September 1993

Female, age 72, at Nikole Demonje Street on 2 October 1993

Female, age 60, at Lovčenska Street on 7 December 1993

Male, age 63, at St Anto Babić on 13 March 1994

Male, age 62, at Omladinskih Radnih Brigada Street on 16 June 1994

Male, age 61, at Prvomajska BB on 16 June 1994

Male, age 67, at Senad Mandić Denda Street, on 17 July 1994

Male, age 63, at Sedrenik Street on 11 December 1994

Male, age 62, at Sedrenik Street on 13 December 1994

Female, age 73, at the intersection of Zmaja od Bosne and Muzejska Streets on 18 December 1994

Men

Male, age 36, at Trg of ZAVNOBiH on 1 February 1993

Male, age 52, at Kobilja Glava on 25 June 1993

Male, age 29, at Stara Cesta Street on 7 October 1993

Male, age 50, and male, age 56, at Brace Ribara Street on 2 November 1993

Male, age 36, at Stara Cesta Street on 14 December 1993

Male, age 27, at Zmaja od Bosne Street on 19 June 1994

Male, age 20, male, age 27, male, age 39, and male, age 34, at Zmaja od Bosne Street on 9 November 1994

Male, age 29, at Sedrenik Street on 8 December 1994

Male, age 46, and male, age 33, at intersection of Franje Račkog and Maršala Tita Streets on 3 March 1995

Male, age 52, at Sedrenik Street on 6 March 1995

45. **RADOVAN KARADŽIĆ** and **RATKO MLADIĆ** individually and in concert with others planned, ordered, instigated or otherwise aided and abetted in the planning, preparation or execution of the sniping of civilians or knew or had reason to know that subordinates were sniping civilians and failed to take necessary and reasonable measures to prevent such acts or to punish the perpetrators thereof.

As to the deliberate attacks by sniper fire against the civilian population and individual civilians, which resulted in death and injury to said civilians, and acts and omissions related thereto, **RADOVAN KARADŽIĆ** and **RATKO MLADIĆ** committed:

> **Count 10:** a **VIOLATION OF THE LAWS OR CUSTOMS OF WAR** (deliberate attack on the civilian population and individual civilians) as recognised by Articles 3, 7(1) and 7(3) of the Statute of the Tribunal.

As to the killing by sniper fire of these civilians, among others, and acts and omissions related thereto, RADOVAN KARADŽIĆ and RATKO MLADIĆ committed:

> **Count 11:** a **CRIME AGAINST HUMANITY** as recognised by Articles 5(a) (murder), 7(1) and 7(3) of the Statute of the Tribunal.

As to the wounding by sniper fire of these civilians, among others, and acts and omissions related thereto, **RADOVAN KARADŽIĆ** and **RATKO MLADIĆ** committed:
Count 12: a **CRIME AGAINST HUMANITY** as recognised by Articles 5(i) (inhumane acts), 7(1) and 7(3) of the Statute of the Tribunal.

PART III

COUNTS 13-16
(HOSTAGES/HUMAN SHIELDS)

46. Between 26 May 1995 and 2 June 1995, Bosnian Serb military personnel, under the direction and control of **RADOVAN KARADŽIĆ** and **RATKO MLADIĆ**, seized 284 UN peacekeepers in Pale, Sarajevo, Goražde and other locations and held them hostage in order to prevent further North Atlantic Treaty Organisation (NATO) airstrikes. Bosnian Serb military personnel held the UN peacekeepers throughout their captivity by force or by the threat of force. In some instances, the UN hostages were assaulted. During and after protracted negotiations with Bosnian Serb leaders, the UN hostages were released in stages between 3 June 1995 and 19 June 1995.

47. After seizing UN peacekeepers in the Pale area, Bosnian Serb military personnel, under the direction and control of **RADOVAN KARADŽIĆ** and **RATKO MLADIĆ**, immediately selected certain UN hostages to use as "human shields," including but not limited to Capt. Patrick A. Rechner (Canada), Capt. Oldrich Zidlik (Czech Republic) Captain Teterevsky (Russia), Maj. Abdul Razak Bello (Nigeria), Capt. Ahmad Manzoor (Pakistan) and Maj. Gunnar Westlund (Sweden). From on or about 26 May 1995 through 27 May 1995, Bosnian Serb military personnel physically secured or otherwise held the UN peacekeepers against their will at potential NATO air targets, including the ammunition bunkers at Jahorinski Potok, the Jahorina radar site and a nearby communications centre in order to render these locations immune from further NATO airstrikes. High level Bosnian Serb political and military delegations inspected and photographed the UN hostages who were handcuffed at the ammunition bunkers at Jahorinski Potok.

48. **RADOVAN KARADŽIĆ** and **RATKO MLADIĆ**, individually and in concert with others planned, instigated, ordered or otherwise aided and abetted in the planning, preparation or execution of the taking of civilians, that is UN peacekeepers, as hostages and, additionally, using them as "human shields" and knew or had reason to know that subordinates were about to take and hold UN peacekeepers as hostages and about to use them as "human shields" or had done so and failed to take necessary and reasonable measures to prevent them from doing so or to punish the perpetrators thereof.

In regard to UN peacekeepers seized and held hostage between 26 May 1995 and 19 June 1995, **RADOVAN KARADŽIĆ** and **RATKO MLADIĆ**, by their acts and omissions, committed:

> **Count 13:** a **GRAVE BREACH** as recognised by Articles 2(h) (taking civilians as hostage), 7(1) and 7(3) of the Statute of the Tribunal.
>
> **Count 14:** a **VIOLATION OF THE LAWS OR CUSTOMS OF WAR** (taking of hostages) as recognised by Articles 3, 7(1) and 7(3) of the Statute of the Tribunal.

In regard to the UN peacekeepers used as "human shields" on 26 and 27 May 1995, **RADOVAN KARADŽIĆ** and **RATKO MLADIĆ**, by their acts and omissions, committed:

> **Count 15:** a **GRAVE BREACH** as recognised by Articles 2(b) (inhuman treatment), 7(1) and 7(3) of the Statute of the Tribunal.
>
> **Count 16:** a **VIOLATION OF THE LAWS OR CUSTOMS OF WAR** (cruel treatment) as recognised by Articles 3, 7(1) and 7(3) of the Statute of the Tribunal.

July 1995
Richard J. Goldstone,
Prosecutor

RATKO MLADIĆ AND RADOVAN KARADŽIĆ

(SREBRENICA)

International Criminal Tribunal for the former Yugoslavia, Indictments and Proceedings, Case No. IT-95-18, 16 November 1995, www.un.org/icty/ind-e.htm. While this is the full text of the Indictment, for Schedules or Annexures appended to the indictments see the ICTY documents on the web.

THE INTERNATIONAL CRIMINAL TRIBUNAL
FOR THE FORMER YUGOSLAVIA

THE PROSECUTOR OF THE TRIBUNAL
AGAINST
RADOVAN KARADŽIĆ
RATKO MLADIĆ

INDICTMENT

Richard J. Goldstone, Prosecutor of the International Criminal Tribunal for the former Yugoslavia, pursuant to his authority under Article 18 of the Statute of the International Criminal Tribunal for the former Yugoslavia ("The Statute of the Tribunal"), charges

RATKO MLADIĆ and RADOVAN KARADŽIĆ

with GENOCIDE, CRIMES AGAINST HUMANITY and VIOLATIONS OF THE LAWS OR CUSTOMS OF WAR, as set forth below:

"SAFE AREA" OF SREBRENICA

1. After war erupted in the Republic of Bosnia and Herzegovina, Bosnian Serb military forces occupied Bosnian Muslim villages in the eastern part of the country, resulting in an exodus of Bosnian Muslims to enclaves in Goražde, Žepa, Tuzla, and Srebrenica. All of the events referred to in this indictment took place in the Republic of Bosnia and Herzegovina.

2. On 16 April 1993, the Security Council of the United Nations, acting pursuant to Chapter VII of its Charter, adopted resolution 819, in which it demanded that all parties to the conflict in the Republic of Bosnia and Herzegovina treat Srebrenica and its surroundings as a safe area which should be free from any armed attack or any other hostile act. Resolution 819 was reaffirmed by Resolution 824 on 6 May 1993 and by Resolution 836 on 4 June 1993.

3. Before the attack by Bosnian Serb forces, as described in this indictment, the estimated Bosnian Muslim population in the safe area of Srebrenica, was approximately 60,000.

ATTACK ON THE SAFE AREA OF SREBRENICA

4. On or about 6 July 1995, the Bosnian Serb army shelled Srebrenica and attacked United Nations observation posts that were manned by Dutch soldiers and located in the safe area. The attack on the Srebrenica safe area by the Bosnian Serb army continued through 11 July 1995, when the first units of the attacking Bosnian Serb forces entered Srebrenica.

5. The Bosnian Muslim men, women and children who remained in Srebrenica after the beginning of the Bosnian Serb attack took two courses of action. Several thousand women, children and some mostly elderly men fled to the UN compound in Potočari, located within the safe area of Srebrenica, where they sought the protection of the Dutch battalion responsible for the compound. They remained at the compound from 11 July 1995 until 13 July 1995, when they were all evacuated by buses and trucks under the control of and operated by Bosnian Serb military personnel.

6. A second group of approximately 15,000 Bosnian Muslim men, with some women and children, gathered at Šušnjari during the evening hours of 11 July 1995 and fled, in a huge column, through the woods towards Tuzla. Approximately one-third of this group consisted of armed Bosnian military personnel and armed civilians. The rest were unarmed civilians.

EVENTS IN POTOČARI

7. On 11 July 1995 and 12 July 1995, **RATKO MLADIĆ** and members of his staff met in Bratunac with Dutch military officers and representatives of the Muslim refugees from Potočari. At these meetings, **RATKO MLADIĆ** informed them, among other things, that Bosnian Muslim soldiers who surrendered their weapons would be treated as prisoners of war according to the Geneva Conventions and that refugees evacuated from Potočari would not be hurt.

8. On or about 12 July 1995, Bosnian Serb military forces burned and looted Bosnian Muslim houses in and around Potočari.

9. On or about 12 July 1995, in the morning hours, Bosnian Serb military forces arrived at the UN military compound in Potočari and its environs.

10. On or about 12 July 1995, **RATKO MLADIĆ** arrived in Potočari, accompanied by his military aides and a television crew. He falsely and repeatedly told Bosnian Muslims in and around Potočari that they would not be harmed and that they would be safely transported out of Srebrenica.

11. On or about 12 July 1995, at the direction and in the presence of **RATKO MLADIĆ**, approximately 50-60 buses and trucks arrived near the UN military compound in Potočari.

Shortly after the arrival of these vehicles, the evacuation process of Bosnian Muslim refugees started. As Muslim women, children and men started to board the buses and trucks, Bosnian Serb military personnel separated the men from the women and children. This selection and separation of Muslim men took place in the presence of and at the direction of **RATKO MLADIĆ**.

12. The Bosnian Muslim men who had been separated from other refugees were taken to divers locations in and around Potočari. On or about 12 July 1995, **RATKO MLADIĆ** and Bosnian Serb military personnel under his command, informed some of these Muslim men that they would be evacuated and exchanged for Bosnian Serbs being held in Tuzla.

13. Most of the Muslim men who had been separated from the other refugees in Potočari were transported to Bratunac and then to the area of Karakaj, where they were massacred by Bosnian Serb military personnel.

14. Between 12 July 1995 and 13 July 1995, Bosnian Serb military personnel summarily executed Bosnian Muslim men and women at divers locations around the UN compound where they had taken refuge. The bodies of those summarily executed were left in fields and buildings in the immediate vicinity of the compound. These arbitrary killings instilled such terror and panic amongst the Muslims remaining there that some of them committed suicide and all the others agreed to leave the enclave.

15. The evacuation of all able-bodied Muslim refugees concluded on 13 July 1995. As a result of the Bosnian Serb attack on the safe area and other actions, the Muslim population of the enclave of Srebrenica was virtually eliminated by Bosnian Serb military personnel.

SURRENDER AND EXECUTIONS

16. Between the evening of 11 July 1995 and the morning of 12 July 1995, the huge column of Muslims which had gathered in Šušnjari fled Srebrenica through the woods towards Tuzla.

17. Bosnian Serb military personnel, supported by armoured personnel carriers, tanks, anti-aircraft guns and artillery, positioned themselves along the Bratunac-Milići road in an effort to interdict the column of Bosnian Muslims fleeing towards Tuzla.

18. As soon as the column reached Bosnian Serb held territory in the vicinity of Buljim, Bosnian Serb military forces attacked it. As a result of this and other attacks by Bosnian Serb military forces, many Muslims were killed and wounded and the column divided into several smaller parts which continued towards Tuzla. Approximately one-third of the column, mostly composed of military personnel, crossed the Bratunac-Milići road near Nova Kasaba and reached safety in Tuzla. The remaining Muslims were trapped behind the Bosnian Serb lines.

19. Thousands of Muslims were captured by or surrendered to Bosnian Serb military forces under the command and control of **RATKO MLADIĆ** and **RADOVAN KARADŽIĆ**. Many of the Muslims who surrendered did so because they were assured that they would be safe if they surrendered. In many instances, assurances of safety were provided to the Muslims by Bosnian Serb military personnel who were with other Bosnian Serb soldiers wearing stolen UN uniforms, and by Muslims who had been captured and ordered to summon their fellow Muslims from the woods.

20. Many of the Bosnian Muslims who were captured by or surrendered to Bosnian Serb military personnel were summarily executed by Bosnian Serb military personnel at the locations of their surrender or capture, or at other locations shortly thereafter. Incidents of such summary executions include, but are not limited to:

20.1 On or about 13 July 1995, near Nezuk in the Republic of Bosnia and Herzegovina, a group of 10 Bosnian Muslim men were captured. Bosnian Serb soldiers summarily executed some of these men, including Mirsad Alispahić and Hajrudin Mešanović.

20.2 On or about 13 July 1995, on the banks of the Jadar River between Konjević Polje and Drinjača, Bosnian Serb soldiers summarily executed 15 Bosnian Muslim men who had surrendered or been captured. Amongst those killed were Hamed Omerović, Azem Mujić and Ismet Ahmetović.

20.3 On or about 13 July 1995, in the vicinity of Konjević Polje, Bosnian Serb soldiers summarily executed hundreds of Muslims, including women and children.

20.4 On or about 17 July 1995 or 18 July 1995, in the vicinity of Konjević Polje, Bosnian Serb soldiers captured about 150–200 Bosnian Muslims and summarily executed about one-half of them.

20.5 On or about 18 July 1995 or 19 July 1995, in the vicinity of Nezuk, about 20 groups, each containing between 5–10 Bosnian Muslim men, surrendered to Bosnian Serb military forces. After the men surrendered, Bosnian Serb soldiers ordered them to line up and summarily executed them.

20.6 On or about 20 July 1995 or 21 July 1995, near the village of Meceš, Bosnian Serb military personnel, using megaphones, urged Bosnian Muslim men who had fled Srebrenica to surrender and assured them that they would be safe. Approximately 350 Bosnian Muslim men responded to these entreaties and surrendered. Bosnian Serb soldiers then took approximately 150 of them, instructed them to dig their own graves and then summarily executed them.

20.7 On or about 21 July 1995 or 22 July 1995, near the village of Meceš, an excavator dug a large pit and Bosnian Serb soldiers ordered approximately 260 Bosnian Muslim men who had been captured to stand around the hole. The Muslim men were then surrounded by armed Bosnian Serb soldiers and ordered not to move or they would be shot. Some of the men moved and were shot. The remaining men were pushed into the hole and buried alive.

21. Many of the Muslims who surrendered to Bosnian Serb military personnel were not killed at the locations of their surrender, but instead were transported to central assembly points where Bosnian Serb soldiers held them under armed guard. These assembly points included, among others, a hangar in Bratunac; soccer fields in Kasaba, Konjević Polje, Kravica, and Vlasenica; a meadow behind the bus station in Sandići and other fields and meadows along the Bratunac-Milići road.

22. Between 12 July 1995 and 14 July 1995, at various of these assembly points, including the hangar in Bratunac and the soccer stadium in Kasaba, **RATKO MLADIĆ** addressed the Bosnian Muslim detainees. He falsely and repeatedly assured them that they would be safe and that they would be exchanged for Bosnian Serb prisoners held by Bosnian government forces.

23. Between 12 July 1995 and 14 July 1995, Bosnian Serb military personnel arbitrarily selected Bosnian Muslim detainees and summarily executed them.

MASS EXECUTIONS NEAR KARAKAJ

24. On or about 14 July 1995, Bosnian Serb military personnel transported thousands of Muslim detainees from Bratunac, Kravica and other locations to an assembly point in a school complex near Karakaj. At this assembly point, Bosnian Serb military personnel ordered the Muslim detainees to take off their jackets, coats and other garments and place them in front of the sports hall. They were then crowded into the school building and adjacent sports hall and held under armed guard.

25. On or about 14 July 1995, at this school complex near Karakaj, **RATKO MLADIĆ** conferred with his military subordinates and addressed some of the Muslims detained there.

26. At various times during 14 July 1995, Bosnian Serb military personnel killed Bosnian Muslim detainees at this school complex.

27. Throughout 14 July 1995, Bosnian Serb military personnel removed all the Muslim detainees, in small groups, from the school building and sports hall and loaded them onto trucks guarded and driven by Bosnian Serb soldiers. Before boarding the trucks, many of the detainees had their hands tied behind their backs or were blindfolded. They were then driven to at least two locations in the vicinity of Karakaj.

28. Once the trucks arrived at these locations, Bosnian Serb military personnel ordered the bound or blindfolded Muslim detainees off the trucks and summarily executed them. The summary executions took place from approximately noon to midnight on 14 July 1995.

29. Bosnian Serb military personnel buried the executed Bosnian Muslim men in mass graves near the execution sites.

30. On or about 14 July 1995, **RATKO MLADIĆ** was present at one of the mass execution sites when Bosnian Serb military personnel summarily executed Bosnian Muslim men.

31. The summary executions of Bosnian Muslim males, which occurred on 14 July 1995 in the vicinity of Karakaj, resulted in the loss of thousands of lives.

THE ACCUSED

32. **RADOVAN KARADŽIĆ** was born on 19 June 1945 in the municipality of Savnik of the Republic of Montenegro. From on or about 13 May 1992 to the present, he has been president of the Bosnian Serb administration in Pale.

33. **RATKO MLADIĆ** was born on 12 March 1943 in Kalinovik municipality of the Republic of Bosnia and Herzegovina. He is a career military officer and holds the rank of general in the Bosnian Serb armed forces. From on or about 14 May 1992 to the present, he has been the commander of the army of the Bosnian Serb administration.

SUPERIOR AUTHORITY

RADOVAN KARADŽIĆ

34. **RADOVAN KARADŽIĆ** was a founding member and president of the Serbian Democratic Party (SDS) of what was then the Socialist Republic of Bosnia and Herzegovina. The SDS was the main political party among the Serbs in Bosnia and Herzegovina. As president of the SDS, he was and is the most powerful official in the party. His duties as president include representing the party, co-ordinating the work of party organs and ensuring the realisation of the programmatic tasks and goals of the party. He continues to hold this post.

35. **RADOVAN KARADŽIĆ** became the first president of the Bosnian Serb administration in Pale on or about 13 May 1992. At the time he assumed this position, his *de jure* powers, as described in the constitution of the Bosnian Serb administration, included, but were not limited to, commanding the army of the Bosnian Serb administration in times of war and peace and having the authority to appoint, promote and discharge officers of the army. As president, he was and is a position of superior authority to **RATKO MLADIĆ** and every

member of the Bosnian Serb army and all units and personnel assigned or attached to the Bosnian Serb army.

36. In addition to his powers described in the constitution, **RADOVAN KARADŽIĆ**'s powers as president of the Bosnian Serb administration are augmented by Article 6 of the Bosnian Serb Act on People's Defence. This Act vested in him, among other powers, the authority to supervise the Territorial Defence both in peace and war and the authority to issue orders for the utilisation of the police in case of war, immediate threat and other emergencies. Article 39 of the same Act empowered him, in cases of imminent threat of war and other emergencies, to deploy Territorial Defence units for the maintenance of law and order.

37. **RADOVAN KARADŽIĆ**'s powers are further augmented by Article 33 of the Bosnian Serb Act on Internal Affairs, which authorised him to activate reserve police in emergency situations.

38. **RADOVAN KARADŽIĆ** has exercised the powers described above and has acted and been dealt with internationally as the president of the Bosnian Serb administration in Pale. In that capacity, he has, inter alia, participated in international negotiations and has personally made agreements on such matters as cease-fires and humanitarian relief, and these agreements have been implemented.

RATKO MLADIĆ

39. **RATKO MLADIĆ** was, in 1991, appointed commander of the 9th Corps of the Yugoslav People's Army (JNA) in Knin in the Republic of Croatia. In May 1992, he assumed command of the forces of the Second Military District of the JNA which then effectively became the Bosnian Serb army. He holds the rank of general and from about 14 May 1992 to the present, has been the commander of the army of the Bosnian Serb administration. In that capacity, he was and is in a position of superior authority to every member of the Bosnian Serb army and all units and personnel assigned or attached to that army.

40. **RATKO MLADIĆ** has demonstrated his control in military matters by negotiating, inter alia, cease-fire and prisoner exchange agreements; agreements relating to the opening of Sarajevo airport; agreements relating to access for humanitarian aid convoys; and anti-sniping agreements, all of which have been implemented.

GENERAL ALLEGATIONS

41. At all times relevant to this indictment, a state of armed conflict and partial occupation existed in the Republic of Bosnia and Herzegovina in the territory of the former Yugoslavia.

42. In each paragraph charging genocide, a crime recognised by Article 4 of the Statute of the Tribunal, the alleged acts or omissions were committed with the intent to destroy, in whole or in part, a national, ethnical, or religious group, as such.

43. In each paragraph charging crimes against humanity, crimes recognised by Article 5 of the Statute of the Tribunal, the alleged acts or omissions were part of a widespread or systematic or large-scale attack directed against a civilian population.

44. **RATKO MLADIĆ** and **RADOVAN KARADŽIĆ** are individually responsible for the crimes alleged against them in this indictment pursuant to Article 7(1) of the Tribunal Statute. Individual criminal responsibility includes committing, planning, instigating, ordering or otherwise aiding and abetting in the planning, preparation or execution of any crimes referred to in Articles 2 to 5 of the Tribunal Statute.

45. **RATKO MLADIĆ** and **RADOVAN KARADŽIĆ** are also, or alternatively, criminally responsible as commanders for the acts of their subordinates pursuant to Article 7(3) of the Tribunal Statute. Command criminal responsibility is the responsibility of a superior officer for the acts of his subordinate if he knew or had reason to know that his subordinate was about to commit such acts or had done so and the superior failed to take the necessary and reasonable measures to prevent such acts or to punish the perpetrators thereof.

46. The general allegations contained in paragraphs 41 through 45 are realleged and incorporated into each of the charges set forth below.

CHARGES

COUNTS 1-2
(GENOCIDE)
(CRIME AGAINST HUMANITY)

47. Between about 12 July 1995 and 13 July 1995, Bosnian Serb military personnel, under the command and control of **RATKO MLADIĆ** and **RADOVAN KARADŽIĆ**, arrived in Potočari where thousands of Muslim men, women and children had sought refuge in and around the UN military compound. Bosnian Serb military personnel, under the command and control of **RATKO MLADIĆ** and **RADOVAN KARADŽIĆ**, summarily executed many Bosnian Muslim refugees who remained in Potočari.

48. Between about 13 July 1995 and 22 July 1995, Bosnian Serb military personnel, under the command and control of **RATKO MLADIĆ** and **RADOVAN KARADŽIĆ**, summarily executed many Bosnian Muslim men who fled to the woods and were later captured or surrendered.

49. Thousands of Bosnian Muslim men, who fled Srebrenica and who surrendered or had been captured, were transported from various assembly locations in and around Srebrenica to a main assembly point at a school complex near Karakaj.

50. On or about 14 July 1995, Bosnian Serb military personnel, under the command and control of **RATKO MLADIĆ** and **RADOVAN KARADŽIĆ**, transported thousands of Muslim men from this school complex to two locations a short distance away. At these locations, Bosnian Serb soldiers, with the knowledge of **RATKO MLADIĆ**, summarily executed these Bosnian Muslim detainees and buried them in mass graves.

51. **RATKO MLADIĆ** and **RADOVAN KARADŽIĆ**, between about 6 July 1995 and 22 July 1995, individually and in concert with others, planned, instigated, ordered or otherwise aided and abetted in the planning, preparation or execution of the following crimes:

a) summary executions of Bosnian Muslim men and women in and around Potočari on 12 July 1995 and 13 July 1995,

b) summary executions, which occurred between 13 July 1995 and 22 July 1995, of Bosnian Muslims who were hors de combat because of injury, surrender or capture after fleeing into the woods towards Tuzla,

c) summary executions of Bosnian Muslim men, which occurred on or about 14 July 1995 at mass execution sites in and around Karakaj.

By their acts and omissions in relation to the events described in paragraphs 13, 14, 20.1-20.7, 23, 26 and 28, **RATKO MLADIĆ** and **RADOVAN KARADŽIĆ** committed:

Count 1: GENOCIDE as recognised by Article 4(2)(a) (killing members of the group) of the Statute of the Tribunal.

Count 2: A CRIME AGAINST HUMANITY as recognised by Article 5(b) (extermination) of the Statute of the Tribunal.

COUNTS 3–4
(CRIME AGAINST HUMANITY)
(VIOLATION OF THE LAWS OR CUSTOMS OF WAR)

52. By their acts and omissions in relation to the summary executions of Bosnian Muslim men and women that occurred in and around Potočari between 12 July 1995 and 13 July 1995, described heretofore in paragraph 13, **RATKO MLADIĆ** and **RADOVAN KARADŽIĆ** committed:

Count 3: A CRIME AGAINST HUMANITY as recognised by Article 5(a) (murder) of the Statute of the Tribunal.

Count 4: A VIOLATION OF THE LAWS OR CUSTOMS OF WAR as recognised by Article 3 (murder) of the Statute of the Tribunal.

COUNTS 5–18
(CRIMES AGAINST HUMANITY)
(VIOLATION OF THE LAWS OR CUSTOMS OF WAR)

53. By their acts and omissions in relation the summary executions of Bosnian Muslims who fled Srebrenica into the woods between 13 July 1995 and 22 July 1995 as described heretofore in paragraphs 20.1 to 20.7, **RATKO MLADIĆ** and **RADOVAN KARADŽIĆ** committed:

Count 5: A CRIME AGAINST HUMANITY (in relation to paragraph 20.1) as recognised by Article 5(a) (murder) of the Statute of the Tribunal.

Counts 6: A VIOLATION OF THE LAWS OR CUSTOMS OF WAR (in relation to paragraph 20.1) as recognised by Article 3 (murder) of the Statute of the Tribunal.

Count 7: A CRIME AGAINST HUMANITY (in relation to paragraph 20.2) as recognised by Article 5(a) (murder) of the Statute of the Tribunal.

Count 8: A VIOLATION OF THE LAWS OR CUSTOMS OF WAR (in relation to paragraph 20.2) as recognised by Article 3 (murder) of the Statute of the Tribunal.

Count 9: A CRIME AGAINST HUMANITY (in relation to paragraph 20.3) as recognised by Article 5(a) (murder) of the Statute of the Tribunal.

Counts 10: A VIOLATION OF THE LAWS OR CUSTOMS OF WAR (in relation to paragraph 20.3) as recognised by Article 3 (murder) of the Statute of the Tribunal.

Count 11: A CRIME AGAINST HUMANITY (in relation to paragraph 20.4) as recognised by Article 5(a) (murder) of the Statute of the Tribunal.

Counts 12: A VIOLATION OF THE LAWS OR CUSTOMS OF WAR (in relation to paragraph 20.4) as recognised by Article 3 (murder) of the Statute of the Tribunal.

Count 13: A CRIME AGAINST HUMANITY (in relation to paragraph 20.5) as recognised by Article 5(a) (murder) of the Statute of the Tribunal.

Counts 14: A VIOLATION OF THE LAWS OR CUSTOMS OF WAR (in relation to paragraph 20.5) as recognised by Article 3 (murder) of the Statute of the Tribunal.

Count 15: A CRIME AGAINST HUMANITY (in relation to paragraph 20.6) as recognised by Article 5(a) (murder) of the Statute of the Tribunal.

Counts 16: A VIOLATION OF THE LAWS OR CUSTOMS OF WAR (in relation to paragraph 20.6) as recognised by Article 3 (murder) of the Statute of the Tribunal.

Count 17: A CRIME AGAINST HUMANITY (in relation to paragraph 20.7) as recognised by Article 5(a) (murder) of the Statute of the Tribunal.

Counts 18: A VIOLATION OF THE LAWS OR CUSTOMS OF WAR (in relation to paragraph 20.7) as recognised by Article 3 (murder) of the Statute of the Tribunal.

COUNTS 19-20
(CRIME AGAINST HUMANITY)
(VIOLATION OF THE LAWS OR CUSTOMS OF WAR)

54. By their acts and omissions in relation to the summary executions of Bosnian Muslim men at mass execution sites in and around Karakaj, on or about 14 July 1995, as described in paragraph 28, **RATKO MLADIĆ** and **RADOVAN KARADŽIĆ** committed:

> <u>Count 19:</u> **A CRIME AGAINST HUMANITY** as recognised by Article 5(a) (murder) of the Statute of the Tribunal.

> <u>Count 20:</u> **A VIOLATION OF THE LAWS OR CUSTOMS OF WAR** as recognised by Article 3 (murder) of the Statute of the Tribunal.

Richard J. Goldstone
Prosecutor
14 November 1995
The Hague,
The Netherlands

INDICTMENT III

SLOBODAN MILOŠEVIĆ
(CROATIA)

International Criminal Tribunal for the former Yugoslavia, Indictments and Proceedings, Case No. IT-01-50, 8 Oct 2001, http://www.un.org/icty/ind-e.htm. While this is the full text of the Indictment, for Schedules or Annexures appended to the indictments see the ICTY documents on the web.

THE INTERNATIONAL CRIMINAL TRIBUNAL
FOR THE FORMER YUGOSLAVIA

THE PROSECUTOR OF THE TRIBUNAL
AGAINST
SLOBODAN MILOŠEVIĆ

INDICTMENT

The Prosecutor of the International Criminal Tribunal for the Former Yugoslavia, pursuant to her authority under Article 18 of the Statute of the International Criminal Tribunal for the Former Yugoslavia ("the Statute of the Tribunal") charges:

SLOBODAN MILOŠEVIĆ

with CRIMES AGAINST HUMANITY, GRAVE BREACHES OF THE GENEVA CON-VENTIONS, and VIOLATIONS OF THE LAWS OR CUSTOMS OF WAR as set forth below:

THE ACCUSED:

1. **Slobodan MILOŠEVIĆ**, son of Svetozar **MILOŠEVIĆ**, was born on 20 August 1941 in Požarevac, in present-day Serbia. In 1964, he graduated from the Law Faculty of the University of Belgrade and began a career in management and banking. Until 1978, he held the posts of deputy director and later general director at Tehnogas, a major oil company in the Socialist Federal Republic of Yugoslavia ("SFRY"). Thereafter, he became president of Beogradska banka (Beobanka), one of the largest banks in the SFRY, a post he held until 1983.

2. **Slobodan MILOŠEVIĆ** joined the League of Communists of Yugoslavia in 1959. In 1984, he became Chairman of the City Committee of the League of Communists of Belgrade. In 1986, he was elected Chairman of the Presidium of the Central Committee of the League of Communists of Serbia and was re-elected in 1988. On 16 July 1990, the League of Communists of Serbia and the Socialist Alliance of Working People of Serbia united, forming a new party named the Socialist Party of Serbia ("SPS"). On 17 July 1990, **Slobodan MILOŠEVIĆ** was elected President of the SPS and has remained in that post until the present date, except during the period 24 May 1991 to 24 October 1992.

3. **Slobodan MILOŠEVIĆ** was elected President of the Presidency of the then Socialist Republic of Serbia on 8 May 1989 and re-elected on 5 December 1989. After the adoption of a new Constitution, on 28 September 1990, the Socialist Republic of Serbia became the Republic of Serbia, and **Slobodan MILOŠEVIĆ** was elected to the newly established office of President of the Republic of Serbia in multi-party elections, held in December 1990. He was re-elected to this office in elections held on 20 December 1992.

4. After serving two terms as President of the Republic of Serbia, **Slobodan MILOŠEVIĆ** was elected President of the Federal Republic of Yugoslavia ("FRY") on 15 July 1997, beginning his official duties on 23 July 1997. Following his defeat in the Federal Republic of Yugoslavia's presidential election of September 2000, **Slobodan MILOŠEVIĆ** relinquished his position on 6 October 2000.

INDIVIDUAL CRIMINAL RESPONSIBILITY

Article 7(1) of the Statute of the Tribunal

5. **Slobodan MILOŠEVIĆ** is individually criminally responsible for the crimes referred to in Articles 2, 3, and 5 of the Statute of the Tribunal and described in this indictment, which he planned, instigated, ordered, committed, or in whose planning, preparation, or execution he otherwise aided and abetted. By using the word committed in this indictment the Prosecutor does not intend to suggest that the accused physically committed any of the crimes charged personally. Committing in this indictment refers to participation in a joint criminal enterprise as co-perpetrator.

6. **Slobodan MILOŠEVIĆ** participated in a joint criminal enterprise as set out in paragraphs 24 to 26. The purpose of this joint criminal enterprise was the forcible removal of the majority of the Croat and other non-Serb population from the approximately one-third of the territory of the Republic of Croatia that he planned to become part of a new Serb-dominated state through the commission of crimes in violation of Articles 2, 3, and 5 of the Statute of the Tribunal. These areas included those regions that were referred to by Serb authorities and are hereinafter referred to as the "Serbian Autonomous District /*Srpska autonomna oblast*/ ("SAO") Krajina", the "SAO Western Slavonia", and the "SAO Slavonia, Baranja and Western Srem" (collectively referred to by Serb authorities after 19 December 1991 as the "Republic of Serbian Krajina /*Republika Srpska krajina*/" ("RSK")), and "Dubrovnik Republic /*Dubrovačka republika*/".

7. This joint criminal enterprise came into existence before 1 August 1991 and continued until at least June 1992. Individuals participating in this joint criminal enterprise included **Slobodan MILOŠEVIĆ**, Borisav JOVIĆ, Branko KOSTIĆ, Veljko KADIJEVIĆ, Blagoje ADŽIĆ, Milan BABIĆ, Milan MARTIĆ, Goran HADŽIĆ, Jovica STANIŠIĆ, Franko

SIMATOVIĆ, also known as "Frenki", Tomislav SIMOVIĆ, Vojislav ŠEŠELJ, Momir BULATOVIĆ, Aleksandar VASILJEVIĆ, Radovan STOJIČIĆ, also known as "Badža", Željko RAŽNJATOVIĆ, also known as "Arkan", and other known and unknown participants.

8. The crimes enumerated in Counts 1 to 32 of this indictment were within the object of the joint criminal enterprise. Alternatively, the crimes enumerated in Counts 1 to 13 and 17 to 32 were the natural and foreseeable consequences of the execution of the object of the joint criminal enterprise and the accused was aware that such crimes were the possible outcome of the execution of the joint criminal enterprise.

9. In order for the joint criminal enterprise to succeed in its objective, **Slobodan MILOŠEVIĆ** worked in concert with or through several individuals in the joint criminal enterprise. Each participant or co-perpetrator within the joint criminal enterprise played his own role or roles that significantly contributed to the overall objective of the enterprise. The roles of the participants or co-perpetrators include, but are not limited to, the following:

10. Borisav JOVIĆ, holding different positions as a member, Vice-President, and President of the SFRY Presidency from 15 May 1989 until April 1992, as President of the SPS from May 1991 until October 1992, and holding other key positions of the SPS until November 1995, and Branko KOSTIĆ, the Vice-President and then Acting President of the SFRY Presidency in the relevant period, together with others, commanded, directed, or otherwise exercised effective control over the Yugoslav People's Army ("JNA") and the Territorial Defence ("TO") units and the volunteer units acting in co-ordination and under supervision of the JNA.

11. General Veljko KADIJEVIĆ, as Federal Secretary for National Defence from 15 May 1988 until 6 January 1992, commanded, directed, or otherwise exercised effective control over the JNA and the TO units and the volunteer units acting in co-ordination and under supervision of the JNA.

12. General Blagoje ADŽIĆ, in his capacity as JNA Chief-of-Staff from October 1989 until 8 May 1992 and Acting Federal Secretary for National Defence from January 1992 until 8 May 1992, together with others commanded, directed, or otherwise exercised effective control over the JNA and the TO units and the volunteer units acting in co-ordination and under supervision of the JNA.

13. General Aleksandar VASILJEVIĆ, in his capacity as a JNA general and chief of the JNA Security Administration until 8 May 1992, in particular the military counter-intelligence service *Kontraobaveštajna služba* ("KOS"), participated in activities designed to stir up hate, fear and violence, which significantly helped attain the overall objectives of the joint criminal enterprise. Agents of the KOS directed and supported the local Croatian

Serb political leaders and the local Serb police and military forces, including the TO staff and volunteers from Serbia.

14. Jovica STANIŠIĆ, in his capacity as chief of the State Security (*Državna bezbednost*) ("DB") of the Republic of Serbia from March 1991 until October 1998, commanded, directed, or otherwise exercised effective control over members of the DB, who participated in the perpetration of the crimes specified in this indictment. In addition, he provided arms, funds, training, or other substantial assistance or support to Serb volunteer units and police units who perpetrated crimes specified in this indictment.

15. Franko SIMATOVIĆ, also known as "Frenki", as head of the special operations component of the DB of the Republic of Serbia, commanded, directed, or otherwise exercised effective control over agents of the DB who perpetrated crimes specified in this indictment. In addition, he provided training, funds, arms, or other substantial assistance or support to members of "Martić's Police" and Serb volunteer units who perpetrated crimes specified in this indictment.

16. Tomislav SIMOVIĆ, in his position as Minister of Defence of the Republic of Serbia from 31 July 1991 until at least 19 December 1991, formed, deployed, and provided substantial assistance or support to Serb volunteer units and other Serb forces involved in the perpetration of crimes specified in this indictment.

17. Milan MARTIĆ, as "Secretary of the Secretariat of Internal Affairs" of the SAO Krajina from 4 January 1991 until 29 May 1991; as "Minister of Defence" of the SAO Krajina from 29 May 1991 until 27 June 1991; and as "Minister of Internal Affairs" for the SAO Krajina (later Republic of Serbian Krajina) from 27 June 1991 until January 1994, established, commanded, directed, and otherwise exercised effective control over members of his police force (referred to as "Martić's Police", "*Martičevci*", "SAO Krajina Police" or "SAO Krajina Militia").

18. Milan BABIĆ, as "President of the Executive Council" of the SAO Krajina from at least 19 January 1991 until 29 May 1991, "President of the Government" of the SAO Krajina from 29 May 1991 until December 1991, and as "President of the Republic" of the Republic of Serbian Krajina from 19 December 1991 until 26 February 1992, organised and administered the actions of the joint criminal enterprise in the SAO Krajina.

19. Goran HADŽIĆ, in his capacity as "President of the Serbian National Council" of the SAO Slavonia, Baranja and Western Srem (SBWS) from 17 March 1991 until at least 25 September 1991, "President of the Government" of the SAO SBWS from at least 25 September 1991 until 26 February 1992, and then as "President of the Republic" of the Republic of Serbian Krajina until January 1994, established, commanded, directed, and otherwise exercised effective control over police (also known as Militia) units and the Serb

National Security (SNB) of the SAO SBWS. He provided funding and other substantial assistance and support to the TO units of the SAO SBWS and the Republic of Serbian Krajina. In addition, he personally participated in crimes specified in paragraphs 50 to 55 in the indictment.

20. Radovan STOJIČIĆ, also known as "Badža", previously the commander of a special police unit in KOSovo, on orders of **Slobodan MILOŠEVIĆ**, went to Croatia in summer 1991 and established the Serb TO units of SBWS, whose members perpetrated crimes as described in this indictment. From early autumn 1991 until December 1991, he personally participated in these crimes as commander of the TO SBWS.

21. Željko RAŽNJATOVIĆ, also known as "Arkan", in 1990 established and commanded the Serbian Volunteer Guard, a volunteer unit commonly known as "Arkanovci" or "Arkan's Tigers", who were under the command of the TO of the SAO SBWS. During the time relevant to this indictment, they maintained a significant military base in Erdut, SAO SBWS, from where members of this unit participated in the crimes described in this indictment. This military base also served as the training centre of other TO units. Željko RAŽNJATOVIĆ himself functioned as the commander of the base in Erdut and personally participated in the crimes specified in paragraphs 50 to 51, 53 to 54, and 56 to 58 in the indictment.

22. Vojislav ŠEŠELJ, as President of the Serbian Radical Party (SRS) from at least February 1991 throughout the time relevant to this indictment recruited or otherwise provided substantial assistance or support to Serb volunteers, commonly known as "chetniks" (*četnici*), "*Šešeljevci*" or "Šešelj's men", who perpetrated crimes as specified in this indictment. In addition, he openly espoused and encouraged creation of a "Greater Serbia" by violence and other unlawful means, and actively participated in war propaganda and spreading inter-ethnic hatred.

23. Momir BULATOVIĆ, as President of the Republic of Montenegro from 1990 until 1998, mobilised and provided substantial assistance to Montenegrin troops, including TO, police and volunteer units, who were deployed to the Republic of Croatia, forming part of the JNA, and who perpetrated crimes as specified in this indictment.

24. From 1987 until late 2000, **Slobodan MILOŠEVIĆ** was the dominant political figure in Serbia. He acquired control of all facets of the Serbian government, including the police and other state security services. In addition, he gained control over the political leaders of Kosovo, Vojvodina, and Montenegro.

25. In his capacity as the President of Serbia and through his leading position in the SPS party, **Slobodan MILOŠEVIĆ** exercised effective control or substantial influence over the above-listed participants in the joint criminal enterprise and either alone or acting in

concert with them and additional known and unknown persons effectively controlled or substantially influenced the actions of the Federal Presidency of the SFRY and later the FRY, the Serbian Ministry of Internal Affairs ("MUP"), the JNA, the Serb-run TO staff in the territories subject to this indictment as well as Serb volunteer groups.

26. **Slobodan MILOŠEVIĆ**, acting alone and in concert with other members of the joint criminal enterprise, participated in the joint criminal enterprise in the following ways:

   a) provided direction and assistance to the political leadership of the SAO SBWS, the SAO Western Slavonia, the SAO Krajina and RSK on the take-over of these areas and the subsequent forcible removal of the Croat and other non-Serb population.

   b) provided financial, material and logistical support for the regular and irregular military forces necessary for the take-over of these areas and the subsequent forcible removal of the Croat and other non-Serb population.

   c) directed organs of the government of the Republic of Serbia to create armed forces separate from the federal armed forces to engage in combat activities outside the Republic of Serbia, in particular in the said areas in Croatia and the subsequent forcible removal of the Croat and other non-Serb population.

   d) participated in the formation, financing, supply, support and direction of special forces of the Republic of Serbia Ministry of Internal Affairs. These special forces were created and supported to assist in the execution of the purpose of the joint criminal enterprise through the commission of crimes which are in violation of Articles 2, 3 and 5 of the Statute of the Tribunal.

   e) participated in providing financial, logistical and political support and direction to Serbian irregular forces and paramilitaries. Such support was given in further-ance of the joint criminal enterprise through the commission of crimes which are in violation of Articles 2, 3 and 5 of the Statute of the Tribunal.

   f) participated in the planning and preparation of the take-over of the SAO SBWS, the SAO Western Slavonia, the SAO Krajina and the Dubrovnik Republic and the subsequent forcible removal of the Croat and other non-Serb population.

   g) exerted effective control or substantial influence over the JNA which participated in the planning, preparation and execution of the forcible removal of the Croat and other non-Serb population from the SAO SBWS, the SAO Western Slavonia, the SAO Krajina and the Dubrovnik Republic.

   h) provided financial, logistical and political support to TO units and Serb volunteer units acting in the SAO SBWS, the SAO Western Slavonia, the SAO Krajina and the Dubrovnik Republic, which assisted in the execution of the purpose of the joint criminal enterprise through the commission of crimes which are in violation of Articles 2, 3 and 5 of the Statute of the Tribunal.

   i) effectively ordered the passage of laws and regulations relative to the involvement of the JNA, the TO and Serb volunteer units in Croatia.

   j) directed, commanded, controlled, or otherwise provided substantial assistance or support to the JNA, the Serb-run TO staff, and volunteer forces deployed in the

SAO SBWS, the SAO Western Slavonia, the SAO Krajina and the Dubrovnik Republic engaged in the execution of the purpose of the joint criminal enterprise through the commission of crimes which are in violation of Articles 2, 3 and 5 of the Statute of the Tribunal.

k) directed, commanded, controlled, or otherwise provided substantial assistance or support to the police forces within the MUP of the Republic of Serbia, including the DB, whose members assisted in the execution of the purpose of the joint criminal enterprise in the SAO SBWS, the SAO Western Slavonia, the SAO Krajina and the Dubrovnik Republic.

l) financed Serb military, police, and irregular soldiers in Croatia who perpetrated crimes as specified in this indictment.

m) controlled, contributed to, or otherwise utilised Serbian state-run media outlets to manipulate Serbian public opinion by spreading exaggerated and false messages of ethnically based attacks by Croats against Serb people in order to create an atmosphere of fear and hatred among Serbs living in Serbia and Croatia. The propaganda generated by the Serbian media was an important tool in contributing to the perpetration of crimes in Croatia.

27. **Slobodan MILOŠEVIĆ** knowingly and wilfully participated in the joint criminal enterprise, sharing the intent of other participants in the joint criminal enterprise or aware of the foreseeable consequences of their actions. On this basis, he bears individual criminal responsibility for these crimes under Article 7 (1) of the Statute of the Tribunal in addition to his responsibility under the same Article for having planned, instigated, ordered or otherwise aided and abetted in the planning, preparation and execution of these crimes.

28. The accused and other participants in the joint criminal enterprise shared the intent and state of mind required for the commission of each of the crimes charged in counts 1 to 32.

Article 7(3) of the Statute of the Tribunal

29. **Slobodan MILOŠEVIĆ**, while holding positions of superior authority, is also individually criminally responsible for the acts or omissions of his subordinates, pursuant to Article 7(3) of the Statute of the Tribunal. A superior is responsible for the criminal acts of his subordinates if he knew or had reason to know that his subordinates were about to commit such acts or had done so, and the superior failed to take the necessary and reasonable measures to prevent such acts or to punish the perpetrators.

30. From at least March 1991 until 15 June 1992, **Slobodan MILOŠEVIĆ** exercised control over the four members of the "Serbian Bloc" within the Presidency of the SFRY (later the FRY). These four individuals were Borisav JOVIĆ, the representative of the Republic of Serbia; Branko KOSTIĆ, the representative of the Republic of Montenegro; Jugoslav KOSTIĆ, the representative of the Autonomous Province of Vojvodina; and Sejdo

BAJRAMOVIĆ, the representative of the Autonomous Province of KOSovo and Metohia. **Slobodan MILOŠEVIĆ** used Borisav JOVIĆ and Branko KOSTIĆ as his primary agents in the Presidency, and through them, he directed the actions of the "Serbian Bloc". From 1 October 1991, in the absence of the representatives of the Presidency from Croatia, Slovenia, Macedonia, and Bosnia and Herzegovina, the four members of the "Serbian Bloc" exercised the powers of the Presidency, including that of collective "Commander-in-Chief" of the JNA. This "Rump Presidency" acted without dissension to execute **Slobodan MILOŠEVIĆ**'s policies. The Federal Presidency had effective control over the JNA as its "Commander-in-Chief" and the TO units and volunteer units acting in co-ordination and under supervision of the JNA. Generals Veljko KADIJEVIĆ and Blagoje ADŽIĆ, who directed and supervised the JNA forces in Croatia, were in constant communication and consultation with the accused.

31. **Slobodan MILOŠEVIĆ** exercised effective control over KOS, the counterintelligence component of the JNA. His control over the leaders of KOS, particularly over General Aleksandar VASILJEVIĆ, enabled the engagement of KOS agents in Croatia. Agents of the KOS carried out the policies of **Slobodan MILOŠEVIĆ** in Croatia by directing the actions of local Croatian Serb political leaders, directing and supporting the local Serb police and security forces, and introducing Serb volunteer groups into Croatia and supporting their activities.

32. **Slobodan MILOŠEVIĆ** is therefore individually criminally responsible under Article 7 (3) of the Statute of the Tribunal for the participation of the members of the JNA, the TO units and the volunteer units acting in co-ordination and under supervision of the JNA in the crimes described in this indictment.

33. From the time **Slobodan MILOŠEVIĆ** came to power in Serbia, he exercised control over key officials in the Serbian MUP, among them Radmilo BOGDANOVIĆ and Zoran SOKOLOVIĆ, who were both, at different times, Minister of Internal Affairs of Serbia, Radovan STOJIČIĆ, the Deputy Minister of Internal Affairs, and Jovica STANIŠIĆ and Franko SIMATOVIĆ, both high-ranking officials in the DB. Through these officials, **Slobodan MILOŠEVIĆ** exercised effective control over agents of the MUP and the DB who directed and supported the actions of local Croatian Serb political leaders, and Serb police and security forces, and introduced Serb volunteer groups into Croatia and supported their activities. The accused **Slobodan MILOŠEVIĆ** is therefore individually criminally responsible under Article 7 (3) of the Statute of the Tribunal for the participation of the members of the Serbian MUP and the DB in the crimes described in this indictment.

THE CHARGES:

COUNT 1
(PERSECUTIONS)

34. From on or about 1 August 1991 until June 1992, **Slobodan MILOŠEVIĆ**, acting alone or in concert with other known and unknown members of a joint criminal enterprise, planned, instigated, ordered, committed, or otherwise aided and abetted the planning, preparation, or execution of the persecutions of the Croat and other non-Serb civilian population in the territories of the SAO SBWS, the SAO Western Slavonia, the SAO Krajina, and the Dubrovnik Republic.

35. Throughout this period, Serb forces, comprised of JNA units, local TO units and TO units from Serbia and Montenegro, local and Serbian MUP police units and paramilitary units, attacked and took control of towns, villages and settlements in these territories listed above. After the take-over, the Serb forces in co-operation with the local Serb authorities established a regime of persecutions designed to drive the Croat and other non-Serb civilian population from these territories.

36. These persecutions were based on political, racial or religious grounds and included the following:

    a. The extermination or murder of **hundreds** of Croat and other non-Serb civilians, including women and elderly persons, in Dalj, Erdut, Klisa, Lovas, Vukovar, Vocin, Bacin, Saborsko and neighbouring villages, Skabrnja, Nadin, Bruska, and Dubrovnik and its environs, as described in detail in paragraphs 38 to 59 and 73 to 75.

    b. The prolonged and routine imprisonment and confinement of **thousands** of Croat and other non-Serb civilians in detention facilities within and outside of Croatia, including prison camps located in Montenegro, Serbia, and Bosnia and Herzegovina, as described in detail in paragraph 64.

    c. The establishment and perpetuation of inhumane living conditions for Croat and other non-Serb civilian detainees within the mentioned detention facilities.

    d. The repeated torture, beatings and killings of Croat and other non-Serb civilian detainees in the mentioned detention facilities.

    e. The prolonged and frequent forced labour of Croat and other non-Serb civilians detained in the mentioned detention facilities or under house arrest in their respective homes in Vukovar, Dalj, Lovas, Erdut, Saborsko, Vocin and Tovarnik. The forced labour included digging graves, loading ammunition for the Serb forces, digging trenches and other forms of manual labour at the frontlines.

    f. The repeated sexual assaults of Croat and other non-Serb civilians by Serb soldiers during arrest and in the mentioned detention facilities.

    g. The unlawful attacks on Dubrovnik and undefended Croat villages throughout the territories specified above.

h. The imposing of restrictive and discriminatory measures against the Croat and other non-Serb civilian population, such as restriction of movement; removal from positions of authority in local government institutions and the police; dismissal from jobs; and arbitrary searches of their homes.

i. The beating and robbing of Croat and other non-Serb civilians.

j. The torture and beatings of Croat and other non-Serb civilians during and after their arrest.

k. The deportation or forcible transfer of at least **170,000** Croat and other non-Serb civilians from the territories specified above, including the deportation to Serbia of at least **5,000** inhabitants from Ilok, **20,000** inhabitants from Vukovar; and the forcible transfer to locations within Croatia of at least **2,500** inhabitants from Erdut, as described in detail in paragraphs 67 to 69.

l. The deliberate destruction of homes, other public and private property, cultural institutions, historic monuments and sacred sites of the Croat and other non-Serb population in Dubrovnik and its environs, Vukovar, Erdut, Lovas, Šarengrad, Bapska, Tovarnik, Vocin, Saborsko, Skabrnja, Nadin, and Bruska, as described in paragraphs 71 and 77 to 82.

37. By these acts and omissions, **Slobodan MILOŠEVIĆ** committed:

Count 1: Persecutions on political, racial, and religious grounds, a **CRIME AGAINST HUMANITY**, punishable under Articles 5(h), and 7(1) and 7(3) of the Statute of the Tribunal.

COUNTS 2 to 5
(EXTERMINATION, MURDER, WILFUL KILLING)

38. From 1 August 1991 until June 1992, **Slobodan MILOŠEVIĆ**, acting alone or in concert with other known and unknown members of a joint criminal enterprise, planned, instigated, ordered, committed, or otherwise aided and abetted the planning, preparation, or execution of the extermination, murder and wilful killings of Croat and other non-Serb civilians in the territories of the SAO Western Slavonia, the SAO Krajina, and the SAO SBWS, as specified in paragraphs 39 through 59 of this indictment.

SAO WESTERN SLAVONIA

39. Beginning August 1991, the Serb forces including the volunteer units "Šešelj's men" and the "White Eagles" were in control of Vocin. On 13 December 1991, while the Serb forces withdrew from Vocin and the surrounding area, they went from house to house, killing a substantial portion of the remaining Croat civilian population. A total of **thirty-two** civilians were killed by these two units before they withdrew on 13 December 1991. The only survivors were those in hiding, whom the Serb forces did not find. The names of the victims are set out in Annex I attached to this indictment.

SAO KRAJINA

40. From about 7 October 1991, the Serb forces, comprised of the JNA, members of the TO and members of the Militia of the SAO Krajina (also known as the SAO Krajina Police and Martić's Police) were in control of the area of Hrvatska Kostajnica. Most of the Croat civilians had fled their homes during the attack in September 1991. Approximately 120 Croat civilians, mostly women, the elderly or the infirm, remained in the villages of Dubica, Cerovljani, and Bacin. On the morning of 20 October 1991, members of the Serb forces rounded up fifty-three civilians in Dubica and detained them in the village fire station. Over the course of the day and night ten were released, because they were either Serbs or had connections with Serbs. On 21 October 1991, the Serb forces took the remaining forty-three detained Croats to a location near the village of Bacin. In addition, the Serb forces brought at least thirteen non-Serb civilians from Bacin and Cerovljani to the same location. All **fifty-six** victims were killed there. At approximately the same time, the Serb forces took away an additional **thirty** civilians from Bacin and **twenty-four** from the villages Dubica and Cerovljani into an unknown location where they killed them. The names of the victims are set out in Annex I attached to this indictment.

41 From early August 1991 until 12 November 1991, the Croat villages of Saborsko, Poljanak and Lipovanić were attacked by Serb forces including JNA, TO and "Martić's Police". As soon as the Serb forces entered the villages, they killed all remaining non-Serb inhabitants they found.

42 On 28 October 1991, TO units entered Lipovanić and killed **eight** civilians. The names of the victims are set out in Annex I attached to this indictment.

43. On 7 November 1991, JNA and TO units, in particular a special JNA unit from Nis, entered the hamlet of Vukovići near Poljanak and executed **nine** civilians. The names of the victims are set out in Annex I attached to this indictment.

44. On 12 November 1991, members of the JNA, "Martić's Police" and the TO entered the village of Saborsko where they killed at least **twenty** Croat civilians. Afterwards, the village was leveled to the ground. The names of the victims are set out in Annex I attached to this indictment.

45. In November 1991, Serb forces comprised of JNA and TO units and "Martić's Police" attacked the village of Skabrnja, near Zadar. On 18 November 1991, the Serb forces entered Skabrnja. Moving from house to house, they killed at least **thirty-eight** non-Serb civilians in their homes or in the streets. The names of the victims are set out in Annex I attached to this indictment.

46. In addition, when Serb forces attacked the neighbouring villages of Nadin the next day, they killed **seven** non-Serb civilians. The names of the victims are set out in Annex I attached to this indictment.

47. Between 18 November and February 1992, all remaining Croat civilians in Skabrnja died. Serb forces killed **twenty-six** of the remaining elderly and infirm Croat civilians. The names of the victims are set out in Annex I attached to this indictment.

48. On 21 December 1991, Serb forces, in particular members of "Martić's Police", entered the village of Bruska and the hamlet of Marinović where they killed **ten** civilians, among them **nine** Croats. The names of the victims are set out in Annex I attached to this indictment.

VUKOVAR HOSPITAL

49. On or about 20 November 1991, as part of the overall persecution campaign, Serb military forces under the command, control or influence of the JNA, the TO SBWS and other participants of the joint criminal enterprise, removed approximately **two hundred and fifty-five** Croats and other non-Serbs from Vukovar Hospital in the aftermath of the Serb take-over of the city. The victims were transported to the JNA barracks and then to the Ovčara farm located about 5 kilometers south of Vukovar. There, members of the Serb forces beat and tortured the victims for hours. During the evening of 20 November 1991, the soldiers transported the victims in groups of 10-20 to a remote execution site between the Ovčara farm and Grabovo, where they shot and killed them. Their bodies were buried in a mass grave. The names of the victims are set out in Annex I attached to this indictment.

SAO SBWS

50. In September and October 1991, the Serb TO forces and Militia of the SAO SBWS arrested Croat civilians and kept them in a detention facility in the police building in Dalj. On 21 September 1991, Goran HADŽIĆ and Željko RAŽNJATOVIĆ visited the detention facility and ordered the release of two of the detainees. Members of the TO of the SAO SBWS led by Željko RAŽNJATOVIĆ shot **eleven** detainees and buried their bodies in a mass grave in the village of Ćelija. The names of the victims are set out in Annex I attached to this indictment.

51. On 4 October 1991, members of the TO of the SAO SBWS led by Željko RAŽNJATOVIĆ entered the detention facility in the police building in Dalj and shot **twenty-eight** Croat civilian detainees. The bodies of the victims were then taken from the building and dumped into the nearby Danube River. The names of the victims are set out in Annex I attached to this indictment.

52. On 18 October 1991, members of the JNA, the TO of the SAO SBWS, and Dušan Silni volunteer unit forced **fifty** Croat civilians, who had been detained for forced labour in

the Zadruga building in Lovas, to march into a minefield on the outskirts of the village of Lovas, located approximately 20 kilometers south-west of the town of Vukovar. On the way to the minefield, **one** detainee was shot dead by these Serb forces. Upon reaching the minefield, the detainees were forced to enter the minefield and sweep their feet in front of them to clear the field of mines. At least one mine exploded, and the Serb forces opened fire on the detainees. **Twenty-one** detainees were killed either through mine explosions or gunfire. The names of the victims are set out in Annex I attached to this indictment.

53. On 9 November 1991, members of the TO of the SAO SBWS led by Željko RAŽNJA-TOVIĆ and members of the Militia of the SAO SBWS arrested ethnic Hungarian and Croat civilians in Erdut, Dalj Planina, and Erdut Planina and took them to the training centre of the TO in Erdut where **twelve** of them were shot dead the following day. The names of the victims are set out in Annex I attached to this indictment. Several days after 9 November 1991, members of the SNB of the SAO SBWS in co-operation with several members of "Arkan's Tigers" arrested and executed three civilians, two of them family members of the original Hungarian victims who had inquired about the fate of their relatives. The bodies of eight of the initial twelve victims were buried in the village of Ćelija and one victim was buried in Daljski Atar. The bodies of the **three** additional victims were thrown in a well in Borovo. The names of the victims are set out in Annex I attached to this indictment. On 3 June 1992, members of the SNB, in co-operation with members of "Arkan's Tigers", arrested Marija Senasi (born 1937), a female family member of the original Hungarian victims who had continued to make inquiries about the fate of her relatives. This woman was subsequently murdered and her body was thrown into an abandoned well in Dalj Planina.

54. On 11 November 1991, members of the TO of SAO SBWS, under the command of Željko RAŽNJATOVIĆ, arrested seven non-Serb civilians in the village of Klisa. Two of the detainees who had Serb relatives were released. The remaining **five** civilians were taken to the TO training centre in Erdut. After their interrogation, the victims were killed and buried in a mass grave in the village of Ćelija. The names of the victims are set out in Annex I attached to this indictment.

55. Between 18 and 20 November 1991, after the termination of the military operations in and around Vukovar, the JNA deported **thousands** of Croat and other non-Serb inhabitants into the territory of the Republic of Serbia. Following a request of Goran HADŽIĆ to retain those non-Serbs who were suspected of participation in the military operations, the JNA transported a large number of inhabitants of Vukovar to the detention facilities in Dalj on around 20 November 1991. There, Serb TO members selected those suspected of participating in the defence of Vukovar. The selected detainees were interrogated, beaten and tortured. At least **thirty-four** were executed. The names of the victims are set out in Annex I attached to this indictment.

56. On 10 December 1991, members of the TO of the SAO SBWS led by Željko RAŽNJA-
TOVIĆ and members of the Militia of the SAO SBWS arrested **five** non-Serb villagers from
Erdut. The victims were taken to the TO training centre in Erdut and subsequently killed.
The bodies of three of the victims were later disposed of in a well in Daljski Atar. The names
of the victims are set out in Annex I attached to this indictment.

57. From 22 December 1991 to 25 December 1991, members of the TO of the SAO SBWS
led by Željko RAŽNJATOVIĆ and members of the Militia of the SAO SBWS arrested
seven ethnic Hungarian and Croat civilians in Erdut and took them to the TO training centre in Erdut. On 26 December 1991, they were shot and killed. The bodies of six of the victims were buried in Daljski Atar. The names of the victims are set out in Annex I attached
to this indictment.

58. On 21 February 1992, members of the TO of the SAO SBWS led by Željko RAŽNJA-
TOVIĆ and members of the Militia of the SAO SBWS arrested **four** non-Serb civilians in
Erdut. All of the victims were interrogated in the Territorial Defence training centre in
Erdut and then killed. The bodies of the victims were buried in a mass grave in Daljski
Atar. The names of the victims are set out in Annex I attached to this indictment.

59. On 4 May 1992, members of the special operations component of the DB, arrested **five**
non-Serb civilians in the village of Grabovac. The civilians were taken away and killed.
Their bodies were later buried in Tikveš Park. The names of the victims are set out in
Annex I attached to this indictment.

60. By the acts and omissions in relation to the incidents referred to in the paragraphs 39
to 49, **Slobodan MILOŠEVIĆ** committed:
> **Count 2:** Extermination, a **CRIME AGAINST HUMANITY**, punishable under
> Articles 5(b) and 7(1) and 7(3) of the Statute of the Tribunal.

61. By the acts and omissions in relation to all incidents referred to in the paragraphs 39
to 59, **Slobodan MILOŠEVIĆ** committed:
> **Count 3:** Murder, a **CRIME AGAINST HUMANITY**, punishable under Articles
> 5(a) and 7(1) and 7(3) of the Statute of the Tribunal.
> **Count 4:** Murder, a **VIOLATION OF THE LAWS OR CUSTOMS OF WAR**, as
> recognised by Common Article 3(1)(a) of the Geneva Conventions of 1949, pun-
> ishable under Articles 3 and 7(1) and 7(3) of the Statute of the Tribunal.

62. By the acts and omissions in relation to all incidents referred to in the paragraphs 39
to 49, 52 to 59, **Slobodan MILOŠEVIĆ** committed:
> **Count 5:** Wilful killing, a **GRAVE BREACH OF THE GENEVA CONVEN-
> TIONS OF 1949**, punishable under Articles 2(a) and 7(1) and 7(3) of the Statute
> of the Tribunal.

COUNTS 6 to 13
(UNLAWFUL CONFINEMENT, IMPRISONMENT, TORTURE and INHUMANE ACTS)

63. From August 1991 until March 1992, **Slobodan MILOŠEVIĆ**, acting alone or in concert with other known and unknown members of a joint criminal enterprise, planned, instigated, ordered, committed, or otherwise aided and abetted the planning, preparation, or execution of the unlawful confinement or imprisonment under inhumane conditions of the Croat and other non-Serb civilian population in the territories of the SAO SBWS, the SAO Western Slavonia, the SAO Krajina, and the Dubrovnik Republic.

64. Serb military forces, comprised of JNA, TO and volunteer units acting in co-operation with local and Serbian police staff and local Serb authorities, arrested and detained **thousands** of Croat and other non-Serb civilians from the territories specified in the following short- and long-term detention facilities:

    a. Military warehouse in Morinje in Montenegro, run by the JNA, approximately **three hundred and twenty** detainees.

    b. Military barracks in Kumbor in Montenegro, a transit detention facility run by the JNA that also included **scores** of long-term detainees.

    c. Military barracks in Bileča in Bosnia and Herzegovina run by the JNA, approximately **one hundred** detainees.

    d. STAJIĆEVO agricultural farm in Serbia run by the JNA, approximately **one thousand and seven hundred** detainees.

    e. Military barracks in Begejci in Serbia run by the JNA, approximately **two hundred and sixty** detainees.

    f. Military barracks in Zrenjanin in Serbia run by the JNA, **scores** of detainees.

    g. Military prison Sremska Mitrovica in Serbia run by the JNA, **hundreds** of detainees.

    h. Prison in Knin, SAO Krajina run by the JNA, approximately **one hundred and fifty** detainees.

    i. Old hospital in Knin, SAO Krajina run by "Martić's Militia", approximately **one hundred and twenty** detainees.

    j. Police buildings and the hangar near the railway station in Dalj, SAO SBWS run by the JNA and TO, **hundreds** of detainees.

    k. Zadruga Building in Lovas, SAO SBWS run by members of the TO and the Dušan Silni volunteer unit, approximately **seventy** detainees.

    l. Territorial Defence training centre in Erdut, also referred to as "Arkan's" military base, SAO SBWS, run by members of the TO and "Arkan's Tigers", approximately **fifty-two** detainees.

    m. Ovčara farm, near Vukovar, SAO SBWS run by the JNA, approximately **three hundred** detainees.

    n. Velepromet warehouse near Vukovar, SAO SBWS run by the JNA, approximately **one hundred** detainees.

o. Military prison in Sid, SAO SBWS run by the JNA, approximately **one hundred** detainees.

p. Police station in Opatovac, SAO SBWS run by the JNA, **scores** of detainees.

q. Stable or workshop in Borovo Selo, SAO SBWS, run by members of the militia and TO, approximately **eighty** detainees.

65. The living conditions in these detention facilities were brutal and characterised by inhumane treatment, overcrowding, starvation, forced labour, inadequate medical care, and constant physical and psychological assault, including mock executions, torture, beatings, and sexual assault.

66. By these acts and omissions, **Slobodan MILOŠEVIĆ** committed:

Count 6: Imprisonment, a **CRIME AGAINST HUMANITY** punishable under Article 5(e) and Article 7 (1) and Article 7 (3) of the Statute of the Tribunal.

Count 7: Torture, a **CRIME AGAINST HUMANITY** punishable under Article 5(f) and Article 7 (1) and Article 7 (3) of the Statute of the Tribunal.

Count 8: Inhumane acts, a **CRIME AGAINST HUMANITY** punishable under Article 5(i) and Article 7 (1) and Article 7 (3) of the Statute of the Tribunal.

Count 9: Unlawful confinement, a **GRAVE BREACH OF THE GENEVA CONVENTIONS OF 1949** punishable under Article 2(g) and Article 7 (1) and Article 7 (3) of the Statute of the Tribunal.

Count 10: Torture, a **GRAVE BREACH OF THE GENEVA CONVENTIONS OF 1949** punishable under Article 2(b) and Article 7 (1) and Article 7 (3) of the Statute of the Tribunal.

Count 11: Wilfully causing great suffering, a **GRAVE BREACH OF THE GENEVA CONVENTIONS OF 1949** punishable under Article 2(c) and Article 7 (1) and Article 7 (3) of the Statute of the Tribunal.

Count 12: Torture, a **VIOLATION OF THE LAWS OR CUSTOMS OF WAR** as recognised by Common Article 3 (1)(a) of the Geneva Conventions of 1949, punishable under Article 3 and Article 7 (1) and Article 7 (3) of the Statute of the Tribunal.

Count 13: Cruel treatment, a **VIOLATION OF THE LAWS OR CUSTOMS OF WAR** as recognised by Common Article 3 (1)(a) of the Geneva Conventions of 1949, punishable under Article 3 and Article 7 (1) and Article 7 (3) of the Statute of the Tribunal.

COUNTS 14 to 16
(DEPORTATION, FORCIBLE TRANSFER)

67. From 1 August 1991 until May 1992, **Slobodan MILOŠEVIĆ**, acting alone or in concert with other known and unknown members of the joint criminal enterprise, planned,

instigated, ordered, committed, or otherwise aided and abetted the planning, preparation, or execution of the deportations or forcible transfers of the Croat and other non-Serb civilian population in the territories of the SAO SBWS, the SAO Western Slavonia, the SAO Krajina, and the Dubrovnik Republic.

68. In order to achieve this objective, Serb forces comprised of JNA, TO and volunteer units, including the "White Eagles", "Šešelj's men", "Dušan Silni" and "Arkan's Tigers", in co-operation with police units, including "Martić's Police", SNB and Serbian MUP, and others under the effective control of **Slobodan MILOŠEVIĆ** or other participants in the joint criminal enterprise, surrounded Croat towns and villages and demanded their inhabitants to surrender their weapons, including legally owned hunting rifles. Then, the town and villages were attacked, even those inhabitants who had complied with the demands. These attacks were intended to compel the population to flee. After taking control of the towns and villages, the Serb forces sometimes rounded up the remaining Croat and other non-Serb civilian population and forcibly transported them to locations in Croatia controlled by the Croatian government or deported them to locations outside Croatia, in particular Serbia and Montenegro. On other occasions, the Serb forces in co-operation with the local Serb authorities imposed restrictive and discriminatory measures on the non-Serb population and engaged in a campaign of terror designed to drive them out of the territory. The majority of the non-Serbs that remained were then deported or forcibly transferred.

69. According to the 1991 census, the Croat and other non-Serb population of these areas was approximately as follows:
SAO Krajina: 28% Croats (70,708), 5% others (13,101).
SAO Western Slavonia: 29% Croats (6864), 11% others (2577).
SAO SBWS: 47% Croats (90,454), 21% others (40,217).

Virtually the whole Croat and non-Serb population of these areas was forcibly removed, deported or killed. According to the 1991 census, the Croat and other non-Serb population of the Dubrovnik Republic was approximately 82% Croats (58,836), 11% others (7,818). The joint criminal enterprise did not achieve its goal of forcibly removing, deporting or killing the entire Croat and non-Serb population of the Dubrovnik Republic.

70. By these acts and omissions, **Slobodan MILOŠEVIĆ** committed:
<u>Count 14:</u> Deportation, a **CRIME AGAINST HUMANITY**, punishable under Articles 5(d) and 7(1) and 7(3) of the Statute of the Tribunal.
<u>Count 15:</u> Inhumane Acts (Forcible Transfers), a **CRIME AGAINST HUMANITY**, punishable under Articles 5(i) and 7(1) and 7(3) of the Statute of the Tribunal.
<u>Count 16:</u> Unlawful Deportation or Transfer, a **GRAVE BREACH OF THE GENEVA CONVENTIONS OF 1949**, punishable under Articles 2(g) and 7(1) and 7(3) of the Statute of the Tribunal.

COUNTS 17 to 20
(WANTON DESTRUCTION,
PLUNDER OF PUBLIC OR PRIVATE PROPERTY)

71. From 1 August 1991 until May 1992, **Slobodan MILOŠEVIĆ**, acting alone or in concert with other known and unknown members of the joint criminal enterprise, planned, instigated, ordered, committed, or otherwise aided and abetted the planning, preparation, or execution of the wanton destruction and plunder of the public and private property of the Croat and other non-Serb population, within the territories of the SAO SBWS, the SAO Western Slavonia and the SAO Krajina although these actions were not justified by military necessity. This intentional and wanton destruction and plunder included the plunder and destruction of homes and religious and cultural buildings, and took place in the following towns and villages:

SAO SBWS, from August until October 1991: the towns and villages Dalj, Ćelija, Vukovar, Erdut, Lovas, Sarengrad, Bapska and Tovarnik.

SAO Western Slavonia, from August to December 1991: the town Vocin.

SAO Krajina, from August to December 1991: the towns and villages Saborsko, Skabrnja, Nadin, and Bruska.

72. By these acts and omissions, **Slobodan MILOŠEVIĆ** committed:

Count 17: Extensive destruction and appropriation of property, not justified by military necessity and carried out unlawfully and wantonly, a **GRAVE BREACH OF THE GENEVA CONVENTIONS OF 1949**, punishable under Articles 2(d) and 7(1) and 7 (3) of the Statute of the Tribunal.

Count 18: Wanton destruction of villages, or devastation not justified by military necessity, a **VIOLATION OF THE LAWS OR CUSTOMS OF WAR**, punishable under Articles 3 (b) and 7(1) and 7(3) of the Statute of the Tribunal.

Count 19: Destruction or wilful damage done to institutions dedicated to education or religion, a **VIOLATION OF THE LAWS OR CUSTOMS OF WAR**, punishable under Articles 3(d) and 7(1) and 7(3) of the Statute of the Tribunal.

Count 20: Plunder of public or private property, a **VIOLATION OF THE LAWS OR CUSTOMS OF WAR**, punishable under Articles 3(e) and 7(1) and 7(3) of the Statute of the Tribunal.

DUBROVNIK

COUNTS 21 to 27
(MURDER, WILFUL KILLING, WILFULLY CAUSING GREAT SUFFERING,
CRUEL TREATMENT, ATTACKS ON CIVILIANS)

73. From 1 October 1991 until 7 December 1991, **Slobodan MILOŠEVIĆ**, acting alone or in concert with other known and unknown members of the joint criminal enterprise, planned, instigated, ordered, committed, or otherwise aided and abetted the planning, prepa-

ration, or execution of a military campaign directed at the city of Dubrovnik and its surroundings in order to achieve the forcible removal of its non-Serb population.

74. In this time period, Serb forces comprised of JNA land, air and naval units, as well as TO and volunteer units and special police units from Serbia and Montenegro subordinated to the JNA and under the effective control of **Slobodan MILOŠEVIĆ** and other members of the joint criminal enterprise, in particular Momir BULATOVIĆ, launched an extensive military attack on the coastal regions of Croatia between the town of Neum, Bosnia and Herzegovina, in the north-west and the Montenegrin border in the south-east. It was the objective of the Serb forces to detach this area from Croatia and to annex it to Montenegro. While the Serb forces seized the territory to the south-east and north-west of the city of Dubrovnik within two weeks, the city itself was under attack throughout the time alleged in this indictment.

75. During an unlawful extensive shelling campaign conducted from high ground east and north of Dubrovnik, with an unobstructed view of the city and its environs, and from JNA naval vessels offshore, forty-three Croat civilians were killed and numerous others wounded. The shelling incidents and the names of the killed civilians are set out in Annex II attached to this indictment.

76. By these acts and omissions, **Slobodan MILOŠEVIĆ** committed:

> **Count 21:** Murder, a **CRIME AGAINST HUMANITY**, punishable under Articles 5(a) and 7(1) and 7(3) of the Statute of the Tribunal.
>
> **Count 22:** Wilful killing, a **GRAVE BREACH OF THE GENEVA CONVENTIONS OF 1949**, punishable under Articles 2(a) and 7(1) and 7(3) of the Statute of the Tribunal.
>
> **Count 23:** Murder, a **VIOLATION OF THE LAWS OR CUSTOMS OF WAR**, as recognised by Common Article 3(1)(a) of the Geneva Conventions of 1949, punishable under Articles 3 and 7(1) and 7(3) of the Statute of the Tribunal.
>
> **Count 24:** Inhumane acts, a **CRIME AGAINST HUMANITY**, punishable under Articles 5(i) and 7(1) and 7(3) of the Statute of the Tribunal.
>
> **Count 25:** Wilfully causing great suffering, a **GRAVE BREACH OF THE GENEVA CONVENTIONS OF 1949**, punishable under Articles 2(c) and 7(1) and 7(3) of the Statute of the Tribunal.
>
> **Count 26:** Cruel treatment, a **VIOLATION OF THE LAWS OR CUSTOMS OF WAR**, as recognised by Common Article 3(1)(a) of the Geneva Conventions of 1949, punishable under Articles 3 and 7(1) and 7(3) of the Statute of the Tribunal.
>
> **Count 27:** Attacks on civilians, a **VIOLATION OF THE LAWS OR CUSTOMS OF WAR**, as recognised by Article 51(2) of Additional Protocol I and Article 13(2) of Additional Protocol II to the Geneva Conventions of 1949, punishable under Articles 3 and 7(1) and 7(3) of the Statute of the Tribunal.

COUNTS 28 to 32
(WANTON DESTRUCTION,
PLUNDER OF PUBLIC OR PRIVATE PROPERTY)

77. From 1 October 1991 until 7 December 1991, during this same shelling attack, **Slobodan MILOŠEVIĆ**, acting alone or in concert with other known and unknown members of the joint criminal enterprise, planned, instigated, ordered, committed, or otherwise aided and abetted the planning, preparation and execution of the wanton destruction or wilful damage and plunder of the public and private property of the Croat and other non-Serb population within the area of the Dubvrovnik Republic. This campaign included the destruction, damage or plunder of homes, religious, historical and cultural buildings and other civilian public or private buildings, not justified by military necessity.

78. During this shelling campaign, approximately 1000 shells fired by the Serb forces impacted in the Old Town area of the city. The Old Town district of Dubrovnik was an UNESCO World Cultural Heritage Site in its entirety. A number of the buildings in the Old Town and the towers on the city walls were marked with the symbols mandated by the Hague Convention on the Protection of Cultural Property in the Event of Armed Conflict (1954). No military targets were located on or within the walls of the Old Town.

79. During the shelling on 8 to 13 November 1991 of the city of Dubrovnik, buildings in the Old Town were damaged, as well as hotels, housing refugees and other civilian structures in other parts of the city.

80. During the shelling on 6 December 1991 of the city of Dubrovnik, at least six buildings in the Old Town were destroyed in their entirety and hundreds more suffered damage. Hotels, housing refugees and other civilian structures were severely damaged or destroyed in other parts of Dubrovnik, specifically in the Lapad and Babin Kuk areas.

81. In October 1991, the Serb forces took control of the Croatian towns and villages Konavle, Župa Dubravačka, and Primorje in the proximity of the city of Dubrovnik. In the aftermath of this take-over, from 2 to 24 October 1991, JNA troops systematically plundered public, commercial and private property in the towns and villages Brgat, Cilipi, Dubravka, Gruda, Močići, Osojnik, Slano, Donja Ljuta, Popovići, Mihanići, Drivenik, Konavle, Plat, Cepikuće, Uskoplje, Gabrili, Pridvoje, Molunat, Donja Cibača, Karasovići and Zvekovica. Much of this property was transported to Montenegro in JNA military vehicles. The JNA thereafter instituted measures to track and maintain the looted property.

82. JNA troops also systematically destroyed public, commercial, and religious buildings as well as private dwellings in the above listed towns and villages. This destruction took place after the cessation of fighting when the areas were securely under the control of the JNA.

83. By these acts and omissions, **Slobodan MILOŠEVIĆ** committed:

<u>Count 28:</u> Extensive destruction and appropriation of property, not justified by military necessity and carried out unlawfully and wantonly, a **GRAVE BREACH OF THE GENEVA CONVENTIONS OF 1949**, punishable under Articles 2(d) and 7(1) and 7(3) of the Statute of the Tribunal.

<u>Count 29:</u> Wanton destruction of villages, or devastation not justified by military necessity, a **VIOLATION OF THE LAWS OR CUSTOMS OF WAR**, punishable under Articles 3(b) and 7(1) and 7(3) of the Statute of the Tribunal.

<u>Count 30:</u> Destruction or wilful damage done to historic monuments and institutions dedicated to education or religion, a **VIOLATION OF THE LAWS OR CUSTOMS OF WAR**, punishable under Articles 3(d) and 7(1) and 7(3) of the Statute of the Tribunal.

<u>Count 31:</u> Plunder of public or private property, a **VIOLATION OF THE LAWS OR CUSTOMS OF WAR**, punishable under Articles 3(e) and 7(1) and 7(3) of the Statute of the Tribunal.

<u>Count 32:</u> Unlawful attacks on civilian objects, a **VIOLATION OF THE LAWS OR CUSTOMS OF WAR**, as recognised by Article 52(1) of Additional Protocol I to the Geneva Conventions of 1949 and customary law, punishable under Articles 3 and 7(1) and 7(3) of the Statute of the Tribunal.

GENERAL ALLEGATIONS:

84. All acts and omissions alleged in this indictment between 1 August 1991 and June 1992 occurred on the territory of the former Yugoslavia.

85. Between at least 1 August 1991 and at least June 1992, a state of armed conflict existed in Croatia. Until 7 October 1991, this armed conflict was internal in nature. From 8 October 1991 an international armed conflict and partial occupation existed in the Republic of Croatia.

86. All acts and omissions charged as Grave Breaches of the Geneva Conventions of 1949 occurred during the international armed conflict and partial occupation of Croatia.

87. At all times relevant to this indictment, the victims of Grave Breaches of the Geneva Conventions of 1949 were persons protected under the provisions of the relevant Geneva Conventions.

88. All acts and omissions charged relative to the destruction of property as Grave Breaches of the Geneva Conventions of 1949 involved "protected property" under the relevant provisions of the Geneva Conventions.

89. At all times relevant to this indictment, **Slobodan MILOŠEVIĆ** was required to abide by the laws and customs governing the conduct of armed conflicts, including the Geneva Conventions of 1949 and the additional protocols thereto.

90. All acts and omissions charged as Crimes against Humanity were part of a widespread and systematic attack directed against the Croat and other non-Serb civilian population of large areas of Croatia.

ADDITIONAL FACTS:

91. The Republic of Croatia, formerly one of the six republics of the SFRY, is located in south-eastern Europe and borders Slovenia and Hungary to the north and north-east and the Federal Republic of Yugoslavia and Bosnia and Herzegovina to the east and south.

92. The territories of the SAO SBWS, the SAO Western Slavonia, the SAO Krajina and the Dubrovnik Republic are indicated in the attached Annex III.

93. In the 1991 census, the population of the Republic of Croatia was 4,784,265 of which 3,736,356 (78.1%) were Croats; 581,663 (12.2%) were Serbs; 43,469 (0.9%) were Muslims; 22,355 (0.5%) were Hungarians; 106,041 (2.2%) were Yugoslavs; and 294,381 (6.1%) were others or undeclared.

94. In April and May 1990, the Republic of Croatia held elections in which the Croatian Democratic Union (HDZ) won a plurality of votes and secured a majority of seats in the Croatian Sabor (parliament). The new Sabor then elected the HDZ candidate Franjo TUDJMAN President of Croatia.

95. In advance of the 1990 elections, the nationalistic Serbian Democratic Party (SDS) was founded in Knin, advocating the autonomy and later secession of predominately-Serb areas from Croatia.

96. Between 19 August and 2 September 1990, Croatian Serbs held a referendum on the issue of Serb "sovereignty and autonomy" in Croatia. The vote took place in predominately Serb areas of Croatia and was limited only to Serb voters. Croats who lived in the affected region were barred from participating in the referendum. The result of the vote was overwhelmingly in support of Serb autonomy. On 30 September 1990, the "Serbian National Council", presided over by Milan BABIĆ, declared "the autonomy of the Serbian people on ethnic and historic territories on which he lives and which are within the current boundaries of the Republic of Croatia as a federal unit of the Socialist Federal Republic of Yugoslavia".

97. On 21 December 1990, Croatian Serbs in Knin announced the creation of a "Serbian Autonomous District" and declared their independence from Croatia. Conflicts between Serbs and Croatian police forces erupted throughout the spring of 1991.

98. In March 1991, the conflict intensified when Serb police forces attempted to consolidate power over areas with significant Serb populations. The Serb police, headed by Milan

MARTIC, took control of a police station in Pakrac and battles erupted when the Croatian government attempted to re-establish its authority in the area. At Plitvice, a bus carrying Croatian policemen was attacked by Serbs and another battle erupted. The JNA deployed troops in the area and issued an ultimatum to the Croatian police to withdraw from Plitvice.

99. In March 1991, the collective Federal Presidency of the SFRY reached deadlock on several issues including the issue of instituting a state of emergency in Yugoslavia. The representatives on the Presidency from the Republic of Serbia, the Republic of Montenegro, the Autonomous Province of Vojvodina, and the Autonomous Province of KOSovo and Metohia all resigned from their posts. In a televised address on 16 March 1991, **Slobodan MILOŠEVIĆ**, in his capacity as President of the Republic of Serbia, declared that Yugoslavia was finished and that Serbia would no longer be bound by decisions of the Federal Presidency.

100. On 19 May 1991, Croatia held a referendum in which the electorate voted overwhelmingly for independence from the SFRY. On 25 June 1991, Croatia and the Republic of Slovenia declared their independence from Yugoslavia. On 25 June 1991, the JNA moved to suppress Slovenia's secession.

101. The European Community sought to mediate in the conflict. On 8 July 1991, an agreement was reached that Croatia and Slovenia would suspend implementation of their independence for 90 days until 8 October 1991. The European Community ultimately recognised Croatia as an independent state on 15 January 1992, and Croatia became a member of the United Nations on 22 May 1992.

102. On 18 July 1991, the Federal Presidency, with the support of the Serbian and Montenegrin governments and General Veljko KADIJEVIĆ, voted to withdraw the JNA from Slovenia, thereby acceding to its secession and the dissolution of the SFRY.

103. **Slobodan MILOŠEVIĆ's** calls for the union of all Serbs in one state coincided with those agitating for the creation of a "Greater Serbia." The Serbs in the Knin Krajina region, in Eastern Slavonia, and in Western Slavonia began receiving increasing support from the government of the Republic of Serbia. By August 1991, Serb volunteer and police forces in these regions were being supplied and led by officials of the Republic of Serbia Ministry of Internal Affairs.

104. In the Knin area, the JNA forces began openly assisting the Serb police forces led by Milan MARTIC. They participated jointly in an attack on the Croatian village of Kijevo in August 1991. Throughout August and September 1991, substantial areas of Croatia came under Serb control as a result of actions by Serb military, volunteer and police forces, conducted with the support of the JNA.

105. In the Serb-occupied regions of Northern Dalmatia, Lika, Kordun, Banija, Western Slavonia, and Baranja, the Croatian and other non-Serb population was systematically driven out and the areas were incorporated into various "Serbian Autonomous Districts". The JNA remained deployed in the areas where the Serb insurgents had taken control, thereby securing their gains.

106. In August 1991, the JNA undertook operations against towns in Eastern Slavonia, resulting in their occupation by JNA and other Serb forces. The Croat and other non-Serb population of these areas was forcibly expelled. In late August, the JNA laid siege to the city of Vukovar. By mid-October 1991, all other predominately Croat towns in Eastern Slavonia had been taken by Serb forces except Vukovar. Non-Serbs were subjected to a brutal occupation regime consisting of persecution, murder, torture and other acts of violence. Almost all of the non-Serb population was eventually killed or forced from the occupied areas.

107. The siege of Vukovar continued until 18 November 1991 when the city fell to the Serb forces. During the course of the three-month siege, the city was largely destroyed by JNA shelling and hundreds of persons were killed. When the JNA/Serb forces occupied the city, hundreds more Croats were killed by Serb troops. The non-Serb population of the city was expelled within days of its fall under Serb control.

108. In Geneva on 23 November 1991, **Slobodan MILOŠEVIĆ**, Federal Secretary of People's Defence Veljko KADIJEVIĆ, and Franjo TUDJMAN entered into an agreement signed under the auspices of the United Nations Special Envoy Cyrus VANCE. This agreement called for the lifting of blockades by Croatian forces on JNA barracks and for the withdrawal of JNA forces from Croatia. Both sides committed themselves to an immediate cease-fire throughout Croatia by units "under their command, control, or political influence" and further bound themselves to ensure that any paramilitary or irregular units associated with their forces would also observe the cease-fire.

109. On 3 January 1992, another cease-fire agreement was signed by Franjo TUDJMAN and **Slobodan MILOŠEVIĆ** paving the way for the implementation of an United Nations peace plan put forward by Cyrus VANCE. Under the Vance Plan, four United Nations Protected Areas (UNPAs) were established in the areas occupied by Serb forces. The Vance Plan called for the withdrawal of the JNA from Croatia and for the return of displaced persons to their homes in the UNPAs. Although the JNA officially withdrew from Croatia in May 1992, large portions of its weaponry and personnel remained in the Serb-held areas and were turned over to the "police" of the Republic of Serbian Krajina (RSK). Displaced persons were not allowed to return to their homes and those few Croats and other non-Serbs who had remained in the Serb-occupied areas were expelled in the following months. The territory of the RSK remained under Serb occupation until large portions of it were re-taken by Croatian forces in two operations in 1995. The remaining area of Serb control in Eastern Slavonia was peacefully re-integrated into Croatia in 1998.

110. The SFRY existed as a sovereign state until 27 April 1992 when the constitution of the Federal Republic of Yugoslavia was adopted, replacing the Constitution of the Socialist Federal Republic of Yugoslavia of 1974.

Dated this day of 2001
At The Hague
The Netherlands

_____

Carla del Ponte
Prosecutor

INDICTMENT IV

SLOBODAN MILOŠEVIĆ

(BOSNIA-HERZEGOVINA)

International Criminal Tribunal for the former Yugoslavia, Indictments and Proceedings, Case No. IT-01-51, 22 November 2001, http://www.un.org/icty/ind-e.htm. While this is the full text of the Indictment, for Schedules or Annexures appended to the indictments see the ICTY documents on the web.

317

THE INTERNATIONAL CRIMINAL TRIBUNAL
FOR THE FORMER YUGOSLAVIA

THE PROSECUTOR OF THE TRIBUNAL
AGAINST
SLOBODAN MILOŠEVIĆ

INDICTMENT

The Prosecutor of the International Criminal Tribunal for the former Yugoslavia, pursuant to her authority under Article 18 of the Statute of the International Criminal Tribunal for the former Yugoslavia ("the Statute of the Tribunal"), charges:

SLOBODAN MILOŠEVIĆ

with GENOCIDE, CRIMES AGAINST HUMANITY, GRAVE BREACHES OF THE GENEVA CONVENTIONS and VIOLATIONS OF THE LAWS OR CUSTOMS OF WAR as set forth below:

THE ACCUSED

1. **Slobodan MILOŠEVIĆ**, son of Svetozar MILOŠEVIĆ, was born on 20 August 1941 in Požarevac, in the present-day Republic of Serbia, one of the constituent republics of the Federal Republic of Yugoslavia ("FRY"). In 1964, he graduated from the Law Faculty of the University of Belgrade and began a career in management and banking. Until 1978, he held the posts of deputy director and later general director at Tehnogas, a major oil company in the then Socialist Federal Republic of Yugoslavia ("SFRY"). Thereafter, he became president of Beogradska banka (Beobanka), one of the largest banks in the SFRY, a post he held until 1983.

2. **Slobodan MILOŠEVIĆ**, joined the League of Communists of Yugoslavia in 1959. In 1984, he became Chairman of the City Committee of the League of Communists of Belgrade. In 1986, he was elected Chairman of the Presidium of the Central Committee of the League of Communists of Serbia and was re-elected in 1988. On 16 July 1990, the League of Communists of Serbia and the Socialist Alliance of Working People of Serbia united, forming a new party named the Socialist Party of Serbia ("SPS"). On 17 July 1990,

Slobodan MILOŠEVIĆ was elected President of the SPS and remained in that post except during the period from 24 May 1991 to 24 October 1992.

3. **Slobodan MILOŠEVIĆ** was elected President of the Presidency of the then Socialist Republic of Serbia on 8 May 1989 and re-elected on 5 December 1989. After the adoption of a new Constitution, on 28 September 1990, the Socialist Republic of Serbia became the Republic of Serbia, and **Slobodan MILOŠEVIĆ** was elected to the newly established office of President of the Republic of Serbia in multi-party elections, held in December 1990. He was re-elected to this office in elections held on 20 December 1992.

4. After serving two terms as President of the Republic of Serbia, **Slobodan MILOŠEVIĆ** was elected President of the Federal Republic of Yugoslavia on 15 July 1997, beginning his official duties on 23 July 1997. Following his defeat in the Federal Republic of Yugoslavia's presidential election of September 2000, **Slobodan MILOŠEVIĆ** relinquished his position on 6 October 2000.

INDIVIDUAL CRIMINAL RESPONSIBILITY

Article 7(1) of the Statute of the Tribunal

5. **Slobodan MILOŠEVIĆ** is individually criminally responsible for the crimes referred to in Articles 2, 3, 4 and 5 of the Statute of the Tribunal as described in this indictment, which he planned, instigated, ordered, committed, or in whose planning, preparation, or execution he otherwise aided and abetted. By using the word "committed" in this indictment, the Prosecutor does not intend to suggest that the accused physically committed any of the crimes charged personally. "Committed" in this indictment refers to participation in a joint criminal enterprise as a co-perpetrator.

6. **Slobodan MILOŠEVIĆ** participated in the joint criminal enterprise as set out below. The purpose of this joint criminal enterprise was the forcible and permanent removal of the majority of non-Serbs, principally Bosnian Muslims and Bosnian Croats, from large areas of the Republic of Bosnia and Herzegovina (hereinafter referred to as "Bosnia and Herzegovina"), through the commission of crimes which are in violation of Articles 2, 3, 4 and 5 of the Statute of the Tribunal.

7. The joint criminal enterprise was in existence by 1 August 1991 and continued until at least 31 December 1995. The individuals participating in this joint criminal enterprise included **Slobodan MILOŠEVIĆ**, Radovan KARADŽIĆ, Momčilo KRAJIŠNIK, Biljana PLAVŠIĆ, General Ratko MLADIĆ, Borisav JOVIĆ, Branko KOSTIĆ, Veljko KADIJE-VIĆ, Blagoje ADŽIĆ, Milan MARTIĆ, Jovica STANIŠIĆ, Franko SIMATOVIĆ, also known as "Frenki," Radovan STOJIČIĆ, also known as "Badža," Vojislav ŠEŠELJ, Željko RAŽNJATOVIĆ, also known as "Arkan," and other known and unknown participants.

8. The crimes enumerated in Counts 1 to 29 of this indictment were within the object of the joint criminal enterprise. Alternatively, the crimes enumerated in Counts 1 to 15 and 19 to 29 were natural and foreseeable consequences of the execution of the object of the joint criminal enterprise and the accused was aware that such crimes were the possible outcome of the execution of the joint criminal enterprise.

9. In order for the joint criminal enterprise to succeed in its objective, **Slobodan MILOŠEVIĆ** worked in concert with or through other individuals in the joint criminal enterprise. Each participant or co-perpetrator within the joint criminal enterprise, sharing the intent to contribute to the enterprise, played his or her own role or roles that significantly contributed to achieving the objective of the enterprise. The roles of the participants or co-perpetrators include, but are not limited to, the following:

10. Radovan KARADŽIĆ was President of the Serbian Democratic Party of Bosnia and Herzegovina (*Srpska demokratska stranka Bosne i Hercegovine* or "SDS") throughout the period of the indictment. On 27 March 1992, KARADŽIĆ became the President of the Bosnian Serb "National Security Council." On 12 May 1992, he was elected President of the three-member Presidency of the self-proclaimed Serbian Republic of Bosnia and Herzegovina (hereinafter referred to as "Republika Srpska") and remained in this position after the Presidency was expanded to five members on 2 June 1992. On 17 December 1992, KARADŽIĆ was elected President of Republika Srpska and remained in that position throughout the period of this indictment. In his capacity as a member of the Bosnian Serb National Security Council, member of the Presidency, as President of Republika Srpska, and in his position of leadership within the SDS party and organs of the Republika Srpska government, Radovan KARADŽIĆ, together with others, commanded, directed, or otherwise exercised effective control over the Territorial Defence ("TO"), the Bosnian Serb army ("VRS") and the police forces of Republika Srpska who participated in the crimes specified in this indictment.

11. Momčilo KRAJIŠNIK, a close associate of Radovan KARADŽIĆ, was a member of the SDS Main Board from 12 July 1991. On 24 October 1991, the day of the founding of the "Assembly of the Serbian People of Bosnia and Herzegovina," (hereinafter referred to as the "Bosnian Serb Assembly") KRAJIŠNIK was elected its President. From 27 March 1992, KRAJIŠNIK was a member of the Bosnian Serb National Security Council. He became a member of the five-member Presidency on 2 June 1992. When the Bosnian Serb Assembly elected Radovan KARADŽIĆ President of Republika Srpska on 17 December 1992, KRAJIŠNIK ceased to be a member of the Presidency, but continued to be one of the most important political leaders in Republika Srpska and remained the President of its National Assembly until 19 October 1996. In his capacity as a member of the Bosnian Serb National Security Council as a member of the Presidency of Republika Srpska, and in his position of leadership within the SDS party and organs of the Republika Srpska government, Momčilo KRAJIŠNIK, together with others, commanded, directed, or otherwise

exercised effective control over the TO, the VRS and the police forces of Republika Srpska who participated in the crimes specified in this indictment.

12. Biljana PLAVŠIĆ, a high-ranking SDS politician, on 28 February 1992, became one of two Acting Presidents of the Serbian Republic of Bosnia and Herzegovina, together with Nikola KOLJEVIĆ. As an Acting President, Biljana PLAVŠIĆ became an ex officio member of the Bosnian Serb National Security Council. On 12 May 1992, she was elected as a member of the three-member Presidency and remained in this position after it was expanded to five members. When the Bosnian Serb Assembly elected Radovan KARADŽIĆ President of Republika Srpska on 17 December 1992, it also elected Biljana PLAVŠIĆ one of two Vice-Presidents, a position she held until 19 July 1996. In her capacity as Vice-President, member of the Bosnian Serb National Security Council as a member of the Presidency of Republika Srpska, and in her position of leadership within the SDS party and organs of the Republika Srpska government, Biljana PLAVŠIĆ, together with others, commanded, directed, or otherwise exercised effective control over the TO, the VRS and the police forces of Republika Srpska who participated in the crimes specified in this indictment.

13. General Ratko MLADIĆ, a military career officer previously stationed in Macedonia and Kosovo, became the commander of the 9th Corps (Knin Corps) of the Yugoslav People's Army ("JNA") in June 1991 and participated in the fighting in Croatia. On 4 October 1991, the SFRY Presidency promoted him to Major General. Subsequently, in May 1992, he assumed command of the forces of the Second Military District of the JNA in Sarajevo. From 12 May 1992 until November 1996, he was the Commander of the Main Staff of the VRS and in this capacity, together with others, commanded, directed, or otherwise exercised effective control over the VRS and other units acting in co-ordination with the VRS who participated in the crimes specified in this indictment.

14. Borisav JOVIĆ was successively the Vice-President, President and then a member of the SFRY Presidency from 15 May 1989 until April 1992, as well as the President of the SPS from May 1991 until October 1992, and a high ranking official of the SPS until November 1995. Borisav JOVIĆ and Branko KOSTIĆ, the Vice-President and then Acting President of the Presidency of the SFRY, together with others during the relevant period, commanded, directed, or otherwise exercised effective control over the JNA and members of the TO and paramilitary units acting in co-ordination with, and under supervision of, the JNA.

15. General Veljko KADIJEVIĆ, as Federal Secretary for National Defence from 15 May 1988 until 6 January 1992, commanded, directed, or otherwise exercised effective control over the JNA and other units acting in co-ordination with the JNA.

16. General Blagoje ADŽIĆ, in his capacity as JNA Chief of Staff from 1990 to 28 February 1992 and Acting Federal Secretary for National Defence from mid-1991 to 28

February 1992, Federal Secretary for National Defence from 28 February 1992 to 27 April 1992 and JNA Chief of Staff from 27 April 1992 to 8 May 1992, together with others, commanded, directed, or otherwise exercised effective control over the JNA and other units acting in co-ordination with the JNA.

17. Jovica STANIŠIĆ, in his capacity as chief of the State Security (*Državna bezbednost* or "DB") of the Republic of Serbia from March 1991 to October 1998, commanded, directed, or otherwise exercised effective control over members of the DB, who participated in the perpetration of the crimes specified in this indictment. In addition, he provided arms, funds, training, or other substantial assistance or support to Serb paramilitary units and police units that were subsequently involved in the crimes specified in this indictment.

18. Franko SIMATOVIĆ, also known as "Frenki," as head of the special operations component of the DB of the Republic of Serbia, commanded, directed, or otherwise exercised effective control over agents of the DB who perpetrated crimes specified in this indictment. In addition, he provided arms, funds, training, or other substantial assistance or support to Serb paramilitary units and police units that were subsequently involved in the crimes charged in this indictment.

19. Radovan STOJIČIĆ also known as "Badža" as Deputy Minister of Interior of Serbia and head of Public Security Service, commanded, directed or otherwise exercised effective control over special forces of the Serbian MUP and volunteer units who participated in the crimes specified in this indictment. In addition, he provided arms, funds, training, or other substantial assistance or support to Serb paramilitary units and police units that were subsequently involved in the crimes specified in this indictment.

20. Milan MARTIĆ, as "Secretary of the Secretariat of Internal Affairs" of the so-called Serbian Autonomous Region ("SAO") Krajina from 4 January 1991 until 29 May 1991; as "Minister of Defence" of the SAO Krajina from 29 May 1991 to 27 June 1991; and as "Minister of Internal Affairs" for the SAO Krajina (later "Republic of Serbian Krajina") from 27 June 1991 to January 1994, established, commanded, directed, and otherwise exercised effective control over members of his police force (referred to as "Martić's Police," "Martić's Militia," "*Martićevci,*" "SAO Krajina Police" or "SAO Krajina Militia") who were subsequently involved in the crimes specified in this indictment.

21. Željko RAŽNJATOVIĆ, also known as "Arkan," in 1990 established and commanded the Serbian Volunteer Guard, a paramilitary unit commonly known as "Arkanovci" or "Arkan's Tigers," who during the time relevant to this indictment operated in Bosnia and Herzegovina and were involved in the crimes charged in this indictment. In addition, he maintained a significant military base in Erdut, Croatia, where he functioned as commander. Other paramilitary groups and TO units were trained at this base and were subsequently involved in the crimes charged in this indictment.

22. Vojislav ŠEŠELJ, as President of the Serbian Radical Party (SRS) from at least February 1991 throughout the time relevant to this indictment recruited or otherwise provided substantial assistance or support to Serb paramilitary units, commonly known as "Šešeljevci" or "Šešelj's men," who perpetrated crimes as specified in this indictment. In addition, he openly espoused and encouraged the creation of a "Greater Serbia" by violence and other unlawful means, and actively participated in war propaganda and spreading inter-ethnic hatred.

23. From 1987 until late 2000, **Slobodan MILOŠEVIĆ** was the dominant political figure in Serbia and the SFRY/FRY. He acquired control of all facets of the Serbian government, including the police and the state security services. In addition, he gained control over the political leaderships of Kosovo, Vojvodina, and Montenegro.

24. In his capacity as the President of Serbia and through his leading position in the SPS party, **Slobodan MILOŠEVIĆ** exercised effective control or substantial influence over the above listed participants in the joint criminal enterprise and either alone or acting in concert with them and additional known and unknown persons effectively controlled or substantially influenced the actions of the Federal Presidency of the SFRY and later the FRY, the Serbian Ministry of Internal Affairs ("MUP"), the JNA, the Yugoslav Army ("VJ") and the VRS, as well as Serb paramilitary groups.

25. **Slobodan MILOŠEVIĆ**, acting alone and in concert with other members of the joint criminal enterprise participated in the joint criminal enterprise in the following ways:
   a) He exerted effective control over elements of the JNA and VJ which participated in the planning, preparation, facilitation and execution of the forcible removal of the majority of non-Serbs, principally Bosnian Muslims and Bosnian Croats, from large areas of Bosnia and Herzegovina.
   b) He provided financial, logistical and political support to the VRS. These forces subsequently participated in the execution of the joint criminal enterprise through the commission of crimes which are in violation of Articles 2, 3, 4 and 5 of the Statute of the Tribunal.
   c) He exercised substantial influence over, and assisted, the political leadership of Republika Srpska in the planning, preparation, facilitation and execution of the take-over of municipalities in Bosnia and Herzegovina and the subsequent forcible removal of the majority of non-Serbs, principally Bosnian Muslims and Bosnian Croats, from those municipalities.
   d) He participated in the planning and preparation of the take-over of municipalities in Bosnia and Herzegovina and the subsequent forcible removal of the majority of non-Serbs, principally Bosnian Muslims and Bosnian Croats, from those municipalities. He provided the financial, material and logistical support necessary for such take-over.
   e) He participated in the formation, financing, supply, support and direction of special forces of the Republic of Serbia Ministry of Internal Affairs. These special

forces participated in the execution of the joint criminal enterprise through the commission of crimes which are in violation of Articles 2, 3, 4 and 5 of the Statute of the Tribunal.

f) He participated in providing financial, logistical and political support and direction to Serbian irregular forces or paramilitaries. These forces participated in the execution of the joint criminal enterprise through the commission of crimes which are in violation of Articles 2, 3, 4 and 5 of the Statute of the Tribunal.

g) He controlled, manipulated or otherwise utilised Serbian state-run media to spread exaggerated and false messages of ethnically based attacks by Bosnian Muslims and Croats against Serb people intended to create an atmosphere of fear and hatred among Serbs living in Serbia, Croatia and Bosnia and Herzegovina which contributed to the forcible removal of the majority of non-Serbs, principally Bosnian Muslims and Bosnian Croats, from large areas of Bosnia and Herzegovina.

26. **Slobodan MILOŠEVIĆ** knowingly and wilfully participated in the joint criminal enterprise, while being aware of the foreseeable consequences of this enterprise. On this basis, he bears individual criminal responsibility for these crimes under Article 7(1) of the Statute of the Tribunal, in addition to his responsibility under the same Article for having planned, instigated, ordered or otherwise aided and abetted in the planning, preparation and execution of these crimes.

Article 7(3) of the Statute of the Tribunal

27. **Slobodan MILOŠEVIĆ**, while holding positions of superior authority, is also individually criminally responsible for the acts or omissions of his subordinates, pursuant to Article 7(3) of the Statute of the Tribunal. A superior is responsible for the criminal acts of his subordinates if he knew or had reason to know that his subordinates were about to commit such acts or had done so, and the superior failed to take the necessary and reasonable measures to prevent such acts or to punish the perpetrators.

28. From at least March 1991 until 15 June 1992, **Slobodan MILOŠEVIĆ** exercised effective control over the four members of the "Serbian Bloc" within the Presidency of the SFRY. These four individuals were Borisav JOVIĆ, the representative of the Republic of Serbia; Branko KOSTIĆ, the representative of the Republic of Montenegro; Jugoslav KOSTIĆ, the representative of the Autonomous Province of Vojvodina; and Sejdo BAJRAMOVIĆ, the representative of the Autonomous Province of Kosovo and Metohija. **Slobodan MILOŠEVIĆ** used Borisav JOVIĆ and Branko KOSTIĆ as his primary agents in the Presidency and through them he directed the actions of the "Serbian Bloc." From 1 October 1991, in the absence of the representatives of the Presidency from Croatia, Slovenia, Macedonia and Bosnia and Herzegovina, the four members of the "Serbian Bloc" exercised the powers of the Presidency, including that of collective "Commander-in-Chief" of the JNA. This "Rump Presidency" acted without dissension to execute **Slobodan**

MILOŠEVIĆ's policies. The Federal Presidency had effective control over the JNA as its "Commander-in-Chief" and other units under the supervision of the JNA. Generals Veljko KADIJEVIĆ and Blagoje ADŽIĆ, who directed and supervised the JNA forces in Bosnia and Herzegovina, were in constant communication and consultation with the accused.

29. On 27 April 1992, the Supreme Defence Council was formed. Throughout the time relevant to this indictment, **Slobodan MILOŠEVIĆ** was a member of the Supreme Defence Council and exercised substantial influence and control over other members of the Council. The Supreme Defence Council and the President of the FRY had de jure control over the JNA and later the VJ. In addition to his de jure powers, at all times relevant to this indictment, **Slobodan MILOŠEVIĆ** exercised de facto control over the JNA and the VJ through his control over the high ranking officers of these armies.

30. **Slobodan MILOŠEVIĆ** is therefore individually criminally responsible, under Article 7(3) of the Statute of the Tribunal, for the participation of the members of the JNA and the VJ and other units under the supervision of the JNA and the VJ in the crimes described in this indictment.

31. From the time **Slobodan MILOŠEVIĆ** came to power in Serbia, he exercised control over key officials in the Serbian MUP, among them Radmilo BOGDANOVIĆ and Zoran SOKOLOVIĆ, who were both, at different times, the Minister of Internal Affairs of Serbia. He also exercised control over Jovica STANIŠIĆ and Franko SIMATOVIĆ, both high-ranking officials in the DB. Through these officials, **Slobodan MILOŠEVIĆ** exercised effective control over agents of the MUP, including the DB, who directed and supported the actions of the special forces and Serb paramilitary groups operating in Bosnia and Herzegovina. The accused **Slobodan MILOŠEVIĆ** is therefore individually criminally responsible, under Article 7(3) of the Statute of the Tribunal, for the participation of the members of the Serbian MUP, including the DB, in the crimes described in this indictment.

THE CHARGES

COUNTS 1 and 2
GENOCIDE OR COMPLICITY IN GENOCIDE

32. From on or about 1 March 1992 until 31 December 1995, **Slobodan MILOŠEVIĆ**, acting alone or in concert with other members of the joint criminal enterprise, planned, instigated, ordered, committed or otherwise aided and abetted the planning, preparation and execution of the destruction, in whole or in part, of the Bosnian Muslim and Bosnian Croat national, ethnical, racial or religious groups, as such, in territories within Bosnia and Herzegovina, including: Bijeljina; Bosanski Novi; Bosanski Šamac; Bratunac; Brčko;

Doboj; Foča; Sarajevo (Ilijaš); Ključ; Kotor Varoš; Sarajevo (Novi Grad); Prijedor; Rogatica; Sanski Most; Srebrenica; Višegrad; Vlasenica and Zvornik. The destruction of these groups was effected by:

a) The widespread killing of thousands of Bosnian Muslims and Bosnian Croats, during and after the take-over of territories within Bosnia and Herzegovina, including those listed above, as specified in Schedule A to this indictment. In many of the territories, educated and leading members of these groups were specifically targeted for execution, often in accordance with pre-prepared lists. After the fall of Srebrenica in July 1995, almost all captured Bosnian Muslim men and boys, altogether several thousands, were executed at the places where they had been captured or at sites to which they had been transported for execution.

b) The killing of thousands of Bosnian Muslims and Bosnian Croats in detention facilities within Bosnia and Herzegovina, including those situated within the territories listed above, as specified in Schedule B to this indictment.

c) The causing of serious bodily and mental harm to thousands of Bosnian Muslims and Bosnian Croats during their confinement in detention facilities within Bosnia and Herzegovina, including those situated within the territories listed above, as specified in Schedule C to this indictment. Members of these groups, during their confinement in detention facilities and during their interrogation at these locations, police stations and military barracks, were continuously subjected to, or forced to witness, inhumane acts, including murder, sexual violence, torture and beatings.

d) The detention of thousands of Bosnian Muslims and Bosnian Croats in detention facilities within Bosnia and Herzegovina, including those situated within the territories listed above, under conditions of life calculated to bring about the partial physical destruction of those groups, namely through starvation, contaminated water, forced labour, inadequate medical care and constant physical and psychological assault.

By these acts and omissions, **Slobodan MILOŠEVIĆ** committed:

Count 1: GENOCIDE, punishable under Articles 4(3)(a) and 7(1) and 7(3) of the Statute of the Tribunal; or

Count 2: COMPLICITY IN GENOCIDE, punishable under Articles 4(3)(e) and 7(1) and 7(3) of the Statute of the Tribunal.

COUNT 3
PERSECUTIONS

33. From on or about 1 March 1992 until 31 December 1995, **Slobodan MILOŠEVIĆ**, acting alone or in concert with members of the joint criminal enterprise, planned, instigated, ordered, committed or otherwise aided and abetted the planning, preparation or execution

of persecutions of non-Serbs, principally Bosnian Muslims and Bosnian Croats, within the territories of Banja Luka; Bihać; Bijeljina; Bileća; Bosanska Dubica; Bosanska Gradiška; Bosanska Krupa; Bosanski Novi; Bosanski Petrovac; Bosanski Šamac; Bratunac; Brčko; Čajniče; Čelinac; Doboj; Donji Vakuf; Foča; Gacko; Goražde; Sarajevo (Hadžići); Sarajevo (Ilidža); Sarajevo (Ilijaš); Ključ; Kalinovik; Kotor Varoš; Nevesinje; Sarajevo (Novi Grad); Sarajevo (Novo Sarajevo); Sarajevo (Pale); Prijedor; Prnjavor; Rogatica; Rudo; Sanski Most; Šekovići; Šipovo; Sokolac; Srebrenica; Teslić; Trebinje; Sarajevo (Trnovo); Višegrad; Vlasenica; Sarajevo (Vogošća) and Zvornik.

34. Throughout this period, Serb forces, comprised of JNA, VJ, VRS units, local TO units, local and Serbian MUP police units and paramilitary units from Serbia and Montenegro, attacked and took control of towns and villages in these territories. After the take-over, the Serb forces in co-operation with the local Serb authorities established a regime of persecutions designed to drive the non-Serb civilian population from these territories.

35. These persecutions were committed on the discriminatory grounds of political affiliation, race or religion and included:
   a) The extermination or murder of thousands of Bosnian Muslim, Bosnian Croat and other non-Serb civilians, including women and the elderly, in those territories listed above, the details of which are set out in Schedules A and B to this indictment.
   b) The prolonged and routine imprisonment and confinement of thousands of Bosnian Muslim, Bosnian Croat and other non-Serb civilians in detention facilities within and outside of Bosnia and Herzegovina, the details of which are set out in Schedule C to this indictment.
   c) The establishment and perpetuation of inhumane living conditions against Bosnian Muslim, Bosnian Croat and other non-Serb civilians, within the above mentioned detention facilities. These living conditions were brutal and characterised by inhumane treatment, overcrowding, starvation, forced labour and systematic physical and psychological abuse, including torture, beatings and sexual assault.
   d) The prolonged and frequent forced labour of Bosnian Muslim, Bosnian Croat and other non-Serb civilians, from these detention facilities. The forced labour included digging graves and trenches and other forms of manual labour at the frontlines.
   e) The cruel and inhumane treatment of Bosnian Muslim, Bosnian Croat and other non-Serb civilians during and after the take-over of the municipalities specified above. Such inhumane treatment included, but was not limited to, sexual violence, torture, physical and psychological abuse and forced existence under inhumane living conditions.
   f) The imposition of restrictive and discriminatory measures against Bosnian Muslims, Bosnian Croats and other non-Serbs, such as, the restriction of freedom of movement; removal from positions of authority in local government institutions

and the police; dismissal from jobs; arbitrary searches of their homes; denial of the right to judicial process and the denial of the right of equal access to public services, including proper medical care.

g) The beating and robbing of Bosnian Muslim, Bosnian Croat and other non-Serb civilians.

h) The forcible transfer and deportation of thousands of Bosnian Muslim, Bosnian Croat and other non-Serb civilians, from the territories listed above, to locations outside of Serb held territories as described in paragraphs 40 and 41 and Schedule D to this indictment.

i) The appropriation and plunder of property belonging to Bosnian Muslim, Bosnian Croat and other non-Serb civilians.

j) The intentional and wanton destruction of homes, other public and private property belonging to Bosnian Muslims and Bosnian Croats, their cultural and religious institutions, historical monuments and other sacred sites, as described in paragraph 42.

k) The obstruction of humanitarian aid, in particular medical and food supplies into the besieged enclaves Bihać, Goražde, Srebrenica and Žepa, and the deprivation of water from the civilians trapped in the enclaves designed to create unbearable living conditions.

By these acts and omissions, **Slobodan MILOŠEVIĆ** committed:

Count 3: Persecutions on political, racial or religious grounds, a **CRIME AGAINST HUMANITY**, punishable under Articles 5(h) and 7(1) and 7(3) of the Statute of the Tribunal.

COUNTS 4 to 7
EXTERMINATION, MURDER AND WILFUL KILLING

36. From on or about 1 March 1992 until 31 December 1995, **Slobodan MILOŠEVIĆ**, acting alone or in concert with other members of the joint criminal enterprise, planned, instigated, ordered, committed or otherwise aided and abetted the planning, preparation or execution of the extermination, murder and wilful killings of non-Serbs, principally Bosnian Muslims and Bosnian Croats living in the territories of Banja Luka; Bihać; Bijeljina; Bileća; Bosanska Gradiška; Bosanska Krupa; Bosanski Novi; Bosanski Petrovac; Bosanski Šamac; Bratunac; Brčko; Čajniče; Čelinac; Doboj; Foča; Gacko; Sarajevo (Ilijaš); Ključ; Kalinovik; Kotor Varoš; Nevesinje; Sarajevo (Novi Grad); Prijedor; Prnjavor; Rogatica; Rudo; Sanski Most; Sokolac; Srebrenica; Teslić; Višegrad; Vlasenica and Zvornik. The extermination, murder and wilful killings of these groups were effected by:

a) The killing of Bosnian Muslims, Bosnian Croats and other non-Serbs in their towns and villages, during and after the take-over of the territories listed above including those specified in Schedule A to this indictment.

b) The killing of Bosnian Muslims, Bosnian Croats and other non-Serbs in detention facilities and during their deportation or forcible transfers, including those specified in Schedule B to this indictment.

By these acts and omissions, **Slobodan MILOŠEVIĆ** committed:

Count 4: Extermination, a **CRIME AGAINST HUMANITY**, punishable under Articles 5(b) and 7(1) and 7(3) of the Statute of the Tribunal.

Count 5: Murder, a **CRIME AGAINST HUMANITY**, punishable under Articles 5(a) and 7(1) and 7(3) of the Statute of the Tribunal.

Count 6: Wilful killing, a **GRAVE BREACH OF THE GENEVA CONVENTIONS OF 1949**, punishable under Articles 2(a) and 7(1) and 7(3) of the Statute of the Tribunal.

Count 7: Murder, a **VIOLATION OF THE LAWS OR CUSTOMS OF WAR**, as recognised by Common Article 3(1)(a) of the Geneva Conventions of 1949, punishable under Articles 3 and 7(1) and 7(3) of the Statute of the Tribunal.

COUNTS 8 to 15
UNLAWFUL CONFINEMENT, IMPRISONMENT, TORTURE, WILFULLY CAUSING GREAT SUFFERING, OTHER INHUMANE ACTS

37. From on or about 1 March 1992 until 31 December 1995, **Slobodan MILOŠEVIĆ**, acting alone or in concert with members of the joint criminal enterprise, planned, instigated, ordered, committed or otherwise aided and abetted the planning, preparation or execution of the unlawful confinement or imprisonment under inhumane conditions of Bosnian Muslims, Bosnian Croats and other non-Serbs within the territories of Banja Luka; Bihać; Bijeljina; Bileća; Bosanska Dubica; Bosanska Krupa; Bosanski Novi; Bosanski Petrovac; Bosanski Šamac; Bratunac; Brčko; Čajniče; Čelinac; Doboj; Donji Vakuf; Foča; Gacko; Ključ; Kalinovik; Kotor Varoš; Nevesinje; Prijedor; Prnjavor; Rogatica; Rudo; Sanski Most; Sokolac; Teslić; Višegrad; Vlasenica and Zvornik.

38. Serb military forces, comprised of JNA, VJ, VRS, TO and paramilitary units acting in co-operation with local police staff and local Serb authorities, arrested and detained thousands of Bosnian Muslim, Bosnian Croat and other non-Serb civilians from the territories listed above. These civilians were held in short and long-term detention, of which the major facilities are specified in Schedule C to this indictment.

39. The living conditions in these detention facilities were brutal and characterised by inhumane treatment, overcrowding, starvation, forced labour, inadequate medical care and systematic physical and psychological assault, including torture, beatings and sexual assault.

By these acts and omissions, **Slobodan MILOŠEVIĆ** committed:

Count 8: Imprisonment, a **CRIME AGAINST HUMANITY**, punishable under Articles 5(e) and 7(1) and 7(3) of the Statute of the Tribunal.

Count 9: Torture, a **CRIME AGAINST HUMANITY**, punishable under Articles 5(f) and 7(1) and 7(3) of the Statute of the Tribunal.

Count 10: Inhumane acts, a **CRIME AGAINST HUMANITY**, punishable under Articles 5(i) and 7(1) and 7(3) of the Statute of the Tribunal.

Count 11: Unlawful Confinement, a **GRAVE BREACH OF THE GENEVA CONVENTIONS OF 1949,** punishable under Articles 2(g) and 7(1) and 7(3) of the Statute of the Tribunal.

Count 12: Torture, a **GRAVE BREACH OF THE GENEVA CONVENTIONS OF 1949,** punishable under Articles 2(b) and 7(1) and 7(3) of the Statute of the Tribunal.

Count 13: Wilfully causing great suffering, a **GRAVE BREACH OF THE GENEVA CONVENTIONS OF 1949,** punishable under Articles 2(c) and 7(1) and 7(3) of the Statute of the Tribunal.

Count 14: Torture, a **VIOLATIONS OF THE LAWS OR CUSTOMS OF WAR** as recognised by Common Article 3(1)(a) of the Geneva Conventions of 1949, punishable under Articles 3 and 7(1) and 7(3) of the Statute of the Tribunal.

Count 15: Cruel Treatment, a **VIOLATIONS OF THE LAWS OR CUSTOMS OF WAR** as recognised by Common Article 3(1)(a) of the Geneva Conventions of 1949, punishable under Articles 3 and 7(1) and 7(3) of the Statute of the Tribunal.

COUNTS 16 to 18
DEPORTATION AND INHUMANE ACTS (FORCIBLE TRANSFERS)

40. From on or about 1 March 1992 until 31 December 1995, **Slobodan MILOŠEVIĆ,** acting alone or in concert with members of the joint criminal enterprise, planned, instigated, ordered, committed or otherwise aided and abetted the planning, preparation or execution of the unlawful forcible transfer, also qualifying as deportation where indicated hereinafter, of tens of thousands of Bosnian Muslim, Bosnian Croat and other non-Serb civilians from their legal domiciles in the territories of Banja Luka (deportation); Bihać; Bijeljina; Bileća (deportation); Bosanska Dubica; Bosanska Gradiška; Bosanska Krupa; Bosanski Novi; Bosanski Petrovac; Bosanski Šamac (deportation); Bratunac; Brčko; Čajniče; Čelinac; Doboj; Donji Vakuf; Foča; Gacko (deportation); Sarajevo (Hadžići); Sarajevo (Ilidža); Sarajevo (Ilijaš); Ključ; Kalinovik; Kotor Varoš; Nevesinje; Sarajevo (Novi Grad); Sarajevo (Novo Sarajevo); Sarajevo (Pale); Prijedor; Prnjavor; Rogatica; Rudo (deportation); Sanski Most; Šekovići; Šipovo; Sokolac; Srebrenica; Teslić; Trebinje; Sarajevo (Trnovo); Višegrad; Vlasenica; Sarajevo (Vogošća) and Zvornik (deportation), to other areas both inside and outside Bosnia and Herzegovina. The details of such acts and omissions are described in Schedule D.

41. In order to achieve this objective, Serb forces comprised of JNA, VJ, VRS and TO, paramilitary units acting in co-operation with local police staff, local Serb authorities and special

forces of the Serbian Ministry of Internal Affairs under the effective control of **Slobodan MILOŠEVIĆ** or other members of the joint criminal enterprise, subjugated villages and towns in Bosnia and Herzegovina and participated with members of the SDS in the disarming of the non-Serb population. The towns and villages, including areas in which the inhabitants complied and offered no resistance, were then attacked. These attacks were intended to compel the non-Serb population to flee. After taking control of the towns and villages, the Serb forces often rounded-up the remaining non-Serb civilian population and forcibly removed them from the area. On other occasions, the Serb forces in co-operation with the local Serb authorities imposed restrictive and discriminatory measures on the non-Serb population and engaged in a campaign of terror designed to drive them out of the territory. The majority of non-Serbs that remained were eventually deported or forcibly transferred from their homes.

By these acts and omissions **Slobodan MILOŠEVIĆ** committed:

> **Count 16:** Deportation, a **CRIME AGAINST HUMANITY**, punishable under Articles 5(d) and 7(1) and 7(3) of the Statute of the Tribunal.
> **Count 17:** Inhumane Acts (Forcible Transfers), a **CRIME AGAINST HUMANITY,** punishable under Articles 5(i) and 7(1) and 7(3) of the Statute of the Tribunal.
> **Count 18:** Unlawful Deportation or Transfer, a **GRAVE BREACH OF THE GENEVA CONVENTIONS OF 1949,** punishable under Articles 2(g) and 7(1) and 7(3) of the Statute of the Tribunal.

COUNTS 19 to 22
WANTON DESTRUCTION,
PLUNDER OF PUBLIC OR PRIVATE PROPERTY

42. From on or about 1 March 1992 until 31 December 1995, **Slobodan MILOŠEVIĆ**, acting alone or in concert with members of the joint criminal enterprise, planned, instigated, ordered, committed or otherwise aided and abetted the planning, preparation or execution of the wanton destruction and plunder of the public and private property of the Bosnian Muslim, Bosnian Croat and other non-Serb populations within the territories of Banja Luka; Bihać; Bijeljina; Bileća; Bosanska Dubica; Bosanska Gradiška; Bosanska Krupa; Bosanski Novi; Bosanski Petrovac; Bosanski Šamac; Bratunac; Brčko; Čajniče; Čelinac; Doboj; Donji Vakuf; Foča; Gacko; Sarajevo (HADŽIĆi); Sarajevo (Ilidža); Sarajevo (Ilijaš); Ključ; Kalinovik; Kotor Varoš; Nevesinje; Sarajevo (Novi Grad); Sarajevo (Novo Sarajevo); Sarajevo (Pale); Prijedor; Prnjavor; Rogatica; Rudo; Sanski Most; Šekovići; Šipovo; Sokolac; Srebrenica; Teslić; Sarajevo (Trnovo); Trebinje; Višegrad; Vlasenica; Sarajevo (Vogošća), and Zvornik. This intentional and wanton destruction and plunder was not justified by military necessity and included:

> a) The appropriation and plunder of property belonging to Bosnian Muslim, Bosnian Croat and other non-Serb civilians, including the coerced signing of documents relinquishing property rights.

b) The intentional and wanton destruction of homes and other property owned by Bosnian Muslim, Bosnian Croat and other non-Serb civilians. Such destruction was employed as a means to compel non-Serbs to flee their legal domiciles and to prevent their subsequent return.

c) The intentional and wanton destruction of religious and cultural buildings of the Bosnian Muslim and Bosnian Croat communities including, but not limited to, mosques, churches, libraries, educational buildings and cultural centres.

By these acts and omissions, **Slobodan MILOŠEVIĆ** committed:

Count 19: Extensive destruction and appropriation of property, not justified by military necessity and carried out unlawfully and wantonly, a **GRAVE BREACH OF THE GENEVA CONVENTIONS OF 1949,** punishable under Articles 2(d) and 7(1) and 7(3) of the Statute of the Tribunal.

Count 20: Wanton destruction of villages, or devastation not justified by military necessity, a **VIOLATION OF THE LAWS OR CUSTOMS OF WAR,** punishable under Articles 3(b) and 7(1) and 7(3) of the Statute of the Tribunal.

Count 21: Wilful destruction or wilful damage done to historic monuments and institutions dedicated to education or religion, a **VIOLATION OF THE LAWS OR CUSTOMS OF WAR,** punishable under Articles 3(d) and 7(1) and 7(3) of the Statute of the Tribunal.

Count 22: Plunder of public or private property, a **VIOLATION OF THE LAWS OR CUSTOMS OF WAR,** punishable under Articles 3(e) and 7(1) and 7(3) of the Statute of the Tribunal.

COUNTS 23 to 29
MURDER, WILFUL KILLING, WILFULLY CAUSING GREAT SUFFERING, CRUEL TREATMENT, ATTACKS ON CIVILIANS

43. Between April 1992 and November 1995, **Slobodan MILOŠEVIĆ,** acting alone or in concert with members of the joint criminal enterprise, planned, instigated, ordered, committed, or otherwise aided and abetted the planning, preparation, or execution of a military campaign of artillery and mortar shelling and sniping onto civilian areas of Sarajevo and upon its civilian population, killing and wounding thousands of civilians of all ages and both sexes.

44. In this time period, the Sarajevo Romanija Corps of the VRS, under the effective control of Radovan KARADŽIĆ and General Ratko MLADIĆ, launched an extensive, forty-four month shelling and sniping attack on Sarajevo, mostly from positions in the hills surrounding the city with an unobstructed view of Sarajevo.

45. The Sarajevo Romanija Corps conducted a protracted campaign of shelling and sniping upon Sarajevo during which civilians were either specifically targeted or the subject of

reckless fire into areas where civilians were known to have been. Among the victims of this campaign were civilians who were, amongst other things, tending vegetable plots, queuing for bread or water, attending funerals, shopping in markets, riding on trams, gathering wood. Specific instances of sniping are described in Schedule E attached to this indictment. Specific instances of shelling are set forth in Schedule F.

By these acts and omissions, **Slobodan MILOŠEVIĆ** committed:

> **Count 23:** Murder, a **CRIME AGAINST HUMANITY**, punishable under Articles 5(a) and 7(1) and 7(3) of the Statute of the Tribunal.
>
> **Count 24:** Inhumane acts, a **CRIME AGAINST HUMANITY**, punishable under Articles 5(i) and 7(1) and 7(3) of the Statute of the Tribunal.
>
> **Count 25:** Wilful killing, a **GRAVE BREACH OF THE GENEVA CONVENTIONS OF 1949,** punishable under Articles 2(a) and 7(1) and 7(3) of the Statute of the Tribunal.
>
> **Count 26:** Wilfully causing great suffering, a **GRAVE BREACH OF THE GENEVA CONVENTIONS OF 1949,** punishable under Articles 2(c) and 7(1) and 7(3) of the Statute of the Tribunal.
>
> **Count 27:** Murder, a **VIOLATION OF THE LAWS OR CUSTOMS OF WAR,** as recognised by Common Article 3(1)(a) of the Geneva Conventions of 1949, punishable under Articles 3 and 7(1) and 7(3) of the Statute of the Tribunal.
>
> **Count 28:** Cruel treatment, a **VIOLATION OF THE LAWS OR CUSTOMS OF WAR,** as recognised by Common Article 3(1)(a) of the Geneva Conventions of 1949, punishable under Articles 3 and 7(1) and 7(3) of the Statute of the Tribunal.
>
> **Count 29:** Attacks on civilians, a **VIOLATION OF THE LAWS OR CUSTOMS OF WAR,** as recognised by Article 51 (2) of Additional Protocol I and Article 13 (2) of Additional Protocol II to the Geneva Conventions of 1949, punishable under Articles 3 and 7(1) and 7(3) of the Statute of the Tribunal.

GENERAL LEGAL ALLEGATIONS

46. All acts and omissions alleged in this indictment occurred on the territory of the former Yugoslavia.

47. At all times relevant to this indictment, a state of international armed conflict and partial occupation existed in Bosnia and Herzegovina.

48. All acts and omissions charged as Grave Breaches of the Geneva Conventions of 1949 occurred during the international armed conflict and partial occupation of Bosnia and Herzegovina. All such acts and omissions were committed against persons protected under the Geneva Conventions.

49. All acts and omissions charged relative to the destruction of property as Grave Breaches of the Geneva Conventions of 1949 involved "protected property" under the relevant provisions of the Geneva Conventions.

50. At all times relevant to this indictment **Slobodan MILOŠEVIĆ** was required to abide by the laws and customs governing the conduct of armed conflicts, including the Geneva Conventions of 1949 and the Additional Protocols thereto.

51. All conduct charged as Crimes against Humanity was part of a widespread or systematic attack directed against the Bosnian Muslim, Bosnian Croat and other non-Serb civilian populations within large areas of Bosnia and Herzegovina.

ADDITIONAL FACTS

52. In November 1990, multi-party elections were held in Bosnia and Herzegovina. At the Republic level, the SDA (Stranka demokratske akcije—Party of Democratic Action) the party of the Bosnian Muslims won 86 seats; the SDS, the party of the Bosnian Serbs, won 72 seats and the HDZ (*Hrvatska demokratska zajednica*—Croatian Democratic Community) won 44 seats in the Assembly.

53. The central idea within the SDS political platform, as articulated by its leaders, including Radovan KARADŽIĆ, Momčilo KRAJIŠNIK and Biljana PLAVŠIĆ, was the unification of all Serbs within one state. The SDS regarded the separation of Bosnia and Herzegovina from the SFRY as a threat to the interests of the Serbs.

54. On 5 February 1991 the Assembly of the Republic of Serbia passed a "Law on Ministries" submitted by **Slobodan MILOŠEVIĆ**. This law established twenty "Ministries" of the Serbian government, including the Ministry for Links with Serbs outside Serbia. This Ministry assisted the SDS to establish the Serb Republic of Bosnia and Herzegovina.

55. The results of the November 1990 elections meant that, as time went on, the SDS would be unable through peaceful means to keep the Republic of Bosnia and Herzegovina in what was becoming a Serb-dominated Yugoslavia. As a result, Serb people within certain areas of Bosnia and Herzegovina, with Serb majorities, began to organise themselves into formal regional structures that they referred to as "Associations of Municipalities." In April 1991 the Association of Municipalities of Bosnian Krajina, centred in Banja Luka, was formed.

56. In March 1991, the collective Presidency of the SFRY reached a deadlock on several issues including the issue of instituting a state of emergency in Yugoslavia. The representatives on the Presidency from the Republic of Serbia, the Republic of Montenegro, the Autonomous Province of Vojvodina, and the Autonomous Province of Kosovo and

Metohija all resigned from their posts. In a televised address on 16 March 1991, **Slobodan MILOŠEVIĆ**, in his capacity as President of the Republic of Serbia, declared that Yugoslavia was finished and that Serbia would no longer be bound by decisions of the Federal Presidency.

57. On 25 March 1991, **Slobodan MILOŠEVIĆ** and Franjo TUDMAN met in Karadjordjevo and discussed the partition of Bosnia and Herzegovina between Serbia and Croatia.

58. On 25 June 1991, Slovenia and Croatia declared their independence. On 26 June, the JNA intervened in Slovenia. In the summer of 1991, fighting broke out in Croatia.

59. In August 1991 Radovan KARADŽIĆ instituted a system of secret communication between the local boards of the SDS and the Main Staff and with the Republic of Serbia. This secret communication protocol was declared mandatory for the transmission of reports and orders.

60. From autumn 1991, the JNA began to withdraw its forces out of Croatia. Forces under the control of the JNA began to re-deploy in Bosnia and Herzegovina. Many of these troops were deployed to areas in which there was no garrison or other JNA facility.

61. As the war continued in Croatia it appeared increasingly likely that Bosnia and Herzegovina would also declare its independence from the SFRY. The SDS, realising it could not prevent the secession of Bosnia and Herzegovina from the SFRY, began the creation of a separate Serbian entity within Bosnia and Herzegovina. During the period from September to November 1991, several Serbian Autonomous Regions (SAO) were formed, some of them on the basis of the Associations of Municipalities referred to above.

62. On 12 September 1991, the Serbian Autonomous Region of Herzegovina was proclaimed. On 16 September 1991, the Autonomous Region of Krajina was proclaimed by the Assembly of the Association of Municipalities of Bosnian Krajina. By 21 November 1991, the Serbian Autonomous Regions and Autonomous Regions consisted of the Autonomous Region of Krajina, the SAO Herzegovina, the SAO Romanija-Birač, the SAO Semberija, and SAO Northern Bosnia.

63. On 3 October 1991, the four members of the SFRY Presidency from Serbia and Montenegro (Borisav JOVIĆ, Jugoslav KOSTIĆ, Sejdo BAJRAMOVIĆ and Branko KOSTIĆ) assumed the function of the SFRY Presidency, circumventing the roles and responsibilities of the Presidency members from Slovenia, Croatia, Bosnia and Herzegovina and Macedonia.

64. On 15 October 1991, at the meeting of the SDS Party Council the decision was reached to form a separate assembly, entitled the "Assembly of the Serbian People of Bosnia and Herzegovina" to secure Serb interests.

65. On or around 22 October 1991, **Slobodan MILOŠEVIĆ**, together with other members of the joint criminal enterprise, continued to advocate for a unitary Serb state governed from Belgrade, Serbia. On the same date the "Rump Presidency" called for the mobilisation of reservists in Serbia and "other regions that want to stay in Yugoslavia."

66. On or about 26 October 1991, Radovan KARADŽIĆ declared a full mobilisation of the TO and the formation of field units in the Serb Republic of Bosnia and Herzegovina.

67. On 24 October 1991, the Assembly of the Serbian People in Bosnia and Herzegovina, dominated by the SDS, decided to conduct a "Plebiscite of the Serbian People in Bosnia and Herzegovina" in order to decide whether to stay in the common state of Yugoslavia with Serbia, Montenegro, the Serbian Autonomous Region of Krajina, SAO Western Slavonia and SAO Eastern Slavonia, Baranja and Western Srem.

68. On 9 and 10 November 1991, the Bosnian Serbs held the plebiscite on the issue of whether Bosnia and Herzegovina should stay in Yugoslavia or become an independent state. The results overwhelmingly showed that the Bosnian Serbs wanted to stay in Yugoslavia.

69. On 21 November 1991, the Assembly of the Serbian People of Bosnia and Herzegovina, proclaimed as part of the territory of the federal Yugoslav state all those municipalities, local communities and populated places, in which over 50% of the people of Serbian nationality had voted, during the plebiscite, to remain in that state as well as those places where citizens of other nationalities had expressed themselves in favour of remaining in Yugoslavia.

70. On 11 December 1991, the Assembly of the Serbian People delivered a detailed request to the JNA to protect with all available means as "integral parts of the State of Yugoslavia" the territories of Bosnia and Herzegovina in which the plebiscite of the Serbian people and other citizens on remaining in a joint Yugoslav state had been conducted.

71. On 19 December 1991, the SDS issued instructions for the "Organisation and Activity of the Organs of the Serbian People in Bosnia and Herzegovina in Extraordinary Circumstances" which provided a plan for the SDS take-over of municipalities in Bosnia and Herzegovina.

72. On 9 January 1992, the Assembly of the Serbian People of Bosnia and Herzegovina adopted a declaration on the Proclamation of the Serbian Republic of Bosnia and Herzegovina. The territory of that republic was declared to include "the territories of the Serbian Autonomous Regions and Districts and of other Serbian ethnic entities in Bosnia and Herzegovina, including the regions in which the Serbian people remained in the minority due to the genocide conducted against it in World War Two", and it was declared to be a

part of the federal Yugoslav state. On 12 August 1992, the name of the Bosnian Serb Republic was changed to Republika Srpska.

73. From 29 February to 2 March 1992, Bosnia and Herzegovina held a referendum on independence. At the urging of the SDS, the majority of Bosnian Serbs boycotted the vote. The referendum resulted in a pro-independence majority.

74. On 18 March 1992, during the 11th session of the Assembly of the Serbian People, a conclusion was reached to "prepare for the next session proposals for the take-over of power in the Republic of Serbian People of Bosnia and Herzegovina."

75. From March 1992 onwards, Serb regular and irregular forces seized control of territories within Bosnia and Herzegovina, including those specified in this indictment.

76. On 6 April 1992, the United States and the European Community formally recognized the independence of Bosnia and Herzegovina.

77. On 27 April 1992, Serbia and Montenegro proclaimed a new Federal Republic of Yugoslavia and declared it the successor state of the Socialist Federal Republic of Yugoslavia.

78. On 12 May 1992, at the 16th Assembly of the Serbian People in Bosnia and Herzegovina, Radovan KARADŽIĆ announced the six strategic objectives of the Serbian People in Bosnia and Herzegovina. These objectives included the eradication of the Drina River as a border between the Serbian states. During the same session, General Ratko MLADIĆ told the Assembly that it would not be possible to separate Serbs from non-Serbs and have the non-Serbs simply leave the territory. He warned that attempting this process would amount to genocide.

79. On 15 May 1992, the United Nations Security Council in its resolution number 752 demanded that all interference from outside Bosnia and Herzegovina by units of the JNA cease immediately and that those units either be withdrawn, be subjected to the authority of the Government of the Republic, or be disbanded and disarmed.

Carla Del Ponte
Prosecutor
Dated this 22nd day of November 2001
At The Hague
The Netherlands

AUTHORS

NORMAN CIGAR Norman Cigar is a Professor of Strategic Studies at the United States Marine Corps Command and Staff College and a Senior Associate with the Public International Law and Policy Group, Washington D.C. He has been a senior political-military analyst for the Deputy Chief of Staff for Intelligence of the Army at the Pentagon and has also served as a consultant to the International Criminal Tribunal for the former Yugoslavia at The Hague. Among other publications he is the author of *Genocide in Bosnia: The Politics of Ethnic Cleansing* as well as *Vojislav Kostunica and Serbia's Future.* He received a D. Phil from the University of Oxford.

PAUL WILLIAMS is an Assistant Professor of Law and International Relations at the American University. He has served as a Senior Associate at the Carnegie Endowment for International Peace where he directed the Public International Law and Policy Program. He has been a Fulbright Research Scholar at the University of Cambridge and has also served in the U.S. Department of State's Office of the Legal Adviser for European and Canadian Affairs. During the course of his legal practice, among other advisory assignments, he has served on the Bosnian delegation to the Dayton peace negotiations and on the Kosovar delegation to the Rambouillet/Paris peace talks. He has also testified as an expert on the crisis in the former Yugoslavia before the U.S. Senate's Foreign Relations Sub-Committee on European Affairs. He is the author of numerous books and articles on public international law. He received a Ph. D. from the University of Cambridge and his J.D. from Stanford Law School.

IVO BANAC is Professor of History at Yale University and Director of the Council on European Studies at the Yale Center for International and Area Studies. His book, *The National Question in Yugoslavia: Origins, History, Politics* (Cornell,1988), ranks as a classic in the history of Southeast Europe.